Economic Growth and Development in Singapore

Economic Growth and Development in Singapore

Past and Future

Gavin Peebles and Peter Wilson

Edward Elgar
Cheltenham, UK • Northampton, MA, USA

Published by
Edward Elgar Publishing Limited
Glensanda House
Montpellier Parade
Cheltenham
Glos GL50 1UA
UK

Edward Elgar Publishing, Inc.
136 West Street
Suite 202
Northampton
Massachusetts 01060
USA

A catalogue record for this book
is available from the British Library

Library of Congress Cataloguing in Publication Data

Peebles, Gavin, 1947–
Economic growth and development in Singapore : past and future / Gavin Peebles and Peter Wilson.
    p. cm.
Includes bibliographical references and index.
1. Singapore – Economic conditions.   2. Singapore – Economic policy.
I. Wilson, Peter, 1951–   . II. Title.
HC445.8P395   2002
338.95957–dc21   2002016659

ISBN 1 84064 741 8 (cased)
ISBN 1 84376 052 5 (paperback)

Printed and bound in Great Britain by MPG Books Ltd, Bodmin, Cornwall

Contents

Figures

Tables

Preface

When we started writing this book in early 2001 the government's official growth forecast was that the economy could grow by as much as 7 per cent in that year. In the previous year growth had been 9.9 per cent and in the year before that 5.9 per cent. It thus seemed that Singapore had recovered well from the Asian financial crisis. By the time we were finishing the book in November 2001 the official growth forecast for 2001 was −3 per cent and for 2002 it was between −2 per cent and 2 per cent. This would be the most significant recession in Singapore's modern history. Forecasts of the number of job losses were revised upwards during the year and are expected to continue well into 2002.

In most countries this would not be thought a good time to call a general election, especially if one was not due until August 2002, as was then the case in Singapore. However, in Singapore things are different and in October 2001 the ruling People's Action Party (PAP) called the 'snappiest of snap elections' by making 25 October Nomination Day and 3 November Polling Day, thus allowing the legal minimum of nine days for canvassing.

As we explain in Appendix B the PAP knew that it could not possibly lose the election and would definitely form the next government. It can be rather tetchy when its share of the votes falls and more opposition candidates enter parliament. There were two out of 83 at that time. The reason for the election was in order to bring in new people into parliament and the cabinet so they would gain experience and exposure and to indicate which of them could play an important role in the post-2007 government, retire 25 PAP MPs as well as allowing ministers to concentrate on economic, not political matters after November.

In the November general election 55 seats were not contested so the PAP had a walkover. On polling day only 29 seats were contested in nine single-seat constituencies and in four 5-seat Group Representation Constituencies (See Appendix B). About two-thirds of the electorate could not vote. Of the 29 contested seats the PAP won 27 with two different opposition parties each retaining a seat with a lower share of the valid vote. Of those who voted, 75 per cent voted for the PAP, the highest share since 1984, but these comparisons are not really valid as the proportion of contested and uncontested seats varies from election to election.

The immediate task of the government will be to deal with job losses and it announced that it would have to take further measures to increase competitiveness by cutting costs and wages. The long-run objective is to create a 'New Singapore' as envisaged by the Prime Minister in August 2001. For both these ends a high-powered ministerial committee has been formed to devise a plan for recovery and transformation of the economy. In this review nothing will be considered sacred and no stone will be left unturned. One of the themes of our book is to show how Singapore got to the position it is in now and the nature of likely future problems and policy challenges.

Note:
All dollar ($) amounts in this book are Singapore dollars unless otherwise indicated.
   One billion is one thousand million (1 000 000 000)
   In June 2002 the value of one Singapore dollar was as follows:

US dollar = 0.57
pound sterling = 0.37
Euro = 0.57
Japanese yen = 67.61
Chinese yuan = 4.68
Malaysian ringgit = 2.15

Any mistakes of fact or interpretation in this book are solely the result of our ignorance and incompetence and are not due to any malicious intent.

Gavin Peebles and Peter Wilson
Singapore
8 November 2001

1. Introduction, themes and structure of the book

1.1 INTRODUCTION

Encouraged by the reception of our first book on Singapore (*The Singapore Economy*, Edward Elgar, 1996), both within and outside Singapore, we offer a new and different analysis of this small but interesting economy. In our first book we tried to provide a macroeconomic and international trade overview of the economy, showing how the different parts fitted together, how the macroeconomic, monetary and exchange rate aspects were related. We also provided some macroeconomic theory to help readers understand the nature of the relationships between these different parts. That book was mainly historical and statistical and had very little institutional and historical detail and only briefly considered the problems associated with some of the policies and institutions that have been credited for Singapore's rapid economic growth. Some reviewers lamented that we were not able to discuss in greater detail some important institutions such as the Central Provident Fund, which has been used for macroeconomic purposes, but has also played an important role in shaping the nature of Singapore society and is not without its problems.

In this volume we offer an historical overview of the growth of the economy and the institutions and policies that made this rapid growth possible. This leads us to an examination of the current state of the economy and its possible future in terms of its prospective growth, structural change and the reforms that are currently being implemented and have been seen by some analysts as a paradigm shift in the government's thinking. An important factor in determining the nature of that future is the values and views of the current political leadership and their responses to current forces acting on the economy, and their own histories as well as that of Singapore. The Singapore system was created by one political party with a small core of policymaking cadres. Some narrations of its history just credit one person, so it is important to keep in mind the background of those who established that ruling party and set out to build a nation. Furthermore, generational changes in the leadership could lead it to consider a range of policies that would not occur to earlier generations. In outlining possible future paths of the economy we will therefore quote several Singaporean politicians and their ideas.

One of the authors of this book once remarked that many books about Singapore just seemed to be a string of quotations linked by a few general comments by the authors. Many writers could not resist quoting Lee Kuan Yew's early passionate defence of democracy, the jury system and individual rights and then his later justification of widespread interference in nearly all aspects of individual life. We will not rehearse such historical quotations but will seek to understand the ideas of the early Singaporean politicians and the views of those now in government and how they see the problems facing them and how they are trying to react to them. It might therefore be helpful to the reader who might not be familiar with the positions and functions of the principal people we will be citing, to mention them here. Their statements, often outside Singapore, give a good indication of the way the government wants the economy to develop. The most important people related to the Singapore government and its economic strategy we cite are the following:

Lee Kuan Yew, English-educated lawyer, founding member of the still-ruling People's Action Party (PAP), defender of those interned under British colonialism and Prime Minister from 1959 to November 1990 when he stood down to become Senior Minister in the Prime Minister's Office. He retains his seat in parliament and is a member of the cabinet. He is generally known as 'SM' in the press and has recently produced two invaluable volumes on his life and the 'Singapore story' (Lee, 1998; 2000). Probably best known for advancing and defending 'Asian Values' in the 1990s which, in 1978, he had said was the necessary antidote against the infection of 'the disruptive individualism of western liberalism' that he thought had already infected Singapore (Hill, 2000, p. 185).

Goh Chok Tong, economist and civil servant who has been prime minister since November 1990. Undergraduate education in Singapore in economics and postgraduate in the United States in development economics. It was thought he would bring a gentler approach to politics and attitudes to opposition politicians but some Singaporeans do not think that has been the case. Generally known as 'PM' in the press. As a young civil servant he contributed a book chapter that argued that '[p]lanned industrialization as a conscious strategy of economic development in Singapore began only in 1961 with the establishment of the Economic Development Board' (Goh, 1969, p. 127). His most frequently used phrase in speeches recently seems to be 'every Singaporean counts'. In May 2001 he received the 'Distinguished Comrade of Labour' award from the trade union movement.

Dr Goh Keng Swee, English educated economist and founding member of the PAP who is often identified as the economic architect of modern Singapore as he has been Minister for Education, Defence and Finance and Deputy Chairman of the Monetary Authority of Singapore at various times. His views are published in three volumes (Goh, 1972; 1977; 1995) and in some academic papers. Now retired.

Dr Richard Hu Tsu Tau, Minister for Finance since 1985, former chairman of the Monetary Authority of Singapore (MAS) and Chairman of the Board of Commissioners of Currency Singapore since 1985 so his signature appears on Singapore's currency notes. Undergraduate education in chemistry in the United States then postgraduate studies in chemical engineering in England. Career with Shell in Singapore and Malaysia before entering politics. Stood down from politics in October 2001 at the age of 75.

Brigadier-General (NS) Lee Hsien Loong, career military officer, in politics since the mid 1980s, currently one of the two Deputy Prime Ministers and, since January 1998, Chairman of the MAS, spearheading the reform and restructuring of the financial sector. Undergraduate education in England in mathematics and computer science then a mid-career programme of education in the United States. Usually serves as acting prime minister when the prime minister is out of the country and is widely expected to be the next prime minister. Some of his speeches on financial reforms are collected in Lee (2000b).

Brigadier-General (NS) George Yong-boon Yeo, Minister for Trade and Industry. Seems to be the face of the young PAP and spokesman for Singapore values and the Singapore spirit against unwanted foreign influences and articulator of the future for Singaporeans. Undergraduate education in engineering in England then MBA in the United States. Although keen on attracting foreign talent (see below) he is against Singaporeans working for foreign publications in Singapore, for example. He was formerly Minister for Information and the Arts and has been described as 'the New Guard's most original thinker' (George, 2000, p. 184).

C. V. Devan Nair, early member of the PAP and detainee under the British, who brought the trade unions under the control of the PAP. Served as Singapore's third President before resigning in March 1985. His speeches when in Singapore are available as Nair (1982) and Nair (1976) is also relevant. Now lives in exile and is a regretful and harsh critic of the political system in Singapore.

Dr Albert Winsemius, a Dutch economist and unpaid economic adviser to the Singapore government for many years and who has been described as the 'founding father of Singapore'. Dr Winsemius does not seem to have written much about his economic philosophy, except Winsemius (1962), but is referred to often in Singapore and also in Lee (2000). Winsemius (1982) refers to Singapore.

Interesting interviews with some of the first generation of PAP leaders and other important contributors to Singapore's early growth and institutional formation can be found in Chew (1996). One feature is that the younger leaders are more likely to have studied in the United States and thus possibly be more open to influences from there.

1.2   THEMES

In this volume we try to supplement and expand our earlier work in a number of ways as we review the nature of Singapore's economic growth experience by examining some related themes about the economy. Our historical focus mainly goes back to August 1965 when the independent nation state, the Republic of Singapore, was established but we do refer to the nature of the island and its economy before then and cite data going back to 1960. Singapore became self-governing in 1959 and was part of Malaysia from September 1963 to August 1965. Our main focus is on the years since 1965 and on the future.

Growth and Development

One important theme, reflected in the title of this volume, is the nature of the relationship between economic growth and development and how this is seen in Singapore. Singapore is always held up as an example of a rapidly growing economy that has, in the recent words of its Senior Minister in his memoirs, moved 'from third world to first' (Lee, 2000) but there are many in the government who do not believe that it is a developed economy. This was noted in Peebles and Wilson (1996, p. 243) where a PAP member of parliament was quoted as saying it absurd to think of Singapore as a developed economy and there has been reluctance within the government to agree to re-classifying Singapore in the official publications of international organisations as more developed (Wilson, 2000a). Singapore was proposed to be reclassified as a developed country by the Organisation of Economic Cooperation and Development in 1996, for example. Haggard (1999, p. 345) finds 'rather odd . . . Singapore's current preoccupation with whether or not it is a developed country'.

The prospect of Singapore's becoming a developed country came to public attention in the early 1990s when the Economic Planning Committee of the Ministry of Trade and Industry published *The Strategic Plan: Towards a Developed Nation* which chose to use the term 'developed nation' in its title (Ministry of Trade and Industry, 1991). This reminds us that when Singapore became a sovereign nation in August 1965 it was not just concerned with economic growth but undertook to create an independent nation that would survive outside Malaysia. The object of the plan was to 'attain the stature and characteristics of a first league developed country within the next 30 to 40 years' (ibid., p. 2). This was seen not just in narrow economic terms but the economic dimension of the objective was that Singapore would aim to 'catch up with – on a moving target basis – the GNP per capita of the United States by 2030 or the Netherlands by 2020'. This objective went beyond the then existing target adopted in 1984 of achieving the 1984 Swiss level of GNP per capita by 1999. The qualitative dimensions were for Singapore to concentrate on the quality of life, Singapore's national identity and to make it a global city. This strategic plan was very long-term and was not seen as a detailed blueprint as there were bound to be many unexpected events in that period and Singapore's size meant it was not able to control events. Although the committee expressed the difficulties of formulating a long-term plan for such a country it did stress that in the past Singapore had implemented three distinct plans that had been 'highly effective in achieving their primary aims' (ibid., p. 15).

The first plan was developed by a visiting team from the United Nations in 1960 led by Dr Albert Winsemius. Its primary objective was job creation, setting up the main planning body, The Economic Development Board, and developing four specific industries that he identified. (See Chapter 2 below for a discussion.)

The second plan came from the Ministry of Trade in 1980 with some advice from Dr Winsemius. By this time the economy was experiencing labour shortages and low productivity as it had embarked on industrialization by attracting multinational companies (MNCs) into labour-intensive sectors. This plan aimed at expanding the number of engineering and technical students at the tertiary level and tried to move employment away from labour-intensive sectors to higher value-added, technology-based sectors by pushing up wages.

The third plan was concerned with the perceived erosion of Singapore's international competitiveness in the early 1980s which preceded the recession of 1985–86. It was prepared by the Economic Committee established by the Ministry of Trade and Industry in 1985, and set out the long-term objectives of building wage flexibility into the economy and the promotion of the services sector.

These plans were brought about by specific problems at specific times: unemployment; labour shortages and low productivity; rising costs and recession. The Strategic Economic Plan of 1991 was much more ambitious and wide-ranging. Since its formulation there have also been many sectoral or topical plans and in the 1990s many strategies which were to realize some of the visions of the Strategic Economic Plan were given such names as Industry 21, Manpower 21, Retail 21, SME21, Technopreneurship 21, Trade 21, Tourism 21, to indicate their relevance for the new century.

The eight strategic thrusts of the 1991 Strategic Economic Plan were

Enhancing human resources
Promoting national teamwork
Becoming internationally oriented
Creating a conducive climate for innovation
Developing manufacturing and service clusters
Spearheading economic redevelopment
Maintaining international competitiveness
Reducing vulnerability

All of these themes reappear in subsequent plans and initiatives. The last one is worth looking at. Vulnerability at that time was seen as the economy's over dependence in certain areas. They were that the bulk of domestic exports came from the MNCs; that a large part of domestic exports went to the United States; that re-exports were still an important part of export earnings and that there was a high degree of reliance on crude oil imports from the Middle East. (The plan was being drawn up when the Gulf War broke out and the Soviet Union collapsed.) The committee thought that this situation had been created through the market mechanism so diversification could result in economic costs. They did identify two areas to increase diversification. MNCs should be encouraged to treat Singapore as a home-base for their activities and that local enterprises should be developed to world standards. These themes recur in subsequent strategies and plans. Vulnerability is still seen as over-reliance on some areas and since the plan was articulated concern has been expressed that in the manufacturing sector and amongst manufacturing exports there is too much specialization on electronic products. We will return to this aspect of the economy later.

Vulnerability does not necessarily come from over-dependence on certain products or markets and other aspects of Singapore's perceived vulnerability should be considered here. Government ministers keep stressing the vulnerability of the economy in language mainly aimed at stressing the importance that people keep voting for the People's Action Party (PAP) who have successfully managed the economy to its present state. People should pay no attention to opposition politicians who are held up as incompetent and incapable of managing the economy and whose sole desire seems to be to get their hands on Singapore's reserves and squander them. Perceived vulnerability, partly due to the country's location and the way it became a sovereign national state in 1965, has always been stressed and has led to commentators attributing to the government 'a siege mentality'. People are kept frightened of the possible consequences of a change in government or even a fall in the percentage vote going to the PAP. The PAP picks the best to run the economy. As Lee Kuan Yew put it in the late 1980s: 'We decide what is right. Never mind what the people think', and shortly after that the then deputy prime minister, Goh Chock Tong, added, that Singapore's '"intellectual elite" will continue to make the key decisions, while the proper role for the "rest of the nation" [is to] conform' (cited from Haas, 1999a, p. 6).

The other factor used to increase this sense of vulnerability and to limit self expression and public action is said to be due to the reliance on foreign investors, so university students have been told they cannot stage demonstrations as that would encourage workers to do the same, then foreign investors would lose confidence and the economy would collapse. National Service must be retained because if it were modified then foreign investors would lose confidence in the economy with the same results. The government seems keen to keep its people in fear of imminent collapse and the return to the low quality of life and standard of living of the colonial era. One aspect of this mentality is the government distrust of academics, especially in the social and political sciences, and of foreign press correspondents who are thought to be trying to influence the electorate and government (Lee 2000, p. 759) and of independent organizations in Singapore. The government wants to have a hand, and nearly always a controlling hand in everything. The Heritage Foundation, which still ranks Singapore as the second most economically free economy in the world, bluntly states that: 'The ruling People's Action Party (PAP) maintains firm control of all political and economic power' (*The 2001 Index of Economic Freedom* at http://database.townhall.com/heritage/index/country.cfm). Note their use of the word 'all'.

One result of Singapore's government-led growth strategy has been the creation of tensions between different groups in society. Locals and foreigners; the PAP itself and opposition parties; government-controlled companies and local, smaller enterprises; heartlanders (the prime Minister's term for the mainly Chinese educated working class who live in public housing estates) and the cosmopolitans (mainly English-speaking professionals who are internationally mobile), between Singapore and Malaysia. Tension between the first two groups has broken out at various times when foreigners have thought to be interfering too much in Singapore resulting in shows of Singapore's independence: the caning of Michael Fay is a good example. See Baratham (1994) and Latif (1994) for two interpretations of the significance of this event that affected American and Singaporean relations and Deck (1999, pp. 135–40) for the diplomatic row and its consequences. The expulsion of foreign journalists and the limiting of the circulation of magazines that are thought to have interfered in Singapore politics or have been unkind in their comments on Singapore's leaders or their wives is another example. The second tension is the basis of Singapore politics and can be seen in such seemingly trivial things as the fact that opposition-held constituencies – there are just two at present – are referred to as 'enemy territory' by the government-friendly press but more seriously in the limiting of public funds for opposition wards. There are problems connected with different perspectives of the progress of the different races also.

One aspect of the economy's vulnerability is that the possible defection of foreign firms and workers make Singapore a less attractive place to produce and work. This might not just be caused by events in Singapore but by changes in the perception of the region in general by foreign investors. One recently heard quip is that Singapore is a great piece of real estate but is just in a lousy neighbourhood. This became more of a worry for the government after the political changes and uncertainties in neighbouring countries that followed the Asian financial crisis. The political nature of Singapore seems to give it the confidence that it can prevent internal events from making the place less attractive to foreign investors but it has much less control over foreigners' perception of the region. In the late 1990s there was a clear shift in the government's tone as it tried to stress the uniqueness of Singapore and to distinguish it from neighbouring countries whereas earlier it had promoted Singapore to foreign investors as a springboard for venturing into the region with the help of government planning agencies. This new foreign policy thrust, which has also led to Singapore negotiating bilateral free-trade agreements with counties outside ASEAN (The Association of South East Asian Nations) founded in 1967.

The government's review of the implications of the finding of the 2000 Census provide another insight into its thinking on the nature of development and required policies. After favourably reviewing the changes in Singapore life over the years 1990 to 2000 BG (NS) George Yeo looked forward to what he expected the census of 2010 to show. He thought that 'we will probably have the economic, educational and cultural profile of a First World country' (*The Straits Times*, 21 February, 2001, p. H3), suggesting that there was still a long way to go to achieve this. He highlighted three major responses to possible problems on the way. First, the government would continue to encourage the importation of foreign talent for both quantitative and qualitative reasons. Second, the process of globalization meant that Singapore should diversify its links outside the immediate region and as Singapore would become a major capital exporter it had to look to such countries as India, China and Australia. The third response was to strengthen 'the Singapore spirit'. The threat of globalization was that more non-Singaporeans would come to live in Singapore just as more Singaporeans went overseas. It was necessary to strengthen the bonds with these overseas Singaporeans. One response was the decision in early 2001 to allow certain overseas Singaporeans to vote in future general elections. This possibility was put on hold in late 2001 as it was argued that the security situation after the terrorist attacks on the United States would make overseas voting too dangerous.

In terms of economic indicators it is easy to rank Singapore using consistent estimates of gross national product (GNP) per capita as published in the latest *World Development Report 2000/20001*. The latest data are for 1999 which will have allowed some time for the Asian economies to start recovery from the Asian Financial crisis. In 1999 Singapore's GNP per capita in purchasing power dollars was $27024 which gave it a ranking of seventh in the world. This amount was 88 per cent of that of the United States, ranked fourth, 98 per cent of that of Switzerland, ranked sixth and 129 per cent of that of Hong Kong, ranked twenty-sixth in that year. Luxembourg, with a GNP per capital in purchasing terms of $38247, is ranked first in the world by this criterion: being small is not a disadvantage. Singapore stands out as being far ahead of neighbouring countries where its GNP per capita was 3.4 times that in Malaysia, 11 times that in Indonesia and 4.8 times that in Thailand. The ratios for the Asian countries today are roughly the same as they were in the 1970s as all these countries have experienced similarly rapid growth since then. In contrast, the ratios to the more developed countries have risen considerably. In 1976 Singapore's GNP per capita was only 34 per cent of that in the United States and 30 per cent of that in Switzerland.

In terms of indicators of development other than narrow economic ones such as GNP per capita or other economic ones such as consumption per capita, Singapore does not rank as highly. We will examine the extent of these differences in Chapter 6. In general, most informal references to and appreciation of development use narrow economic indicators such as GNP per capita but individuals use other ways for themselves in assessing development. If, using the approach of the many millions of visitors to Singapore who assess its level of development by looking as its buildings, its transport system and shops, then Singapore already looks like a developed city that can be favourably compared to the cities of Western countries. If we take development to mean the ability to respond to external economic shocks and prevent major economic damage then, again,

Singapore, would be ranked as developed. The Asian financial crisis which swept over the region after July 1997 did not lead to a major recession in Singapore. Growth stopped for a year and unemployment rose but did not reach crisis proportion and by the year 2000 the growth rate of real GDP returned to 9.9 per cent and foreign investments kept coming into the economy. Even a huge economy such as Japan perhaps does not deserve to be characterized as developed in this sense as it has been unable to respond successfully to an almost decade-long period of slow growth and declining prestige (Peebles, 1999b).

In January 2001 Singapore started a two-year term as a member of the 15-member United Nations Security Council and was its president for the month of January. This can be taken as recognition of developed status but we should note that such small countries as Jamaica, Tunisia and Ireland are also current members of the Security Council.

Institutional Foundations of Growth and their Possible Future

A second theme we examine is the nature of the institutions that have been able to secure rapid growth for Singapore and their relevance for the future. Are the institutions and policies that have been used successfully to secure economic growth in the past appropriate for the future development of Singapore as an economy and society? What reforms are being implemented, why, and what impact are they likely to have on the economy? How will the government's role change if it proceeds with plans for further liberalization and divestment of government-owned companies and statutory boards? The government is aware that the world has changed, partly because of the adoption of internet technology and the importance of research and innovation so that for Singapore to be successful in the future it must be 'part of the knowledge-based world.' (Lee, 2000, p. 763).

One aspect of prime ministerial behaviour that the present prime minister has inherited from his predecessor is the tendency to reveal more about Singapore policies and government thinking to journalists outside Singapore than at home. He has also adopted the Senior Minister's tendency to use 'you' to mean 'one' or 'me' or 'we'. This assumption makes the following revealing comments in a face-to-face interview with the *Financial Times* in 2000 intelligible. 'We have no choice. This is becoming a smaller and smaller world, and if Singapore is to survive into the future in this new economy, new world, it's got to embrace the cultures of the world. We are embracing globalisation and the IT revolution, convinced that they present more opportunities than costs.' And 'Can we be more entrepreneurial, more innovative, more creative within that model which we decide to have for Singapore? I think that's a basic question. Can you do it? I won't have the answer. Ten years from now, you can come back and ask me if we succeeded' (Goh Chock Tong quoted from McNulty, 2000).

When we look at the future of the economy we are not making our own predictions but will examine the trends in demography, technology and globalization that have been identified and look at how they may change the nature of the economy. In addition, we look at the government's own visions for the future of the economy. The extent of government intervention, planning and economic activity has been an important factor in the economy's past growth and it would be fair to say that Singapore is a planned economy that has used supply-side socialism for its development. Although all current government plans might not be realized they will, nevertheless, give us an idea of likely future developments in the economy.

Nature of the Economy and Different Perceptions of Singapore

Another theme we wish to pursue is to establish the nature of the economy and how that perception differs from that of other people and how their own perceptions differ so much. Between us we have lived in Asia for 33 years altogether and have worked in Singapore for 23 years. Our impressions of the economy are based on personal observation as well as hearing the views of the government, reading the analyses of people both within and outside Singapore, and becoming familiar with the economy and its data for our publications and our university teaching. Such institutions as the Central Provident Fund, the Inland Revenue Authority, government-linked companies such as the Development Bank of Singapore, the co-operatives operated by the trade union movement, the nature of immigration, taxation and academic bureaucracies, the standards of private and public medical care have all been part of our recent lives and are not just represented by abbreviations or acronyms on the printed page of some newspaper or book. Another consequence of our living in Singapore is that we will stress events that the outsider might think trivial and not at all commensurate with the great forces of demography, saving, investment, technology, trade and globalization that have transformed Singapore. Such seemingly trivial events and their interpretation by Singaporeans are important. Another consequence is that we have been able to see the introduction of certain policies and their effects and the extent to which they have been abandoned. Often analysts will highlight the introduction of a policy and leave the reader believing that it had the intended effect or that it was never withdrawn or significantly modified. That is not always the case.

It is surprising sometimes what influential people say about Singapore and the extent of disagreement over basic aspects of the economy they reveal. Partly this is due to the lack of official information on the role of government organizations in the economy and the confusing and incomplete way in which some information is presented, especially the government budget, balance of payments statistics and others. One government reaction to the Asian Financial Crisis was to call for more transparency in Singapore business and it is true that some government bodies have been more willing to talk about their policies and objectives, but this desired openness does not seem to have had an affect on the presentation of some statistical information.

In their very useful exercise in ranking the degree of economic freedom of different economies, Gwartney and Lawson (1997, p. 165) remark of Singapore that: 'Most of the enterprises are private (state-operated enterprises produce only a small portion of the total output) and there are few restraints limiting the entry into business.' This would be a great surprise to anyone who knows Singapore and what other people believe. Compare this view with that of Cardarelli et al. (2000, p. 9) who argue that: 'One likely cause of the weakness in microeconomic environment in the very high degree of government involvement in Singapore economy.' Not only do they believe there is a great degree of government involvement (note that they say 'involvement', not 'intervention') but that that factor has had harmful effects on the economy. They identify this involvement through the fact that public sector enterprises have been very active in production when they say that 'the business landscape in Singapore is characterised by heavy government presence, through the Statutory Boards and a large number of Government Linked Corporations (GLCs)'. The word 'presence' means that the government is in the business of production and is not only intervening through subsidies to foreign firms. It also obtains and allocates land and financial resources, forms companies and joint ventures with foreign investors and so on. Cardarelli et al. (2000, pp. 10–11) go on to show that government ownership of companies is higher in Singapore than in other Asian countries and that 'their overwhelming power is likely to have crowded out local private enterprise and thus prevented the development of a large and dynamic network of local corporations, contributing to the widely perceived lack of corporate dynamism in Singapore' (ibid., p. 11). One of our themes will be to examine how the government has tried, and is likely to try, to increase the degree of corporate dynamism in Singapore. This perceived lack of local dynamism is not only due to the presence of many public enterprises and bodies which have been accused of being rather conservative and risk-adverse in their activities but also to the fact that much of Singapore's technological base has been imported with the MNCs that have transformed the Singapore economy, and not through indigenous innovation and enterprise.

In another comprehensive ranking of economies by their degree of economic freedom, in which Singapore is again ranked second after Hong Kong, Johnson et al. (1999, p. 346) evade the issue of the importance of GLCs. They argue that as 'neither the level of government ownership nor its level of expenditures for the GLCs is known exactly [as if it ever could be]; therefore, until the extent of the government's involvement in the GLCs is known with greater accuracy, Singapore is graded solely on the level of government consumption as a percentage of GDP, which remains very low by global standards'. This misses the point in a number of ways. We do not need to have an exact measure of something to know that it is significant in some way. We can find out the extent of government ownership and do have some idea of the significance of the output of public enterprises. Furthermore the amount of government consumption in GDP is not an accurate measure of the extent of government activity and influence over the allocation of resources. We should look at the proportion of resources the government can obtain and allocate, such as land, a large part of private saving and the extent to which it decides how these resources will be used, not relying on the decisions of private individuals. Alten (1995) did not take such a defeatist approach and apart from trying to identify the significance of the public sector in production using measures of ownership and control over GLCs he also looked at its role as 'provider of public merit goods', 'entrepreneur', 'planner' and facilitator' amongst other functions. In addition he surveyed managing directors of MNCs in Singapore to learn their views on how important the government was in a number of areas and how much and how the government affected their business. He attributes an important role to the government and concludes that 'Singapore's economic development is, above all, a political process, decided upon and guided by a strong government determined to overcome the country's backward economic status and to enter the first league of industrialised nations in the beginning of the next century' (Alten, 1995, p. 230).

For many years the annual review of the Singapore economy by the American Department of Commerce has stated that GLCs produce as much as 60 per cent of GDP (*Singapore Economic Trends Report*, p. 5), an estimate taken from a report from the Ministry for Finance of 1993. The Singapore government has not commented on this estimate until very recently when, in answer to a question in parliament, the Minister for Trade and Industry stated that it was wrong and, referring to then unpublished estimates stated that GLCs contributed only 13 per cent of GDP and foreign-controlled companies 42 per cent (*The Straits Times*, 24 February, 2001, p. H6, and Department of Statistics (2001) where they were subsequently published). The government is out to refute the view that GLCs have stifled local entrepreneurship. It is surprising to see that the 60 per cent figure was still being used in the foreign press as late as late March 2001 (Richardson, 2001, p. 24) in a publication that has been heavily fined for its reporting on Singapore. See Davies (1999, pp. 101–3) and Seow (1998, pp. 173–7) for accounts of the most recent attacks on it.

GLCs are not the only part of the pubic sector and we must keep in mind the economic role of statutory boards and ministries. One point to keep in mind is not necessarily the overall contribution to GDP of GLCs but their importance in certain industries and sectors where they can have a dominant market position (Department of Statistics, 2001, p. 1). These new estimates show the extreme importance in production of the MNCs. Foreign-controlled companies are those of which 50 per cent or more of their voting shares are owned by foreigners and can be branches or subsidiaries of foreign companies. We will see in subsequent chapters their even greater importance in different sectors.

The official view can be summarized in Table 1.1. A GLC is defined as a company if 'it is a subsidiary or associate, by virtue of share ownership, of Temasek Holdings (the government holding company) or a statutory board' (Department of Statistics, 2001, p. 3). Government ownership is considered to be the situation when the holding company holds more than 20 per cent of the voting shares. This seems to ignore the fact that there are three other government holding companies and that some companies are directly owned by government ministries. The public sector is the central government and statutory boards. The main facts that emerged from these estimates are that only 33 per cent of GDP in 1998 was produced by local-controlled, non-state firms and that as much as 42 per cent of GDP came from foreign firms. Whether one concludes that GLCs have not crowded out local enterprise or not, it must be admitted that not much is produced by the indigenous private sector. Rectifying that is one of the current challenges facing the government.

Table 1.1   Production of GDP by type of ownership, 1998

	Share of GDP %
Public sector	8.9
Corporate sector	87.5
Foreign-controlled companies	41.5
Local-controlled companies	46.0
of which GLCs	12.9
of which Others	33.1
Owner-occupied dwellings	3.6

Source: Department of Statistics (2001, p. 8). Cited with permission.

It would be pointless presenting time series data showing that the share of the public sector has fallen from 16 per cent of GDP in 1990 to the 9 per cent of 1998 as this has mainly been accomplished by converting some statutory boards into companies, some of which, such as the Port of Singapore Authority, the government still completely owns. This has increased the share of GLCs in output slightly.

The nature of corporate ownership and the sectors in which they are significant can be seen by looking at the nature of the largest firms in terms of their sales or turnover. The largest ten according to *Singapore 1000: Year 2000/2001* published by DP Information are shown in Table 1.2.

Table 1.2   Largest firms in Singapore in terms of annual sales or turnover

Company	Sales or turnover $ billion per year
Caltex Trading Pte Ltd.	32.10
Shell Eastern Trading (Pte) Ltd.	12.56
Hewlett-Packard Singapore (Private) Limited	11.60
Singapore Airlines Limited	8.90
SK Energy Asia P(Pte) Ltd.	7.60
Flextronics International Limited	7.56
Neptune Orient Lines Limited	7.25
BP Singapore Limited	7.56
Toshiba Capital (Asia) Ltd.	6.43
Mitsui Oil (Asia) Pte Ltd.	6.02

The significance of foreign-owned petroleum trading firms is clear. SK Energy Asia is a Korean firm that was only established in Singapore in 1990. The largest firm in the manufacturing sector is an American-owned electronics firm which is the second largest employer in Singapore, Hewlett-Packard Singapore. Flextronics International is an American electronics contract manufacturer with its headquarters in Singapore and operations in the United States. Singapore Airlines is a GLC as is Neptune Orient Lines, a shipping and logistics firm where the current prime minister made his reputation as an administrator. An important GLC such as SingTel ranks only eighteenth with a turnover of $4.87 billion but would rank first amongst Singapore listed companies by market capitalization. Singapore-owned private firms, especially in manufacturing, do not feature near the top of the list. Two privately owned local banks are listed at twenty-ninth and thirty-sixth place. This review shows the significance of foreign firms in petroleum trading, electronics and chemical production.

The main reason for the differing views on the significance of the public sector is that the Singapore experience is often used to illustrate and support a particular view of economic development. In the case above, Gwartney and Lawson (1997) rank Singapore as the second most economically free economy in the world, after Hong Kong, and so it would be inappropriate to show the extent of the government's business operations, its control of the economy and the restriction of entry into production that that control has meant in the past. Public enterprises are usually thought of as socialistic and therefore inefficient so could not be part of a strategy that produced such high rates of economic growth as Singapore has achieved. Its public enterprises have not required massive subsidies from the state budget and statutory boards, with one exception, generated surpluses. Some had monopoly positions which, according to some analysts, were used to extract a surplus from the local population through their pricing policies for the purpose of development (Ermisch and Huff, 1999). Or, as Asher (1999, p. 1) puts it: 'The Statutory boards and the GLCs have used their monopoly power and absence of competition policies to set prices significantly above marginal cost to generate surpluses. As a result, their prices contain elements of taxation.' Evidence suggests that there is a 'relative lack of domestic competition in Singapore' (Cardarelli et al., 2000, p. 12) which is hard to reconcile with a high degree of economic freedom.

Surprisingly, The Heritage Foundation, which still ranks Singapore as the second most free economy in the world, states that GLCs 'dominate Singapore's economy, constituting up to 70 per cent of Singapore-owned companies and generating up to 60 per cent of GDP' and that there 'is increasing evidence of government intervention in Singapore's economy' which led to it being downgraded on this criterion (*The 2001 Index of Economic Freedom*). Their reaction to the new estimates will be of interest.

To some observers Singapore is an economically free paradise of a corporately organized economy which provides an efficient pro-business environment, especially for chosen foreign investors. To others it is an Orwellian nightmare of repressive social control of the local population in the interest of foreign capital (Tremewan, 1994; Terzani, 1998, pp. 161–3 and Chee, 2001) and where the 'official policy of the government is to keep the wage share in national income as low as possible, and correspondingly keep the share of capital as high as possible' (Asher, 1999, p. 1). This contrast and the nature of the political system has encouraged such writers as Haas to assume 'the task of presenting the Singapore puzzle out of respect for the successes of the country and chagrin over the excesses' (Haas, 1999b, p. 11). The nature of these 'excesses' were identified by the Dutch Labour Party in its criticism of PAP rule and in its attempt to expel the PAP from the Socialist International in 1976. It is ironic that a report was published by the trade union movement in Singapore in 1976 (Nair, 1976, pp. 250–67) in a volume of rebuttals and Singaporean documents entitled *Socialism that*

Works: The Singapore Way, edited by C.V. Devan Nair and including the text of the Dutch Labour Party's complaints. The Singapore defence for its excesses in closing down newspapers, controlling the press, holding people in detention without trial, suppressing the trade union movement, student associations and suppressing intellectual freedom was that in the 1960s and early 1970s it was virtually in a state of war with communists. The point is that many of these policies remain today and Singaporeans see no justification for them, neither does the editor of that volume, C.V. Devan Nair, who served as Singapore's third President, referred to as 'Comrade President' by his brothers in the movement. He is now living in exile in Canada and is a harsh critic of how the Singapore political system has developed and sees it as the main impediment to development (Nair, 1994, and the interview with him in Chew, 1996, pp. 99–110).

Another conclusion drawn from Singapore's experience is the argument that democracy and a free press are not necessary for economic development and that 'soft authoritarianism' and discipline is better. This view is most closely associated with Lee Kuan Yew, Prime Minister from 1959 to 1990, and now Senior Minister. What Singaporeans are asking now is whether the degree of restriction and control that was used in the past was really necessary for the achievement of high growth and, more importantly, will that approach hinder future development of the economy? Here, again, the distinction between high growth rates and economic development and economic performance is important.

Another view sometimes drawn from Singapore's growth achievements is that socialism, the Singapore way, works. This was the claim of Dr Goh Keng Swee, widely regarded as the economic architect of modern Singapore, in an essay in a volume with that title (Nair, 1976, pp. 77–85). But that socialism has only worked as the government enthusiastically welcomed the creations of other countries' capitalist struggles: the efficient, globally-orientated foreign companies that have been attracted to Singapore by its supply-side socialist policies. Singapore has retained the bad aspects of socialism in the form of a one-party state, restrictions on some freedoms, the lack of independent interest groups described as civil society, government-controlled local media, no really independent trade unions and the seeming subservience of everything to economic growth and development as defined by the government. It has not replicated their dismal economic inefficiency. The argument formerly heard in Singapore is that democracy and a free press are not important for achieving growth, but will such a situation and the old approaches to politics and civil society serve the economy well in the future? Singaporeans such as Chee (2001, pp. 3–43) argue that Singapore could only be considered a developed county if it were a democracy and adopts the arguments of those such as A.K. Sen that democracy, or rather political freedoms of a higher level than found in Singapore, promote growth and that the evidence is that authoritarianism does not promote a good economic performance and that there is no real Asian tradition to rely on to justify Authoritarianism of the kind found in Singapore (Sen, 1997, pp. 1–2). With reference to Singapore we will have to ask whether its high growth rates really do indicate good economic performance.

Those economies that have emerged from the collapse of socialism have been attempting to develop opposition political parties, civilized political behaviour, civil society and truly independent broadcast and print media. They think they are important for both their future growth and development and entry into the international economic environment, a place where Singapore has always been. It is ironic that these factors were held up in Singapore, partly under the guise of Asian values, as the requisite for growth. Some of them such as huge savings rates, one-party rule, press and broadcast media that put the survival of the party first were key features of socialist economies and it is perhaps no surprise that Paul Krugman was led to compare Singapore with the former Soviet Union in his assessment of the nature of the Asian miracle. We will look at this argument and the controversy it provoked in Chapter 3. Will Singapore follow the trend of political liberalization or will it try to keep some of these old approaches in place?

The government has realized that such things as the internet have changed its ability to control the flow of much information and entertainment. The Singapore government, as did the Chinese, approached a Scottish company that had developed technology that allowed it to identify very quickly who was accessing what on the whole internet. The company declined to do business. In early 1999 it was revealed that SingNet (an internet provider and subsidiary of the GLC SingTel) together with the Ministry of Home Affairs scanned the files of all their 200 000 subscribers. This was widely reported in the press which might indicate the transparency of the system but it also puts people on guard that their computers could again be scanned in a more subtle way. Internet access to overseas sites and internet communication is vital for the development of Singapore so it has talked less more recently about the potential of foreign viruses (ideas, not destructive programmes) that could affect Singapore. Internally, however, it tightened the rules relating to internet use by its own citizens in August 2001, especially in the political arena. Only registered political parties are allowed to use their web sites to announce their policies and discuss issues and so on. No other site can endorse candidates, display party material and slogans. This has been interpreted by some web sites that they can be prosecuted for political postings or statements put in their discussion groups and so two web sites decided to close down when the legislation was announced. One of the organizers of such a web site was also associated with a private organization recently established by former journalists and academics that aimed at monitoring the local press and providing an annual report on its standards. That organization closed down as it was unable to raise funds leading one former member to observe that there was a 'decreasing space for civil society in spite of all the talk about opening up with Singapore 21' (*The Straits Times*, 13 September, 2001, p. H4).

The Asian Financial Crisis

Throughout the book there will be reference to the Asian financial crisis. In some places it will be where we show how a particular sector was affected by this event or where we examine the policies adopted in reaction to it, how long-term strategies might be affected by it, or how the government has taken advantage of the crisis. The impact of the crisis has not finished and it has had a continuing and major effect on the political as well as economic sectors of Singapore's neighbours. Thailand became a client of the International Monetary Fund and is still suffering from its weaknesses in the financial sector and overinvestment in certain sectors. Malaysia spurned foreign help, became rather anti-Western, introduced capital control, pegged the currency and froze financial assets held by many Singaporeans. Politically, the deputy Prime Minister was removed and jailed, thus creating a new focus for new opposition political parties. Indonesia lost three Presidents and a colony and is suffering from an independence movement in various unstable provinces. Hong Kong retained its linked exchange rate system and so had to suffer domestic deflation caused by a severe recession as neighbouring currencies collapsed. South Korea became an IMF client and recovered quite quickly. Japan seems to be impotent in the face of a near-decade of stagnation. Throughout this there was no major crisis in Singapore. The banks and the financial system were not affected although they did experience an increase in non-performing loans, trade declined and so there was no growth in 1998. There was mild deflation, controlled depreciation of the currency and an increase in unemployment but there was no crisis. Expected government fiscal deficits did not emerge. In the early days of the crisis there were those who predicted it would turn into a worldwide recession that would be more severe than that of the 1930s. However, small, vulnerable Singapore did not bear the brunt of the crisis. This brought the risk of people becoming complacent about any future regional or international crisis as the government seemed able to ride the storm quite safely. Being small is not a disadvantage. Many of the reforms we are seeing now predated the crisis in conception but the crisis, and the reaction to it in other countries, might have forced the pace slightly.

It would be wrong to attribute the current significant changes in strategy in Singapore to the impact of the crisis on Singapore itself, but more to technological and global changes and the way neighbouring countries have suffered from it, have declined in their attractiveness to foreign investors and how they have reacted themselves.

Intellectual Foundations of Singapore

This will be a minor theme that will be alluded to in places when we seek to link a certain set of policies to a possible intellectual ancestor or any other countries' experiences. Such a link might be purely accidental and perhaps not very clear. The PAP sees itself as a pragmatic party that does not draw on any ideology. Dr Goh Keng Swee has identified Adam Smith as his main influence and that Smith's ideas are enough for any developing economy, but for a more advanced one such as Singapore, David Ricardo could be consulted. We leave it to the reader to see if he or she can see any model or set of intellectual influences from which Singapore has drawn its approach to economic growth and the extent to which there are contradictions in any claims of intellectual influence. Goh Keng Swee has argued that Singapore is a socialist economy that works (Goh, 1977, pp. 94–106) and this might be hard to reconcile with the views of Adam Smith, though it has been said that one could construct a socialist tract from the *Wealth of Nations*. Goh's views, expressed in a speech to the Singapore Manufacturers' Association in 1969 were as follows:

> What I want to do first tonight is to give an account of facts and figures to suggest that the PAP government are good socialists notwithstanding our genial relations with the capitalists. It is one of the fundamental tenets of socialism that the state should own a good part of the national wealth, particularly what is called the means of production. In this regard, that is state ownership of the means of production, it is my submission that the socialist sate of Singapore is not lagging behind the achievements of socialist governments in other parts of the world, probably ahead of most of them. In parenthesis, may I say when I use the term 'socialist' I exclude Communist states. (Goh, 1972, p. 183)

1.3   STRUCTURE OF THE BOOK

The book is organized in the following way. Chapter 2 reviews the nature of the institutions and policies that generated Singapore's growth and the role the political system has played. We intend to show the importance of the public sector in production and of the government in mobilizing and allocating resources; an importance that is not captured by just looking at the share of the public sector or GLCs in production. Further evidence of this latter feature will appear in subsequent more specialized chapters. We ask how the political system might change in the future and whether this will improve or hinder growth and development prospects.

Chapter 3 looks at the nature of economic growth. Much one-sided attention has been paid to the result of economic activity in the form of output growth rates but recently a debate has arisen about the efficiency with which those high growth rates had been achieved and whether such rapid growth is sustainable. We review some of this debate but argue that what is more important than the exact conclusions of the rapidly proliferating and contradictory academic studies is the nature of the government's response to that debate, the policies it adopted and what it thinks the growth prospects are. We thus review some official projections for future growth rates.

Chapter 4 looks at the structural changes in the economy in terms of expenditure components and the type of production. Expenditure patterns have changed in order to achieve extremely high rates of domestic saving and capital formation which has been accompanied by large current account surpluses leading to the rapid accumulation of foreign reserves which, on a per capita basis, are the highest in the world. We look at the possible justifications of such a policy later. In terms of the future structure of production we identify the extent and nature of the rise of the manufacturing and financial sectors and then look at some recent government statements of its strategy towards manufacturing.

Chapter 5 reviews the nature of the monetary, financial and fiscal aspects that accompanied and supported rapid growth and how the financial system is being restructured at present. The fiscal system and taxation policy reflects the PAP's desire to command financial resources and to avoid what it considers would be the debilitating effects of having a social welfare system. The nature of the actual social welfare system has had an important impact on the welfare of the population and so in Chapter 6 we examine aspects of welfare. That chapter also introduces other indicators of development apart from the narrowly economic, based on income per capita. One important point to note is that even these are misleading. What Singaporeans are interested in from their economic activity is not so much the level of income per capita and its growth rate but the level of their incomes. The presence of many foreign companies and foreign workers in the economy means that about one-third of GDP is earned by foreigners so that the income per capita of Singaporeans is less than the usual figure of GNP per capita that is used in international comparisons. Of course, other countries should adjust their GNP data to identify the earnings of their nationals and in some they would also have to reduce the GNP per person, but probably not by as much as the Singapore figures are reduced. In addition, if we think of development levels in terms of how much people can consume now and were to make international comparisons of consumption per capita then Singapore's GNP figures would be very misleading as its growth strategy has required the highest saving rates in the world such that personal consumption is only about 40 per cent of GDP and government consumption is only about 10 per cent. The extent to which Singaporeans have and will be able to benefit from these high saving rates will be examined in a subsequent chapter. We also look at the changes in the distribution of income in Singapore as its experience has not followed some expectations and here, again, there have been contradictory statements about this experience.

Chapters 7 and 8 look at trade policy and the role it has played in growth as well as international financial and exchange rate aspects. Here the important issues for the future of the economy are its ability to develop further an international financial centre and the future role of the Singapore dollar, that is, the possible further internationalization of the Singapore dollar and what the government feels about this and the possibility of regional monetary cooperation. In Chapter 9 we review the nature of the Asian financial crisis recession in Singapore and how the government responded to it and the nature of the unexpected and severe recession in the economy in the year 2001. We conjecture that this might be seen in the future as a pivotal year in Singapore's development. We review some of our earlier conjectures and look at the likely changes in the future economy if the government implements those policies that it sees necessary to create a 'New Singapore'.

In trying to make this a more general and lighter book than our first offering we have tried not to clutter the text with a source for every statement of fact or interpretation although they are given when we feel it is a point that might not be obvious or might need direct justification. We have provided a list of suggested reading for each chapter that gives the main sources and more can be found in the references.

Appendix A provides some summary time series data that appear in the figures and the text, and the main sources of data on the economy. The annual macroeconomic data we use are the latest revisions of February 2001, which means that in subsequent official publications different numbers will appear. Our annual data run to the year 2000 and we cite quarterly data that include the first two quarters of 2001. Appendix B outlines the electoral systems for parliament and the presidency and the results of elections. Appendix C provides recommendations for readings for each chapter. We include some items of fiction and political texts in these suggestions as we want the reader to obtain a feeling for what life is like in Singapore as expressed by novelists and non-government politicians as well as by the official press.

In our earlier volume we limited ourselves to referring to a very limited number of web sites. In this volume they have become much more important, not only for information and data about Singapore but for access to newspapers, journals and speeches. We have tried not to clutter up the text with too many references for the points we make but we stand by our statements.

2. Foundations for growth

In this chapter we examine the particular nature of Singapore before and at the beginning of its modern period of economic growth and the distinctive institutions and policies the PAP adapted and adopted in order to achieve the economy's high and sustained rate of growth and its structural transformation. One purpose is to show that many characterizations of Singapore as a free-market economy with few state enterprises or state control that is commonly found in writers from the United States, who rank Singapore as the second most economically free economy in the world, are misleading. Many aspects of the government's influence over the economy's resources are not revealed in such numbers as the proportion of GLCs or the public sector in output, which we examined in the previous chapter. Ownership is not the main factor but rather how the government can mobilize resources and allocate them where it sees fit. Another aspect to note is the close links between the business sector, especially the financial sector, and the political elite and the view that the bureaucracy has little independent strength, points argued by Hamilton-Hart (2000). In this context it is relevant to note which sectors of the economy have been protected by the government and the way it has recently faced up to the inefficiencies this has caused and the strong measures it is taking to reform the financial and banking sectors.

2.1 GEOGRAPHIC AND DEMOGRAPHIC ASPECTS

Cohorts of students have been taught that Singapore is a small, open economy with no natural resources. The geography of this flat, little island and the pressures on them from the education system have probably limited the extent of their weekly travels and have blinded them to the obvious fact that Singapore is surrounded by the sea which is an important natural resource. It was the sea and its resources that attracted early settlers who turned it into a fishing village; it was the sea that allowed Sir Stamford Raffles to arrive and establish Singapore; it was the sea that attracted him as it made Singapore an ideal port for his purposes of trade and it is the sea that facilitates the huge amount of trade that passes though Singapore today. Although air and road transport are used for this purpose the sea remains vital. As Adam Smith pointed out, as sea transport is much cheaper than terrestrial transport it is no surprise that major civilizations and great cities are situated on the coast or on navigable rivers. Sea transport facilitated trade thus increasing the extent of the market, reducing costs through specialisation and increasing the variety of products available. This insight of Smith's is one of the reasons for the view of Dr Goh Keng Swee, that developing countries need go no further than Adam Smith for economic advice, although more advanced ones, such as Singapore, could look at David Ricardo (Goh, 1995, p. 263). See Peebles (1998b, pp. 182–7) for a critical discussion of this view. Both Smith and Ricardo approved of free trade and open trading economies. Lingle and Wickman (1999, p. 61) see Singapore's policies after 1965 as an attempt to '"emulate" Hong Kong's policies' as a 'Ricardian free port'. Furthermore, Smith believed that economic growth, not a large volume of output, was the factor that produced high wages, hence the emphasis on the need for sustained further growth in Singapore found in the writings of Dr Goh.

It is only recently that the government has taken seriously the work of making the sea an even more valuable resource by turning some of it into potable water that would reduce its dependence on imports of water from Malaysia, some of which it treats and re-exports to Malaysia at a higher price. Such desalinated water is, in fact, cheaper than imported water.

Singapore was a small city that has become a slightly larger, but still a very small, city-state. The fact that by the 1950s it was a city has been important in influencing its development. Although not completely urban even now, it has not had the burden of a large, backward agricultural sector. In the 1960s those who chose to live by raising chickens, pigs and vegetables in their kampungs were relocated to government housing once the public housing programme got underway. Singapore's agricultural sector today does not show up in the aggregate national income statistics as it is so small, but there is a sector that produces chickens, eggs, raises high-value seafood, vegetables and fruits. This constitutes a minute part of Singapore's total food needs which are met virtually entirely from abroad. The primary sector also concentrates on developing ornamental fish and orchids, of which Singapore is a major world source. This development has been done through a government statutory board (more on these later) under the Ministry of National Development, which had earlier developed Agrotechnology Parks (note they are not called farms) to support this sector. The point to note is that even here the paradigm of goverement mobilization and creation of resources through government agencies also applies to a very small sector of the economy. Despite the insignificance of agriculture in GDP there is a public sector research institute working in the field of molecular agro biology. The former head of the EDB recently described it as 'a criminal waste of taxpayers money' (*The Straits Times*, 2 August, 2001, p. H8). It was subsequently merged with the Institute of Molecular and Cell Biology with a total number of 200 scientists.

By the 1930s Singapore was a major entrepot exporting rubber, tin and petroleum and was a significant and world-renowned distributor of such regional products as copra, rattan, gutta percha, arecanuts, and black pepper (Huff, 1994, p. 86). Globalization is nothing novel to Singaporeans. This entrepot trade required good ports, transport facilities and financing, which was mainly provided by European, not local, banks and insurance. Manufacturing was limited and after the Second World War the earnings of the ports, from facilitating the trade and the expenditures of the British forces, were an important part of the economy. In the 1950s Singapore was a city with a good infrastructure, a colonial civil service and banks but, no doubt, probably due to colonial neglect, very poor living conditions for part of the local population. Population growth was high in the period 1946–57, at a rate then said to be the fastest in the world. This is seen by some in retrospect as a problem but is also an indicator that people had confidence in the economy's future and this was to provide a growing pool of labour for the late 1960s and early 1970s when the inflow of foreign investment started Singapore's industrialization. It seems that this rapid labour growth did not reduce wages (Huff, 1994, p. 293).

Post-war Singapore was never a backward fishing village waiting to be transformed by Lee Kuan Yew into a modern economy as claimed by Keenan (1997) when she describes him as 'an authoritarian Asian leader who transformed a fishing village into an economic powerhouse'. The reputation of the journal, which still has a limit imposed on the numbers it can sell in Singapore, has led others to repeat this view. The King of Thailand would not have sent 20 of his sons to a fishing village for education in the late nineteenth century. A fishing village could not have staged a manned air flight as early as 1911, albeit with a plane that was imported in parts by sea, or be the landing site of a Vickers Vimy airplane in 1919 which was en route from England to Australia. In the 1930s Singapore was credited with having 'the finest airport in the British Empire' (Brazil, 1999, p. 165). Although the Japanese occupation of Singapore was devastating for much of the population and their property it did not reduce the place to rubble and destroy its infrastructure.

In August 1967, two years after Singapore became an independent, sovereign nation and just before it started industrialization by relying on multinational corporations and developing the financial sector, Lee Kuan Yew, speaking to American businessmen in Chicago, pointed out that 'Singapore had grown from a village of 120 fishermen in 1819 to become a metropolis of two million' (Lee, 2000, p. 74).

The reference to Singapore's population of two million in 1967 should remind us of the implications of Singapore being a small city. One often hears description of the massive social problems caused by high unemployment in Singapore in the mid-1960s and references to unemployment rates of, say, 10 per cent (it was 8.2 per cent in 1970 and the highest rate seems to be the 8.9 per cent of 1966 (Huff, 1994, p. 291) although one official source puts it at 10.2 per cent in 1970). These high unemployment rates are sometimes compared to the double-digit rates found in Europe in the 1990s. But 10 per cent of a very small labour force is a small number of people. The increasing inflow of labour-intensive foreign investment into the manufacturing sector starting in 1968 was able to absorb the unemployed rapidly and create jobs for those who were entering the labour force and for those who would lose jobs due the withdrawal of British forces in the late 1960s and early 1970s. Within four years of 1970 the unemployment rate had fallen to 3.9 per cent and the year 1973 is general thought to be one when Singapore became a labour-shortage economy. In 1971 the workforce in manufacturing was 2.3 times greater than in 1967 (Goh, 1977, p. 16). A small amount of direct investment is more significant in a small economy. Furthermore, Singapore's small size means that retrenched workers can remain in their homes and change jobs, an option not open to many people in structurally depressed areas of large economies who face high costs of relocation associated with taking up new employment in different regions. A simple comparison of macroeconomic statistics from Singapore such as unemployment, growth rates and per capita GNP with those of huge national economies should be made with great care. Singapore should grow more rapidly than large countries, given the amount of foreign investment it is still able to attract and its ability to attract foreign workers of the type needed to support this investment.

By the year 2000 Singapore's population just exceeded 4 million, of whom 81 per cent were Singapore residents (citizens and permanent residents) and the rest were foreigners living in Singapore for more than one year. Whereas the number of non-Singaporeans in 2000 was 2.4 times its 1990 level the number of Singaporeans was only 1.2 times its 1990 amount. The average annual growth rate in the total population over the period 1990 to 2000 was 2.8 per cent a year but the growth rate of citizens was only 1.3 per cent a year. The growth rate of the non-resident population was 9.3 per cent per year and by 2000 29 per cent of the working population, that is 612 200 people, were foreigners compared to 16 per cent in 1990.

With falling indigenous population growth rates caused by higher incomes, the need felt by many married couples that both have to work, and the perceived high cost of children, the government abandoned its policy of encouraging small families to an active pronatalist policy and came to rely on the importation of foreign workers and the selective encouragement to settlement in Singapore of workers with talents specific to the features of the government's economic development plans. An important aspect of this is that although Singapore is a small city it has been an independent, sovereign nation since 1965 and thus has control over the nature of the immigrants it allows to settle and the terms of citizenship and permanent residence. With the exception of cities in communist countries such as Shenzhen in China, where immigration can be regulated by internal residence permits, other cities in Asia cannot easily restrict immigration from the poorer rural areas. Singapore can also restrict the importation and use in its territory of motor vehicles, which is not feasible in other cities.

A second feature of Singapore's size and city status is that its economic development has been based on good city planning in providing housing and the required infrastructure, mainly for export-oriented, foreign firms. Again, a small amount of investment goes a long way and with the governments powers of land acquisition and use of government agencies to coordinate urban development Singapore has become a modern city. In the year 2000 it was ranked as the third best city in Asia in terms of quality of life and is known for its 'clean and green' image and for tourists as 'Asia for beginners'. Roads generally lack the terrible congestion found elsewhere in Asia and public transport is good but slow.

One aspect of Singapore's vulnerability that the government is constantly repeating is due to this city-state aspect. Taking a longer perspective, Lee Kuan Yew has pointed out the poor record of survival of city-states and cities in national economies and has answered the question 'Will Singapore the independent city-state disappear?' by replying that 'the island of Singapore will not, but the sovereign nation it has become, able to make its way and play its role in the world, could vanish' (Lee, 2000, p. 762). Lee is not clear as to why he thinks city-states are so vulnerable. Is it the external threat that was the downfall of the ancient Greek states or is it vulnerability to internal change? After all, such city-states as Athens evolved from being oligarchies to monarchies and then to democracies and Lee does not think democracy is conducive to stability, discipline and economic growth. Singapore shares another feature found in ancient city-states but to a lesser degree. In Athens the number of foreign workers and slaves outnumbered the number of citizens who alone were allowed to take part in politics and enjoyed a comfortable life. Singapore does not have such an extreme degree of imbalance between citizens and foreigners but such dependence has caused concern. Some Singaporeans see too much dependence on foreign workers and too much westernization which is thought necessary to attract them to work in Singapore and do not like the government's policy of providing the art and entertainment facilities for them, something which nearly every international advisory panel has suggested. The bars and restaurants of Boat Quay, where Nick Leeson, the 'rogue trader' (Leeson, 1996) who brought down Barings Bank through his unauthorized dealings in Singapore, went to unwind at night, are part of the tourist infrastructure but are not universally liked by Singaporeans. Chee (2001, pp. 11–13, 66–8) indicates some reasons for Singaporeans' resentment of foreign workers.

Another consequence of the presence of foreign workers is one which the government admits could be a greater problem in the future. Lower paid workers face competition from workers from much poorer neighbouring countries. The government's policy is to provide training schemes so they can 'upgrade' (a keyword in Singapore). The higher paid administrative and managerial workers, especially in the field of information technology at present, are free to move elsewhere so they can command salaries linked to the highest in the world in their field. In 2000 there were 200 000 Singaporeans living outside Singapore. This would include retirees, students and workers. There is no way of knowing what proportion of them would return to Singapore. There are no public data of the extent of emigration and the nature of those who leave Singapore. These forces will have implications for the distribution of income and the nature of the workforce and will be examined in Chapter 5.

2.2 POLITICAL ASPECTS

A recent book about Singapore characterized it in its title as 'government-made' (Low, 1998). This is one of the more accurate descriptions of Singapore that can be put in a simple phrase. Since 1959 that government has been formed by the People's Action Party and from 1959 to 1990 its Prime Minister was Lee Kuan Yew. It is relevant to examine briefly the nature of this party, why it adopted the development strategy it did and how this has moulded Singapore society and whether it has possibly created an environment inimical to future development of the economy as a knowledge-based economy.

The PAP was formed in 1954 by mainly English educated professionals as an anti-colonial party in order to contest the 1955 Legislative Assembly General Elections, and which later wanted to establish an independent, non-communist, socialist Malaya. Many members were influenced by Fabian Socialism and some were further to the left and have been characterized as communists. In the 1960s the PAP was allied with communists in order to gain the support of the Chinese-educated population. These factors have influenced the party. In terms of the latter association it has been said that it 'is true that the PAP learned about party organisation and control from the communists' (George, 2000, p. 119). Another link would be Lee Kuan Yew's enthusiasm for the thinking of Mao Zedong whose ideas he studied in English and in the Legislative Assembly in Singapore in 1957 referred to him as the 'great Chinese theoretician' (Barr, 2000, pp. 167–8). The PAP has been described as a Leninist, cadre party into which people are invited if it is thought they are suitable parliamentary or ministerial material required for managing the economy. There are only about 15000 PAP members at present. The PAP was a member of the Socialist International until withdrawing in June 1976 which prevented its expulsion which had been proposed by the Dutch Labour Party.

The legacy of the Fabian socialist influence is that early leaders of the PAP thought the government should have an active role in developing the economy, and that public housing and medical care was a necessity. Lau (1981, pp. 43–88) analyses the pragmatic socialism of Lee Kuan Yew and Goh Keng Swee. Much economic activity was initiated by statutory boards and government-created companies, now called government-linked companies (GLCs). The PAP did not implement radical socialist redistribution policies through high taxes on higher earners or on corporate profits to generate revenues for the provision of social welfare and unemployment. It sought to benefit the general population through job creation and the provision of public housing, education and medical services. This was done by attracting the epitome of global capitalism – mobile, multinational enterprises which were wooed with tax incentives, the provision of infrastructure and a well-trained and non-belligerent work force. Sources of finance other than high taxes on earned incomes were used for the social provisions (see Chapter 5). Dr Goh Keng Swee described himself as a democratic socialist (Chew, 1996, pp. 148–9) and Lee Kuan Yew was thought of as a communist when he was at Cambridge and associated with members of the Labour Party and Labour Club there and was even involved in campaigning for a Labour Party candidate in a by-election. (Barr, 2000, pp. 65–6). Lee's early views and their subsequent versions have dominated the nature of Singapore's political life and it could be said that he has created 'authoritarian capitalism' (Lingle, 1996), although this seems to downplay the socialist origins of the PAP and organizations. Barr (2000, pp. 63–5) argues that apart from socialist influences the most important factor behind Lee's approach is that of the 'Challenge and Response' thesis of Arnold Toynbee which has led to Singapore being governed under the fear of crisis, internal and external enemies and the need to respond to some new crisis which needs all to 'stand up for Singapore' and support the PAP.

Although there are democratic institutions and regular parliamentary elections, things are arranged so that the opposition parties could never form a government (they do not even try), there are restrictions on the domestic press and broadcast media so the opposition can rarely present its view to their fellow citizens and such a medium as a video tape made by a political party is illegal. As the PAP forms the government it has no problems getting its ministers or MPs presented in the media.

The problems facing the political opposition in Singapore are documented in Seow (1994), Chee (1994, 1995, 1998, 2001), George (2000) and reports of various human rights organizations. The way the Singapore press was made subservient to the government is recalled in Seow (1998), Davies (1999) and Chee (2001). The trade union movement, organized under the national Trades Union Congress (NTUC) and headed by a PAP minister has become, in the view of the World Bank, 'in effect a branch of the ruling People's Action Party' (World Bank, 1993, p. 165). Nearly all union members are in unions that are affiliated to the NTUC. Union members who actively support any opposition parties cannot hold positions in NTUC affiliated unions. Their expectation is that they would lose their jobs as well. This process of pulling nearly all independent organizations under the control of the PAP, which has always been able to use the organs of the state to enforce this trend, has been discussed by many. See Haas (1999b) for a recent collection of analyses in which he tries to assess the extent to which this is the result of Lee's character, aspects of which can be examined in Lee (1998 and 2000) and Barr (2000) and whether his permanent retreat from political activity will change this.

The PAP's domination of parliament is documented in Appendix B as many outside observers do not realize its extent, particularly the fact that at the time of a general election the PAP has already won the election as non-PAP parties do not put up enough candidates to defeat it. They do this in the hope that this will encourage people to vote against the PAP knowing they will still get a PAP government but more non-PAP members in parliament. The largest number of elected non-PAP members of parliament has been the four out of 81 seats after the 1991 general election. This was reduced to two out of 83 in 1997. This means that many Singaporeans are not allowed to vote at all. In the 1997 general election 60 per cent of the electorate could not vote at all and in 1991 the figure was 50 per cent. This rate of disenfranchisement has increased since 1980 and it is possible to find a 44-year-old citizen who has never been allowed to vote in a general election (*The Straits Times*, 14 April, 2001, p. H8). When there is a contest voting is compulsory. In the views of some this makes a mockery of the claim that Singapore is a democracy and is a challenge to the prime minister's slogan that 'every Singaporean counts', when a majority of Singaporeans do not have their vote counted as it does not exist.

When asked about this situation and his long-term service at the head of government, when he is outside Singapore, Lee replies that he is not a dictator as he has to face re-election every five years or so (on all 12 occasions he has 'won') and that anyone can stand against him. This is not accurate. Mr Lee is a member of a Group Representation Constituency (GRC) that requires a team of six people to contest the election, an innovation he introduced for the 1988 General Election. Under this system a person who wishes to stand against Mr Lee must be part of a group of candidates, either all of the same political party or all independents, one member of which must belong to a minority community. As opposition parties find it hard enough to get a reasonable number of candidates it is difficult to find enough for the many large GRCs and a potentially good candidate risks losing because of his partners. The opposite is true for the PAP which can put an unpresentable candidate who is thought to have potential into a GRC which is held by the Senior Minister, the Prime Minister or a popular minister. In the 1997 general election Mr Lee and his team were returned to parliament unopposed, meaning that his constituents were not allowed to vote at all and show the degree of support for his party. This allowed him, and the future Prime Minister who was also returned through a walk-over, to spend more time on other matters and give their support to other PAP candidates elsewhere. Mr Lee is re-elected so it might not be appropriate to call him a dictator but another aspect of such behaviour relates to the style of governing, It is now clear that Mr Lee and Dr Goh Keng Swee decided to negotiate the 'expulsion' of Singapore from Malaysia without consulting any of their Cabinet colleagues who were used as a way of hiding these actions and to pretend that Singapore was asking to remain in Malaysia. See Barr (2000, pp. 79–80) and the interview with Goh Keng Swee, which first revealed these actions, and Toh Chin Chye, who revealed that he had not known what was really going on, in Chew (1996) and Lee (1998, pp. 628–47). Barr (2000) interprets these events and the subsequent political cover up in the context of his analysis of Lee's core beliefs in Toynbee's 'Challenge and Response' thesis as a perfect opportunity to face Singaporeans with the challenge to survive, convince them to make immediate sacrifices as well as minimizing his personal embarrassment as he had been the one who had manipulated Singapore into Malaysia in the first place (Barr, 2000, pp. 80–81). Singapore's parliament did not meet until 8 December 1965, four months after separation.

The government's justification of such a system is mainly based on economic considerations. By having no real political activity between elections ministers are free to concentrate on managing the economy, which is what they are recruited to do. Politicking generally only emerges at election time. The PAP, which decides when a general election will be held, knows well in advance when that will be and usually gives the opposition parties very little notice so they are not able to prepare election materials and meetings. There are 21 registered political parties in Singapore but not all of them are active and in 1997, for example, only six parties contested the elections.

Another justification for the GRC system, described by Singapore's third President after his removal from office as fecund gerrymandering, is that it allows the PAP to bring into government a man, usually a man as there a very few women in parliament, who, lacking charisma or the common touch and looking awkward and gawky, might not have much hope in a single fight against a well-chosen adversary. However the PAP wants him in as it believes he is a good manager because of his experience, often in the military. The people cannot be trusted to choose as they really do not know their own best interests or do not have the required information to make complicated decisions, so their leaders are chosen for them and are ensured of entry into parliament.

It has been truly said that all politics is local politics and the PAP has taken this to heart in the way it manages public housing estates and provides benefits such as upgrading of public housing flats and related, urban developments (which have a crucial impact on the value of most people's main assets – the lease on their public flat), and benefits such as student grants and aid to the elderly. This management and distribution of funds is done by Community Development Councils (CDCs). In order to help voters understand that their member of parliament is not just their representative in the national parliament but the person who can decide how their estates will be developed and disburse these state funds, all CDCs are headed by an elected member of parliament – except the two opposition-held wards. These are headed by unelected members of the PAP who are usually previously defeated but potential candidates for those constituencies. The CDCs have been told not to work with the elected members of parliament for the ward if they are not PAP members of parliament – there are only two at present and both are single-member constituencies. They both have complained of the lack of cooperation of statutory boards in providing services for their wards. In all wards, the PAP has access to election returns that are so disaggregated that they show the votes for the PAP at the level of groups of blocks of flats, even in PAP constituencies, so that those blocks which did not return what was thought to be an acceptably high share of votes for the PAP, can be discriminated against when state funds are used on upgrading projects. More recently, the government has appointed five unelected mayors to administer different areas and it would not be difficult to guess which political party they are associated with.

From the point of view of Singapore's development strategy based on foreign investment by large global capitalist enterprises, the dominance of the PAP can be seen to reduce uncertainty involved in any large investment, and sometimes a single investment by a foreign firm can be US$1000 million and would require a long pay-back period. There is not going to be a change in government through which a populist, redistributive party gained power. Singapore is regularly rated as the least risky economy to invest in. For example, The Economist Intelligence Unit's ranking for the end of 2000 ranked Singapore as the least risky followed by Hong Kong, Chile, Botswana and the United Arab Emirates. Amongst the most risky were Iraq, Myanmar, Indonesia, Pakistan and Russia so it can be seen that, by their criteria at least, being small is not a disadvantage (*The Economist*, 10 March, 2001, p. 116). Similarly, the World Bank ranks Singapore as a very low risk country with a high institutional investor credit rating (World Bank, 2000, Table 17, p. 307).

The Singapore example is often held up as one that shows that democracy is not a prerequisite for growth but that case can only be based on the evidence available and only supports the view that this situation has produced high output growth rates so far. Whether it has produced a developed society and equally rapid improvement in the standards of the indigenous population, and whether it is suited to the demands of a different future are another matter. A consequence of Singapore's political system is that people are very reluctant to become involved in politics or in organizations that might be construed as trying to play a political role. Even the PAP continually complains of the difficulty it has in recruiting members suitable enough for election to parliament or government office.

The PAP is proud to state that its policies are essentially pragmatic, meaning that they do not push policies that are derived from ideology but only ones that they think will contribute to the economic growth of Singapore. Goh Keng Swee's economic theory is 'the primacy of economic growth' and that 'unless you have economic growth, you die' (quoted from Chew, 1996, p. 149). Here the influence of Adam Smith is likely as he believed that only in growing societies would wages be high, and in opulent but stagnant ones wages would be low. One aspect of this pragmatism is that they do not feel that they have 'to re-invent the wheel' and will examine ideas from anywhere and see whether they can be adapted to Singaporean circumstances. This has meant that there has been, and still is, a great deal of reliance on foreign advisers. In 1960 the United Nations Development Programme (UNDP) visited Singapore to advise it on industrialization. It was led by Dr Albert Winsemius, a Dutch economist, who became a regular visitor to Singapore for 23 years and 'was to play a major role in our economic planning' (Lee, 1998, p. 347). Part of that role was not only advising but also promoting Singapore, especially to potential investors from Holland such as Phillips which now has significant investments in Singapore. *The Straits Times* called him 'Singapore's economic engineer'

(*The Straits Times*, 23 September, 1996) and elsewhere he has been described as the 'founding father' of Singapore (Tamboer, 1996). He had no contract with the government. It was Dr Winesmius who pushed the government to develop the ports so they could handle containers and in this respect the Singapore ports now rival Rotterdam itself in the extent of its throughput. He identified four industries to develop and recommended the establishment of a single coordinating agency that would attract foreign investors, so in August 1961 the Economic Development Board (EDB) was established, with the aid of the UNDP and the International Labour Office, as a statutory board. This organization has been crucial in Singapore's development. The first managing director of the EDB was an Israeli, E.J. Mayer, and another Israeli acted as occasional consultant (Schein, 1996, pp. 34, 40–42). Lee Kuan Yew had talks with Israeli econo-mists and advisers in these early days of planning. It could be argued that what later were called 'Asian Values' and were associated with his views came more from those experiences than from any Confucian heritage which, after all, was alien to the early PAP leaders. Another suggestion is found in Hill (2000) who argues convincingly that Singapore later adopted the general idea of 'Asian Values' from the works of Western social scien-tists in the 1960s and 1970s who had argued that neo-Confucianism was more conducive to industrialization than had been supposed. Lee Kuan Yew recalls how he learned of the nature of some Asian societies though his visits to American universities and talks with Western academics (Lee, 2000, pp. 512–13). Dr Goh Keng Swee identified the values that Singapore upholds and which are often presented as Asian as those of the Victorian era in Britain. Backman (1999, p. 21) offers a cynical redefinition of what 'Asian Values' actually are.

One of the most important views that Lee Kuan Yew remembers receiv-ing from these talks with Israelis was the necessity of identifying and select-ing the best people and working out how to manage and train them (Schein, 1996, p. 35). The best are often selected by government ministries, statutory boards and companies at graduation and given generous scholarships for further education abroad with the condition of being bonded to that organ-ization for a number of years on return to Singapore. They are managed by being probably the highest paid civil servants in the world and ministers are the highest paid in the world with all their salaries being linked to those of top earners in a number of professions. The generous payment of civil ser-vants was identified by the World Bank as one reason for the Asian miracle and in Singapore it is justified as being necessary to keep people from moving into the private sector. One criticism of this form of recruitment often heard in Singapore is that these scholars have little business experi-ence after their return to Singapore, remain out of touch with the concerns of ordinary Singaporeans and become rather arrogant. To some extent in the past they have had their lives planned for them and a career path laid out, leading them to lack a spirit of adventure.

Despite the origin of these 'basics' (Lee Kuan Yew's phrase) in their modern justification in a government White Paper on 'Shared Values' political leaders are described as *junzi,* Confucian gentleman, despite the general failure of promoting Confucianism in Singapore schools. See Peebles (1998b, pp. 196–7) for a discussion. Another view offered by the Israelis was that one reason other countries have not followed such good advice of selecting the best as leaders was that they become 'enamored of various theories or they don't want to do the difficult parts of that prescription', in the words of E.J. Mayer addressed to Lee Kuan Yew (Schein, 1995, p. 34). Hence PAP pragmatism.

Israelis also played a crucial role in helping Goh Keng Swee design the Singapore Armed Forces and with the decision to make it a conscript service as this had not been the intention of the government (Chew, 1996, p. 148) and Lee (2000, pp. 40–44). All adult male Singaporeans and Permanent Residents are required to serve two or two-and-a-half years in the services or related organizations such as Civil Defence. Subsequently they must do training and be ready for active service until the age of 40 or 50. Employers have learned to cope with these demands on their employees. National Service (NS) is seen as an essential part of creating a Singaporean identity and nation. It also allows young men to learn skills that might later be useful. In terms of selecting the elite, military scholarships were used to recruit scholars who would study abroad at top universities and then be bonded to the military for eight years during which time they would again do specialist courses abroad including degrees in public or business administration. Such people were then available for the civil service or in the public sector if they did not wish to remain in the military. Four of the most prominent younger ministers are former career military men – two Brigadier Generals, one Lieutenant-Colonel and one Rear Admiral.

In 1983 the civil services adopted the recruitment and promotion methods and criteria used by the Shell company which Lee Kuan Yew had observed. It is interesting to note that on the very day that Singapore became a sovereign nation, Monday, 9 August 1965, even before he had declared this to the world, Lee Kuan Yew had already given letters to the Indian diplomatic representative requesting advisers to train an army and to the diplomat from Egypt asking for an adviser to help build a coastal defence force (Lee, 1998, 15).

The role of foreigners in modern Singapore, apart from those who live and work there, is different from in the early days when establishing institutions and mobilizing adequate resources was the key task. Recently, their role has been related to advising on reforms to the existing system and on the industries that might be attracted to Singapore and how to get them. For example, in the 1990s there were International Advisory Panels for the banking and financial sectors and the education system. In the case of banking most of their recommendations were adopted. Some Singaporeans find it ironical that the government will pay large fees for foreign advisors who have no vested interest in the success of Singapore when there are equally qualified Singaporeans who do not generally have their views recognized in public. The negative aspect of this is often made by the PAP to foreigners who discuss Singaporean affairs in public: 'If we listen to you Singapore will fail and we will lose everything and be finished but you can just go home.' This is a typical reaction to an unsolicited and what is seen as a critical suggestion or interpretation of policy offered by a foreigner. All good policies must be seen to come from the PAP, it seems. Using foreign advisory panels does have an interesting political function. The government can say they are following the best advice and they have to adopt possibly unpopular policies because they reflect the best the world can offer. This means that they can ignore the fact that opposition politicians have long advocated some of the policies that were later adopted on the basis of this foreign advice. For example, it was suggested that the two main universities, both statutory boards, should be given more autonomy over some of their affairs. This had been advocated by the Workers' Party and others for years, but the PAP's saying it was adopting the practice of the world's best universities based on foreign advice meant any independent indigenous source of ideas could be marginalized or ignored.

The other role international advisory panels play today and how they affect the economy can be seen by the recent moves by the government to build a 'fourth pillar' for the economy around life sciences. Foreigners were asked which sectors of the economy could be expanded, which companies might be interested in investing in this area and how research should be organized. There is even a ministerial committee concerned with life sciences and ministers, civil servants and COEs of statutory boards have been sent on courses on the basic science, such as genetics, underlying life sciences and the education system will be told to increase the coverage of such topics in its curricula, even down to the kindergarten level. Ministers have regular meetings with foreign businessmen and members of several foreign business councils are part of the National Wages Council.

Another aspect of this pragmatism is that Singapore is keen to take advantage of problems faced by neighbouring countries. Hong Kong has always been seen as a source of immigrants as they would support the racial structure of Singapore (77 per cent of the resident population are Chinese,

14 per cent are Malay, 8 per cent are Indian and 1 per cent are 'other') and are thought to be more entrepreneurial than Singaporeans. Hong Kong has been particularly vulnerable to problems that might encourage emigration. The brutal suppression of students in China in 1989, the uncertainty related to the return of sovereignty to China in July 1997 and the effects of the Asian financial crisis on the economy have affected Hong Kong. As BG (NS) George Yeo remarked on the effects of the Asian financial crisis: 'All over the region now, bright, able, dynamic entrepreneurial people have gone bankrupt or are without jobs. . . . Should we not selectively encourage some of them to come into Singapore so that when the tide comes in again, we will have that thick layer of entrepreneurs and foreign talent to take our economy even further into the next century?' (George, 2000, p. 185).

Another important aspect of that pragmatism has been the government's policy towards the general use of English although there have been campaigns to promote Mandarin, known as *Hua yu*, for the Chinese, in Singapore. English is one of the four official languages, the other three being Mandarin, Tamil and Malay, which is the national language. The use of the English language has been very important as a way of attracting foreign investment, most of which comes from the United States, Japan and Europe. It is interesting to note that during the 1990s English-speaking economies performed well with Ireland being hailed as a 'Celtic tiger', Australia avoiding the effects of the Asian financial crisis, and Britain performing better than continental Europe. Not to forget that Singapore, with strong trade and investment links with the United States, was the least affected regional economy during the financial crisis.

2.3   POLITICS AND DEVELOPMENT: PAST, PRESENT AND FUTURE

The past nature of politics in Singapore is easy to characterize as PAP dominance but it is harder to say how that dominance has affected the nature of society and to identify the extent to which it has been necessary for creating government-led economic growth. Of course, the PAP, usually through the arguments of Lee Kuan Yee, claim that the PAP dominance and its micro-level social engineering were indispensable. The negative aspects of that dominance are regularly rehearsed in Singapore: a reluctance to enter politics even as a member of the PAP; the fear to speak out on social and political issues; a lack of independent organizations that are usually characterized as civil society; an expectation that the government will solve any problem, which has bred a lack of independence in thought and in entrepreneurship. The churches are forbidden from commenting publicly on social issues and when church members and a few lawyers became involved in upholding the rights of Filipino women working in Singapore as domestic helpers in 1987 they were arrested under the Internal Security Act and were accused of being part of a 'Marxist Conspiracy'. This later led to staged publicly broadcast 'confessions' not untypical of one-party socialist states and which in the view of Seow (1994, pp. 230–32) was ineptly handled by the government and backfired on them. In March 2001 the government classified two civil society organizations, the Think Centre and Open Singapore Centre, as political associations which would mean restrictions on the sources and amount of donations they could solicit.

The PAP recognizes the negative legacy of what some people see as its domineering, all-intrusive bullying and talks of allowing more room for people to express themselves and to form civil society organizations – as long as they stay outside politics, which is virtually impossible. Current understanding of what might happen to the political scene is clouded by the mixed signals the PAP has been sending out. It was thought that under Goh Chok Tong there would be a more tolerant approach but the same things continue to happen to those very few who join the political arena: loss of employment if they work at a statutory board; biased reporting of their ideas by the local media, if they are even mentioned there at all; flurries of law suits and investigations by the tax authorities; derogatory comments on their motives and ideas by the PAP. In the political realm Singapore has some institution found in developed countries such as an elected parliament and regular elections. In late 2000 another institution found in some developed countries was adopted with great fanfare to show the government's willingness to accept more public comment. This was 'Speaker's Corner' modelled on that in Hyde Park in London. It was established in a small city-centre park next to a police station. This would give Singaporeans a chance to debate political and social issues in public without first having to apply for an entertainment license issued by the police. All they need to do was to prove at the nearby police post that they were a citizen and give notification of their topics and be reminded they were subject to the usual laws of slander and those concerning religious harmony. A member of an opposition party had chosen to serve two short jail sentences rather than pay a fine when he had been charged for speaking in pubic without a license. This might seem like a trivial change but in Singapore it was significant and attracted the attention of most international media organizations. Casual review of the newspapers and visits suggests that interest in this venue has declined. Opposition party members have declined to use it so far. One prominent figure involved in trying to develop the influence of civil society organizations has been called up for police interviews concerning an incident at the corner when it was felt that too many people turned up, which was probably taken as indicating some degree of organization. This might not seem significant but that event was enough for the *Asian Wall Street Journal* (13 February, 2001) on its editorial page to comment that 'Singaporeans may now learn that it's OK to hold forth at Speaker's Corner, so long as there's no audience. If that's the outcome, civil rights advocates who thought the Speaker's Corner was a step forward will likely decide that they were duped.'

It has been argued, by Samuel Huntington in particular, that the demise of Lee Kuan Yew will be the major turning point and that the Singaporean system will not survive him and it will not be able to maintain an uncorrupted political system and will be subject to a process of 'degeneration and decay' (*The Business Times*, 29 May, 2000). Hamilton-Hart (2000) argues that the exiting system of government 'may be showing signs of decay' and that 'Lee Kuan Yew's personal power is in fact something that plausibly threatens the system of government rather than sustains it' (Hamilton-Hart, 2000, p. 204). So, one view is that it is the lack of Lee Kuan Yew that will cause decay and the other is that the lingering of Lee Kuan Yew is causing problems already. Given the nature of the future Singapore leadership that Lee Kuan Yew has planned it is no surprise to learn that he dismisses these views. What is of concern to some Singaporeans is whether any future leadership will give them more room to express themselves in the fields of the arts and politics and give them more access to the popular media through which they can contact the bulk of the population and not the limited number who use the internet to access alternative views on Singapore. In the past such freedoms were seen as irrelevant as they did not promote economic growth and were of no intrinsic value. To some extent this view has been modified, but the economic imperative remains and the building of theatres and museums and attracting foreign theatrical productions is seen as part of a move to make Singapore an arts hub of Asia to boost the tourist industry and to please the growing expatriate population.

One long-term prediction of the nature of Singapore from one of its former presidents links future economic performance with the possible continuance of the existing political system when he writes

> As things are, one can only wonder how much longer successful economic performance and a loutish political style can sleep together in the same bed. While one dreams of electronic paradises to come, the other enacts, in political nightmares, vengeful vendettas against foes real or imaginary, mostly the latter. Alas, both must perish in fatal embrace, on the same bed. C.V. Devan Nair (1994, p. *xxx*)

Since that was written economic growth has continued and there has been a general election that showed the accuracy of his description of the PAP's political style. See Appendix B for some details. Whether his long-run prediction is as accurate, one wonders and fears.

2.4 MAJOR INSTITUTIONS

Here we briefly describe some of the most important institutions behind Singapore's growth and the role they have played in mobilising and coordinating the use of resources. They will feature in subsequent sections when we discuss particular aspects of their roles.

The Economic Development Board has played the most important part in planning the development of the Singapore economy. Not only does it woo foreign investors it also acts as a coordinating agency with other public sector bodies to ensure that they respond to the needs of foreign investors. In its early days it quickly gained a reputation for professionalism and an ability to respond very quickly to enquiries and make decisions so that foreign investors found they could start operations within a very short period, much sooner than if they had gone to other countries. The EDB enters into joint ventures with foreign firms thus receiving revenue which makes up for the fact that many investors are given generous tax breaks. It also conducts training courses for workers.

Another important institution is the Jurong Town Corporation (JTC). Jurong is the eastern part of Singapore where the swamps were first drained and industrial estates were built. The JTC now operates throughout Singapore by building and managing industrial and commercial premises as well as the Science Parks. It can offer ready-built factories or will prepare land and the required supporting infrastructure for those investors who require specific features in their factories. This has become more important as some factories such as those in the three wafer fabrication parks require buildings that are not subject to vibrations and must be protected from the outside environment.

A very important feature of the Singapore economy that allows these two organizations and others to do their work efficiently is the government policy towards land. Over the period 1968–81 the British military were organizing their withdrawal and handing over the land and bases, together making up about 11 per cent of the land area, including valuable docks and an airport. The government ensured that these resources were immediately put to productive economic use by attracting foreign investors into them or to locate nearby. In addition the government has used its power of compulsory land acquisition to the extent that now about 80 per cent of Singapore's land area is state land. Such state land ownership is usually associated with socialist states but it is also the case in Hong Kong when it was a British colony where all the land, with the exception of one small plot, was crown land. The government has been able to acquire land to convert it to the needs of foreign investors or for developing infrastructure. Most recently there have been many acquisitions necessary for the construction of the North-East railway line. Privately-owned factories were acquired and demolished to make space for new industrial parks. The extent of state ownership of land gives the government an important other source of revenue as it can sell leases. Some have called these powers of land acquisition 'draconian' as the government was able to acquire land in the period 1973–87 at prices that prevailed in 1973 (Phang, 1996, pp. 491–4). The government does not believe it has abused these powers, but has perhaps misused some of the land it acquired. Overenthusiasm for modernization led it to demolish many unique, old buildings to replace them with the ubiquitous skyscraper box, thus destroying what attracted many tourists to Singapore. It has tried to rectify this by redeveloping areas such as Chinatown but the result to many is to turn the areas into theme parks. The significance of this aspect of Singapore's resource mobilization was again stressed when, in June 2001, a new statutory board, the Singapore Land Authority (SLA), was created by merging four government departments.

The policy of increasing the extent of state land ownership could have two explanations apart from the influence of socialist ideas of the PAP. During and after the Second World War Lee Kuan Yew observed that those who bought properties using rapidly depreciating Japanese occupation currency from desperate sellers became very rich once peace returned. Once he realized that Singapore would grow rapidly it would have become clear that large private landowners could become very rich with the potential to branch out into such businesses as publishing and broadcasting and even become a source of funds for opposition political parties. Businessmen in Singapore are reluctant to indulge in politics as the government and PAP members have extensive commercial interests in the economy and any potential challenger could suffer economic damage. Another possible explanation, more academic and economic rather than political in nature, is the possible influence of the socialist background of the PAP and the view that land rent is unearned income, is not a cost and does not serve to create more of it. As Goh Keng Swee said, more advanced economies such as Singapore could look to Ricardo. Perhaps it is this context he had in mind since it was Ricardo who developed such a view to be picked up by Henry George and turned into a political movement in America that would tax land rents and still attracts the attention of some economists today. In fact, Phang (1996) argues that Singapore's land policies are an implementation of and justification for Georgist policies but is not able to identify whether there was any academic influence on the early PAP leaders. She believes that Henry George would approve of the government's policy towards capturing land rents for the community but would not like the extent of the government's involvement in the economy through 'industrial policy, zoning, compulsory saving, housing subsidies etc.' (Phang, 1996, p. 500).

Another aspect of the government's policy towards land has been land reclamation which has increased the land area by 13 per cent from 1965 to 1999. This might not seem a large increase but it has been valuable land that has been allocated to modern container ports and, in the form of Jurong Island, the linking of seven islands to create a huge offshore petrochemicals complex, which is still expanding and attracting more foreign investors in activities that are related to refining, chemicals and pharmaceuticals. A large area of land has been created in the sea just next to the Central Business District and financial centre and in 2001 the first plots were sold to developers. The earth for reclamation is largely imported from Indonesia.

In the early days of Singapore's modern economic growth the government played the role of entrepreneur in the sense of establishing organizations necessary to support economic growth. The indigenous capitalist sector was limited to the financial and trading sectors and there was little experience in manufacturing. The manufacturing sector was built up by relying on foreign firms but large amounts of the necessary support was from the public sector. The Public Utilities Board (PUB) was established as a statutory board to supply gas, electricity and water. In October 1995 the PS was corporatized and it became the PUB becoming the regulatory agency for the supply of water, gas and electricity with the electricity supply coming from three newly-created generation companies and supply from one. The Port of Singapore Authority (PSA) operated the ports, the Housing and Development Board (HDB) provided public housing in which about 86 per cent of Singaporeans live and 90 per cent of them own their flats. Public housing is not cheap and the government has used it for purposes of social engineering in deciding who can live where, to put limits on to whom it can be re-sold in order to prevent the concentration of certain races in one place, to make it hard for single people to obtain it and to encourage children to live near their parents.

Statutory boards are seen as potentially more efficient than government departments as they can adopt incentive systems for both their overall performance and for their staff. For example, in September 1992 the Internal Revenue Department was converted into a statutory board known as the Inland Revenue Authority of Singapore (IRAS). The previous performance of the Internal Revenue Department had been quite poor and in 1991 nearly 50 per cent of tax returns had not been assessed and the amount of arrears was growing rapidly (Asher, 1999, p. 15). The IRAS is paid a fee by the government which is linked to performance and it is thought that statutory board status improved staff morale and was the impetus for technological upgrading for which there are further plans and a move towards self assessment. See *IRAS Annual Report 1999* from http://www.iras.gov.sg.

In addition to statutory boards the government created its own companies which are now called Government-linked Companies (GLCs) and which are owned by four major government holding companies and statutory boards. The extent of public ownership of these GLCs has changed over time as some have had shares sold to the public with the government retaining substantial shareholdings. It has proved very difficult to compile a complete list of GLCs, with some of them in defence-related areas or strategic sectors being exempted for having to file with the Registrar of Companies (Low, 1998, p. 159). Low (1998, p. 161) estimates the number of GLCs and statutory boards in 1985 to be 361 rising to a peak of 720 in 1994 and then falling to 592 in 1996. Alten (1995, p. 201) cites the number of GLCs in which the government holding companies and statutory boards had holdings at 505, a figure from a government publication, and estimates the number in 1990 to be 616 (ibid., p. 201). After the 1985 recession the Public Sector Divestment Committee recommended in 1987 the selling of shares in many GLCs but the government has retained significant holdings in many listed companies such as Singapore Telecommunications (79.7 per cent, Semb Corporation Industries (58.8 per cent), Singapore Airlines (53.8 per cent) and Singapore National Printers Corporation (49.0 per cent) and others at present (Cardarelli et al., 2000, p. 11). There is room for the government to sell more of its holdings to provide its people with a greater shareholder stake in the economy, which it did in 1993 when it sold shares in SingTel, and provide more shares for trading.

GLCs have had problems in implementing the government's policy of regionalization when they try to buy into foreign companies. One reason is their natural conservative nature and the other is the reluctance of foreign countries to see GLCs take large stakes in some of their industries as they are perceived to be too closely connected with the Singapore government. The number of statutory boards in 2001 exceeded that of mid 1986. As the government reduces is ownership of well established GLCs it continues to take up joint shareholdings with new foreign firms attracted to Singapore so just examining the trend of government share divestment would not give an accurate picture of the government's involvement in the economy. Taking up joint ventures with foreign investors is not to gain control of the newly created firms but will generate revenues for the government. The GLCs owned by Temasek Holdings alone accounted for about 10 per cent of GDP and about 27 per cent of the stock market capitalization in 2000 despite years of privatization.

Board members and senior executives of GLCs are appointed by the government and are mainly civil servants, politicians or military officers, and multiple directorships are common. Singapore's best known company, Singapore Airlines, was established by the government and is the best known GLC with the government retaining 53.8 per cent of its shares. All statutory boards except the HDB generate surpluses, part of which are passed on to the government. It has been argued the monopoly position of many of them has been used to extract a surplus from the working population to finance Singapore's development – just as in socialist countries the pricing of agricultural and industrial products was used to exploit agriculture for a similar purpose.

GLCs are significant in areas of the economy that are thought to be strategic such as military equipment, aerospace repair, steelmaking and shipbuilding and repair. SIA is thought of as having national strategic importance but it has even been proposed recently that the government should not be adverse to see foreign majority ownership but it would be interesting to see whether this would ever happen.

The continuing significance of statutory boards in economic activity can be shown by the fact that in 1999, of the 472.6 hectares of state land that were alienated to statutory boards and to the private sector, as much as 84 per cent was bought by statutory boards.

The public sector's role has not been limited to providing infrastructure, housing, education, health and entrepreneurship in those sections of industry where indigenous capital or expertise was lacking but can also be seen in the nature of the financial system and the mobilization and allocation of saving. The Development Bank of Singapore (DBSBank) was established in 1968 as a development financing institution and was used to channel funds to areas of the economy thought important for development. The Post Office Saving Bank (POSBank), originally established in 1877 but turned into a statutory board in 1972, has served as the main retail bank for the local population and has always had more accounts in it than the total population of Singapore. It is a savings bank and the only bank whose deposits are guaranteed by the government. It is required to hold a significant part of its assets in government securities, loans to GLCs or statutory boards and deposits at DBSBank. One of its two main objectives was 'to mobilize domestic savings for the purpose of public development' (Luckett et al., 1994, p. 62).

Another socialistic aspect of Singapore is its co-operative movement, with 972 000 members in 1998 and which has significant firms in retailing and insurance. Goh Keng Swee was behind the idea of letting unions run co-operatives and here again the guiding hand of the government is very clear as they are part of the NTUC. In the retail sector NTUC Far Price is the largest supermarket retailer and has about 400000 members/owners and operates 80 stores. Membership is only open to members of trade unions under NTUC and they benefit by receiving a rebate on their purchases, as is the case with most retail cooperatives, and a dividend on their shares. Its shops are open to any customer and it sees itself as having an important social role by keeping down the cost of living of the poorest members of society and its pricing policy puts competitive pressure on new entrants into retailing. It believes it served to moderate the increase in food prices that would be expected during the recent recession as the Singapore dollar was allowed to depreciate about 20 per cent against the American dollar (Tan, K.L., 1998). This supermarket chain was established by the NTUC in 1973 and has grown by its merger with other labour organizations' retail co-operatives that were established after 1973, which was a time of high imported inflation. The other significant cooperative is NTUC Income, an insurance company, with 518 000 members. It develops products that fit in with the government's changes in the Central Provident Fund scheme. NTUC also operates the largest taxi cab company. These co-operatives are firms that sell goods and services to non-members whereas there are many small organizations that call themselves co-operatives that are social clubs for members only. Other co-operatives are found in housing and credit provision.

The local banking system has been protected from foreign competition and has been very profitable, but in the government's view it led this sector to be 'inward-looking' and the banks 'were doing well, protected from competition' (Lee, 2000, p. 99). As part of its policy to try to increase the efficiency of the local banking sector the government, which thinks there is room for only two large domestic banks, compared to the current 'big four' sold POSBank, a statutory board to DBS, a major GLC in November 1998. It has also encouraged the employment of foreigners to lead the banking sector to greater levels of efficiency and to venture abroad (Lee, 2000, pp. 99–100).

Another important institution that will feature in later chapters is the Central Provident Fund, which first started operating in July 1955, this is a mandatory retirement plan for all employees into which both employers and employees are required to contribute. Funds are held in government bonds and in virtually every year of its existence contributions have exceeded withdrawals by a significant amount. Members own their own funds which are available for financing retirement, for private investment, property purchase or education in Singapore. The rates of contributions have been adjusted over the long run to increase this amount of 'forced saving' and changed in the short run as a tool of macroeconomic policy. Although designed as a scheme for providing funds for retirement, various reforms have allowed members to withdraw part of their funds for the purchase of housing, their own investment in a limited number of financial instruments, and education fees in Singapore. We will return to this institution in later chapters.

We can see that the government has had access to large amounts of domestic savings and has played a role in determining their use. The estimates of the government's 'take' from the economy in studies of economic freedom that look at income tax rates or tax revenues grossly underestimate the government's 'take' (as there are many other non-tax charges) and give a misleading impression of the extent of the government's command over financial resources. The government has generally kept tax rates on personal incomes and profits low to encourage business but has been able to raise more revenue through the leasing of land, the surpluses of statutory boards, charges for road usage and automobile purchase and others. In Asher's view 'Singapore cannot be regarded as a low tax country. Anecdotal evidence suggest that this is indeed how management consultancy and other such firms portray Singapore' (Asher, 1999, p. 4).

Related, in a way, to the CPF system to the extent that it has played an important role in influencing the earnings of the working population, is the National Wages Council which was established in 1972 as an independent tripartite organization that is not part of the government, nor is it a statutory board. It does not report to parliament nor to any minister though its recommendations are endorsed by the cabinet. In the late 1990s there were 30 members, being equally drawn from the government, from the trade unions and from the business community where of the ten employers' representatives two represented Japanese companies, two German and two American. It has been chaired by a university professor, Professor Lim Chong Yah, since its establishment. It makes annual recommendations which have been both quantitative and qualitative on the extent of wage and salary adjustments. It does not plan wage changes for any sectors of the economy and its suggestions, unlike CPF components of wages which are mandatory and set by the government, are overall national guidelines which have been influenced by the Council's concern with the international competitiveness of the economy and the belief it should build flexibility into wages in Singapore (Lim, 1998, pp. 44–5).

In the nexus between saving, much of which is channelled through the public sector, and investment an interesting and important institution plays a role that is not as transparent as many Singaporeans would like. This is the Government of Singapore Investment Corporation Pte Ltd (GIC), a private company established in 1981 and wholly owned by the Ministry of

Finance. It states that it has the responsibility of managing the foreign reserves of Singapore which are said to exceed $120 billion. See their web site at: http://www.gic.com.sg/we/index.html. By 2001 these reserves reached $140 billion.

Recent changes have meant that the GIC is three different companies with one specializing in real estate investment and another in 'venture capital, infrastructure, mezzanine financing, management buy-outs and buy-ins, distressed debts and corporate restructurings' (GIC web site). So we can see that the GIC puts funds into areas that would not usually be thought of as being suitable for a nation's official foreign reserves, which are about $120 billion. Hence, there is the view that the GIC manages more than this amount (Peebles, 2000b, 2001a). The GIC, whose board of directors is made up of senior cabinet ministers, is not required to report to parliament nor to the people on its activities or its performance. The most Singaporeans hear of its performance is typified by a recent comment by the Minister of Finance who said that the company 'gets more than adequate returns' and that the results and accounts are not published because they contain 'information which our competitors would love to have'. He pointed out that this information is available to the President and the Auditor-Gerneral [and presumably to the board of directors] 'so there is no problem of secrecy' (*The Straits Times*, 13 March, 2000, p. H9). The performance of the company could be revealed without the detailed accounts being made public, one supposes. Information about the type of commercial assets it buys crops up in the foreign press when rules of disclosure require this and they are reported back to Singaporeans through the local press. It has recently been providing venture capital funds for technology start-ups in Singapore so not all its investments are outside Singapore. According to private sector estimates the return on Singapore's reserves are amongst the lowest in Asia at 1.5 per cent a year from 1965 to 1995 (*The Straits Times*, 2 March, 2001, p. S13).

In early 2001 the newspapers in Singapore were suggesting that the GIC become more transparent and this was obviously a signal that something might happen. The response was that the Senior Minister gave an interview in which he described some aspects of the GIC. The interesting thing to note is that he gave this interview to a foreign newspaper which was published in *The Asian Wall Street Journal* (26 April, 2001, pp. 1, 8) and that the local newspapers referred to the interview the following day. He made a number of interesting points, one of which was headlined as the 'GIC to open up to attract top foreign talent' (*The Straits Times*, 27 April, 2001, p. 1) which compares with the previous day's 'Singapore's Investment entity begins to open to outsiders' (*The Asian Wall Street Journal*, 26 April, 2001, p. 1). This 'opening' is aimed at attracting foreign workers into joining CIC where already about 40 per cent are non-Singaporeans and there was no intention of 'opening up' the actions to Singaporeans. In the Senior Minister's own words: 'The ultimate shareholders are the electorate. It is not in the people's interest, in the nation's interest, to detail our assets and their yearly returns' (*The Straits Times*, 27 April, 2001, p. 1). This seems to contradict the generally accepted ideas in capitalist societies that shareholders of publicly listed companies have a right to know how their companies and their equity stake are being managed and have a right to elect the board of directors, and goes against the government's attempts to make local companies more transparent in their annual reports. But the GIC is not a publicly listed company for that reason, no doubt.

2.5 THE FOUNDATIONS FOR SUSTAINED GROWTH

The above sections show the early nature of Singapore and the institutions that were put in place from the early 1960s to the early 1980s. The relative importance of each institution, policy, foresight or luck in starting Singapore's rapid growth that will be examined in the next chapter is hard to unravel. The early PAP leaders were amazed how quickly unemployment fell once the MNCs started arriving in the late 1960s. The arrival of some of the MNCs was attributed to luck as Singapore was chosen over Taiwan and Hong Kong in the late 1960s because of the continuing political chaos on the Chinese mainland. The period from the mid 1960s to 1973 was one of rapid world trade growth and the MNCs that came to Singapore were export-oriented, of course. This increase in economic activity increased government revenue in 1973/74 to 4.4 times its level of 1965. Increases in tax revenues were not used to redistribute income but, together with other institutions such as the Central Provident Fund, were used to increase the rate of domestic saving and investment and the DBS and POSBank to support government growth policies. In 1974 annual contributions to the CPF system were nearly 15 times their 1965 level and the number of members in 1974 was 2.5 times the 1965 level. Public housing pricing policies probably made it necessary for wives to work and would tend to increase the female participation rate and there was relatively rapid growth in this and in the overall labour force growth. The announcement of the withdrawal of British forces was at that time seen as a serious problem for the economy but in hindsight it was one of the main contributing factors to economic growth. The government had already put in place institutions to handle the transfer of land and assets to productive use and to its own military, had very competent public servants to make the best use of them and was committed to growth. In addition to receiving the physical assets there was £50 million in economic aid in the form of grants and interest-free loans (Myint, 1972, p. 128).

The extent to which these factors caused sustained long-run growth is the subject of the next chapter.

3. The growth experience

In this chapter we look at quantitative aspects of Singapore's aggregate growth and make some comparison with a few selected countries. In Chapter 1 we saw that in per capita terms Singapore ranked seventh in the world in 1999 for GNP per capita in purchasing power terms. We thus look at the factors contributing to this rapid growth and the debate about the efficiency with which that growth has been achieved and what the government thinks this implies for the nature of the future growth of the economy.

3.1 OUTPUT GROWTH

Singapore's output growth rate has been high and remarkably consistent over a long period, thus increasing considerably the size of the economy measured simply in terms of real domestic output. In 2000 real GDP was 24 times its 1960 level and 10 times its 1970 level. It had increased by 140 per cent in the decade of the 1960s. Real GNP (GDP plus Net Factor Income from Abroad) was 25.1 times its 1960 level in 2000 and 10.4 times its 1970 level in 2000, indicating a slightly higher growth rate of GNP than GDP over the long period. Real GNP per capita in 2000 was 10.3 times its 1960 level and 5.4 times its 1970 level. The implied average growth rate of real GNP per capita over the period 1960–2000 is 6 per cent a year which is sufficient to double per capita real incomes every 12 years. As we will argue in subsequent chapters GNP per capita is not a good measure of incomes of Singaporeans and should be used with caution when comparisons with other countries are made but here we can just note its significant growth.

Table 3.1 gives some indication of these growth rates for decades and longer periods. In terms of real GDP growth we can see that growth was most rapid during the decade of the 1970s with the average for the 1960s being not much less. In the period after 1980 the growth rates were lower but not significantly so. These decade averages are from official publications and differ slightly from other estimates we have seen. The average annual growth rate for real GDP for the entire period 1960–2000 was 8.5 per cent and real GNP increased by a slightly greater amount over this long period.

Table 3.1   *Indicators of real output growth and income by decades and periods, 1960–2000*

	Index of real GDP	Average annual growth rate of real GDP for the decade/period (%)	Index of real GNP	Index of real GNP per capita
1960	100		100	100
1970	241	8.7 (1960–69 average)	240	190
1980	570	9.4 (1970–79 average)	527	359
1990	1 152	7.4 (1980–89 average)	1 197	647
2000	2 424	7.6 (1990–99 average)	2 506	1 027
Ratio 2000/1960	24.2	8.5 (1960–2000 average)	25.1	10.3
Ratio 2000/1970	10.1	8.0 (1970–2000 average)	10.4	5.4

Sources: Calculated from *Economic Survey of Singapore 1992*, p. xii and *Economic Survey of Singapore 2000*, p. 1. GNP data were deflated by the Consumer Price Index. See also Appendix A for data.

Figure 3.1 shows the annual growth rates of real GDP and it can be seen that the periods of significant slowdown in the growth rate were in the years 1964, 1985 and 1998 when output growth rates were −4.3 per cent, −1.6 and 0.1 respectively. So there have only been two years of falling output, 1964 and 1985, and during the Asian financial crisis growth was halted only in the year 1998. In the recovery from the slowdown of 1998 GDP grew 5.9 per cent in 1999 and 9.9 per cent in 2000. There is no sign of a regular cycle in this growth rate but every ten years or so the growth rate has fallen: 1964 saw a fall in output, in 1975 the growth rate was only 4 per cent and in 1985 the recession saw output fall 1.6 per cent. The next year of low growth, 1998, was more than ten years after the previous slowdown. As Figure 3.1 shows the years 1966 to 1973 all saw real growth rates in excess of 10 per cent a year. This was the period of the first flood of foreign investment and a period of rapid growth in world trade. From 1976 to 1984 the GDP growth rates were around the 8 per cent level. Koh (1990) has studied the length of cycles in Singapore time series and argues that downturns are particularly severe and prolonged but we agree with Kapur's criticism that the standard methods used are not appropriate for Singapore as the periods between the low and high points of the cycle are not periods of stagnation but are of sustained growth (Kapur, 1996, p. 78). Figure 3.1 shows that departures from high growth rates are quickly reversed.

Figure 3.2 shows the rate of inflation as measured by the Consumer Price

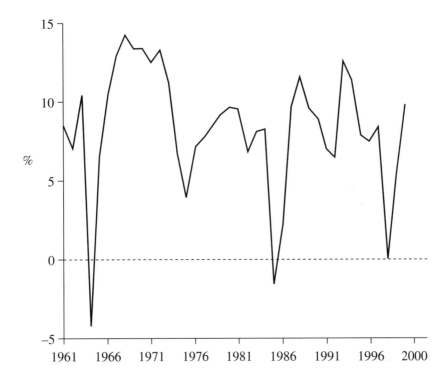

Source: Table A.1 in Appendix A.

Figure 3.1   Annual real GDP growth, 1961–2000

Index. This indicates that the rapid rate of output growth has been associated with a low long-term inflation rate. From 1960 to 2000 the average
annual inflation rate was 3.4 per cent, but it can be seen that there were two
periods of significant deviation from this low average. In 1973 and 1974
consumer prices rose 19.6 and 22.3 per cent in each year. This was the time
of significant increases in world commodity prices, especially in food, and
of an OPEC-induced increase in oil prices. The second period in the years
1980 and 1981, when the CPI rose 8.5 and 8.2 per cent, respectively, is
attributed to the effect of the second oil shock of 1979. Prices fell on an
annual basis in 1969, 1976, 1986 and 1998, and in the 1990s, a generally low
inflation world environment, the inflation rate has been quite low, never
exceeding the 3.4 per cent experienced in both 1990 and 1991. Since the
early 1980s the domestic inflation rate has been closely associated with
movements in the domestic economy with the output gap being the best
explanation of variations in inflation. The CPI inflation rate and the output

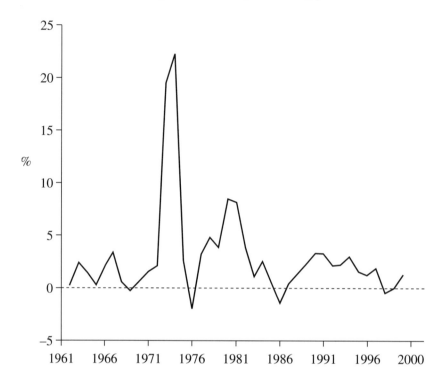

Source: Table A.1 in Appendix A.

Figure 3.2   Annual consumer price inflation, 1961–2000

gap, as measured by the MAS on a quarterly basis, have a correlation
coefficient of $r = 0.73$ over the period 1983Q1 to 2001Q1 (*MAS Quarterly
Bulletin, September 2000*, p. 22). How Singapore has managed its inflation
rate in what is such an open economy where the import component of much
of its output, especially its direct exports, is high, and most food is
imported, will be examined in Chapter 8.

So far we have looked at output growth rates and seen that they have been
impressive. Let us not forget absolute amounts of production as they will
show Singapore's significance in terms of its contribution to world output
and how its significance is greater than that of much larger economies
including Ghana, for example, which was thought to have better growth
potential than Singapore in the early 1960s. Table 3.2 shows a comparison
with some selected countries for the year 1999 using World Bank data,
which have been used for consistency and which are in comparable purchasing power dollars.

Table 3.2   Comparison of the economic size of selected economies measured by GNP at PPP, 1999

	GNP $billions	Singapore's GNP as a percentage of that country's GNP	(Population millions)
Singapore	87.1	100.0	3
USA	8 350.1	1.04	273
UK	1 234.4	7.1	59
Australia	426.4	20.4	19
Hong Kong	144.0	60.3	7
Thailand	345.4	25.2	62
Malaysia	180.8	48.2	23
Egypt	206.2	42.2	62
Philippines	292.2	29.8	77
Ghana	34.0	256	19

Source: Calculated from *World Bank Development Report 2000/2001*, Table 1, World Bank (2000).

Singapore's total output in 1999 was 1.04 per cent of that of the American economy, meaning that if the latter grew 2.1 per cent in a year it would add the equivalent of two years' of Singapore's GNP to world output.

3. 2   INPUT GROWTH AND THEIR CONTRIBUTIONS TO GROWTH

There are no official data of the capital stock for Singapore so it is difficult to assess its absolute size (a different concept to formalize, anyway), its growth rate and its possible contribution to output growth. Different studies have used different methods and assumptions about depreciation rates to derive their own series of the capital stock. We can get a feel for possible dimensions by looking at the estimates of the Department of Statistics which are put in terms of annual growth rates and cover the period 1973 to 1996 only, and are shown in Table 3.3.

We can see the relative stability of the output growth rate and that its lowest rate was in the period 1980–85 which includes the year of 1985 when real output fell. For the entire period 1973–96 the capital stock grew more rapidly than real output and this was true for the period 1973–85 when it grew significantly more rapidly. The high rate of growth of the capital stock

Table 3.3   Annual growth rates of real GDP and capital and labour inputs,
*   Singapore*

	Real GDP, % per annum	Capital input, % per annum	Labour input, % per annum
1973–96	7.4	8.8	3.4
1973–80	7.3	10.4	4.0
1980–85	6.0	11.2	1.7
1985–90	8.1	5.6	3.0
1990–96	8.0	7.8	4.4

Source: Department of Statistics: Singapore (1997b, Appendix 2) cited with permission.

in the first half of the 1980s was mainly due to a significant investing in construction and works and investment in housing. After 1985 the capital stock growth rate fell and was less than that of output growth, In all periods the capital stock grew more rapidly than the labour force leading to a significant increase in capital per workers. Over the period 1973–96 an annual average growth rate of the capital stock of 8.8 per cent would increase the capital stock to nearly seven times its 1973 level and GDP would have increased to five times its 1973 level. Most studies do not publish their estimates of the capital stock but Rao and Lee (1995) is an exception; using their data it can be shown that by the first half of the 1990s the capital–output ratio (K/Y) reached 2.5 (Peebles, 2000b). Figures in Sarel (1997, pp. 18–20) imply that Singapore had the highest capital–output ratio compared to those of Indonesia, Malaysia, Philippines and Thailand of roughly 2.8 by 1996. This is about the same as that of the United States. The Singapore capital–output ratio is seen to rise over the period 1978–85 and then to remain roughly constant from about 1987–96. That pattern is consistent with the estimates of the incremental capital–output ratio cited below from Peebles (2000b).

Singapore's rapid rate of capital accumulation was made possible by high domestic saving and an inflow of foreign direct investment. We will examine how it was possible for the saving and investment rates to increase in the next chapter but Table 3.4 gives us an indication of the large increase in the amount of Gross Fixed Capital Formation as a proportion of GDP.

By 1970 the real amount of Fixed Capital Formation had reached one-third of GDP and was nearly nine times the amount that was being achieved in 1960. Since then the rate of capital accumulation has exceeded 33 per cent and in 1980 was 38.5 per cent of GDP and as much as 41.3 per cent in 1985. It increased rapidly in the late 1970s and early 1980s.

Table 3.4   Share in GDP of Gross Fixed Capital Formation, selected years

	1960	1965	1970	1980	1985	1990	2000
GFCF as a per cent of GDP	10.2	22.7	33.1	38.5	41.3	32.5	34.0

Sources: Calculated from *Economic Survey of Singapore 1992*, p. 114, *Economic Survey of Singapore 2000*, p. 105, *Yearbook of Statistics 1995*, p. 58 from data in constant prices and TRENDS data base.

The composition of capital formation has also changed as shown in Table 3.5. Residential building construction has become less significant but non-residential buildings remain as significant in the 1990s as in the earlier period. Machinery and equipment investment has become more significant as the significance of construction and works has fallen from the high rates of the 1960s and early 1970s. In the debate about the efficiency of Singapore's saving and investment (see below), Singaporeans often stress that a high proportion of capital formation was in the form of residential buildings in the 1970s and early 1980s (in 1985 35 per cent of total fixed capital formation was in the form of residential buildings) and this investment would not directly contribute to increasing labour productivity in the way that investment in machinery and equipment might.

Table 3.5   Composition of Gross Fixed Capital Formation, per cent of total, selected years, 1960–2000

	1960	1970	1980	1985	1990	2000
Construction and works	72.0	55.4	43.6	64.4	39.2	47.8
Residential buildings	43.0	27.6	15.4	34.8	16.6	20.4
Non-residential buildings	11.9	16.8	20.5	20.9	17.1	18.6
Other construction and works	17.5	11.1	7.6	8.9	5.6	7.9
Transport equipment	12.2	9.8	24.3	11.1	16.5	7.4
Machinery and equipment	25.8	38.5	32.6	26.6	44.3	45.6

Sources: Calculated from *Economic Survey of Singapore 1992*, p. 118 and *Economic Survey of Singapore 2000*, p. 107, *Yearbook of Statistics 1995*, p. 60 from data in constant prices.

The growth in Singapore's labour force has been based on three factors: indigenous population growth, an increase in the labour force participation rates and the inflow of foreign workers. As the economy matured, and partly as a result of government policies, indigenous population growth rates have fallen so the latter two factors have become more important. In 1965 the population had a child dependency ratio of 86.2 per cent meaning that the number of residents under 15 years was 86 per cent of the number of residents in the age group 15–59 years, meaning they would enter the labour force in the late 1960s and 1970s as foreign, labour-intensive capital started arriving. Sine then the population growth rate has fallen and the population has aged so that by 1995 the child dependency ratio had fallen to 34.2 per cent.

The participation rate of the population has increased from an average of 58 per cent in the 1970s to 63 per cent in the 1980s to nearly 65 per cent in the 1990s. Most of this has been due to an increase in the female participation rate. The corresponding figures for the male participation rate were 79.6 per cent in the 1970s, 80 per cent in the 1980s and 78 per cent in the 1990s, roughly constant, but those for females increased from 36.5 per cent in the 1970s to 46 per cent in the 1980s and to 51 per cent in the 1990s. In 1970 the female participation rate was only 28.2 per cent but by 1974 it had jumped to 37.1 per cent. This was the period of the inflow of labour-intensive assembly type jobs in electronics that increased the demand for female factory labour. In fact, the location of the factories was decided by the government in relation to the location of large numbers of young women and mothers whose children were already at school in the newly-built housing estates (Lee, 2000, pp. 119–120). Despite the changing structure of the economy, female labour force participation has continued to increase significantly. One factor behind this has been the educational system that has shown no bias against females. By 1999 females made up 43.2 per cent of the student population of the two public sector universities and 43.7 per cent of the students at the four polytechnics. In the universities only 21 per cent of the teachers are female, however, and in the polytechnics the proportion is 35 per cent. These labour force participation rates are probably at their limit and there seems little hope of significantly increasing the indigenous population growth rate despite the government's recent policies of subsidizing children by giving payments into special accounts set up by parents for the first five years of their babies' lives. The current birth rate is below the populating replacement rate. The government's clearly stated policy is to rely on the recruitment of suitable foreign workers to meet the needs of those sectors that it tries to attract to Singapore and develop.

3.3   THE TFP DEBATE

In 1994 the concept of Total Factor Productivity (TFP) and its role in contributing to economic growth in Asia became a prominent concept in the analysis of the Asian miracle because of the arguments of Paul Krugman

(1994b). This popular and influential paper was based mainly on earlier statistical studies by Alwyn Young (1992, 1994a, 1994b, 1995). Krugman argued that productivity growth had played no role in the economic growth of Singapore and that the total amount of output growth could be explained by the increase in the quantities of inputs of capital and labour alone, Young's major finding. In contrast, Hong Kong, which was studied in one of Young's papers, was claimed to show significant TFP growth. Earlier studies of Singapore had also identified the lack of TFP growth so this was no real surprise to see similar results in later studies. See Peebles and Wilson (1996, pp. 200–210) for a summary of these earlier studies. What made the difference was that Krugman brought some of these studies to the attention of a broader audience at the time that Asian economic growth was being described as a miracle (World Bank, 1993). More importantly, in terms of the reaction he provoked, was probably the way he likened Singapore's growth experience to that of the former Soviet Union – and he pointed out what happened to that economy – being based solely on the increase in factor inputs and not on efficiency. As he put it,

> all of Singapore's growth can be explained by increases in measured inputs. There is no sign at all of increased efficiency. In this sense, the growth of Lee Kuan Yew's Singapore is an economic twin of the growth of Stalin's Soviet Union growth achieved purely through mobilization of resources. Of course, Singapore today is far more prosperous than the U.S.S.R. ever was – even at its peak in the Brezhnev years – because Singapore is closer to, though still below, the efficiency of Western economies. (Krugman 1994b, p. 71)

Krugman took Young's historical estimates and argued they would be relevant to the future growth of Singapore. He argued that further improvement in the quality of the labour force was limited, there was no scope for increasing the participation rate, the existing investment ratio of 40 per cent was high enough and one could not envisage increasing it any more so that 'one can immediately conclude that Singapore is unlikely to achieve future growth rates comparable to those of the past' (Krugman, 1994b, p. 71). That is not a particularly radical conclusion as it is generally known, even in Singapore, that developed economies tend to grow more slowly than developing ones, so it was perhaps the comparison with Stalinist economies, and we know what happened to them, that caused attention to be directed towards his critique. On re-reading Krugman's paper it is clear that he did not predict for Singapore the same fate as the Soviet Union, nor did he predict the Asian financial crisis. Economists are modest people – really – and his conclusion was just that Singapore's future growth rates were 'unlikely' to be as high as in the past and since this was true for other Asian economies so their future world role, in international politics in particular, would not be as great as had been predicted by those who casually used the phrase 'Asian century'.

One reaction to Krugman is for economists to review the earlier studies of TFP and their methods to see whether they told the same story. Chen (1997) is a survey article of the most relevant studies. Felipe (1999) also surveys other studies and takes a more sceptical view on the different methods used, coming to the conclusion that it seems that anyone can show anything they want. Studies by Kim and Lau (1994) and Lau (1998) are at the extreme of arguing that there had been no TFP contribution to growth in Singapore – none elsewhere in Asia except Japan, either. The World Bank study also found large negative technical efficiency change in Singapore (World Bank, 1993, p. 69) but this had been largely overlooked by readers.

Another reaction was to update the earlier studies using either the same or different methods and more recent or different data sets. One difficulty found by all studies of Singapore is that there is no official series for the capital stock so different studies will produce different data sets that might have overstated the growth rate of the capital stock hence reducing the esti- mate of the contribution of TFP. Most of those more recent studies of Singapore claimed to have found higher rates of TFP growth in the period studied by Young by using revised data sets, or have found higher TFP growth rates for the period after about 1990 than for the earlier periods examined by Young. For example, Marti claims an estimate of 1.49 per cent per annum contribution of TFP for the period 1970–85 (Young's period) and 1.45 per cent for 1970–90 (Felipe, 1999, p. 18). These are higher rates than identified by Young. Gapinski (1999, pp. 134–9) uses a method that accounts for the role of trade in affecting TFP. For the period 1960–90 his estimates without taking international trade into the estimates show that TFP accounted for only 14 per cent of Singapore's output growth but when trade is taken into account the contribution of TFP to growth in Singapore was 56.7 per cent – the highest ratio in his sample of 13 countries! This latter finding has been cited in what can be thought of as a semi-official Singaporean refutation of the thesis of no TFP contribution (Toh and Ng, 2001, pp. 13–16). Sarel (1997) is another study that challenges the findings of Young about Singapore and proposes an estimate of TFP's contribution of 2.23 percentage points of per capita output growth over the period 1978–96 (compared to Young's 0.7 per cent for a different period) but his estimates for the more recent period 1991–96 shows no marked increases as it is only 2.46 per cent, which accounts for half the rate of growth of per capita output (Sarel, 1997, pp. 29–30).

In contrast, studies have claimed to see an increase in the significance of TFP in more recent years. For the period 1987–94 Rao and Lee (1995, p. 95) estimated that TFP had contributed 30 per cent of the observed annual growth rate of GDP compared to only 7 per cent for the earlier period 1976–84. That study also concluded that there had been an increase in TFP's contribution in the manufacturing sector in the latter period (32 per cent of growth) compared to a negative contribution of −5 per cent of growth. In contrast, Mahadevan and Kalirajan (2000), using a different technique and methods for the 28 industries in the manufacturing sector, found that TFP's contribution declined in the late 1980s and became negative in the 1990s concluding that their findings supported those of Young (1995) and contradicted those of Rao and Lee (1995). However, Rao and Owyong (1998), using an econometric technique, argued that there was a structural break in TFP's significance in 1986 resulting in its substantial improvement which they say is compatible with the findings of Rao and Lee (1995) and is attributed to government policies adopted after the 1985–86 recession. However, a study by Bloch and Tang (2000) for the manufacturing sector over the period 1975–94 supports the pessimistic view of the efficiency of that sector: 'factor accumulation, in particular capital growth, accounts for almost all the rapid output growth in Singapore manufacturing. Technical progress as measured by total factor productivity growth is found to be either very low or negative' (Bloch and Tang, 2000, p. 52). A further interesting conclusion of their study is that the rapid output growth has been mainly due to increasing returns to scale and the rapid growth of factor inputs. Scale economies are particularly found in MNCs which have the world for their market and that the MNCs have not done much to promote technical change in, or technology transfer to, the domestic sector.

There is an incredible range for, and growing number of estimates of, the role of TFP in Singapore's growth and it seems one is free to pick the ones one likes to support the position one chooses to take. What is more relevant for policy development in Singapore is not so much which studies are correct but what the Singapore government thought of the points being made in the debate. Singapore seems to have taken the view that, historically, Young, Krugman and others were correct in identifying TFP's insignificant historical contributions to output growth but that, here at least, history was no guide to what would happen in the future, because the government could react to these findings and warnings. It has been reported that in 1995 Lee Kuan Yew said to Krugman: 'you're right so far, but our total factor productivity growth will be much higher in the future because of the investments we're making in education' (quoted from Lovell and Tang (1999, p. 35) who refer to a report in *The Wall Street Journal* of 1995 on ibid., p. 40.)

It was not only on the basis of the hope that education would ensure future TFP growth that Singapore could be optimistic. The characteristic Singapore response of planning was brought into play to boost TFP. In

November 1995 the Ministry of Trade and Industry announced its approach to this matter. One was to create in April 1996 the Singapore Productivity and Standards Board (PSB), a statutory board, by merging the National Productivity Board and the Singapore Institute for Standards and Industrial Research. Its mission is to 'raise productivity so as to enhance Singapore's competitiveness and economic growth for a better quality of life for the people' (*Singapore 1997*, p. 128). It has five major initiatives: productivity promotion, manpower development; technology application; industry development; standards and quality development and incentives management. A new board and programme would mean nothing without a target and it was announced that its aim would be to sustain TFP's contribution at 2 per cent a year and contribute to 7 per cent annual growth. That would mean that TFP's contribution would be about 28–29 per cent, regarded as 'quite modest and achievable' by Rao and Lee (1995, p. 97).

Not only was a board with a mission established but monitoring and publication of TFP was undertaken by the Department of Statistics resulting in an Occasional Paper 'Multifactor Productivity Growth in Singapore: Concepts Methodology and Trends' in October 1997. This paper prefers the term Multifactor Productivity (MFP) used by the Australian Bureau of Statistics and the US Bureau of Labor Statistics. We use both the terms TFP and MFP according to the source cited. They are the same concept. The Department of Statistics used the most simple and basic growth accounting method shown below to estimate MFP as a residual given by the observed rate of growth of output minus the growth of capital and labour with each weighted by its share in GDP. Estimates can be made for individual years or sub-periods for which average value of shares would be used.

MFP growth = Real GDP growth
minus average share of capital input times growth in capital input
minus average share of labour input times growth rate in labour input.

To illustrate using the data for the period 1973–96 the figures are as follows:

MFP = GDP growth   − Capital contribution   − labour contribution
(1.0) =   (7.4)   − 0.551(8.8)   − 0.449(3.4)

where all the numbers in brackets are average annual percentage growth rates and 0.511 is the share of capital and 0.499 the labour share. MFP therefore contributed 13.5 per cent of GDP growth (1.0/7.4) over this long period.

This method assumes constant returns to scale, competitive markets and just two factors of production. As MFP is estimated as a residual it is sensitive to the weights chosen and the accuracy of the growth rates of the factor inputs. The paper contains the raw data and estimates for the period 1974 to 1996. As the factor inputs are not adjusted this means that 'besides technical progress, the measure of MFP growth derived would include the effects of improvements in the quality of and compositional changes in the inputs such as increased educational attainment of the workforce' (ibid., p. 10). Table 3.6 shows the estimates of contributions to growth for various periods.

Table 3.6   Factor input contributions to real GDP growth rate, 1973–96, selected periods

Period	Contribution to real GDP growth (in per cent of the growth rate) of			MFP contribution in percentage points of GDP growth
	Capital input	Labour input	MFP	
1973–96	66.5	20.0	13.5	1.0
1973–80	85.3	22.2	−7.4	−0.5
1980–85	98.6	11.8	−10.3	−0.6
1985–90	37.3	16.2	46.5	3.8
1990–96	51.1	26.1	22.8	1.8

Source: Department of Statistics (1997b, Table 1 and Appendix 2), cited with permission.

Some interesting features stand out. Over the entire period studied capital accumulation accounted for two-thirds of growth and MFP only 14 per cent, a positive contribution but lower than found in the other studies that reviewed the data. In the early period of development, 1973–85, capital accumulation was even more significant and the quantities of the factors of production explained more than the entire observed growth rate, which was Krugman's main point. The period 1980–85 was one of very significant public sector investment, especially in housing and includes the recession of 1985–86. The period 1985–90 includes the rapid recovery from that recession and it is in this period that MFP makes its most important contribution to growth, just because recovery meant that output would be growing at higher than trend rates and returning to trend levels. The period 1990–96 shows an MFP contribution of 23 per cent to the growth rate, lower than the objective of nearly 30 per cent adopted in 1995. The other way to see this is to note that in the period 1990–96 MFP contributed 1.8 percentage points of GDP growth, just lower than the objective of 2 per cent adopted in 1995.

The annual data show that yearly movements in MFP closely follow the

GDP growth rate and as can be seen is much more volatile than the contributions of the factors. An interesting point is that this simple method of computing MFP is still used and annual estimates are published in the official *Yearbook of Statistics* starting with the issue published in 2000. Table 3.7 shows these annual estimates in the form of the contribution in percentage points of the GDP growth rate. These growth rates are logarithmically derived and so will differ from other expressions of the GDP growth rate.

Table 3.7   Estimates of contributions to real GDP growth, 1994–2000

	1994	1995	1996	1997	1998	1999	2000
GDP growth rate	10.8	7.7	7.3	8.2	0.1	5.7	9.4
Capital contribution	4.0	4.2	5.1	5.1	3.9	3.2	3.3
Labour contribution	2.1	2.3	2.9	2.9	1.4	−0.2	1.9
MFP	4.7	1.1	−0.7	0.3	−5.2	2.7	4.2
MFP contribution as a per cent of GDP growth rate	43.4	14.3	−9.6	3.7	−5 200	47.4	44.7

Source: *Yearbook of Statistics 2001*, p. 50 and last row calculated from there.

With the exception of 1994 and 1999 and after, the MFP contribution to growth has never reached the desired 2 per cent points rate. In 1999, for example, it did and accounted for 47.4 per cent of the observed growth rate in that year. The recession of 1998 produced a huge negative MFP contribution which is misleading for assessing trends.

The Monetary Authority of Singapore has made its own econometric estimates of TFP for the period 1960–86 and puts the TFP contribution to growth at an average of 0.9 per cent which is a comparatively low figure (Monetary Authority of Singapore, 2000d, p. 20). The Department of Statistics estimates shown in Table 3.6 above for its longest period 1973–96 was roughly the same at 1 per cent but, as we have seen, was higher for later periods being 3.8 per cent for 1985–90 and 1.8 per cent for 1990–96.

Here we have seen what could be thought of as the technocrats' reaction to studies that seemed to show that Singapore was not a very efficient economy. They did their own calculations trying to show that things were not as bad as the earlier studies had shown, provided references to other studies for ministerial speeches and did something about measuring and monitoring the supposed crucial variable and set up institutions and policies to improve things. All quite civilized and progressive. In the political real world the reaction was different. According to Seow (1998, pp. 132–3) a government minister was 'saddened' that the newspaper of a local political party had reproduced two articles 'written by foreigners against Singapore'. These were two articles from *The Economist*, one of which related to Young's 'tale of two cities' article – a scholarly work – the conclusions of which the politicians were probably trying to make available to an audience that did not have time to read *The Economist*. In this arena the works were 'against Singapore', not just analyses of the results of past policies of the government. This again reflects the government's way of taking any criticism or comment it does not like, even though they might suspect it is correct, as an attack 'against Singapore'. *The Economist* later had its circulation restricted and Seow attributes this partly to the fact that it was the convenient source of the articles reproduced in the political arena (Seow, 1998, p. 133).

Another factor behind Singapore's growth that we refer to throughout this book is the contribution of foreign workers. The main guesses of their significance have been based on their share in the workforce of their share in GDP (see Section 6.1) and, until recently, there have been no attempts to assess their contribution to growth. In the build up to the November 2001 general election the government repeatedly emphasized the importance of foreign workers to the economy as this had become a contentious election issue. During the campaign estimates of the contributions of foreigners to growth were released. Lee Kuan Yew stated that he initiated the policy of taking in foreign workers and takes full responsibility for it. He cited recent growth accounting estimates by economists at the Ministry of Trade and Industry of foreigners' contributions to growth. Table 3.8 summarizes them. The figures are annual percentage growth rates based on quarterly data and they show the contribution to the growth rate in percentage points of growth and the figures in brackets show the percentage contribution to the growth rate of each input.

Table 3.8   Estimates of contributions to GDP growth, stressing foreign labour, 1986–2000

Period	GDP growth	Capital stock	Local labour	Foreign workers with employment passes	Foreign workers with work permits	Total factor productivity
1986Q1–	8.46	1.10	1.30	0.45	0.16	5.45
1990Q4	(100)	(13.0)	(15.4)	(5.3)	(1.9)	(64.4)
1991Q1–	7.79	2.06	1.10	2.87	0.30	1.47
2000Q4	(100)	(26.4)	(14.1)	(36.8)	(3.9)	(18.9)

Source: Estimates by the Ministry of Trade and Industry, Singapore cited from *The Straits Times*, 1 November, 2001, p. S12.

The overall results are not too different from the estimates presented in Table 3.6 when we look at the 1990s. TFP in Table 3.8 contributed about 19 per cent of growth in 1991–2000 whereas earlier estimates put its contribution at about 23 per cent. It is the breakdown of the labour contribution that is of interest here. It is claimed that foreign workers with employment passes (that is those who were generally earning more than $2000 a month – those earning more than $3500 a month are called professionals) contributed 39 per cent of the growth in the 1990s, which is higher than the contribution of either capital or TFP. Foreign labour made up 29.2 per cent of the working population in 2000. Local labour contributed only 14 per cent of the growth rate. Foreign workers with work permits, who are usually employed as domestic servants, in the retail trade or in jobs such as cleaning and gardening contributed just 3.8 per cent of the growth of GDP in the 1990s. The contribution to growth by foreign workers was substantially higher in the 1990s that in the late 1980s. These estimates, published in local newspapers just before a general election, underscore the importance of foreign labour to Singapore's growth and the fact that the PAP wanted people not to forget it.

3.4   CAPITAL–OUTPUT RATIOS AS ESTIMATES OF EFFICIENCY

One way to get a general feel of the efficiency of investment in an economy is to compute the Incremental Capital–Output Ratio which shows how much extra capital was required to increase output by one unit in a given year. The lower the ratio the more efficient that investment is seen to be. As there are no data for net investment in Singapore, and because of serious methodological and conceptual problems with this measure, we should keep in mind the warning of Hooley (1995, p. 249) that all results 'should be treated with considerable discretion'. He found that Singapore's ICOR over the period 1977–89 was, on average, the lowest of those of the Southeast Asian (SEA) countries but higher than that found in East Asia – Korea and Taiwan. Despite his warnings, Hooley (1995, p. 250) was willing to conclude that a 'reasonable inference from the consistently higher ICOR in SEA is that investment efficiency is below that in East Asia'. However, compared to the other SEA countries, Singapore's performance was the best, although worse than that in East Asia.

Arndt (1991) presents a comparison of the ICORs for many Asian economies for the 1980s using the average investment ratio for this decade and the average growth rate which removes the problems associated with using annual observations noted by Hooley (1995). Singapore's ICOR at 7.1 was the highest apart from the Philippines, and Arndt remarks that it even exceeded India's 3.8. He recognizes that the 1980s might not be a fair basis for comparison as it contained two recession years (at least by Singapore standards) and much investment was in housing which might not produce as much of an increase in GDP as other types of investment (Arndt 1991, pp. 156–7). A fairer method would be to use decade averages as is done in Table 3.9 which is based on that in Peebles (2000b).

Table 3.9   Estimates of the Incremental Capital–Output Ratio, by decade

	Average ratio of GFCF to GDP, %	Average annual growth rate of GDP %	Average ICOR
1960–69	19.6	8.1	2.4
1970–79	35.2	8.3	4.2
1980–89	39.2	6.3	6.2
1990–99	36.6	8.0	4.6

Source: Calculated from data in TRENDS database, Department of Statistics, Singapore in Peebles (2000b).

The data reflect the higher ICOR for the 1980s found in other studies and show a subsequent fall compared to the 1980s when growth picked up after the recovery from the recession. This fall is consistent with studies cited above and Lee (2000) that argued that productivity performance has improved after 1990. The figure of 4.6 in the 1990s derived above is compatible with that of 'about 5' cited in a speech by Lee Hsien Loong (2000a, p. 3) referring to the then estimates of an unpublished report by the Ministry of Trade and Industry, Singapore which are probably those of Toh and Ng (2000, p. 12) who estimates it for 1990–98 at 'about 5'. In his speech Lee Hsien Loong gave comparable figures of an average of 9 for Hong Kong and 18 for Japan for the 1990s. These are also the figures found in Toh and Ng (2000, p. 12).

More recently the Heritage Foundation has returned to the views of Young and in particular his comparisons between the efficiency of investment in Hong Kong and Singapore. In their annual *Index of Economic Freedom* report for 2000 the foundation ranked Hong Kong as the most free in the world with the same score as in 1999 and reduced Singapore's score but still put it in second place. Gerald O'Driscoll, one of the three authors of the report, summarized a key difference between these two economic systems by saying: 'Hongkong pursues a persistent laissez-faire policy. In Singapore there are government-directed investments, almost twice the rate invested in Hongkong. Yet, the real per capita GDP is higher in Hongkong than in Singapore. In other words, the Singapore government has wasted the savings of its citizens' (*The Straits Times,* 1 December, 1999, p. 23). The authors of the report further argued that: 'since Singaporean growth rates were no higher for all the compulsory investment required of its citizens, it is fair to say that the government effectively dissipated all the forced savings' (*2000 Index of Economic Freedom: Executive Summary*: Gwartney et al., 2000, p. 8, from www.heritge.org/index/execsum.htm.). Toh and Ng (2000) dispute this interpretation and even the statement that real per capita GDP is higher in Hong Kong than in Singapore.

3.5   TFP AND FUTURE GROWTH

On the basis of their estimates the MAS has taken a figure of 1 per cent as a reasonable guide for the minimal attainable contribution of TFP to growth. The planned rate is 2 per cent. On the basis of estimates of expected labour force growth and the view that future investment will be sufficient just to increase the capital–labour ratio slightly they have made projections of Singapore's long-run growth potential. Two scenarios are envisaged: under Scenario I TFP's contribution remains at 1 per cent and under Scenario II it increases by 0.1 percentage points a year so that it would reach the planned rate of 2 per cent in ten years' time. Table 3.10 assembles their estimates.

Table 3.10   Average potential real GDP growth rate, 2000–2030, per cent per annum

	Scenario I TFP remains at 1 per cent	Scenario II TFP increases to 2 per cent by 2010
2000–2005	5.6	6.1
2010–2015	4.1	5.8
2025–2030	2.8	4.4

Source: Adapted from *MAS Economics Department Quarterly Bulletin,* December, pp. 20–21.

The projections show that the long-run potential growth rates fall, as predicted by the work of Young and others and stressed by Krugman. The extent of the fall is greater under Scenario I, of course. Under Scenario II in 30 years time the economy could be growing at 4.4 per cent per annum. What that means in terms of potential living standards depends on population growth. The demographic assumptions underlying these projections are that by about 2030 the annual rate of growth of the residential population will fall to only 0.3 per cent. Under the more optimistic scenario total GDP can still grow at 4.4 per cent a year so that with almost no population and labour force growth this lower rate can provide a high rate of per capita income growth.

If we take the two scenarios and interpret them as implying it might be possible for GDP to grow 4.5 per cent per annum after 2000 this means that GDP will be double its 2000 level by the year 2016 when the total resident population is likely to be about only 17 per cent higher than in 2000. That implies that per capita GDP could be 70 per cent higher than in 2000 in just 16 years time.

These general conclusions should not have been a surprise as *The Strategic Economic Plan* of 1991 had already made long-run projections of growth rates but this was before the concept of TFP had become the focus it was for later projections. The earlier projections are worth reviewing to see the extent they differ from the later ones described above. Table 3.11 shows that they were drawn up under two different possible scenarios and for different future population levels and are in terms of GNP.

Table 3.11   Projected growth rates of GNP, 1990–2030, per cent per annum

	Optimistic scenario			Pessimistic scenario		
Population in 2030	3.4 million	4.0 million	4.4 million	3.4 million	4.0 million	4.4 million
1990–1995	6.7	7.1	7.3	5.7	6.1	6.3
1995–2000	5.6	6.0	6.2	4.6	5.0	5.2
2000–2010	4.4	4.8	5.0	3.5	3.9	4.1
2010–2020	3.9	4.3	4.5	3.0	3.4	3.6
2020–2030	3.7	4.0	4.3	2.7	3.1	3.3

Source: *The Strategic Economic Plan*, Ministry of Trade and Industry: Singapore, Tables 1 and 2.

The Plan did not describe the exact nature of the assumptions underlying the two scenarios except to say they were 'based on some technical assumptions'. In terms of total GNP the pessimistic scenario means that the annual average growth rate is about 1 percentage point below that of the optimistic scenario. The greater the expected population in 2030, the faster the growth rate. In comparisons with the later Monetary Authority projections then the most similar is the optimistic scenario with a projected population of 4.4 million as by the decade 2020–2030 growth would be at about 4.4 per cent per annum. What is interesting to note is that the government had such long-range growth projections in mind in the early 1990s which showed that long-run potential annual growth of around 4 per cent a year would be roughly half of the long-run rate achieved over the period 1970–2000. Therefore, Krugman's point that growth would fall should have been no surprise as the government knew that as countries become more developed their growth rates slow down (*Strategic Plan*, p. 45).

The long-term per capita projections are also interesting and are shown in Table 3.12.

Table 3.12   Projected growth rates of GNP per capita, 1990–2030, per cent per annum

	Optimistic	Pessimistic
1990–1995	5.4	4.4
1995–2000	4.6	3.6
2000–2010	3.7	2.9
2010–2020	3.5	2.6
2020–2030	3.5	2.5

Source: *The Strategic Economic Plan*, Ministry of Trade and Industry: Singapore, Table 6.

Again, the pessimistic projections are about 1 percentage point lower than those under the optimistic scenario. We can get a feel for what they would mean to future per capita GNP by taking the pessimistic scenario and projections forward to 2030 from 2000. If GNP per capita grew at the pessimistic rates then in 2030 GNP per capita would be 2.2 times its year 2000 level, double its current level within a generation! The important question is who would receive what share of the vastly increased amount of income?

3.6   CONSEQUENCES OF THE TFP DEBATE

The government has seemed to have taken the facts and arguments of Young and Krugman into account and not to have differed from them to any great extent. It might seem, however, that they have not considered Young's tentative explanation for Singapore's poor TFP performance. Young (1992, pp. 25–6, 41–3) offered the hypothesis that Singapore's industrial policies had caused a too rapid a rate of structural transformation within manufacturing so that before the full benefits of higher productivity in one sector could be achieved the economy was being pushed into other sectors so that it suffered from 'industrial targeting taken to excess'

(Young, 1992, p. 43). The government has not stopped such industrial targeting policies. However, there might be more symbiosis today between the new sectors and existing sectors than there was between, for example, textiles and electronics when that transformation started in the late 1960s.

In the next chapter we look at the nature of the structural changes that accompanied Singapore's economic growth both from the perspective of the structure of demand and how high rates of saving and investment were achieved and also in terms of the structure of production. We then look at the areas the government is currently targeting for future development and how they see the future structure of the economy.

4. Structural change

As we saw in the previous chapter Singapore's rapid output growth rates have been accompanied by one of the highest rates of investment in the world. Furthermore, there have been considerable changes in the structure of production, especially since the early 1960s before industrialization started. In this chapter we first examine changes in the expenditure structure of the economy in order to establish the extent of and reasons behind the increase in saving and investment and how these changes have affected domestic consumption. We also look at the likely future trends in saving and how they might limit future growth. We then look at the changes in the structure of production and especially in the development of the manufacturing sector and the role of foreign investment. We also look at the change in the distribution of income in general terms; information that has only been recently published.

4.1 COMPOSITION OF EXPENDITURES

Standard national income accounting categorizes expenditures in the economy into private consumption (C), government consumption (G), investment (I), which consists of gross fixed capital formation and the change in inventories (increase in stocks, which can be positive or negative), and exports (EX), foreign demand. All these expenditures include imported items. This demand for output is met from two sources of supply which are domestic production, Gross Domestic Product (GDP) and imports (IM).

Hence: $C + G + I + EX = GDP + IM$
Therefore, $GDP = C + G + I + (EX - IM)$ where the bracketed term is called Net Exports.

This form of presenting the accounts does not let us see separately the import content of each type of expenditure, such as C, G, I or EX. In Singapore, many items of consumption, such as food and clothing, are imported. Some parts of fixed investment, especially machinery and equipment, have a large import component. It is important for fiscal policy formulation to know the different import content of each type of expenditure if it is thought demand needs stimulation at a time of recession. In general, estimates of the overall marginal propensity to import (MPI) for Singapore have been very high. Historical estimates using total imports will produce an MPI that exceeds unity because of the significance of re-exports in the economy (Lim et al., 1988, p. 460), a situation also found in Hong Kong. More relevant is the propensity to import goods which are retained for domestic production as intermediate goods or investment goods or used for consumption. In this case the MPI is about 0.8. This is a very high import leakage and is one reason why the government consumption expenditure multiplier, historically estimated at only 0.64999 in the short run and 0.7850 in the long run (Lim et al., 1988, pp. 460, 469). More recent government econometric estimates by the Ministry of Trade and Industry of such government expenditure multipliers put it at about 0.63 (*The Business Times*, 13 February, 2001, p. 12). See also Wilson (1995).

One recent argument that has emerged in Singapore, just before the budget of 2001, is that as net exports are only 11 per cent of GDP (the figure claimed) then domestic demand is more important and can be stimulated to offset any slowdown in export growth. This view misses the point that each domestic expenditure category has its own import component that is not shown separately in the accounts as they are all aggregated and deducted from exports to produce net exports. What needs to be shown is how any increase in the expenditures C, G, I or EX result in higher GDP in Singapore or in higher production in other countries, which is reflected in the increase in imports into Singapore. Imports do not generate incomes in Singapore, net exports do and as GDP is the sum of values added in Singapore (which equal incomes generated in Singapore) it is the resulting amount of net exports that are presented in the expenditure version of the accounts. The size of net exports does not indicate the relative importance of external demand, which is given by exports, compared to the domestic components of demand. Imports are important as they allow Singapore to export, reversing the cliché taught to students that countries need to export in order to import. In Singapore production needs a huge amount of direct, retained imports.

To get a feel of the extent to which structural change has increased the importance of foreign demand for Singapore and to show the relative size of the demand components we can present the approximate figures for 2000 in billions of dollars. It is important to see the importance of external demand as, as we have seen above, even commentators in Singapore have been confused by concentrating on net exports.

$$GDP = C + G + I + (EX - IM)$$
$$159 = 64 + 17 + 50 + 29$$

In this standard way of presenting the account net exports do not seem as important as some elements of domestic demand but when we re-write the underlying relationship in terms of demand and supply we get the following (numbers do not add up precisely because of rounding and that exports and imports come from the balance of payments accounts).

$$\text{Demand} = \text{Supply}$$
$$\text{EX} + \text{C} + \text{G} + \text{I} = \text{GDP} + \text{IM}$$
$$287 + 64 + 17 + 50 = 159 + 257$$

It can be seen that export demand is four times the amount of domestic private consumption and 5.7 times the amount of investment. The important question is to what extent changes in the demand for output on the left-hand side of the equation are translated into higher output in Singapore or just result in an increase in imports. All expenditures have an import component.

Table 4.1 shows the import component of each item of final expenditure for the year 1990. A one-dollar increase in total final expenditure requires a 54 cent increase in imports. The most import dependent items of expenditure are exported petroleum and for total exports each dollar requires 60 cents of imports. As would be expected the import leakage for services is the lowest and is similar to that of government consumption.

We can see the association between domestic and external demand and growth in GDP for the last few years which included the recessionary impact of the Asian financial crisis in Table 4.2 which shows the percentage changes of these demand components over the previous year's level.

Table 4.1   Import component of each dollar of final expenditure

Total	0.54
Domestic consumption (1 + 2 + 3)	0.46
1. Consumption	0.33
Private	0.34
Government	0.30
2. Gross Fixed Capital Formation	0.63
3. Change in stocks	0.84
Exports	0.60
Manufacturing	0.69
Petroleum	0.90
Non-oil	0.62
Services	0.29

Source: MAS Quarterly Bulletin, March (Monetary Authority of Singapore, 2001b, p. 35).

They do not directly indicate their relative importance in changing GDP because they are of different amounts: a 5 per cent increase in external demand might have a greater impact on GDP than a 10 per cent increase in private consumption. This means that a given percentage change in external demand translates into a greater increase in demand than the same percentage change in any other kind of demand. Of the increase in total demand of 14 per cent in 2000 domestic demand contributed 3.0 points and external demand 11 points (*Economic Survey of Singapore 2000*, p. 17).

Table 4.2   Changes in domestic and external demand and real GDP growth, 1997–2000

	1997	1998	1999	2000
Total demand	7.6	−5.4	6.5	14.0
Total domestic demand	10.2	−7.8	5.3	10.7
Final domestic demand	8.3	−3.4	1.3	8.5
Consumption	6.4	−0.8	5.2	10.3
Public	7.1	8.0	5.0	13.7
Private	6.2	−2.9	5.3	9.4
Gross Fixed Capital Formation	10.6	−6.4	−3.9	5.9
Public	22.9	8.4	4.1	−2.9
Private	8.1	−9.9	−6.1	8.6
Increase in stocks	1.7	−4.2	3.4	1.8
External demand	6.6	−4.4	6.9	15.2
Increase in real GDP	8.5	0.1	5.9	9.9

Sources: Economic Survey of Singapore 1999, p. 19 and *Economic Survey of Singapore 2000*, p. 17.

The table shows that in 1998 all elements of demand fell except public capital formation. Private capital formation fell in both 1998 and 1999. In both 1999 and 2000 the percentage increase in external demand exceeded the increase in domestic demand. The greater the increase in external demand the greater the growth rate of real GDP as shown by the 9.9 per cent increase in real GDP in 2000. There is bound to be an association between increases in external demand and the components of domestic demand. External demand is exogenous to the domestic economy and when it increases it will change GDP which in turn increase incomes in Singapore. Such income increases will increase induced items of demand such as private consumption and, with a lag, possibly government consumption as it is thought it follows previous changes in tax revenue which

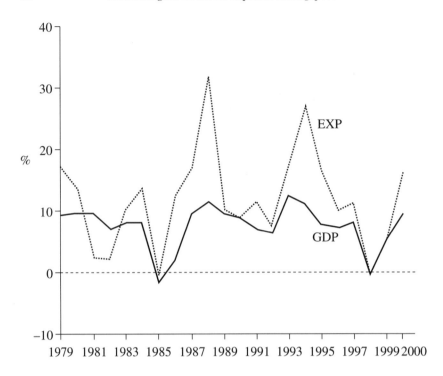

Sources: Table A.1 in Appendix A and TRENDS data base.

Figure 4.1   Export growth and real GDP growth, 1979–2000

will be greater the greater the increase in GDP. Growing external demand is likely to increase investment also.

Figure 4.1 shows the association between real GDP growth and the growth rate of exports over the period 1979–2000, showing the close positive association on which Singapore has been categorized as having export-led growth. More sophisticated studies support this visual impression. What is important is how Singaporeans see this relationship. The recently appointed new chairman of the Economic Development Board, when talking of the economy in general, recently said that: 'We are really totally at the mercy of the world economy. How well we do depends a lot particularly on how the US is performing' (Singapore Economic Development Board website at http://www.sedb.com.sg.home.htm.).

Before reviewing the changes in the components of expenditures it is worth remembering that the measure of private consumption in the accounts is the consumption of Singaporean households and non-profit institutions, both within and outside Singapore, and excludes the purchases by non-residents, mainly tourists. Having identified the amount spent on consumption items the statisticians add residents' consumption purchases when they are abroad and deduct non-residents' expenditures. Singaporeans' expenditures abroad were about 10 per cent of the amount spent on consumption in Singapore in 2000 and non-residents' expenditures were about 15 per cent of private consumption, a not insignificant amount. Singaporeans' consumption expenditures abroad would be added to imports and non-residents' expenditures would be added to exports to ensure they are included in the accounts in their proper place.

As Table 4.3 shows, changes in consumption expenditures by non-residents are associated with changes in the number of visitors, which illustrates the importance of tourism to the domestic consumption sector. The amount spent is not perfectly correlated with the number of visitors since it would depend on their length of stay and how much they chose to spend, which will be associated with the country they come from. A second implication of the large number of tourists that visit Singapore, 7.69 million in 2000, is that as the government is moving towards greater reliance on indirect taxes the taxable base of consumption is larger than the domestic population figures would imply, as tourists cannot reclaim and do not reclaim all of the indirect taxes they pay while they are in Singapore, however briefly.

Table 4.3   Annual changes in visitor arrivals and non-residents'
consumption expenditures, 1997–2000

	1997	1998	1999	2000
Change in visitor arrivals, per cent	−1.3	−13.3	11.5	10.5
Change in non-resident's expenditures, per cent	−10.4	−12.7	6.9	12.8

Sources: Economic Survey of Singapore 1999, pp. 116, 162 and *Economic Survey of Singapore 2000*, pp. 107, 157.

We can now look at the incredible changes in the structure of expenditures in Singapore since 1960 which are summarized in Table 4.4.

Figure 4.2 shows the remarkable increase in gross national saving (GNS) and investment as ratios of GNP since 1960. In 1960 and 1961 GNS was negative, but by 1975 it had reached 25 per cent of GNP. In 1985 GNS exceeded domestic investment for the first time so the Current Account balance became positive (see Table A.2). 1987 saw a negative Current Account balance but since then it has been positive and large. As the main

Table 4.4   *Expenditures as a percentage of GDP: averages by decades and various years*

	Private consumption	Government consumption	Investment	Net exports
1960–69	74	10	29	−6
1970–79	59	12	42	−9
1980–89	48	11	42	1
1990–99	43	10	37	11
1997	40.9	9.9	42.3	8.9
1998	39.5	10.6	34.9	16.9
1999	39.3	10.5	35.2	17.5
2000	39.1	10.9	35.2	16.8

Note: Figures might not add to 100 because of the statistical discrepancy. See also Peebles (2002).

Sources: Updated from Peebles (2000b) and calculated from *Economic Survey of Singapore 2000*, p. 105.

element of the Current Account is Net Exports the information in Table 4.4 is also relevant.

Table 4.4 shows the changes in consumption associated with this dramatic rise in saving with it falling from about 74 per cent of GDP in the 1960s to around 40 per cent at present. The government's consumption share has remained roughly constant but net exports have increased substantially. This is no surprise as Singapore's development strategy has been based on attracting export-oriented foreign firms. The contrast of the position today with that in the 1960s and 1970s is quite marked. The data for the 1960s are subject to a wide margin of error and do not add up because of the large statistical discrepancy but it is clear that in the 1960s total demand exceeded domestic production and Singapore was borrowing from abroad because net exports were negative. This can be attributed to the high level of domestic consumption in the 1960s because investment was still low. By the 1970s net exports were still negative but consumption had fallen to allow a marked increase in investment. Continued high investment rates with constant government consumption and a falling private consumption share have been reflected in the increase in Net Exports. During recent recessionary times net exports were boosted in 1998 by a greater fall in imports than in exports. The implications of such a high amount of net exports for the size of the Current Account and the balance of payments will be examined in Chapter 8.

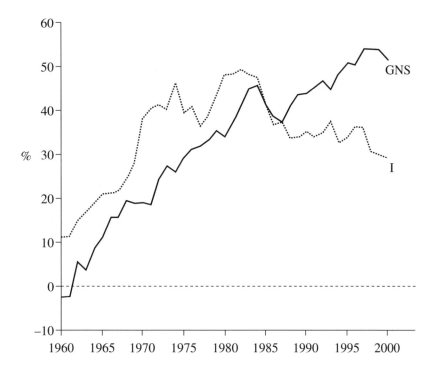

Sources: Table A.2 and its sources.

Figure 4.2 Saving and investment as ratios of GNP, 1960–2000

4.2 THE GENERATION AND USE OF NATIONAL SAVING

With such a large fall in the private consumption share it is obvious that domestic saving must have risen over this long period. Domestic saving finances domestic investment and lending abroad and as these latter two shares have risen then saving must have risen to make this possible. We can look at two aspects of saving: Gross Domestic Saving (GDS) which is GDP minus domestic consumption and Gross National Saving which is GNP minus domestic consumption. In modern Singapore GNP has consistently exceeded GDP since 1984 as Net Factor Income from Abroad (NFIA) has become positive, thus providing another source for saving in excess of what can be made out of the smaller amount of domestic production. See Table A.2 for the remarkable increase in NFIA, especially in the 1990s. The fact that NFIA has been positive since 1984 implies that if there is any significant repatriation of profits by foreign firms in Singapore, as well as wages earned by foreign workers, they have been offset by greater earnings of Singapore factors of production that are produced outside Singapore. It has been the government's policy since the early 1990s to encourage local firms to operate outside Singapore. Table 4.5 gives a snapshot picture of the significance of the two savings concepts, their origin and relationship.

Table 4.5   Sources and use of Gross Domestic Saving and Gross National Saving, various years 1960–2000

Million dollars	1960	1970	1980	1990	2000
GDP at market prices	2 149.0	5 804.9	25 090.7	66 464.4	159 041.8
Plus Net Factor Income from Abroad	39.4	56.2	−1 044.2	1 824.0	10 554.7
Equals GNP at market prices	2 189.0	5 861.1	24 046.5	68 228.4	169 596.5
Minus private and government consumption	2 083.0	4 612.1	15 358.7	37 626.2	80 185.6
Plus statistical discrepancy	−123.0	−127.4	−178.2	109.1	283.7
Plus Current Net Transfers from Abroad	−35.3	8.1	−257.8	−763.3	−2 342.1
Equals Gross National Saving	−52.3	1 129.7	8 251.8	30 008.0	87 352.5
Gross Domestic Saving (= GNS minus NFIA)	−56.4	1 065.4	9 553.8	28 947.3	79 139.9
GNS as a percentage of GNP	−2.4	19.3	34.3	44.0	51.5
GDS as a percentage of GDP	−2.6	18.4	38.1	43.6	49.8
Use of GNS					
GNS plus Net Capital Transfers from abroad	−52.3	1 129.7	8 281.7	29 968.4	87 072.0
Equals Gross Capital Formation	244.5	2 244.5	11 627.6	24 348.8	49 776.4
Plus Net Borrowing from (+) or Lending (−) to Abroad	296.8	1 114.8	3 345.6	−5 619.6	−37 295.6

Sources: Derived from *Economic Survey of Singapore 1992*, p. 120 and *Economic Survey of Singapore 2000*, p. 112.

It is clear that in the 1990s NFIA has become significant and thus increases GNP above GDP, by about 6.6 per cent in 2000, and this has allowed GNS to exceed GDS. We can see that Singapore's gross saving rates are more than half of output and are the highest in the world. Since the mid-1980s Singapore has been lending to the rest of the world as GNS has exceeded the amount of domestic investment. In 1960, 1970 and 1980 domestic investment exceeded national saving so this had to be supplemented by borrowing from abroad. In 1990 domestic investment was 81 per cent of GNS meaning that nearly 20 per cent of Singapore's saving was being invested abroad. By 2000 57 per cent of GNS was being invested in the domestic economy, meaning that 43 per cent was being lent abroad. The total amount of that year, $37 296 million dollars was 22 per cent of GNP.

4.3 EXPLAINING THE INCREASE IN THE SAVING RATE

As in many other areas of research on the Singapore economy there are significant differences amongst researchers on the reasons for the marked increase in the national saving rate. The main reason is also the cause of disagreement in other areas: the lack of official data that everyone could accept and start to interpret. In the case of national saving this is because there are no official data that allow us to assess the relative importance of the public and private sectors in generating saving. The differences among analysts are mainly about the relative importance of pubic saving and whether the increase in the saving rate can be attributed to 'forced saving' due to the compulsory public provident fund system, the Central Provident Fund (CPF). Other issues over which there are different opinions are whether this scheme has just crowded out private voluntary saving and whether Ricardian equivalence holds in Singapore. If it does hold then this would mean that increases in public saving would lead to lower levels of private saving and that public saving could not be the explanation of Singapore's high saving rate. The Ricardian equivalence hypothesis is often explained in terms of the effect of an increase in public sector dissaving through its financing say, a tax cut, by selling bonds to the public. The public has foresight and realizes that taxes will have to be increased in the future to repay the bonds so their net wealth has not changed (Barro, 1974) and there is no reason for them to increase consumption so they will just save the tax cut and national saving will remain the same. In Singapore, the government consistently runs budget surpluses so if this public saving is to affect private sector behaviour and reduce their saving people must believe that they, or their descendants, could receive these surpluses and that public saving is increasing their wealth so they can consume more now, that is, save less. There is no way people can know this. In the case of the CPF there is a stronger link between the scheme and private sector behaviour. People do know that they will receive their savings, generally after the age of 55, so it is more plausible to argue that this compulsory saving could reduce private voluntary saving.

Again, what is important in understanding what might happen in Singapore is not to be found in the range of estimates of different academics or analysts but what the government itself believes on the basis of the information it has that is not made available to the public.

The sources of national saving are: public sector saving; household saving which has a voluntary element; and the so-called 'forced' element of CPF saving and corporate or business saving. Different concepts of what constitutes the public sector and how the government's budget surplus should be defined have led to different views of the importance of public sector saving in national saving. The common approach is to start with some measure of public sector saving and then attribute the residual to the private sector but it is very difficult to disaggregate this into household and corporate saving. See Peebles (2000b and 2001a) for a discussion of these problems and a survey of the range of different estimates of the relative importance of different sources of GNS or GDS.

Asher has consistently made the point that public sector saving is extremely significant as he measures government saving as its Current Account Balance which includes receipts from leasing land (Asher, 1999, p. 4). He points out that conventionally measured tax revenue is a relatively small proportion of GDP (16–18 per cent in the 1990s) but when correctly measured the government's total revenue in 1997 was as much as 38.5 per cent of GDP or even 43.4 per cent if other government revenue sources are taken into account (Asher, 1999, pp. 4 and 22). This means that over the period 1985–97 government saving averaged 41.2 per cent of GNS. Asher does not include the surpluses of the statutory boards nor CPF savings in this estimate so concludes that there is 'an extremely high degree of concentration of the nation's savings in the hands of the government' (Asher, 1999, p. 4).

Huff (1994, p. 332) concluded that the 'driving force in Singapore's savings process was pubic sector savings – the current surplus in the con-solidated accounts of the public sector', meaning that the surpluses of the seven major statutory boards are included whereas CPF funds are attri-buted to the private sector. He estimated that by 1985 public sector saving was 67 per cent of GNS (Asher puts it at about 45 per cent), CPF saving was 25 per cent and so the rate of private sector saving (private and corpo-rate) was only 8 per cent (Huff, 1994, p. 333). Asher and Huff attribute to the public sector the most significant role in gross saving as do Ramesh and Asher (2000). Chen and Tan (1998, Table 2 and p. 313) also estimate a significant public sector contribution: 71 per cent of GDS in 1985, for example, but declining to nearly 50 per cent in the 1990s. The World Bank's famous study of the Asian Miracle (World Bank, 1993) puts public saving at about 44 per cent of GDP on average in the period 1981–90, agreeing with those studies that stress the significance of public saving. Toh's esti-mates of the significance of public saving are in the middle of the range though he does conclude that: 'Public sector saving has consistently played [sic] a significant role in contributing to national saving' and that it hit 'a peak of 59 per cent in 1986' – presumably of total saving: as the 1985 proportion was 53 per cent (Toh, 1997, p. 9). He includes statutory board surpluses in public sector saving and refers to the share of public sector saving in total saving as 'disproportionately high' (Toh, 1997, p. 29).

In contrast with the above view, Low and Aw (1996, 1997) have argued that private saving is the main source of GNS with government saving being estimated as less than one-quarter of GNS (Low and Aw, 1997, pp. 98–9). They conclude that: 'Voluntary savings by households and firms are not insignificant, reflecting the people's penchant for thrift rather than a trait decreed by government fiat' (Low and Aw, 1997, p. 99). They are trying to downplay the significance of CPF saving and not necessarily denying the significance of the public sector as they also state that: 'The claim that the CPF is the reason for the high gross savings rate is at best intuitive. In view of the healthy budget surpluses generated by prudent budgetary practices, the outcome can also be attributed to government savings' (Low and Aw, 1996, p. 5) and that: 'The Singapore government has appeared to have performed extremely well in generating gross savings, controlling CPF rates and formulating and implementing budgetary policies' (Low and Aw, 1996, p. 15).

Such differences are reflected in explanations of why the saving rate increased so significantly. The Monetary Authority of Singapore stresses that the two most important long-run factors have been demographic change and the high and sustained rates of economic growth. The demographic changes at the early period of modern growth saw a significant fall in dependents, both young and old, in the population and the rise of working-age savers. The other factors stressed by the MAS are the persistence of high income growth rates as this is thought to encourage saving, and the importance of government saving. These three factors together explain about one half of the excess of Singapore's high saving rate over that of the average figure for OECD countries (Monetary Authority of Singapore, *Annual Report 1993/1994*, pp. 46–8). The residual must be due to a higher private sector propensity to save. The MAS stresses that the corporate structure in Singapore leads to high business saving and might be an important factor. Family-owned, private businesses are more common in Singapore than in OECD countries and their reluctance to rely on outside finance might have led them to generate funds for investment internally.

The demographic factor is considered by Faruqee and Husain (1998) who note that in the case of Singapore the upward trend is strongly associated with the growth rate of per capita income. The CPF system was thought to have had a long-run impact on the aggregate rate in Singapore 'but most of the rise in compulsory saving was offset by a reduction in voluntary saving' (Faruqee and Husain, 1998, p. 209). Changes in the CPF rates were one factor in explaining the upward trend in private saving.

Financial deepening was found to have had a marginally positive impact on the increase in the saving rate. Demographic factors alone could not explain the upward trend in aggregate saving in Singapore. Heller and Symansky (1998) concentrated on the demographic factor in aggregate private saving behaviour of the Asian 'tigers'. A review of earlier studies of developed and high-income countries reveals that most do find a significant and large effect of the dependency rate on private saving with increases in the elderly dependency rate being more significant in reducing saving rates.

Despite this emphasis on demographic changes many analysts still stress the government' role. Chandavarkar's survey of the literature led him to conclude that the 'phenomenal rise in the national saving rate is largely accounted for by "forced saving" through the CPF' (Chandavarkar, 1993, p. 17). Toh believes that 'this involuntary saving [CPF] is another important factor [apart from public sector saving] in raising the saving rate in Singapore' (Toh, 1997, p. 9). Ermisch and Huff (1999) attribute Singapore's high saving rate to forced saving, which was obtained by 'a combination of manipulation of the internal terms of trade and financial repression' (Ermisch and Huff, 1999, p. 31).

Table 4.6   Saving variables as a percentage of GDP, 1995–99

	1995	1996	1997	1998	1999
Gross National Saving	51.9	52.0	57.2	58.2	58.0
Government	11.8	12.3	11.0	10.1	10.2
Private sector and other	40.1	39.8	46.2	48.1	47.8
CPF saving	7.1	5.1	5.0	4.1	2.2

Source: Cardarelli et al. (2000, Statistical Appendix, Table 4).

As argued above, the main reason for such different views is the lack of official data. Recently, however, some data have been published outside Singapore. The data came from the Singapore government and were provided to the International Monetary Fund but we are told that they do not 'necessarily reflect the views of the Government of Singapore or the Executive Board of the IMF' (Cardarelli et al., 2000, Statistical Appendix, cover page). The relevant form of the data provided are reproduced in Table 4.6. They were expressed in a rather unusual way with GNS being expressed as a proportion of GDP, leading to a higher saving rate than would be found by the usual ratios of either GNS/GNP or GDS/GDP.

The figures imply the private sector is much more important than government saving which seems to have been defined in a very narrow way as the budget surplus. The highest rate for government saving was the 24 per cent of GNS of 1996. The CPF saving rate is the change in the amounts due to members. Using data from the Pacific Economic Development Council, Rao (2001, p. 14) argues that Singapore has a relatively high public sector saving rate which from his table can be seen to be about 46 per cent of total saving in the early 1980s and 43 per cent in 1996 (Rao, 2001, p. 15).

Investigation of the Ricardian equivalence hypothesis has produced mixed results. Husain (1995, pp. 49–51) believed that 'any increase in public saving is fully reflected by an increase in gross national saving', meaning that Ricardian equivalence does not hold but later remarked that the 'joint null hypotheses of rational expectations and Ricardian equivalence could not be rejected'. Chen and Tan (1998) report regression results explaining the private saving rate (as a percentage of GDP) and the public saving rate using a number of standard determinants and annual data for the years 1974–96. The private saving rate is the residual obtained after deducting an estimate of the public saving rate so it includes both household and corporate saving and is sensitive to the exact definition of public saving, and they estimate the public saving rate for 1995 as 20.8 per cent of GDP and the private savings rate at 30.0 per cent (Chen and Tan, 1998, p. 322). As they are both expressed as a percentage of GDP this means that the amount of private saving is 50 per cent more than the amount of public saving or that public saving is 41 per cent of GDS. In contrast, Low (1998, p. 135) puts government saving for 1995 at 25.2 per cent of GDS and private saving at 74.8 per cent. Low and Aw (1996, p. 6) put government saving at 22.7 per cent of GDS in 1995 and private saving at 77.3 per cent. As they are both expressed as a proportion of the same variable, GDS, we can see that Low and Low and Aw believe that private saving was about three times the amount of public saving.

The regression results for the private saving rate estimated by Chen and Tan show that the most significant explanatory variable is the terms of trade which has a positive effect and that the effective CPF rate and the growth rate of GDP have roughly similar, significant, positive effects on the private savings rate. Interestingly their variable for the public saving rate has a coefficient of exactly 1 (no t statistic is given) meaning that 'public savings and private savings were almost perfect substitutes, and high public savings did not contribute to the high overall savings rate. This is consistent with Ricardian Equivalence' (Chen and Tan, 1998, p. 316). Chen and Tan (1998, p. 315) are aware of an MAS study that found that income was not a major determinant of the rising saving rate in Singapore. They do not indicate that that study came to the complete opposite conclusion about Ricardian Equivalence. The view of the MAS is that there 'is little evidence of this phenomenon [Ricardian equivalence] in Singapore' (*Annual Report*

1993/94, p. 48). Chen and Tan (1998, pp. 316–19) interpret their results by saying that a 1 per cent change in any particular explanatory variable will bring about a given percentage change in the saving rate that is equal to the value of the estimated coefficient. This seems to be wrong. The important variables are all percentage ratios so what the coefficients show is by how much a 1 percentage point change in, say, the effective CPF rate, will change the private saving rate which from subsequent estimates is 0.565 percentage points (Peebles, 2000b).

Chen and Tan interpret the coefficient of exactly minus one for the public saving rate in their regression of the private saving rate as evidence for Ricardian equivalence. This is not strictly correct. If one takes the proposition literally then a one-dollar increase in public saving would be offset by a one-dollar fall in private saving so any regression in dollar amounts should show a coefficient of minus one. What they have done, however, is to regress savings rates on each other and these are not dollar amounts, nor does a 1 percentage point in each represent the same number of dollars. The average for the private saving rate over the sample period is 24.4 per cent and that of public saving is 16.8 per cent.

4.4   THE FUTURE OF SAVING RATES

The most important influences in the long-term development of saving rates is likely to be demographic factors and growth rates. Heller and Symansky (1998) concentrated on the demographic factor in aggregate private saving behaviour of the Asian 'tigers' and their survey of earlier studies of developed and high-income countries shows that most do find a significant and large effect of the dependency rate on private saving with increases in the elderly dependency rate being more significant in reducing saving rates. They identify that for Singapore, where demographic change will eventually produce one of the world's most rapidly ageing populations, such changes are likely to have a positive effect on saving up to about the year 2010. Thereafter it will tend to reduce the saving rate. The range of the negative estimates from eight different studies is that the reduction in the National Saving rate in percentage points of GDP compared to 1995 is from about 8 to 22 percentage points by the year 2025. Of these eight studies two predict a positive impact of demographic change on National Saving in Singapore up to the year 2025.

The MAS believes that demographic factors will have a slight positive impact on savings rates up to 2005 with the saving rate staying around 40 per cent – but it has exceeded 50 per cent in the years since they made this prediction. The rate will decline to about 22–23 per cent of GDP by 2030

(*Annual Report 1993/94*, p. 48). If per capita income growth rates are lower in the future this factor could lead to a greater fall in the saving rate. The ageing population will require higher government expenditures and so lead to smaller public sector surpluses. The MAS projects that by about 2020 the positive saving-investment balance that Singapore achieved in 1988 will disappear and saving will fall below domestic investment (*MAS Annual Report 1995/96*, p. 46). At around 2025 the domestic saving rate is expected to be 26–28 per cent of GDP and the investment rate to be 28–30 per cent of GDP (*MAS Annual Report 1995/96*, p. 45).

Toh carried out an econometric study of the determents of the GDS rate and the non-compulsory savings rate in Singapore over the period 1970–95 in which he shows that the dependency ratio (the ratio of those under 15 and over 55 years to the total population) has exerted negative effect on saving (Toh, 1997, pp. 39–41). A simulation exercise on household saving suggests that it will tend to increase up until the year 2030 and the negative effect of ageing will only appear in about the year 2015. In that econometric study variables such as the real interest rate and the extent of financial deregulation had no significant impact on saving.

So there is a reasonable degree of consensus that Singapore will not be able to maintain such incredibly high national saving rates as at present and that saving will even be unable to finance domestic investment. The important policy question is whether household saving will be adequate to finance the retirement years of the ageing population and the role the CPF has played in the economy and whether it is sufficient to cope with future demographic changes.

4.5   THE CPF SYSTEM AND SAVING

The Central Provident Fund was established by law in 1953 under the colonial administration and started operations in July 1955. It was initially intended as a fully-funded pension plan for civil servants but has been expanded in coverage and scope immensely under the PAP and has become an important part of social and economic policy and has been used for macroeconomic purposes. Employers and employees both contribute to the member's account at rates that have changed significantly over time. All employees are required to be members and permanent residents can be members and the self-employed can join also. The scheme implies no transfers between economic classes and is not redistributive, aimed at reducing income inequality and does not guarantee any minimum pension on retirement. The scheme has attracted positive attention by such political parties as Britain's New Labour and is thoroughly condemned by others as a further means used by the PAP to ensure workers' enslavement to the state and capital in such an analysis as that of Tremewan (1994, pp. 53–62). For a Singaporean criticism of the failures, inadequacies and distorting effects of the CPF system see Chee (2001, pp. 139–65). The balances in each member's account are available for withdrawal at the age of 55 or on leaving Singapore or West Malaysia permanently. On the death of a member balances are inherited by the next of kin and if due to physical or mental incapacity a member can no longer work, funds can be drawn on. CPF funds must be held in government bonds or as advanced deposits at the MAS, awaiting a suitable issue of such bonds. It is thought that CPF funds are mostly invested abroad. Over the years there have been many changes in the rules relating to the use of members' balances. The first significant change came in 1968 when they could be used for purchasing public housing and this was extended to private residences in 1981. From 1986 balances could be used to buy non-residential properties and from 1993 to buy land for the purpose of building their own houses. From 1984 part of the members' balances had to be put in a special account which could be drawn on for financing the member's or family members' health needs. From 1989 balances could be borrowed for tertiary education fees of the member's family in Singapore but have to be repaid upon graduation. Further significant changes started in 1978 when members were allowed to buy shares up to a maximum of $5000 in Singapore Bus Services Ltd and then from 1986 members were allowed to use their own funds for buying selected listed shares, unit trusts and gold or holding them in fixed deposits at approved local banks. Over time the nature and range of financial assets that members can hold has been broadened with the aim of encouraging the growth of the unit trust sector and insurance provision in Singapore and to allow members to get a better return than the CPF had been paying them. The interest rate paid to members is based on short-term local bank interest rates and this has meant that over the long period the real rate of return on members' balances has been very low (1.7 per cent a year over the period 1984–93, compared to rates of 10.6 per cent for the USA and 11.8 for the UK (Cardarelli et al., 2000, p. 58). Because the rate paid to members is lower than what is thought to be the return the government gets on using these funds, there is an implicit tax on members' funds and because of other features of the system. Asher (1999, p. 2) cites the view that the CPF system could be defined as taxation. Balances used by members for their own investments have to be paid back into their accounts with interest and only capital gains can be retained for the member to determine the use of. So we can see that the CPF system has been used to obtain funds from the population at low rates, restrict their consumption and direct it into areas such as house purchase, education and health care that the government seems to think households would ignore. It has also used the liberalization of the use of this large fund as an incentive for attracting foreign fund managers to Singapore. At the end of 2000 there were 2.9 million members of the CPF (including active and non-active) whose balances amounted to $90.298 billion (57 per cent of 2000's GDP and equal to 65 per cent of Official Foreign Reserves).

These balances have been built up over the years at various rates of contribution, changes in which are shown in Table 4.7. It should be noted that these rates are those paid to members who are under 55 years of age and that lower rates are paid to older age groups. Furthermore there is a maximum amount payable because since 1986 these rates do not apply to salaries of more than $6000 a month and anyone earning more than that is just assumed to be earning $6000.

Over the period up to 1986 these rates were steadily increased to reach 50 per cent of the total of wage and salary levels. During this period the national saving rate was increasing also and it is this simple association that has led people to attribute to the CPF, in the form of 'forced' saving, an important role in increasing national saving.

A question proposed above was whether CPF saving has merely replaced voluntary saving as members do know they will be able to use their balances in the future. A survey of early studies found some on each side of the argument but, based on criticisms of those studies that concluded that the CPF scheme did not discourage private saving, it was concluded that it 'is empirically proven that mandatory CPF saving does adversely affect voluntary saving' (Lim and Associates, 1988, 234). Tohs's econometric estimates led him to conclude that 'compulsory saving has crowded out voluntary saving' but this was not on a dollar-to-dollar basis as 'every dollar of compulsory saving will reduce voluntary saving by about 55 cents' (Toh, 1997, pp. 37 and 41) so that he can support his claim cited above that compulsory saving has contributed to higher national saving

In an analysis of long-run trends in aggregate saving in Singapore, Faruqee and Husain (1998, p. 209) concluded that in the long run over the period 1970–92 'most of the rise in compulsory saving was offset by a reduction in voluntary saving'. Husain (1995, p. 49) concluded that 'consumers fully offset any changes in CPF saving by changes in voluntary (non-CPF) saving, probably because of the variety of purposes for which CPF saving may be used, particularly in recent years, which make it highly substitutable with voluntary saving'.

Cao and Ng (1995) present an econometric study of voluntary saving behaviour using quarterly per capita data for the period 1977Q3 to 1994Q2. The main aim is 'to verify whether voluntary private saving in Singapore has been perfectly substituted by the government compulsary [sic] CPF

Table 4.7   Central Provident Fund contribution rates, 1955–2001

Effective date	Employer contribution %	Employee contribution %	Total %
July 1955	5	5	10
September 1968	6.5	6.5	13
January 1970	8	8	16
January 1971	10	10	20
July 1972	12	12	24
July 1973	13	13	26
July 1974	15	15	30
July 1975	15	15	30
July 1976	15	15	30
July 1977	15.5	15.5	31
July 1978	16.5	16.5	33
July 1979	20.5	16.5	37
July 1980	20.5	18	38.5
July 1981	20.5	22	42.5
July 1982	22	23	45
July 1983	23	23	46
July 1984	25	25	50
July 1985	25	25	50
April 1986	10	25	35
July 1987	10	25	35
July 1988	12	24	36
July 1989	15	23	38
July 1990	16.5	23	39.5
July 1991	17.5	22.5	40
July 1992	18	22	40
July 1993	18.5	21.5	40
July 1994	20	20	40
July 1995	20	20	40
July 1996	20	20	40
January 1999	10	20	30
April 2000	12	20	32
January 2001	16	20	36

Sources: Central Provident Fund Annual Report 1998, Annex A, and their website http://www.cpf.gov.sg/cpf_info. See also Tan (1999, p. 369) and Low and Aw (1997, pp. 34–5).

saving' (Cao and Ng, 1995, p. 232). They concluded that 'the high CPF saving has not distorted people's behaviour of voluntary saving' and that 'we may conclude that high gross private saving in Singapore (which consists of both CPF saving and voluntary private saving) has not been due to high compulsory CPF saving' (Cao and Ng, 1995, pp. 232–3).

Table 4.7 shows the complete history of CPF contribution rates for those under the age of 55. These rates do not apply to all members. The 30 year period from 1955 saw the total rate increase from only 10 per cent to as much as 50 per cent of salary for a short period in the mid 1980s. We can also see when there were significant change in rates. The first was in April 1986 when the employers' rate was reduced from 25 per cent to 10 per cent as part the anti-recessionary macroeconomic policies of that year. Such reductions are usually called 'cost-cutting' measures but could better be described as 'income redistributive' or 'profit enhancing' as they do not reduce any real business costs and their aim is to maintain the profitability of firms in Singapore and to try to minimize the number of workers laid off. After the recovery from that recession it took until July 1994 for the earlier announced, long-term policy of having balanced contribution rates of 20 per cent from employers and employees to be reached. The next significant cut was again part of anti-recessionary cost cutting measures announced in late 1998 when there was a 10 percentage point cut in the employers' contribution which came into effect in January 1999. This lasted 15 months until 2 percentage points were restored in April 2000 and a further 4 points in January 2001. The fears of much slower growth in 2001 has led the government to postpone further restoration of the rate to later than expected.

The government can use the CPF system to give members occasional bonuses, known as 'top-ups' to their accounts when the economy performs well and has begun to differentiate these payments by the status of the recipients, such as whether the person is doing national service and the size of the public housing unit the recipient lives in. These transfers from government surpluses have been quite small, a few hundred dollars a time, and infrequent and are not intended to return government surpluses to the taxpayers or redistribute it to those whose balances are very low. The latest top-up announced in August 2000 to apply to about 1.9 million people and to come into affect in two contributions over 2001 was more significant ranging from $500–$1500 a person with $200 extra for an active national service man. Members must have made a minimum contribution to their account in the year before this to qualify and quite a few had not. It was seen as a pre-election handout by many.

4.6 THE CPF AND THE ADEQUACY OF PRIVATE SAVING

The national saving rate in Singapore is the highest in the world, and the extent to which this has allowed investment abroad has increased official foreign reserves to the highest per capita rate in the world. It has been argued that the original intention of the CPF to provide retirement funds has been thwarted by the policy of allowing such funds to be used for housing, thus turning contributions into a source of mortgage payments. This had led to the characterizations of Singaporeans as being 'asset rich but cash poor' as government policy has aimed at increasing (enhancing) the value (price) of public housing as it is the most important asset ordinary Singaporeans will hold. One effect is that cash balances in members' accounts will be low and on retirement the amount of cash there will provide a very low replacement rate on earning. Wong and Park (1997, pp. 113–14) calculate for the mid 1990s that members with average balances who purchase an annuity at age 55 will be able to receive $521 a month for 20 years which is 35 per cent of their last monthly earnings of $1500 or about $600 a month for those whose last monthly earnings were $2000 (30 per cent replacement rate). The higher the salary the lower the replacement rate offered by the annuity. These are very low replacement rates compared to the standard recommendation of 60–70 per cent of last salary (Wong and Park, 1997, p. 114).

Discussions of income distribution and the adequacy of CPF saving for retirement is a sensitive issue in Singapore and most media discussion focuses on household wealth in the form of the value of their HDB flat, and the range of consumer durables they are able to afford and the extent to which such ownership has increased over the years. The extent of this sensitivity can be seen from the way a Singaporean academic was treated when he published a comment in the *Jakarta Post* in 1994 in which he said he believed many Singaporean households had inadequate savings and some were living from hand to mouth. The fact that this opinion was published outside Singapore might have added to the robustness of the response from the Singaporean propaganda machine where he was challenged to support his views with 'facts and figures'. He was told that his research was flawed and newspapers and television programmes stressed the extent of ownership of major electrical appliances and essential consumer durables in low-income households. He eventually withdrew his views under this pressure.

The interesting thing about this episode is that not long after, in October 1996, the Prime Minister, himself, in a speech to the Consumer Association of Singapore (CASE), said that he thought that Singaporean households were buying too many consumer durables and were not saving enough. (Economists in Singapore might have been tempted to reduce the shock of these claims of inadequate household saving by defining the purchase of consumer durables as saving and investment as is done in many studies of household saving, but this would not alter the fact that financial saving rates were too low and were falling – the main point the Prime Minister wished to make.) The Prime Minister pointed out that in 1988 households were voluntarily saving 11 per cent of income with a further 24 per cent of income going into the CPF – a total saving rate of 35 per cent. By 1993 households were voluntarily saving only 5 per cent of gross income, with 25 per cent of income going into the CPF – a total saving rate of 30 per cent. That is, voluntary saving rates have approximately halved over this short period whereas the total saving rate only fell 5 percentage points as it was maintained by the CPF system. This enforces the view quoted above that private saving is mostly CPF saving (five times as much) and that private voluntary saving is declining. This is a challenge to those who argue that private voluntary saving is an important part of overall saving. A private survey for 1993 also put voluntary saving at only 6 per cent of income. The Prime Minister pointed out that in order to produce a retirement income of two-thirds of final salary people needed to save voluntarily about 10–12 per cent of income and that CPF savings might not be enough for retirement. He also said that many households saved nothing apart from their CPF savings and he knew many elderly people who were now destitute, as they had not saved enough. He blamed many households for over-consumption (*The Sunday Times*, 6 October, 1996, p. 1). The newspapers and the analytical television programmes did not tell him he must be wrong as they had earlier established that there was no real problem and there was no attempt to debate the implications of his data and the extent to which they supported the academic's earlier view.

How this could happen in Singapore is well explained by Gomez (2000). It is believed by many that CPF funds and private saving are inadequate for financing retirement. The most common source of money for retired people is their children. A government ministry survey in 1995 showed that about 60 per cent of the elderly in the survey had no CPF savings, 56 per cent who did have some balances believed what they had was inadequate, and that three-quarters received money from their children and 64 per cent of them said this was the most important source of money (Cardarelli et al., 2000, p. 56). Most of this help is likely to be voluntary but to reinforce this filial aspect of behaviour the government adopted in 1995 a bill proposed by a nominated member of parliament which has allowed parents to sue their children for financial support. Under the Maintenance of Parents Act, which started operating in mid 1996, up until early 1999 there were 424 applications of which 328, about 77 per cent, were successful. About two-thirds of the applicants were Chinese. Monthly payments ordered ranged from \$10–\$1500 and as any parent can receive support from more than one child the range of payments reeived was from \$20 to \$2700 a month (*The Sunday Times*, 4 April, 1999).

4.7   THE FUTURE OF THE CPF

The great paradox of Singapore is that it has the highest national saving rate in the world and a compulsory saving system, but the government worries about the adequacy of the personal savings for retirement of a large part of the population. This is easily explained by remembering that much of the national savings by the private sector, CPF funds, have been used for house purchase and that many working families have had low life-time earnings so, even with forced saving, would not have been able to build up large sums for retirement.

The way the system has been used to allow households to buy public housing has been criticized for many years and has produced the 'asset rich, cash poor' households. There are not likely to be major changes in the system in the short run but we can expect additional modifications and supplements to it. As the government regards the employers' contribution as a cost it will retain the system so that there remains some flexibility in wage costs although other methods are being adopted to increase the degree of wage flexibility. The last two recessions have seen cuts in these contributions and rapid recovery in the economy. The two main thrusts of change will be to add other savings schemes and to try to ensure than what funds members have can be used to obtain higher returns that will be sustained over the long run.

The first approach can be seen in the introduction of a new saving scheme known as the Supplementary Retirements Scheme (SRS), details of which were released on 31 January 2001 and which came into effect from 1 April 2001. This scheme is open to all Singaporeans, Singapore Permanent Residents (including those who are working outside Singapore) and foreigners (who are not allowed to be members of the CPF) and provides a further way of saving that has tax advantages. Contributions are voluntary and of any amount up to a limit, and must come from earned income, not from such income as rental or interest income. People's savings must be put into investment products that are offered by any bank or fund manager as long as they are made through the chosen four local banks which have been appointed as SRS Operators. SRS savings can be withdrawn at any time but will lose favourable tax treatment and it is hoped that people will keep their funds until the statutory retirement age which is 62 years. Accompanying these changes are further changes that are aimed at providing more destinations for these funds and, it is to be hoped, higher sustained returns. The MAS is working on reforms that would allow more freedom of action for foreign funds managers in an attempt to attract more of them into the financial sector and offer more products. The legislation for this is expected in the second half of 2001 and has been described as 'quite dramatic,' and one fund manager remarked that there would be 12 to 24 months of 'constructive chaos' (*The Asian Wall Street Journal*, 29 March, 2001, p. M5).

Another solution to the 'asset-rich, cash-poor' problem for elderly households has been to publicize the ideas of reverse mortgaging their homes but so far very few companies or banks have offered this service. NTUC Income only offers reverse mortgages on privately owned housing.

It is less likely that the CPF system will be used in the future as a cost-cutting measure, despite the successes attributed to such policies during the last two policies by the government which has now realized that it is a rather blunt instrument. The current policy of both the government and the trade union movement is to push companies into building a larger flexible component in wages which could be cut in future recessions so that CPF contributions could be maintained. The government has a two-year period in which it hopes employers will adopt this system which, at the end of 2000, had been introduced by 29 per cent of employers in the unionized sector and only 2.4 per cent in the non-unionized sector. The government and the trade union movement are unhappy with this slow rate of adoption.

4.8   STRUCTURAL CHANGE IN PRODUCTION

Table 4.8 shows the significant changes in the structure of production from 1960 to 1995 using consistent data. Quarrying has been omitted as it is not at all important and, in fact, in modern versions of the production data agriculture, fishing and quarrying are put together as 'Other goods industries'. In 2000 only 0.6 per cent of the working population

Table 4.8   Structure of production as proportion of GDP, selected years, 1965–95

% of GDP	1960	1970	1980	1985	1990	1995
Agriculture and fishing	3.6	1.9	1.0	0.6	0.2	0.2
Manufacturing	16.6	25.0	29.7	23.7	28.6	27.8
Utilities	1.7	1.7	1.8	1.8	1.8	1.7
Construction	5.3	10.0	7.5	11.3	5.5	7.4
Commerce	24.6	23.4	20.1	18.0	18.8	18.3
Transport and communications	8.8	6.7	11.0	12.3	12.8	13.1
Financial and business services	14.0	16.9	20.5	27.3	26.3	26.8
Other services	19.6	14.4	11.4	11.6	10.8	10.5

Sources: Calculated from *Economic Survey of Singapore 1992*, p. 112, *Economic Survey of Singapore 1997*, p. 111 and *Yearbook of Statistics Singapore 1995*, p. 57.

worked in agriculture, fishing, mining and quarrying and utilities and other undefined activities. We can see the rise of the manufacturing sector to its peak in 1980 and the importance of construction in the 1970s and its peak in the share of production in 1985. Financial and business services increased in significance from the early 1980s.

In terms of employment, by mid 2000, manufacturing jobs accounted for 21 per cent of the labour force and construction provided as much as 13 per cent. Table 4.9 shows the structure of employment in 2000 according to the modern categories of employment. It shows that there is still a significant amount of employment in commerce and other services.

Table 4.9   Employment by industry, June 2000

		%
Total employment	2 094 814	
Manufacturing	434 901	20.8
Construction	274 015	13.1
Wholesale and retail trade	286 791	13.4
Hotels and restaurants	114 478	5.5
Transport and storage and communications	196 541	9.4
Financial intermediation	96 303	4.6
Real estate, renting and business activities	226 215	10.8
Community, social and personal services	452 703	21.6
Others	12 866	0.6

Source: Calculated from *Economic Survey of Singapore 2000*, p. 115.

Table 4.9 shows that employment in manufacturing and construction and utilities comprised about 34 per cent of the workforce and brings out the important point that although the manufacturing sector is important in terms of generating output and exports it is supported by a service sector that employs two-thirds of the workforce.

4.9   THE MANUFACTURING SECTOR

Singapore's manufacturing sector has been built up by attracting export-oriented foreign firms into sectors chosen by the government with the advice of its international advisory panels and business councils. This has had important consequences for the nature of the manufacturing sector. By 1999, the year of the most recent survey, wholly-owned foreign firms, 631 of them, made up only 16 per cent of the number of establishments in the manufacturing sector but had 55 per cent of net fixed assets, produced 72 per cent of value added and 82 per cent of direct manufacturing exports (*Report on the Census of Industrial Production 1999,* Table 7). These figures do not include the contribution of those firms that are less than wholly foreign-owned and so could have a significant foreign ownership. Wholly locally-owned firms produced only 15 per cent of the manufacturing sector's value added and provided only 7 per cent of direct exports. Foreign firms tend to be much larger than local firms and generally have the latest, world-class technology. In the important disk drive sector which started developing in Singapore only in 1986 but quite soon after the invention of the device in 1980, for example, there were just 10 establishments in 1997 (the peak had been 15 in 1992) but the average number of workers per establishment was 3626 (McKendrick et al., 2000, p. 158). This is a significant size and differentiates Singapore from Hong Kong where manufacturing enterprises used to be much smaller. The attraction of top-class foreign firms in one sector such as hard disk drives has encouraged other foreign firms to locate in Singapore as suppliers and has allowed a lot of technology transfer to the local manufacturing sector. Some of this was done by government agencies linking local firms to the MNCs as suppliers. (McKendrick et al., 2000, p. 159) identify about 90 firms that supply the disk drive industry in Singapore. Another consequence of the high technology nature of the foreign firms is that many employees of the MNCs learned skills which they could then apply to their own ventures if they decided to become an entrepreneur. Singapore's best known private sector firm, Creative Technologies, was founded and developed by a former employee of a foreign MNC. It employs about 5500 people in Singapore and the United States but is contemplating reducing its workforce by about 10 per cent in mid 2001.

The manufacturing sector was a strong force behind the recovery from the Asian finanical crisis recession. Table 4.10 shows the extent of vola-tility in its output by showing changes over the previous year's value of

Table 4.10   Indicators of manufacturing sector's recent performance, 1997–2000

	1997	1998	1999	2000
Change in employment %	−0.4	−3.9	−3.4	2.1
Change in output %	5.6	−4.0	10.2	18.9
Change in value-added %	5.1	−0.1	18.3	18.4
Change in direct exports %	4.8	−1.2	13.1	18.3

Sources: Economic Survey of Singapore 2000, p. 149 and *Economic Survey of Singapore 1999*, p. 154.

selected important indicators. Despite continued falls in the number of workers over the period 1997–99 output growth was positive in both 1997 and 1999 and was very high in the year of 9.9 per cent GDP growth in 2000.

The manufacturing sector consists of a number of important clusters: electronics, chemicals and engineering being the most important. Petrol refining started in Singapore in the early 1960s and has been developed by the government, and although refining itself is less important now it has been used as a basis for attracting related industries such as petrochemicals and chemicals. Electronics started in the late 1960s when National Semiconductors and Texas Instruments chose Singapore over Taiwan and Hong Kong.

Table 4.11   Significance of different industries in the manufacturing sector, 1999

Industry	Workforce % of total	Value added % of total	Direct exports % of total
Printing and reproduction of recorded media	5.1	3.8	0.8
Refined petroleum products	1.0	4.4	4.3
Chemical and chemical products, of which	4.6	17.5	13.1
Petrochemicals and petrochemical products	1.1	2.1	3.3
Pharmaceutical products	0.5	12.6	6.8
Other chemicals and chemical products	3.0	2.8	2.9
Fabricated metal products except machinery and equipment	11.2	5.1	2.3
Machinery and equipment	10.7	5.3	4.4
Electrical machinery and apparatus	3.2	1.9	1.5
Electronic products and components	31.2	43.6	62.2
Medical, precision and optical instruments, watches and clocks	2.5	3.1	2.6
Transport equipment	10.3	5.9	3.8

Source: Calculated from *Report on the Census of Industrial Production 1999*, Table 11.

Table 4.11 shows the relative importance of the major industries in manufacturing in terms of their share in employment, in value added of the manufacturing sector and their share in direct exports. It can be seen that electronics dominates both as a share of value added and as a share of direct exports and, together with the chemicals sector, produce 61 per cent of manufacturing valued added and 75 per cent of direct exports of manufactured products. These two sectors played an important role in sustaining the economy during the recessionary period and the recovery in 2000. In each of the four years 1997–2000 the chemicals sector grew 25.8 per cent, 25.3 per cent, 27.1 per cent and 6.8 per cent. These are remarkably high growth rates. Electronics grew by 3.2 per cent, −3.1 per cent, 24.2 per cent and 25.2 per cent in each of these years.

Table 4.12   Value added and remuneration per worker by selected industry, 1999

	Value added per worker $	Remuneration per worker $
Printing and reproduction of recorded media	76819	35727
Refined petroleum products	489433	92999
Chemical and chemical products, of which	388316	62435
Petrochemicals and petrochemical products	194813	71109
Pharmaceutical products	2393771	53658
Other chemicals and chemical products	96137	60778
Fabricated metal products except machinery and equipment	46862	27186
Machinery and equipment	50584	33162
Electrical machinery and apparatus	60743	33607
Electronic products and components	143954	31996
Medical, precision and optical instruments, watches and clocks	124953	34804
Transport equipment	58991	34950
Total manufacturing	103072	33107

Source: Report on the Census of Industrial Production 1999, Table 12.

A comparison of the share in value added with the share in employment of such sectors as pharmaceuticals and electronics suggests they would be among the higher output per worker sectors, which is the case. In 1999, for example, value added per worker in pharmaceutical products was $2.394 million and in electronics is was $143 954. Table 4.12 shows value added per worker and remuneration per worker for the same industries as in Table 4.11. For the entire manufacturing sector the average value added per worker was $103 072 and remuneration per worker was $33 107. All those industries that produced more than the average amount of value added per worker, and there were just six, are included in both tables. It can be seen that the large electronics sector did not provide a higher than average remuneration per worker and higher than average remunerations tended to be in chemicals and petrochemical-related industries. These differences might be the basis for the government's choice of new targeted industries.

The significant of electronics in the manufacturing sector and especially its importance in direct exports has often been taken as one of the indicators of the vulnerability of the economy to fluctuations in global demand for electronics products. It is clear that Singapore's annual growth rates are strongly influenced by what is happening in global electronics demand and to a greater extent than found in other electronics exporting countries such as Taiwan, Malaysia and South Korea (Ministry of Trade and Industry, 1999, p. 5). The roots of this specialization can be linked to Dr Goh Keng Swee's view that Singapore should not become more diversified and when asked, in relation to the electronics sector, whether Singapore should become more diversified replied: 'No. There is an advantage in specialization. Because of our size' (quoted from Chew, 1996, p. 149). Again, we see the influence of Adam Smith. What should be added is that 'electronics' is just a statistical category of different products and although 'electronics' might be a large part of exports, say, its composition can change over time and there can be less dependence on any given type of product or market. Between 1986 and 1996 Singapore was regularly producing 45–50 per cent of the world's supply of hard disk drives each year (McKendrick et al., 2000, p. 155). Seagate was the first hard drive producer to locate in Singapore in 1982, and chose Singapore over Hong Kong and Korea. Its senior vice-president at the time relates that decision to the impression on him of the officers of the EDB and the generous investment incentives that were offered. Seagate had been dissatisfied by the quality of labour in California and was impressed by the availability of cheap, disciplined workers in Singapore. As it was building up a new sector in Singapore where there was no supply base and as they recruited management talent only one had ever seen a disk drive (McKendrick et al., 2000, p. 156). Seagate's early success attracted other, mainly American, disk drive manufacturers, and by the late 1990s four of the five most important disk drive producers in the world had manufacturing plants in Singapore. However, some have reduced their workforce recently and one transferred its manufacturing operations to Malaysia. This has resulted in an increase in the production-based integration between Singapore and Malaysia because of such relocations, and it is clear that changes in the amount of bilateral trade between the two countries are highly correlated with swings in global semi-conductor sales (*Economic Survey of Singapore 2000*, pp. 89–90).

There has been continuing diversification into other electronic products since then. The electronics sector consists of electronics, computers, telecommunications equipment, semiconductors, data storage devices, computer peripherals and printed circuit board assembly.

4.10   THE FUTURE OF MANUFACTURING

Deliberate diversification is taking place in the manufacturing sector. Even within the electronics sector this is clear with the EDB being more keen to attract companies producing components that will be crucial for the next wave of electronic products. Hard drives for desk-top personal computers are being replaced by such things that will be used in smaller, portable, wireless, internet-connected communicators and cellular telephones. A major event in this shift was the attraction by the EDB of a joint venture between Toshiba and Matsushita which will establish a plant to manufacture liquid-crystal display (LCD) panels. This will be the first wholly-owned Japanese LCD plant outside Japan and is expected to cost about $1800 million. The joint venture was established in March 2001 and it is expected that it will start production as early as July 2002. We can expect to see more diversification within the electronics sector but in the short run it is expected to remain an important part of the manufacturing sector. The new Chairman of the EDB Teo Ming Kian said in 1999 that: 'As a form of diversification, certainly we want to look at the other sectors, but while we would want to build up the other sectors, we would not want to deliberately suppress the electronics sector.' In terms of the manufacturing investments that the EDB will seek this means that about 40 per cent is expected to go into electronics, compared to the current approximately 50 per cent, with 20 per cent going into each of the sectors of chemicals, engineering and biomedical sciences, compared to their current shares of 24 per cent, 17 per cent and 9 per cent, respectively (EDB web site at www.sedb.com.sg/home.htm). The feeling in the Ministry of Trade and Industry is that the global electronics industry will have reached a peak by about 2020 and so it is seeking new sectors to expand. Despite this, the plan Industry21 envisages an electronics sector that will have attracted 150 new projects by 2010 to be able to produce $150 billion in an output-based annual growth rate of 8 per cent until then (EDB web site at www.swdb.com.sg.industry21/el_htm). This will be 2.2 times the level of output in 1999 of $68.7 billion. The way this sector is developing has grown out of some of the basic aspects of Singapore's growth strategy. In early 2001 two firms announced that they would establish research and manufacturing units in Singapore. One of these firms, Affymetrix, has as an executive vice president someone who was formerly with Seagate and which uses a combination of wafer fabrication and DNA synthesis technologies in building GeneChips. Such technology uses computers more intensively than other medical-related products. The other firm was co-founded by someone who was on the government's Biomedical Sciences International Advisory Council.

The EDB has chosen life sciences, also known as biomedical sciences, to be the fourth pillar of the economy and is recruiting firms into this sector which can draw on the existing experience in pharmaceuticals, medical equipment in the manufacturing sector and the fact that several foreign medical schools, private hospitals and research institutes have been attracted to Singapore. It has no quantitative targets for output as this is a relatively new field, but the EDB wants Singapore 'to be noted for expertise in research and development and the manufacturing of drugs and medical devices. Our goal is to be home to 15 world-class biomedical science companies by 2010. Singapore aims to be the regional centre for clinical trials and drug development' (EDB web site at www.swdb.com.sg/industry21/in_htm).

The chemical sector will continue to expand over the next decade as more of the capacity on Jurong Island comes on stream. This is a major land reclamation area undertaken by Jurong Town Corporation, a statutory board, linking seven islands for the petroleum and related sectors. The aim under the plan Industry21 is for chemicals to generate an output of more than $75 billion by the year 2010 (EDB web site at www.swdb.com.sg/industry2_/ch.htm). This is considerably more than the output of $29 billion of 1999.

In terms of engineering, Industry21 plans to 'nurture five new industries, attract 20 global engineering centres and 50 manufacturing headquarters to Singapore, and to raise the value-added per worker in this industry to match that of advanced countries by the year 2010' (EDB web site at www.swdb.com.sg/industry21_en.htm).

The government has always stressed that its objective in the near term is to try to keep manufacturing at about 25 per cent of GDP and 20 per cent of total employment. There are a number of reasons for this. One is just the view that manufacturing jobs are the only 'real' type of jobs, which in Singapore is supported with the view that a large part of the labour force would not be suitable for advanced service sector employment. The more sophisticated justification is the view that manufacturing is necessary for developing a related sophisticated service sector that will include logistics, research and product development and marketing. As the Chairman of the EDB put it:

> We need really to have a critical mass of manufacturing activities, especially if we want to build ourselves into a technologically sophisticated knowledge-based economy. The point really is we don't think we can just simply abandon manufacturing and say let's move on to services. To make sure that we continue to generate the intellectual property, to be able to exploit that intellectual property, we must have a good foundation, a good manufacturing base to do so . . . therefore, in that aspect that's critical. (EDB web site at www.sedb.com.sg.hone.htm).

One model of market-driven structural change that would horrify Singapore is that of Hong Kong where the manufacturing sector has shrunk to be less than 7 per cent of GDP. This occurred as firms in Hong Kong moved their physical manufacturing capacity into the Pearl River delta to take advantage of cheaper labour. The contribution of this to Hong Kong, apart from the profits that are re-emitted to the firms that remain there, is the need for services related to this activity such as transportation, financing, insurance, marketing, design, research and product development. The fear in Singapore is that if it lost manufacturing capacity to neighbouring countries it would be because the MNCs would be able to move out in their entirety and there would be no associated service employment in Singapore, the demand for inputs from local firms would fall or they would have to be exported to neighbouring countries, and they would pay no taxes in Singapore. The hope is that if MNCs do relocate some manufacturing activities they would keep headquarters in Singapore, and possibly re-import components for further assembly here. It was often thought that services jobs could not be exported to countries with lower labour costs but now with well developed electronic links countries will be able to move service jobs in banking, ticketing, invoicing and answering customer telephone queries.

4.11   THE SERVICES SECTOR

We can think of the main components of this sector as retail and wholesale commerce, hotels and restaurants, transportation and communications, finance and business services and education and medical services. We will examine the important financial services sector in Chapter 6. The small domestic market and the low consumption share in spending means that retailing and restaurants depend on the tourist trade. Hotels obviously have such a dependence and the government has built up facilities for the holding of major international conventions and conferences. Singapore is often ranked as the best convention venue in Asia. Transportation serves both tourist, other visitors and the huge amount of trade Singapore generates.

4.12   FACTOR INCOMES AND STRUCTURAL CHANGE

For many years the national accounts were only available in terms of the expenditure and production forms and we had little idea of the factor distribution of output as compensation of employees (wages and salaries and employer's contribution to CFP and private pension or insurance funds) and the gross operating surplus of corporations, both public and private. Unfortunately the data now available do not show the surpluses of the public and private sectors separately. It was generally felt that the wage share would be lower than that found in more developed economies. When the data were finally released this conjecture was supported because Singapore's wage share, at 43 per cent of GDP in 1997, for example, was substantially lower than that in the developed countries such as the United States where it was 58 per cent and Japan at 55 per cent, and lower than Hong Kong where it was 46 per cent. The corresponding high profit share for Singapore was interpreted as being 'consistent with the observation that Singapore is a high-saving and high-investment economy'. With the exception of Thailand, the agricultural nature of which means it should not be compared with the other countries used by the Department of Statistics, the Profit-to-Remuneration ratio was the highest (at 1.11) of eight economies with the nearest being Hong Kong at 1.05. This is taken to mean that 'Singapore has the most competitive wage structure with the lowest remuneration share' (*The Income Approach to Gross Domestic Product*, Department of Statistics, 1998b, p. 22). Furthermore, the high profit share is taken to mean that 'Singapore has been able to remain competitive, and provides adequate returns to corporations operating in Singapore' (ibid., p. 23). These two statements in an official statistical report encapsulate the government's view that competitiveness can be associated with a low wage share and that it is important to maintain corporate profitability because, although not mentioned directly, many of those corporations are foreign owned. Many government polices can be understood in these terms.

Furthermore, the statisticians observed a relationship between changes in the profit-to-remuneration ratio and output growth. Figure 4.3 shows the share of GDP being paid as compensation to employees and the gross operating surplus share. They concluded that a rise in the compensation rate compared to the surplus, as observed over the period 1980–85, predicted a slowdown in growth. At the time of publication they did not have data later than 1997 but as the figure shows the compensation rate rose in 1998 and the operating surplus fell and this was a year of slow growth. The statisticians do not offer a theory of why changes in the factor distribution of income should cause variations in the growth rate but this relationship can be seen to underlie government policy. The reaction to the 1985–86 recession was to 'cut costs' with the aim of increasing the compensation rate and as the figure shows this was achieved and output growth rates increased. This incidence has formed the basis of thinking about anti-recession policies in Singapore.

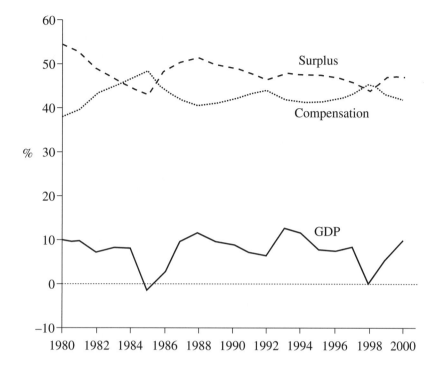

Sources: See text and Table A.1.

Figure 4.3 Factor shares and GDP growth, 1980–2000

4.13 CHANGE IN OCCUPATIONAL STRUCTURE

Changes in the structure of production and changes in the nature of technology have changed the types of jobs being performed in the economy. Such changes will have effects on both earnings and the quality of life. Higher skilled jobs pay more, are usually safer and performed indoors in a more pleasant environment although they can be more stressful for some. A review of the changing occupational structure in very general terms over the last decade shown in Table 4.13 indicates that Singaporeans are moving into administrative, professional and technical occupations at a greater rate than the total workforce. Residents moved out of such occupations as cleaners and labourers (although the proportion of the total workforce in these jobs increased), production and sales and service jobs. These changes 'reflect the concentration of non-resident workers in the low-skilled jobs'

(*Singapore Census of Population, Advanced Data Release No. 4*, p. 4). The construction sector is a significant employer of non-residents and employs about 13 per cent of the workforce and increased its share of the workforce from 8 per cent in 1990.

Table 4.13   Occupational distribution by residential status, per cent of total, 1990 and 2000

	Total		Residents	
	1990	2000	1990	2000
Administrative and managerial	8.6	11.9	9.4	14.3
Professional	4.9	8.9	5.3	10.1
Technical and related	10.8	14.9	12.2	19.1
Clerical	13.0	11.0	15.1	14.4
Sales and service	12.7	10.1	14.4	12.3
Production and related	30.8	24.4	27.7	19.3
Cleaners and labourers	15.0	16.0	10.9	6.8
Others	4.8	2.6	5.1	3.6

Source: Singapore Census of Population, Advanced Data Release No. 4, p. 4.

These changes are related to the general move of jobs away from the goods-producing industries, especially manufacturing, towards services where business services saw a significant increase in its share of employment. The overall skill level of the resident workforce has increased thus increasing their earnings. Interestingly, most of this increase has not been due to movements from low-skill sectors to higher-skill sectors but to movements into higher-skilled occupations within given sectors. The former is called the 'between' or 'industry shift effect' while the latter is called the 'within' or 'occupational mix effect'. The former would be illustrated by the case of developing countries when workers move out of low-skill, low-paying jobs in the agricultural or self-employed sectors into manufacturing jobs. The second case is where the same worker moves into a more skilled job in the same sector or the newcomers into that sector have higher skills than those who leave. The evidence for Singapore over the period 1983–96 is that 90 per cent of the change in the economy's aggregate skill level came from the occupational mix effect, and only 10 per cent from the industry shift effect (Wong, 1997, pp. 85–6). We can envisage the Singapore case when we think of the nature of electronics production where 30 years ago the workers would be performing assembly jobs on imported components, perhaps ten years later they would also be doing the final testing of the assembled units, whereas today they are working in a high-technology, sealed environment that is the most advanced in the world producing the latest foreign designed wafers or chips. Such jobs are paid more but still require workers to work 12-hour rotating shifts and to wear complete body covering suits often known as 'bunny suits' in the trade, which are not popular with some workers. In some cases the increase in skills would be as the same worker moves upwards and in other cases, more likely in the long run, it is the replacement of the older workers by better qualified younger ones. Some workers in these plants will now be engaging in research and development, something very rare 30 years ago. For those workers who move upward it is likely to be through in-house training or government skill enhancement programmes, and for those new workers it can be attributed to investment in the education system to provide the type of workers foreign firms need. Many of the jobs in the foreign owned electronics plants that are planned to keep coming in the first decade of this century require polytechnic level qualifications and technical institute certificates. This is likely to mean further expansion of the education sector. The government expects that the types of jobs that will be created over the next 10–15 years will require that 65 per cent of the labour force have at least a post-secondary education compared to the present rate of about 35 per cent (Hu, 2001, p. 10).

The welfare of the working population depends on the nature of the jobs available, their remuneration as well as the taxation and social welfare systems amongst other things. The next chapter analyses monetary, financial and fiscal aspects which, together with some of the issues we have examined in this chapter, will be relevant for the welfare of the population – a topic which will be covered in Chapter 6.

5. Monetary, financial and fiscal aspects

In this chapter we overview the nature of the monetary system and make a suggestion and a conjecture about the nature of money in the future in Singapore. The financial system has become an important part of the economy and its development and reform is a major current concern of the government. This is particularly true of the domestic banking system which has suffered from being protected from competition for many years. Singapore's fiscal system has a number of characteristics that are featured uncritically in appraisals of its economic polices: persistent budget surpluses, leading to large reserves accumulation which are uncritically accepted as a good thing; very conservative spending policies; a very limited social welfare system; low tax rates on incomes and profits, although as we have seen in Section 2.5 the view that Singapore is a low tax country is disputed by some tax experts. We examine the fiscal system and its contribution to growth and some of its possible future changes.

5.1 SINGAPORE'S MONETARY SYSTEM

The Singapore dollar came into existence only in June 1967, nearly two years after separation from Malaysia, under the Currency Act of that year. As a British colony Singapore was part of the Straits Settlements and Malay States since 1938 so its currency was issued by the Board of Commissioners of Currency, Malaya. In April 1967 the Board of Commissioners of Currency, Singapore (BCCS) was established with the sole currency-issuing power in Singapore. After 1967 Singapore, Malaysia and Brunei issued their own separate currencies but they were linked to the pound sterling at the same rate and so were interchangeable at par and were used as customary currencies in each country. In the early 1970s there was considerable instability in world currency markets and exchange rates but in 1971 Singapore still kept its currency pegged to the pound sterling, which meant a revaluation against the American dollar. In 1972 the pound sterling was floated and Singapore switched to the American dollar as its intervention currency as Dr Winsemius had suggested breaking the link with sterling as part of the policy of developing the financial sector. In May 1973 Malaysia terminated its currency interchangeability agreement with Singapore, effectively floating it against the Singapore dollar. It thought the system was slowing down the development of Malaysian institutions as it was still mainly a producer of primary commodities whereas Singapore was then relying more on trade and services (Monetary Authority of Singapore, 2000a, p. 26). The Brunei ringgit remains at par with the Singapore dollar and each currency can be used in either country to this day. In June 1973 the Singapore dollar was allowed to float and, in the face of speculative inflows, appreciated, which, at a time of high world inflation, was an intention of the policy. Since the early 1980s, at least, the use of the exchange rate to counter imported inflation has become the centrepiece of Singapore's monetary policy, which basically is exchange rate policy.

The floating of the Singapore dollar in June 1973 should have led people to realize that, despite the currency being issued by an institution known as a currency board, it was not a currency board currency. Using the criteria suggested by Peebles (1994) and comparing the situation with that of Hong Kong, Peebles and Wilson (1996, pp. 130–32) argued, not particularly originally as a few others had made the point, that Singapore did not operate a currency board system and in effect had a managed floating system for its exchange rate. At that time the Monetary Authority of Singapore was still trying to associate the Singapore system with the currency board institution mainly because the BCCS accounts do show that it holds foreign currency reserves that exceed the amount of currency in circulation, which is one feature of a currency board system. The rates at which the BCCS deals, however, are based on those in the free market, which is influenced by MAS intervention at the time, of course, but are not fixed as a matter of policy. Today, the MAS is more willing to state that the Singapore dollar does not meet the criteria for a currency board currency (Monetary Authority of Singapore, 2000a, p. 24). The reputation the Singapore dollar has gained as a strong currency is not because it is a currency board currency that happens to be linked to a strong currency or that it has been backed by foreign currency reserves held by the BCCS, for they only cover the currency issue. It has been gained through the policies of the MAS, the continued increase in demand for exports and the inflow of foreign capital and control over the rate of domestic consumption. Some role must also be attributed to limits on access to Singapore dollars by non-residents thus preventing any short-run speculation and instability. This is part of the policy of not allowing the internationalization of the Singapore dollar that will be examined in more detail in Section 8.6. The nature of money in Singapore and its link with the exchange rate policy which result from the economy being open to trade and capital flows is analysed in Peebles and

Wilson (1996, chapters 5 and 6) and the model we recommend for thinking about these aspects of policy are covered in chapter 4 of that work.

It has been traditional to argue from the open nature of the Singapore economy and the use of a managed floating exchange rate that the money supply will be exogenous, adapting itself to changes in demand. Analysts saw little role for a monetary policy that aimed at stabilizing the economy. Empirical studies and interpretations referred to by Peebles and Wilson (1996, pp. 150–52) supported this view. It has always been the view of Dr Goh Keng Swee and he frequently said, and has been quoted on this many times, that the MAS was the only central bank in the world that did not worry about the size of its money supply. These views of the nature of money in Singapore have been confirmed empirically again by Ong and Wan (2000) whose tests for causality between GDP and three measures of the money supply show that there is unidirectional causality from GDP to M2 and M3 whereas for M1 there is a feedback relationship. These results are similar to those found for the United Kingdom, a relatively open economy, and contrast with those of the United States, a less open economy and a reserve currency nation, where a greater causal role for monetary aggregates has been found.

5.2   THE FUTURE OF THE SINGAPORE CURRENCY

Is it, perhaps, time for Singapore to think about the way Singapore currency is issued? The BCCS has retained this role but by now it could be transferred to the MAS, the central bank. It is hard to find a role for the BCCS except that of currency design and issue. Its vision is 'to be a premier currency-issuing authority that provides a world-class currency service, and to establish an electronic legal tender system by 2008' (BCCS website at http://www.bccssin.com/bccsinfo.html). This role could be carried out by a branch of the MAS. Furthermore, it has recently been authoritatively disclosed that the BCCS does not even manage its own reserves because, as the GIC gained experience '[b]y 1987 it was able to manage the reserves of the Board of Commissioners for [*sic*] Currency of Singapore and the long-term assets of the MAS as well' (Lee, 2000, p. 97). It is the MAS that intervenes in the foreign exchange market to influence various exchange rates, not the BCCS. We feel that there would be no great loss of confidence in the Singapore dollar if it were to be issued by the central bank, which is consistently voted one of the most successful central banks in the world, although it could never be described as independent. We are not recommending the winding up of the BCCS but suggesting that it could be done. The year 2005 would be 40 years since Singapore's nationhood was achieved and there would be time for plans to be put in place for any such change by then. The year 2007 would be the fortieth anniversary of the first issue of the Singapore dollar so that could be a suitable year and the year 2011 would be the fortieth anniversary of the foundation of the MAS.

5.3   THE FUTURE OF MONEY IN SINGAPORE

Whether the BCCS or the MAS is to be the future currency issuing body, one aspect of Singapore's future money is likely to be a greater emphasis on an 'electronic legal transfer system'. This is the phrase in the BCCS's vision and government ministers have often stated the objective of turning Singapore into a cashless society. This is thought to be feasible because of the technological and social changes already underway and what is thought to be Singaporeans' increasing familiarity with and willingness to use inter-net-based means of communication, although the extent of this might have been overestimated by the government.

Table 5.1   Ratio of monetary aggregates to GDP, end of year, selected years, 1970–2000

	1970	1980	1990	1997	1998	1999	2000
Currency in active circulation/GDP %	11.7	12.5	10.7	7.6	7.4	8.0	7.1
M3/GDP %	70.1	81.8	124.1	114.6	126.3	131.0	115.0

Sources: Calculated from *Economic Survey of Singapore 1999*, p. 167, *Economic Survey of Singapore 2000*, pp. 105, 132.

Table 5.1 shows the fall in the ratio of currency in active circulation to GDP over the last 30 years with most of the fall occurring in the 1990s. The ratio of M3, the broadest measure of the concept of 'money' has risen, of course, and Singapore is one of the most monetized economies in Asia. The money ratios that are usually taken as indicators of financial development are nearly at the rates found in OECD countries (Arif and Khalid, 2000, p. 112). The M3 series includes types of monies which are less used for trans-actions but form part of people's portfolio of financial assets. Other series such as that for M2 are not consistent over time because of intuitional changes, but see Peebles and Wilson (1996, pp. 132–45) for the earlier evo-lution of monetary aggregates in Singapore.

There has been a trend to a less-cash society brought about by the use of electronic means of fund transfer at the retail level as that is generally where cash is most frequently used. Singapore probably has a smaller underground economy that other countries and, apart from in tiny Brunei, its currency is not used in other countries in the way the American dollar is used, which increases the demand for it. The most important step along the way to less cash use occurred in 1986 when the five main banks established a cashless shopping and payment system known as NETS (Network for Electronic Transfers). Cards that are linked to one's bank account and which can also be used at one's bank's Automatic Teller Machines (ATMs) to obtain cash and do banking transactions, pay fines, apply for shares and to bid for the right to buy an automobile, are accepted in most major retail establishments for cashless, automatically deducted payments. This trend has been reinforced by the move by many government agencies that deal with the public and expect on-the-spot payment for their services, such as the Immigration Department, to refuse to accept cash and insist on NETS payments. Other government initiatives have moved people away from using cash. In 1984 the Committee on Minimizing Cash Transactions for Manpower Savings (COMMICT) recommended the greater use of GIRO payments for wages and salary payment for government employees (Tan, 1999, pp. 92–3). Such use of employees' bank accounts as the recipient of their salaries is a feature of developed economies where very few wages are paid in cash today. Even many small payments such as bus and train fares can be made without cash but experiments to encourage students to use cash cards for small daily expenses such as meals have not been successful. Futurists envisage cellular phones, which are infesting Singapore at a faster rate than in most countries, as the medium through which even small value transactions could be done without using cash. That would require us to own such a device, and as Singapore is the host to may producers of components for these phones we should not be surprised to see Singapore supporting this form of what it would call technological progress.

The move to a cashless economy could be seen as part of the 'electronic paradises' dreamt of by technocrats and envisaged by C.V. Devan Nair (quoted in Section 2.3) but would be less welcome by many. Apart from removing choice in how a transaction is conducted and requiring everyone to be a client of the transferring institution or purchasing and using the required technology, such transactions will always leave an electronic record and even the innocent might be compromised by having their privacy invaded. Many people fear that those records will be accessible to the authorities. In contrast, Kolar (1993) believes that a cashless society would be the ideal environment for free banking to operate in. Competing, privately-owned banks would offer electronic domestic and international transaction and money storage facilities. The power of the central bank would be removed and it would be hard to conceive of what the 'money supply' is, something that has happened already. The main opponents of such a move would be the general public, and it is hard to see how much weight their opposition to this policy would be given in Singapore, and financial institutions who benefit by the time lags associated with clearing cheques. It is hard to see Singapore ever supporting free banking and the competitive issue of money.

In the future considerations of money supply and monetary conditions are likely to become more important. The view expressed by Dr Goh Keng Swee that the MAS is the only central bank in the world that does not care about the size of the money supply has been modified somewhat. Although some econometric studies continue to show that monetary aggregates are exogenous (Ong and Wan, 2000) there has been other econometric evidence that some monetary series lead output changes and that domestic interest rates 'could have an impact on activity in the tradable sectors' (Monetary Authority of Singapore, 2001c, p. 68). Official increased interest in monetary matters was signalled in early 2000 when the Economics Department of the MAS announced it had created a Monetary Model of Singapore (MMS). This model is not in the public domain. This has encouraged the development of other methods of monitoring monetary conditions. Many central banks have constructed Monetary Conditions Indexes since the mid 1990s and Singapore has followed this trend but has chosen to call its indicator a 'Domestic Liquidity Indicator' (DLI). It is a weighted average of the Singapore dollar Nominal Effective Exchange Rate and the three-month interbank interest rates. The weights are determined econometrically once a target macroeconomic variable has been chosen, such as GDP. The purpose of the DLI is to give a general indication of liquidity conditions and is to be taken as an indicator, not as an instrument or target, nor as the focus of MAS policy (Monetary Authority of Singapore, 2001d, pp. 70–73). Further research could be aimed at establishing whether this indicator is a predictor of GDP, CPI or unemployment changes and outperforms other such indicators such as the Composite Leading Index which is based on a larger number of variables.

5.4 FINANCIAL SECTOR

The financial sector has become an important part of the economy and by 2000 accounted for nearly 12 per cent of GDP, a figure higher than the usual 4–8 per cent said by Arif and Khalid (2000, p. 123) to be found in developed economies. In other years, such as 1993 and particularly in 1997 when the sector grew rapidly due to increased instability caused by the onset of the Asian financial crisis, this sector can be more significant (see

Table 5.2). In terms of output the most significant sub-sector is banking which produces 46 per cent of the output of the financial sector. Stock, futures and commodity brokers produce only 9 per cent of its output, investment advisers 3.8 per cent and insurance produces 18.5 per cent.

Table 5.2   Indicators of the financial services sector, 1997–2000

	1997	1998	1999	2000
Growth of real output over previous year %	18.6	−8.6	0.8	4.1
Change in employment, number of workers	8 100	−2 000	4 700	8 100

Source: Economic Survey of Singapore 2000, pp. 102 and 113.

The financial sector has been built up in the Singaporean way of offering tax breaks for foreign firms and the advice of foreign advisers, particularly Dr Albert Winesmius in the late 1960s who pushed the government to take advantage of its location which meant it could fill a time gap that then existed during which there were no financial sectors open for trading. Many of the foreign financial institutions in Singapore are not concerned with the domestic economy because it is so small, but use it as a base for international business. This is particularly true of those offshore banks that started operating in the Asian dollar market from 1968 through parts of their banks known as Asian Currency Units (ACU). They are part of the bank that own them and are granted tax concessions but are separate accounting units. They mainly deal with non-residents but can lend to residents if they receive approval. By 1998 there were 227 banks that had ACUs with total deposits of US$504 billion compared with US$30 million in 1968 (Tan, 1999, p. 172). Subsequent years saw contraction but a small increase in 2000 brought total deposits to US$486 billion which reflects the impact of the Asian financial crisis on this business. The total number of commercial banks operating at the end of 2000 was 134 (eight of which were local banks), compared to 145 in 1998 and the number of foreign banks had fallen from 142 to 125 in the same period. There were 58 merchant banks and 12 finance companies.

Other parts of the financial sector are the foreign exchange market, securities and derivate trading, domestic commercial banking, fund management, unit trusts and insurance. Singapore has one stock exchange that trades both securities and derivates.

The foreign exchange market has a turnover that puts it as the fourth most active in the world and in 2000 average daily turnover was slightly below US$100 billion, considerably lower than the rate of US$167 billion in 1997, a year of instability and booming business for this sector. Most of the trade is in the American dollar against the yen, euro and sterling and in 2000 only 10 per cent of turnover was in Singapore dollars for American dollars.

The stock exchange is not particularly large as many enterprises were statutory boards or GLCs and so were not created through share issue and now a large part of their shareholding is held by one or other of the four government holding companies. At the end of 1999 over 370 companies were listed on its two boards (SES and SESDAQ for smaller firms) and total market capitalization was $434 billion which was 3.4 times the amount of that year's GDP. Some government companies have been listed on the market and about 27 per cent of the market's capitalization is shares in companies owned by Temasek Holdings Ltd., the main government holding company.

Singapore has a reputation for its derivatives trading market that used to be called the Singapore International Monetary Exchange (SIMEX) on which Nick Leeson famously traded Nikkei 225 and Japanese Government Bonds futures in the early 1990s. In the early 1980s the government surveyed financial institutions to gauge their interest in having a futures market. Advice was taken from the Chicago Mercantile Exchange's International Money Market and the committee established in 1982 to implement the establishment of the market had a chairman from Chicago. Futures trading started in 1984 and in 1985 there were only four types of contracts (three in currencies and one in gold). Subsequently, many more contacts have been added including contracts on oil and Stock Index Futures (Tan, 1999, pp. 315–21). In 1999 SIMEX was merged with the Stock Exchange of Singapore (SES) and the exchange was demutualized to become the Singapore Exchange (SGX) and in 2000 it became a public-listed company. SIMEX is now Singapore Exchange Derivates Trading Limited (SGX-DT). During its lifetime SIMEX benefited from incentives schemes aimed at both SIMEX itself and its members and at local firms to encourage them to use its products (Tan, 1999, p. 323). In 2000, 91 per cent of the turnover of SGX-DT was in just four contacts: Eurodollar Interest Rate, Euroyen Interest Rate, the Nikkei-225 Futures contract and the MSCI Taiwan Stock Index Futures contract. Now one can eventually trade in the Singapore Straits Times Index contract which was launched in June 2000.

Singapore has a very underdeveloped bond market because of the nature of its growth strategy using statutory boards and GLCs. They have generally been profitable and have not required bond financing. Many of the GLCs and statutory boards have built up very large cash reserves which they just left deposited with local banks. In order to promote the development of the bond market the government has encouraged its firms to issue bonds in Singapore and a number of statutory boards have done so. The government itself, which runs a surplus, has sold bonds of various maturities to set benchmarks for the rate of interest and to give traders something to trade in. In contrast to the extent of domestic bond issue the Asian Dollar Bond market has been more active (Tan, 1999, p. 236). Most of these bond issues are in American dollars (Tan, 1999, pp. 184–5). In the budget of 2001 the government took steps that are expected to lead to a marked expansion of the local bond market as it lifted restriction on the way Singapore dollar bond issuers can swap their proceeds in foreign currencies and reduce the cost of issuing short-term bonds.

The GIC has been told to put some of its funds under management in Singapore to develop that sector and together with tax incentives for foreign fund managers and continual relaxation of the CPF investment scheme it is hoped to build up that sector. However, the extension of the use of members' CPF balances has not led to rapid growth in fund management or unit trust ownership but has led to a boom in the insurance sector which has recently been liberalized after years of protection during which no new products were offered and there were hardly any new entrants to the sector.

One sector that has occupied government thinking recently and has been the object of much attention and reform is the domestic commercial banking sector. Reforms in this sector have been analysed as an indicator of the extent to which the government is formulating a new paradigm about its role in the economy; how to manage a more liberalized sector in the era of increased international competition due to technological change and how it would react to increased foreign involvement in what has been thought of as a strategic domestic sector. This sector has been dominated by four local banking groups ('the big four') one of them, DBS, a GLC, and three, family-controlled banks. They have been protected from foreign competition by restrictions on the number and activities of foreign banks in Singapore but with the advent of internet banking they were likely to be subject to a greater degree of competition anyway. As the Senior Minister put it, these banks were profitable not because they were efficient but because he chose to protect them from competition. While talking with foreign bankers and businessmen in the 1990s he realized that protection had weakened the domestic banking sector and he concluded 'that they [local banks] were not awake to the dangers of being inbred and of failing to be outward and forward-looking in an age of rapid globalisation. They were doing well, protected from competition. They wanted the government to continue to restrict foreign banks from opening more branches or even ATMs (automatic teller machines)' (Lee, 2000, p. 99). He has since continued his public criticism of local banks. This prompted him to propose reforming the banking sector and entrusted this responsibility to the Deputy Prime Minister, Lee Hsien Loong who took over as chairman of the MAS in January 1998.

5.5 THE FUTURE OF BANKING

From about 1997 the government considered reforms of the banking sector with advice from the usual International Advisory panels and the first stage of reform was launched in 1999 with an initial three-year period, 1999–2001, although a five-year period is envisaged. The main thrust is to introduce more competition into commercial banking without losing domestic banks and to make those banks which survive this competition more transparent and more focused in their business activities. For this latter end the government has required them to disclose hidden assets that they did not report on their balance sheets and has said that it will pass legislation if they do not voluntarily divest themselves of non-core businesses. Once this legislation has been passed local banks will have three years to divest themselves of non-core businesses.

The government has stated that it expects there to be room for only two large local banking groups in the retail market. It is clear which one of them will be. In November 1998 the government sold the Post Office Bank (POSBank), a statutory board since 1972, to DBS, a GLC, for a price that was felt to be rather high at 37 per cent more than the value of its net tangible assets. It subsequently emerged that this was because DBS had to undertake that there would be no redundancies from the merger. POSBank had been in existence since 1877 as a savings bank to encourage personal saving and 'to channel these savings into national development' (Tan, 1999, p. 400). It offered loans at rates lower than that of commercial banks. It has increased its range of services substantially and it has always had more account holders than there are Singaporeans, with 5 866 200 in June 1998, for example. The advantages to depositors of receiving tax-free interest on deposits, and the fact that out of all bank deposits only POSBank deposits were guaranteed by the government, will be removed as a result of the merger. In 1996 POSBank was rated the second-best quality service provider out of 15 government service providers (Tan, 1999, p. 409), but since the merger there have been many complaints about deteriorating service both at branches and through its internet and telephone services. One way banks are seeking to reduce costs is to allow the withdrawal of cash with one's bankcard when one makes purchases at supermarkets or shops and some will allow withdrawals with no minimum purchase. This suggests that cash is still important for many people's transactions. Banks will do less cash business and will pay the supermarkets and shops for this. Such services have been available in other countries such as Australia for a while now. Restructuring the banking system has produced the first ever hostile takeover bid of a large listed company in mid 2001 when the third largest bank bid for a controlling stake in the smallest banking group. This followed its earlier failed merger attempt that would have created a banking group larger than DBS (*Asiaweek*, 22 June, 2001, p. 10). In June 2001 what has been called 'a merger frenzy' erupted when DBS made an offer for the fourth biggest bank which was followed by an alternate offer from the second largest local bank There was a cultural clash during these merger attempts when statements by the American advisers to DBS about the private banks in Singapore were thought to be too blunt for Singapore sensibilities and the DBS had to issue a public apology and gave compensation of $1 million to each of the two banks (which will be given to charity) that were thought to have been slighted by the Americans' comments.

The strategy of increasing competition is to gradually allow more foreign banks into the domestic retail sector. The MAS announced it would issue up to six Qualifying Full Bank Licenses by 2001 and in 1999 four such licences were issued. This allows these banks to have 10 locations and off-premise ATMs of which up to five can be branches. They can set up to two new branches and three off-premise ATMs and can relocate their existing branches. In mid 2001 the number of branches they can set up was increased to 15 which is likely to increase the extent of competition in retail banking. They can also set up a network linking their own ATMs among themselves (Tan, 1999, p. 354). As they have not been allowed to share the existing widespread ATM networks nor the NETS system of the local banks, although they are negotiating to try do this later at the moment, there has not been much extra competition. The government's view is that it would like local banks to retain at least 50 per cent of the local market and at present they have just over 60 per cent of the market. The government has also abolished the 40 per cent limit on foreign ownership of domestic banks and as it has said it is willing to sell off some of its 37 per cent share in DBS there has been speculation that some local banks might become foreign-owned. The MAS has announced it might give foreign banks access to the local ATM network in two to three years time when it reviews the situation. At present the four foreign banks that do retail business have just 56 ATM machines between them and the local network has more than 1000. Local banks are strongly opposing these measures (*The Business Times*, 17 October, 2001, p. 1).

One task the government has set Singapore companies is to 'go regional' as the Singapore market is too small for their expansion to efficient size, and it expects its companies to show a lead in this effort. The Asian Financial Crisis caused great problems for banks in neighbouring countries and DBS has been active in buying up some of them and now has subsidiaries in Thailand, Hong Kong, the Philippines and Indonesia. To this end DBS appointed an American as its COE and other local banks have employed foreigners as they feel they are more familiar with business in a competitive international environment. DBS is already the largest banking group in South-east Asia with activities in 13 countries and about five million customers. It has 10 000 employees.

One reason for this liberalization and its likely intensification in this year and in the future is that Singapore expects to conclude more bilateral free trade agreements with Australia, Japan, Mexico and the United States this year. (One with New Zealand has already been concluded.) The United States is likely to be pressing for more access to Singapore's service sectors, including banking, which have traditionally been protected.

The liberalization of the banking sector raises an issue that has relevance to other sectors of the economy. At the beginning of its reforms in about 1997 the government admitted that it had overregulated the financial sector and that this had stifled innovation and that Singapore was lagging behind Hong Kong. Dr Richard Hu used a few times the comment that had been heard in many places when people compared the approaches of these two places: in Hong Kong, what is not expressly forbidden is taken as permitted, whereas in Singapore what is not expressly permitted is thought to be forbidden. See also Lee (2000, pp. 97–101) for this and why the government did not start reforms earlier. Dr Hu promised that Singapore would move to showing a lighter touch in its regulation of the financial sector. His soon-to-be successor at the MAS, Lee Hsien Loong, announced in November 1997 that: 'We must shift our emphasis. We need to regulate the financial sector with a lighter touch, accept more calculated risks, and give the industry more room to innovate and stretch the envelope. The process should start now, notwithstanding the current regional uncertainties' (Lee, 2000b, p. 5). Now, this new approach to regulation is not just limited to the financial sector if the government goes ahead with its plans to privatize statutory boards and GLCs. If these become independent, privately owned, commercial organizations they cannot be ordered by the government to behave in a particular way, whether it be cutting their prices or fees and charges, or venturing into certain foreign countries. Furthermore, these companies might have a high degree of market power so they need to be regulated in a way that differs from when they were public enterprises. This will be very relevant to such sectors as telecommunications, which has been liberalized by allowing competition against the former government monopoly, SingTel, and in energy production, especially electricity, where liberalization is planned. Monopoly or oligopolistic industries will need regulation and this is something the civil service will have to learn how to do. It also means that the government will lose what has been a fundamental part of anti-recessionary macroeconomic policy, that is, the power to order statutory boards and GLCs to reduce their prices in order to enhance the profits of all companies.

When asked what the financial landscape might look like in 2004, the end of the first stage of reform, the Chairman of the MAS was rather cautious when he was asked whether 'we are talking about a completely level playing field for local and foreign banks?' (*The Business Times*, 20 July, 2001, p. 12). He replied:

> I can't say. If you ask the banks, they will say their greatest concern is with ATMs because once you open up the ATM network, then straightaway a foreign bank can have 1,000 points of access, which will be a very big change. So this time we decided not to open up the ATM market – we said we are not doing it for now. We'll have to see how things are in a few years' time.
>
> I am sure we will continue to liberalise. I'm not sure whether we will reach a position where the playing field is completely level. It depends on the way the industry develops. If it turns out to be feasible to maintain local banks and keep banks with significant Singapore market shares, significant Singapore ownership and control in our system. I think that would be good. And if they can hold this position without any extra props, that's even better.
>
> And I think given time, eventually, and with luck, we should be able to get to that position without extra props; that means completely level but we keep certain banks which are defined as Singapore banks.
>
> But if the industry goes a different way, the consolidation process will still continue. It if turns out that Singapore banks are simply not big enough and we have to be the size of, say, Australia to have really big banks, then we'll have to calculate our options. It will be a more uncomfortable world for us. But we will have to see what we can do to preserve our position. (Lee Hsien Loong, *The Business Times*, 20 July, 2001, p. 12)

5.6   FISCAL FEATURES

The principle ideas that have shaped Singapore's fiscal policy are conservative, Victorian values in that it should avoid budget deficits and always aim for surpluses; allow increases in expenditures only after increases in revenues have been ensured; in forecasting, to underestimate revenues and overestimate expenditures so that larger surpluses than forecast are the usual case; and not have a welfare system under which people think they have a right to be supported by the government in hard times or old age. The stress for running budget surpluses is constantly articulated by Dr Richard Hu, the Minister for Finance, as the resulting reserves are all that Singapore has, but is probably the philosophy of the whole cabinet. The avoidance of budget deficits can be seen in Dr Goh Keng Swee's antipathy to anything in economics that is later than Ricardo which would include Keynes whose ideas Dr Goh does not think relevant to Singapore. Ricardo thought that there were only two things necessary to make England the richest nation in the world: free trade in food and the abolition of the national debt.

The opposition to a social security system has also been part of Dr Goh's ideas and is now entrenched in the minds of the current cabinet so that one member of it can say in 1996: 'If we are moved by one compassionate concern after another, it is a slippery path to perdition' (quoted from Ramesh, 2000, p. 243). Such antipathy to a general welfare system is justified to the people by invoking the negative models of Australia, New Zealand and the United Kingdom that are often mentioned as examples of the nature of the end of that 'slippery path'. The positive justification is that such a system of minimal social security and fostering the belief that nothing its due as a right would help to build a rugged and self-sufficient society where 'Singaporeans look after each other', in the words of the prime minister, meaning help not by transfers through taxes but by voluntary support. The expected voluntary aspect of support for the elderly has been reinforced by the Maintenance of Parents Act, and encouraged by tax incentives for children to support or live with or near their parents. Support for those for whom social welfare is thought to be acceptable, the disabled and the elderly destitute, those living below subsistence level and those who cannot support themselves because of specific problems is provided by the government on a discretionary basis to voluntary welfare organizations who then administer the system of small payouts to help those who cannot cope (Ramesh, 2000, p. 252). Vagrants are taken off the streets and put in residential homes. There is no unemployment benefit, meaning that during recessions there is no call on the state budget for extra expenditures which, in many countries, is an important reason for budget deficits at such times. There are no publicly funded pensions, except for holders of political positions, the judiciary, top civil servants and military officers.

The retirement needs of the general population are supposed to be met by their CPF funds and their own saving but, as we have seen, these are felt to be inadequate in many cases, even by the government. On this basis we would expect the social welfare expenditures in Singapore to be lower than elsewhere and, according to Ramesh, the average amount spent by the government on income maintenance social welfare each year over the period 1990–95 was indeed very low at 0.53 per cent of GDP compared to an average of 8.2 per cent for OECD countries (Ramesh, 2000, p. 244). The extent to which there is public assistance for the disadvantaged can be seen in the numbers for 2000. The total number of people who received public assistance was 2409 consisting of 1930 aged destitutes, 178 people who were unfit for work, 78 abandoned/distressed wives and orphans, 211 handicapped and disabled people and 12 widows with children under 12 years of age (*Yearbook of Statistics Singapore 2001*, p. 269). We can see that the main category of recipients are aged destitutes and this number is likely to increase in the future. As women outlive men there will be more women in this position as they will probably not have had a history of high earnings and large CPF contributions. Possible high levels of structural unemployment following from the marked slowdown of the economy in 2001 might prod the government to think about adopting some limited system of support for the unemployed. During the build up to the election the government did mention a suggestion by the Workers' Party that people be allowed to use their CPF funds during periods of unemployment but this has not been endorsed by the government. Until now, the problem of hardship caused by unemployment has been dealt with by support for retraining programmes and rebates on rents and utility charges for those who live in public housing, small handouts on a case-by-case basis but these might miss those who might need the most support when they are unemployed.

Government revenues come in the form of operating revenues from taxes on incomes and assets and from fees and charges on the population. Another significant additional source of revenue is the revenue from the lease of land which is not often included in government operating revenue, thus giving a misleading impression of how much the government takes from the economy. Asher has always argued that revenue from the lease of land should be regarded as current income for the government. In 1997 total operating revenue was 20.2 per cent of GDP but with revenue from the lease of land at 15.9 per cent of GDP the total government revenue was 38.5 per cent of GDP. Over the years 1991–97 total revenue conceived this way averaged 34.6 per cent of GDP (calculated from Asher, 1999, Table A2).

The government's rule of thumb is to keep expenditures at less than 20 per cent of GDP. As a result, over the long run government budget surpluses have averaged 4.3 per cent of GDP each year. Deficits were experienced after the mid 1980s recession in the years 1986–88 but did not recur during the recent slowdown and there were budget surpluses every year after 1988 (Monetary Authority of Singapore, 2001a, p. 10). Measurers of economic freedom are impressed by the low 'take' by the government from the population and identify it with the low amount of operating revenue or the low level of government expenditure, or the low marginal tax rates. However, it could be argued that even if these are low, regular budget surpluses are a violation of economic freedom. Which of these countries shows more economic freedom? One in which the government is elected and supported by a large majority of the entire population and which takes 40 per cent of GDP and spends 40 per cent of GDP or one which takes 25 per cent of GDP and spends 18 per cent?

Table 5.3 indicates the extent of budget surpluses in the 1990s where the surplus is just the difference between operating revenue and operating and development expenditures. The very high surpluses of the years 1992–95, which were associated with very rapid real GDP growth in those years, were not repeated in the later 1990s as growth rates fell. The budget data are for the associated fiscal year and have been expressed as a percentage of the relevant GDP computed by the MAS and show the developments in 2000 by each quarter. On a quarterly basis the government does not always run a surplus and the first quarter of each year tends to produce a deficit just as that quarter's GDP tends to be less than that of the previous quarter. The MAS estimate is that the surplus for FY2001 will be 3.7 per cent of GDP.

Let us look at how the government obtains its operating revenue and see what changes there have been in the 1990s as the data are now presented in a consistent way for this period, and there have been a few new sources of revenue introduced in the 1990s. Table 5.4 shows the total amount of operating revenue and the percentage of this total contributed by each item. It can been seen that there has been a fall in the proportion of revenue that comes from taxes and therefore an increase in the proportion coming from fees and charges. This reflects the government's attempt to keep taxes low and the principle that people should pay for the use of public goods. For, example, one item of 'Fees and Charges' is the revenue from the Certificate of Entitlement that was introduced in early 1990. This is an extra licence that must be bought from the government in order to buy a vehicle. The government sets the number of licenses available each month and sells them at auction. The aim is to limit the growth of the vehicle population to about 3 per cent a year. The government uses other means to make motorists pay for vehicle ownership and use. The item 'Taxes on Motor Vehicles' includes road tax, additional registration fees and other charges but does not include import duties on motor vehicles, which are significant, and which are included in the item 'Custom and Excise Duties'.

Detailed data on income tax receipts are not available separately for individuals and corporations but it is estimated that about two-thirds of income tax revenue comes from corporations (Asher, 1999, p. 6). Only a relatively small proportion of the labour force pays personal income tax. For example, in 1999 only 566060 residents paid personal income tax which was 28.6 per cent of the labour force, which is much lower than the ratio of over 60 per cent estimated for the mid 1980s by Asher (1999, p. 7). Residents contribute 99 per cent of all personal tax receipts and on average pay more than

Table 5.3   Real GDP growth rates and budget surpluses as a percentage of GDP, selected fiscal years

	1992	1993	1994	1995	1996	1997	1998	1999	2000	2000 QI	2000 Q2	2000 Q3	2000 Q4	2001 QI
GDP growth rate %	6.5	12.7	11.4	8.0	7.6	8.5	0.1	5.9	9.9	9.8	8.4	10.3	11.0	4.5
Budget surplus as % of GDP	6.8	8.0	8.9	6.4	4.3	4.3	0.7	3.8	3.4	−4.4	9.1	13.0	−4.0	−1.5

Sources: MAS Quarterly Economic Bulletin, June 2001, Tables 1 and 7 (Monetary Authority of Singapore, 2001c).

Table 5.4   Amount and structure of government operating revenue, selected years, 1990–2000

	1990	1995	1999	2000
Total operating revenue $ million	13 102	24 782	28 619	33 527
Total operating revenue as a percentage of GDP	20.5	21.0	20.1	21.0
Percentage of total revenue				
Tax revenue	80.4	79.0	75.4	75.4
Income tax	37.5	35.3	40.6	40.0
Corporate and personal income tax	33.6	32.8	32.6	36.5
Contributions by statutory boards	3.9	2.5	8.1	3.6
Assets taxes	8.5	7.4	4.1	4.4
Taxes on motor vehicles	10.2	7.3	4.7	6.5
Customs and excise duties	10.0	6.5	5.4	5.3
Betting taxes	4.0	4.0	4.6	4.3
Stamp duty	5.0	5.5	4.5	4.1
Goods and services tax	0	6.6	6.2	6.7
Others	5.3	6.3	5.4	4.0
Fees and charges	11.4	14.8	13.0	16.6
Other receipts	8.2	6.2	11.6	8.0

Sources: Calculated from *Economic Survey of Singapore 1992*, p. 125 and *Economic Survey of Singapore 2000*, p. 125.

non-residents. (Calculated from Internal Revenue Authority of Singapore *Annual Report 1999*, Appendix 8.) The government's stated figure is that 35 per cent of economically active residents pay income tax and that it would not like to see this proportion fall as 'we would like everybody to pay some tax, no matter how low it is, so they have some responsibility for the public budget' (Dr Richard Hu, Minister for Finance, quoted from *The Business Times*, 24 February, 2001, p. 3). Of the 86 164 companies assessed for corporate taxes in 1999 only 26 per cent paid taxes. In addition statutory boards are required to contribute to the government. These amounts are negotiated each year and are not based on any tax rate and, as can be seen from Table 5.5 which shows the annual changes in the amount collected, can vary very significantly from year to year.

An important change to the tax revenue structure occurred in April 1994 with the introduction of a Goods and Services Tax (GST) at a rate of 3 per cent. The government stated then that it would not increase the rate for at least five years and has not increased it at all to date. This move to a greater reliance on indirect taxes follows a global trend. Rebates on income taxes were given to offset some of the effects of higher prices. By 2000 GST was providing 8.9 per cent of total tax revenue. The government's long-term plan is to increased the share of indirect taxes in total tax revenue from the

Table 5.5   Annual percentage changes in items of government operating revenue, 1997–2000

	1997	1998	1999	2000
Total operating revenue	9.2	−7.8	1.4	17.1
Tax revenue	11.5	−9.4	−2.6	17.1
Income tax	20.2	−4.3	6.0	15.5
Corporate and personal income tax	6.9	2.9	−4.9	31.3
Contributions by statutory boards	206.1	−39.9	97.6	−48.3
Assets taxes	47.5	−23.0	−36.1	25.7
Taxes on motor vehicles	−27.7	−12.4	−13.6	63.0
Customs and excise duties	1.8	−3.9	−4.7	14.9
Betting taxes	9.1	0.8	3.4	10.9
Stamp duty	−7.6	−36.2	18.4	7.8
Goods and services tax	11.2	−15.1	5.2	26.3
Others	16.1	−2.2	−28.4	−12.1
Fees and charges	−0.6	−16.8	11.3	49.3
Other receipts	3.8	26.3	22.4	−19.1

Source: Economic Survey of Singapore 2000, p. 125.

present 40 per cent to 50 per cent. This is not likely to be done through an increase in the GST rate but through other indirect taxes such as those on vehicles and possibly higher taxes on tobacco products and alcohol. A problem experienced in many countries is that the cost of collecting indirect taxes can be quite high for small businesses so in Singapore all companies with a turnover of less than one million dollars are exempt from registering for GST.

The Asian financial crisis and the marked slowdown in the economy in 1998 had an affect on some components of operating revenue but, as we have seen, there was no overall government budget deficit in this period. Table 5.5 shows the annual changes in the main categories of government operating revenue. Those that showed the greatest fall in 1998 are the ones one would expect to be more susceptible to the business cycle and a marked fall in property prices and transactions.

Changes in fiscal policy during the 1990s have had an affect on the macroeconomic nature of the economy. The policy of reducing tax rates on incomes and moving towards more revenue from indirect taxes have made some revenues less responsive to changes in total income, GDP. This became clear during the recovery from the recent recession when operating revenue did not increase at the rate it had done after the 1985–86 recession, suggesting that the strength of automatic stabilizers in the economy has weakened. There have been two reasons for this reduction in the responsiveness of revenue to changes in output when we measure this as the dollar increase in revenue caused by a one dollar increase in GDP. This depends positively on the elasticity of revenue with respect to output and the ratio of that type of revenue to output.[1] The elasticity term can be estimated econometrically and the MAS has found that there has indeed been a fall in the elasticity for direct and indirect taxes as well as non-tax items of revenue. For example, the elasticity of direct tax revenue to output has fallen from 3.35 in 1995 to 2.14 in 2000, that for indirect taxes has fallen from 2.40 to 1.87 and for non-tax operating revenue (generally fees and charges) it has fallen from 2.00 to 0.95 (MAS *Quarterly Bulletin*, March 2001, p.15). Furthermore, the ratio of personal and corporate tax revenue to output has fallen, mainly due to reductions of corporate tax rates and the reduction of the number of tax bands for personal taxes. Both these changes contribute to a fall in the change in revenue for a given change in aggregate income, GDP.

Table 5.6   Structure of operating expenditure, selected years, 1990–2000

	1990	1995	1999	2000
Total operating expenditure $million	7 062	10 834	13 907	18 897
Total operating expenditure as a percentage of GDP	11.1	9.2	9.9	11.9
Percentage of total expenditure				
Security	48.2	48.4	50.8	47.0
Social and community services	36.9	37.9	34.9	32.0
Education	24.7	24.6	21.3	20.6
Health	6.5	6.3	6.3	5.2
Environment	2.7	2.5	2.3	1.9
Public housing	0.6	1.5	1.2	0.9
Others	2.4	2.9	3.8	3.2
Economic services	6.1	6.3	8.2	16.2
National development	3.5	3.3	1.6	0.7
Communication and information technology	0.4	0.7	3.3	12.8
Trade and industry	1.8	2.0	2.5	2.1
Manpower	0.4	0.3	0.8	0.5
General services	5.2	6.6	6.0	4.8
Pensions	3.6	–	–	–

Sources: Calculated from *Economic Survey of Singapore 1992*, p. 126 and *Economic Survey of Singapore 2000*, p. 126.

Table 5.6 shows the structure of operating expenditures which are mainly expenditures on labour and grants. Operating expenditures have been kept relatively constant during this period and the most important item is security. This is the necessary expenditure on the support of the military, most of which is made up of national servicemen who would not be paid a market wage for their service. Education naturally takes up a significant share of operating expenditures as the educational system is dominated by the public sector. It appears from the data for 2000 that economic services have become more significant but this can be better analysed by looking how these expenditures changed during the Asian financial crisis and Table 5.7 shows how these elements change year-to-year. The government was not afraid to reduce operating expenditures in the years 1998 and 1999 on important services it provides such as education and health, also probably benefiting by wage reductions in these years. In 2000 there were significant increases in expenditures on security, education and health among the social and community services. These were due to the government decision to deal with some longstanding problems that have not yet been solved. Education and health expenditures increased as the government recruited more teachers, of which there is a shortage, and gave significant pay increases to doctors in the public sector because there has also been a significant shortage there, with many doctors leaving for the private sector, and this is likely to continue to be a problem. The large increase in expenditures on economic services of 167 per cent in 2000 seems mainly due to the increase in that on communication and information technology by the huge amount of 430 per cent. The reasons for this are worth examining as they relate to the nature of the way the government has tried to liberalize parts of the economy and might have a long-run impact on investment in certain sectors of the economy.

Table 5.7   Changes in elements of operating expenditures, 1997–2000

Percentage increase over previous year	1997	1998	1999	2000
Total expenditure	23.7	−6.1	−2.3	35.9
Security	7.3	7.8	−1.8	25.8
Social and community services	20.1	−0.3	−7.5	24.4
Education	17.7	−0.8	−10.8	31.5
Health	39.5	−4.6	−6.4	13.2
Environment	5.0	5.0	0.9	11.0
Public housing	29.7	−14.4	1.6	9.8
Others	10.0	15.8	3.9	16.2
Economic services	5.7	1.4	17.1	167.0
National development	−1.6	−10.7	−5.6	−40.4
Communication and information technology	12.3	2.0	44.2	430.1
Trade and industry	6.6	−0.5	1.8	14.8
Manpower	3.7	73.1	39.2	−17.0
General services	2.9	7.3	3.1	8.6

Source: Economic Survey of Singapore 2000, p. 126.

The story behind this huge increase goes back a few years. The government decided to end the monopoly of its company SingTel over land-based telephone services and announced that it would create a duopoly market from April 2000 and guarantee to maintain this market structure for two years. For the loss of its monopoly the government gave SingTel $1.5 billion in compensation and this shows up in the higher operating expenses of the government in 1997. This set a precedent. The other company that was allowed to enter the market was StarHub, a consortium of British, Singaporean and Japanese telecommunications companies that then had to undertake a large investment programme of laying fixed lines. In late January 2000, on a Friday night after the stock exchange had closed, the government held a surprise press conference and announced it had changed its mind and would open the telecommunications market to open competition from April 2000 and not stand by its commitment to maintain the duopoly structure. This change led the government to announce it would compensate both companies for the loss of a duopoly market and appointed financial advisers to assess the compensation which was set at $1.9 billion, thus increasing operating expenditures. At the time fears were expressed that this abandonment of a specific government commitment could harm any future investments but the government's response was that in the short run, at least, the investment that would come from the new entrants to the fixed line and mobile phone markets would be about $3 billion.

Table 5.8 shows the structure of government development expenditures. These expenditures do not include loans to statutory boards but do include capital grants to them and aided institutions for development activities. For the budget for the financial year 2001/2002 62 per cent of development expenditures were directly made by government ministries and the rest, 38 per cent, were by statutory boards and aided institutions. Recent capital grants to the statutory boards have been mainly for road and rail development projects. Both ministries and statutory boards can be involved in development expenditures on the same types of projects, such as public housing, for example. In the budget for 2001/2002 the coverage of the development expenditure item has changed so that in the future the figures will not be directly compatible as future expenditures will not include land-related items whereas those used here do.

The main trend we can see is an increase in expenditures on security (that is national defence and domestic security, not social security) and in expenditures on social and community services. Here we can see a significant increase in expenditure on education as in the 1990s the government embarked on a widespread programme of school building and upgrading. In addition, the two public universities were upgraded with extra buildings

Table 5.8   *Structure of development expenditures, selected years,*
            1990–2000

	1990	1995	1999	2000
Total development expenditure $million	4218	4671	11039	9118
Total development expenditure as a percentage of GDP	6.6	4.0	7.8	5.7
Percentage of total expenditure				
Security	6.3	8.1	13.8	16.5
Social and community services	36.3	43.8	47.1	42.2
Education	5.4	16.7	13.6	16.9
Health	1.1	7.0	1.0	1.4
Environment	5.0	6.1	9.5	6.4
Public housing	22.7	10.7	20.6	15.0
Others	2.0	3.4	2.3	2.5
Economic services	51.0	38.9	29.8	37.1
National development	37.7	8.0	2.3	3.3
Communication and information technology	7.9	16.9	4.9	9.1
Trade and industry	4.7	8.3	14.1	17.5
Manpower	0.2	0.4	0.1	0.1
Research and development	0.5	5.7	8.5	10.2
General services	6.3	9.2	9.4	4.2

Sources: Calculated from *Economic Survey of Singapore 1992*, p. 127 and *Economic Survey of Singapore 2000*, p. 127.

for academic, social and residential purposes being built. There has been a strong commitment to the development of the educational infrastructure in the government's path towards a knowledge-based economy. As the share of expenditures on social services rose that on economic services naturally fell, especially on national development, which could be connected with the divestment of some GLCs.

Table 5.9 shows that the government was willing to allow large year-to-year changes in selected items of development expenditure during the Asian financial crisis with a large increase in 1997 and then a reduction in total expenditure in 2000 when the economy's growth rate recovered to 9.9 per cent. Some of the large year-to-year changes will be related to the timing of certain projects such as those associated with communications and information technology and purchases of properties by certain ministries. In the year following such large acquisitions of buildings and land, expenditures by certain ministries and therefore in certain expenditure groups will be much lower of course. This means that many year-to-year changes are not based on short-run adjustments but are the results of earlier decided plans and their eventual timing.

Table 5.9   Changes in elements of development expenditures, 1997–2000

Percentage increase over previous year	1997	1998	1999	2000
Total expenditure	54.7	−1.4	4.6	−17.4
Security	54.6	8.1	15.5	−0.6
Social and community services	−9.9	51.3	21.7	−26.0
Education	40.7	51.5	9.3	2.5
Health	−25.2	−13.1	−51.6	10.7
Environment	24.7	39.8	15.3	−44.6
Public housing	−29.7	105.6	54.4	−39.9
Others	−52.5	−0.5	−8.5	−10.6
Economic services	61.2	32.1	−22.3	2.8
National development	−32.7	−3.3	122.4	19.8
Communication and information technology	60.2	37.5	−68.9	54.1
Trade and industry	131.8	34.8	−1.0	3.0
Manpower	233.3	66.7	126.0	369.9
Research and development	25.9	23.1	15.4	−36.0
General services	242.0	−78.5	39.2	−62.9

Source: Economic Survey of Singapore 2000, p. 127.

5.7   GOVERNMENT FINANCIAL ACCUMULATION

Singapore is often singled out as having the highest per capita official foreign exchange reserves to illustrate the conservative nature of its budget policies. The extent of the government's financial accumulation is likely to be greater than the $139.3 billion (US$80.36 billion) that had accumulated by the end of the year 2000 (*Yearbook of Statistics*, 2001, p. 180). In a table showing the extent of government debt in the *Economic Survey of Singapore 1999*, p. 137) there appeared a column headed 'Memo: Financial Assets (as at end March)' for each of the years after 1997. These figures had not been published in the equivalent table of the previous year's *Economic Survey* and were omitted from this year's volume. They do not appear in the *Yearbook of Statistics*. What they show is that in March 1999 the provisional estimate of the extent of the government's financial assets was $365.53 billion. These assets are almost certainly under the management of the GIC.

5.8   FISCAL FUTURE

Singapore's budget for the forthcoming financial year is presented towards the end of February each year and although its contents are covered in detail in the press, budgets are nearly always described as 'boring' and 'dull' by commentators. This is taken as a sign of the strength of the economy in that drastic actions are not needed in its fiscal policy and there are no crises of impending huge deficits nor much opposition to its contents, although it is debated in parliament and PAP members do criticize some aspects of each budget. Anti-recessionary policies are often announced as off-budget measures whenever they are needed. It is possible that the budget presented to parliament in February 2001 will be seen as a watershed in that it departed from earlier concerns and signalled a shift in the government's strategy towards local firms and other sectors of the economy. There was more excitement about this budget than we have seen in ten years and it was described by one journalist as 'the best ever' (*The Business Times*, 24 February, 2001, p. 1). His main reason was that it offered something to everyone in the form of tax reductions and rebates on charges for those living in public housing. Although the government had then already expressed concern about the possible impact on Singapore of a marked slowdown or even recession in the United States, these tax cuts should not be seen as intended as having any demand-side expansionary effect on output. It was described as moderately expansionary and was thought to add just 0.2 percentage points to the year's GDP growth rate. The Minister for Finance was presenting the budget in the light of the previous year's GDP growth rate of 9.9 per cent, greater than expected increases in revenues, and possibly with an eye on the possibility of an earlier than necessary general election. That is how many of the individual tax reductions were interpreted.

Unlike in previous budgets there was nothing of significance aimed at encouraging the fund management sector that the government had been trying to build up by encouraging foreigners to set up in Singapore and manage state funds. In the case of this budget the top priorities were to create 'the best conditions for private enterprise to flourish'. As we saw in Chapter 1 in the week before this budget the government had argued that GLCs had not crowded out the private sector but now it was focusing on direct fiscal steps to encourage its growth. The Minister noted firstly that other countries had been reducing their corporate tax rates in order to attract foreign investment and so in the face of this competitive pressure he cut the corporate tax rate from 25.5 per cent to 24.5 per cent, which was completely unexpected. The main reason was that some countries regard a corporate tax rate of less than 25 per cent as unfair and equivalent to creating a 'tax haven'. This policy was not only aimed at attracting further foreign investors but, as the minister made clear, the thrust of his budget was to stimulate local, small firms and he did this through a tax exemption scheme that will mean that about two-thirds of existing firms would pay half the amount of tax for the same level of earnings. The key word was 'entrepreneurship' and other changes such as help for the self employed were made to encourage self-employment and company creation. Earlier the government had eventually responded to many appeals that people should be allowed to run small businesses from their homes and, realizing that these would probably be internet-based retailing and consulting businesses not bakeries or motorcycle repair shops, had allowed this. Special tax treatment of stock options was granted, indicating the government's hope that there will be an upsurge in the establishment of small, technologically-orientated firms where stock options will serve as a strong motivating force. The tax breaks are only available to those companies that offer stock options to at least half of their employees. The scheme will be reviewed within five years time and the last year or so of Silicon valley companies' experiences with the impact of stock options on their employees might have faded from memory. The focus is on creating an entrepreneurial, knowledge-based private sector. Two other thrusts are though fostering even more general education, retraining for displaced workers and more spending on research and development with the government funding promising local small firms. The top individual tax rate was reduced from 28 per cent to 26 per cent and larger tax exemptions were allowed and restored a tax rebate. This budget also featured large top-ups to citizens' CPF balances and rebates on charges for those living in public housing, all aimed at benefiting lower income families.

5.9   IMPLICATIONS

The previous three chapters have looked at the main factors that are thought to contribute to increasing a population's economic welfare: the growth rate of the economy and personal incomes, the nature of structural change and types of jobs available, the impact of monetary factors such as inflation and the nature of the fiscal system on disposable personal incomes and wealth. The next chapter attempts to assess the significance of broader indicators of welfare and development apart from those already discussed above. For many indicators we would like to discuss there are no hard data available and so we move further into the realm of personal interpretation and experience than most economists are comfortable with.

NOTE

1.   The dollar change in revenue (T) per unit of output Y is dT/dY and this can be shown to be equal to $[(dT/dY)(Y/T)](T/Y)$. The expression in the square bracket is the elasticity of T with respect to output and the last term in the ratio of the revenue to output

6. Development indicators and welfare

According to conventional wisdom, the process of economic development has something to do with the achievement of sustained growth in GNP per capita, a period of structural change involving, amongst other things, a rise in the importance of manufacturing industry and high-income services in national income and employment, and a demonstrable improvement in welfare or well-being for a substantial proportion of the population. In Chapter 1 we saw how, according to the World Bank, the growth of output has put Singapore in the top seven countries in the world ranked by GNP per capita (Table 6.1). Indeed, Singapore is one of the few countries historically to have achieved rapid growth in output over successive decades, even in the 1990s when expectations were that growth would fall to a more sustainable rate.

Table 6.1   Ranking by GNP per capita, 1999

Country	Rank	GNP per capita US$	Country	Rank	GNP per capita US$
USA	4	30600	France	24	21897
Switzerland	6	27486	Finland	25	21209
Singapore	**7**	**27024**	UK	27	20883
Norway	8	26522	Sweden	28	20824
Denmark	12	24280	Italy	29	20751
Belgium	13	24200	Ireland	34	19180
Japan	14	24041	Spain	41	16730
Austria	15	23808	New Zealand	42	16566
Canada	16	23725	Portugal	45	15147
Netherlands	17	23052	Korea	49	14637
Australia	20	22448	Greece	50	14595
Germany	21	22404			

Note: GNP per capita is based on purchasing power parity estimates.

Source: World Bank (2000, Table 1).

In Chapter 4 we also saw that, apart from certain quirks arising from its history as an entrepot trading centre and island city state bereft of natural resources, Singapore's structural change began predictably with labour-intensive industrialization in the late 1960s and the economy has moved steadily up the value-added ladder ever since. These changes were associated with a significant increase in the rate of domestic saving, which reduced the relative importance of private consumption in output, and the CPF system, which allowed the government to guide the use of these funds for expenditures it approved of. Singaporeans have tended to move into more professional jobs with higher levels of skill while the less attractive, low-paying and dangerous jobs have been taken up by foreigners. This has improved the welfare of its citizens. Foreign workers are commonly employed in the construction sector and in the maintenance of parks and roadside greenery. There is no historical legacy in Singapore of coal, gold, uranium or diamond mining which produce hard, unhealthy jobs and can leave a terrible environmental legacy.

In this chapter we look at economic indicators, such as GNP per capita, which purport to measure welfare or the quality of life, the extent to which they have increased in Singapore over time and how they compare to the situation in other countries. We also ask a fundamental question about Singapore's development status: why has Singapore, unlike South Korea, not been re-classified as a fully developed country?

6.1   INDIGENOUS GNP PER CAPITA

Economists would be the first to agree that output measures are not necessarily good indicators of the standard of living of a country's citizens. However, as a general rule, the more output a country produces the higher is the standard of living, as both private incomes are higher and the potential tax base from which the government can transfer resources to less privileged sectors of society is greater and this puts a smaller burden on those who pay taxes. But the positive correlation between income per capita and the standard of living will also include outliers. A 'rich' country might score low on the welfare indexes for a number of reasons: people are producing a lot because they are working long hours or have multiple jobs; the distribution of income is very unequal leading to a high degree of resentment and possibly a high level of crime; job security may be low with long spells of unemployment, and so on.

Singapore produces a lot of output for its size but who benefits from it and to what extent? Since a large part of Singapore's GDP is produced by foreign companies and workers and so is not earned by Singaporeans, the

Department of Statistics has come up with a concept of 'Indigenous GNP' (IGNP). In 2000, for example, 35 per cent of GDP was owned by foreigners (*Yearbook of Statistics Singapore*, 2000, Table 5.1, Table 5.2). This means that indigenous GDP was only 65 per cent of GDP. Singaporeans earn incomes from the factors of production they choose to employ outside Singapore, so if we add the inflow of factor incomes to IGDP, we get IGNP. In 2000 this was 74 per cent of GNP. We can then divide IGNP by the number of Singaporeans to get a feel for how much Singaporeans earn from economic activity both within and outside Singapore. In 2000 GNP per capita was \$42 212 whereas IGNP per capita was \$38 445 (Table A.1) which means that the GNP per capita figures overstate the average per capita income of Singaporeans by about 10 per cent. Contrast this with equivalent calculations for 1966 when IGNP per capita was 95 per cent of GNP per capita (*Economic and Social Statistics, Singapore 1960–1982*, p. 55) so the GNP figure overstated Singapore's GNP per capita by only 5 per cent then.

A further problem is that growth and welfare comparisons between Singapore and other countries need to take into account its city-state characteristics. In many ways it seems more appropriate to compare Singapore's development with other cities such as New York, Tokyo or Shanghai. After all, Singapore has benefited from capital and expertise from outside and has been able to draw on nearby countries for labour in forms ranging from domestic maids, who release trained women to undertake higher productivity work, to the 'reserve army' of immigrant workers on short-term contracts in the construction industry, to managers of MNCs and academics. There are even thousands of daily commuters from neighbouring Malaysia. It is also easier to provide welfare and other social infrastructure (and measures of social control) in a small city of 3–4 million which has no poor agricultural sector to contend with. But the fact remains that, notwithstanding its city characteristics, Singapore has been an independent sovereign entity since 1965, with none of the political ambiguities which have clouded the issue for Hong Kong and Taiwan.

6.2   HUMAN DEVELOPMENT

A broader measure of economic welfare than GNP per capita is the United Nations Human Development Index (HDI) which is published in its annual *Human Development Report*. This combines life expectancy at birth, adult literacy and educational enrolment, and a measure of income discounted above a certain threshold. This is a useful measure of average achievements in basic human development in one simple composite index and provides a ranking of countries into 'high', 'medium' and 'low' levels of human development.

Table 6.2   Singapore's ranking in the Human Development Index, 1998

HDI rank	Life expectancy	Literacy rate	Education	Difference rank
1 Canada	79.1	99.0	100	8
2 Norway	78.3	99.0	97	1
3 USA	76.8	99.0	94	−1
4 Australia	78.3	99.0	114	9
5 Iceland	79.1	99.0	89	1
6 Sweden	78.7	99.0	102	15
7 Belgium	77.3	99.0	106	4
8 Netherlands	78.0	99.0	99	6
9 Japan	80.0	99.0	85	1
10 UK	77.3	99.0	105	13
11 Finland	77.0	99.0	101	8
12 France	78.2	99.0	93	5
13 Switzerland	78.7	99.0	80	−9
14 Germany	77.3	99.0	90	1
15 Denmark	75.7	99.0	93	−8
16 Austria	77.1	99.0	86	−4
17 Luxembourg	76.8	99.0	69	−16
18 Ireland	76.6	99.0	91	−2
19 Italy	78.3	98.3	83	3
20 New Zealand	77.1	99.0	96	7
21 Spain	78.1	97.4	94	9
22 Cyprus	77.9	96.6	81	3
23 Israel	77.9	95.7	81	3
24 Singapore	**77.3**	**91.8**	**73**	**−16**

Notes: Life expectancy is at birth in years; the adult literacy rate is the percentage of those aged 15 and above who are literate; education is the combined primary, secondary and tertiary gross enrolment ratio as a percentage of the number of children in the relevant age groups; difference is the difference between the ranking of the country in terms of real GDP per capita in purchasing power parity US$ and the HDI rank.

Source: United Nations (2000).

In the *Human Development Report 2000* Singapore was ranked 24 out of 174 countries based on data for 1998 (Table 6.2). This placed the Republic in the 'high' human development category just below Spain, Cyprus and Israel, but above Hong Kong, Korea and Brunei. With a score of −16 for the difference between the ranking based on real GDP per capita in purchasing power parity US$ and the rank in terms of the HDI, this implies that Singapore was more 'advanced' in terms of income than in social development. Other countries which have large negative difference numbers include the middle eastern oil exporters: United Arab Emirates (-21), Qatar (-24) and Kuwait (-31). So does Luxembourg (-16). Singapore has the highest HDI value in South-east Asia and the Pacific.

Since 1995 two further indexes of human development have been included in the Human Development Report: a gender-related development index which uses the same variables as the HDI but takes into account inequality in achievements between men and women, and a gender-empowerment index. This captures gender inequality in economic and political opportunities or gender inequality in key areas of economic and political participation and decision-making, such as seats in parliament held by women, the number of female administrators and managers, professional and technical workers, and women's GDP per capita. For Singapore, as with most countries in the world, the gender adjusted index is lower than the HDI, indicating gender inequality, but Singapore has the same ranking on both indexes. In common with a number of other Asian countries, Singapore does much worse in terms of the gender-empowerment index with a ranking of 38 out of 70 countries. This is better than the Philippines and Malaysia, but in the 'high' HDI category only Japan, Korea, Chile, Uruguay, Hungary and Greece came lower.

As far as gender inequality is concerned (Mukhopadhaya, 2001b), at the end of the 1970s the female to male earnings ratio was about 74 per cent, higher than that in the USA and higher than the average of the OECD countries. But by the mid 1990s this ratio had hardly increased (75 per cent) compared to other developed countries, so Singapore now lagged well behind the USA and to a lesser degree behind most other OECD countries. Female participation rates have increased substantially in the 1980s and 1990s, especially among the higher educated, but this has also widened income inequality among females, and female employment in male-dominated industries is still low, especially among those over 35 years old.

The HDI is a useful summary measure of the level of human development, but a country's position in the rankings can be sensitive to the precise way in which it is compiled. Table 6.3 reproduces some country rankings based on GDP per capita and different versions of the HDI for 1992 from Crafts (1997b, Table 6). Singapore slips from 16 in terms of GDP per head to 21 when the figures are adjusted to take into account hours worked per member of the labour force. The adjustment for hours worked is based on the suggestion by Nordhaus and Tobin (1972) that some allowance is needed for time spent on market work to allow for the opportunity cost of leisure. Such adjustments are especially important in comparisons which include countries such as Singapore and the other east Asian 'tigers' (see Crafts 1997b, p. 78), where participation rates and hours worked per member of the labour force have been rising substantially since the 1950s compared to more advanced countries. Nonetheless, even when the adjustments are made, Singapore still ranks above Portugal, Korea and Taiwan in 1992, and would probably be ranked higher in more recent years.

Table 6.3   Comparative welfare rankings for Singapore, 1992

	GDP/head	GDP/hour	DW
USA	1	9	10
Switzerland	2	6	1
Japan	3	18	4
Germany	4	4	7
Hong Kong	5	19	13
Denmark	6	11	17
Canada	7	7	5
France	8	2	7
Norway	9	5	5
Belgium	10	1	10
Austria	11	8	10
Sweden	12	10	2
Netherlands	13	3	3
Australia	14	12	9
Italy	15	14	18
Singapore	**16**	**21**	**24**
UK	17	15	15
Finland	18	17	14
Spain	19	13	19
Ireland	20	16	20
Taiwan	21	23	16
Portugal	22	22	22
Korea	24	24	23

Notes: GDP per head is in 1990 international dollars based on purchasing power parity estimates; GDP per hour is a revised version of Maddison (1995); DW is an amended version of Dasgupta and Weale (1992) including standardized unemployment.

Source: Crafts (1997b, Table 6).

Singapore does better from a longer-run perspective. Since 1975 Singapore's ranking on the HDI has risen by a total of 22 per cent, with 7 per cent growth on average between 1990 and 1998. This can be compared with the fastest progress for a country starting in the 'medium' human development category, China at 36 per cent, and the fastest starting in the 'high' human development category, Ireland at 13 per cent. Moreover, if the

HDI is benchmarked back to 1870 (Crafts 1997a), Singapore and Taiwan were the biggest gainers out of a sample of 16 developed countries and 23 other countries between 1950 and 1992 in terms of their HDI rankings.

There is also a suspicion that HDI indexes are a little unfair to Singapore, partly because it is more difficult to achieve an increase in the HDI if the country starts from a relatively high base and undergoes rapid change, but also because of the use of inappropriate or incorrect indicators in the index itself. Smith (1993), for example, argues that Singapore's relatively low HDI ranking for 1992 is due largely to a low score on educational attainment which does not adequately capture improvements in education. It is ironic that of the 'high' HDI countries in that year only Qatar and Kuwait score lower than Singapore, despite the fact that raising average educational levels has been at the heart of Singapore's economic success. On any disaggregated measure of welfare or 'basic needs', such as nutrition level, access to health care, housing, social infrastructure, level of crime, absolute poverty, number of beggars, Singapore is likely to score highly in comparison with other countries. This is also true if a range of educational indicators are used, as in Smith (1993, Table 3).

6.3   STRESS

Singapore is a very densely populated city. Although not completely urban the rural parts are not suitable for extensive leisure activities. Eighty-six per cent of the population lives in public housing. These are flats which are mainly high-rise buildings many of them of more than 30 storey. Plans are to build even taller residential blocks and perhaps more underground buildings. Their quality is quite good and are better than the public housing flats built in Britain in the 1960s. The government continually upgrades them. This kind of living, however, can be quite stressful for many people. The pace of working life is fast and urban areas are quite noisy. One joke is that Singapore's national bird should be the crane, as there are so many building sites and so much building going on at any time.

Other factors can contribute to the perception that Singapore is a stressful society. Singapore is not unique in pushing its children hard in terms of academic achievements, another example is Japan, but a growing number of students and their parents, it seems, are consulting psychiatrists for help:

> Behind Singapore's neat streets and orderly society lies a serious health problem. A highly competitive primary-school system and anxieties among children about less-than-perfect grades is driving more of the country's youth into the armchairs of psychiatrists. Ministry of Health statistics reveal that the number of new cases of young people under 18 visiting psychiatrists at government-run

outpatient clinics doubled from 1126 cases in 1990 to 2491 cases in 2000. Half were of primary-school age. (Saywell, 2001)

One other area of recent concern has been the rise in attempted suicides among women, children and teenagers, with a fourfold increase in the number of children aged 10–14 who have succeeded in killing themselves since the early 1980s (*The Sunday Times*, 7 July, 2001, p. 30). The reasons are largely anecdotal and wide-ranged but include boy and girl relationships, stress at school, unhappy homes, unrealistic expectations and bullying. Actual suicide rates in Singapore are, however, still quite low by international standards (Table 6.4). The male suicide rate of 14.3 per 100000 is still well below the average of developed countries (20.1) and is not exceptional in terms of the regional average (13.8) or compared to Japan (26) and Korea (17.8). The female rate (8) is higher than the developed country average (6.9) but is also high in other East Asian countries. Switzerland, a country which at times Singapore seems to want to emulate, has high suicide rates by developed country standards.

Table 6.4 Male and female suicide rates in Singapore compared to other countries

Country (per 100000)	Year	Males	Female	Country	Year	Males	Female
Singapore	1997	14.3	8.0	Canada	1997	19.6	5.1
China	1994	14.3	17.9	Norway	1995	19.1	6.2
Hong Kong	1996	15.9	9.1	Switzerland	1996	29.2	11.6
Japan	1997	26.0	11.9	USA	1997	18.7	4.4
Korea	1997	17.8	8.0	Australia	1995	19.0	5.1
Thailand	1994	5.6	2.4	Netherlands	1997	13.5	5.9
Philippines	1993	2.5	1.7				
Average		13.8	8.4			20.1	6.9

Note: The average for the Asian countries is based on the sample given in the table. The average for the developed countries is based on a sample of 24 developed countries.

Source: World Health Organization (2000).

6.4 CRIME

Economic factors and the nature of a country's development can affect its crime rate and that in turn can influence the welfare of its citizens. High unemployment (which Singapore does not have) and wide and widening income disparities (which Singapore may have) are often associated with crimes against property. Unemployment can cause stress, depression and lead to suicide and murder. A push to become a developed nation might put too much stress on the workforce.

Singapore has always claimed to be a relatively low-crime country because of its strict laws, many of which were retained from the British colonialists, such as caning for vandalism and many other crimes. The streets are safe. Caning for vandalism such as writing graffiti on walls, was aimed at deterring political agitators in the 1950s and 1960s and was extended by the PAP in 1966 to 'political' activities like hanging banners in the street. Baratham (1994) and Latif (1994) provide two different Singaporean perspectives on caning or 'flogging' as 'caning' is used in schools and reformatories. Baratham reserves the terms 'lashing' or 'flogging' for the judicial punishment and 'thrashing' or 'caning' for private parental punishments, which he says are the normal form of domestic punishment of children in Singapore (Baratham, 1994, p. 70). Singapore imposes the death penalty on those possessing more than certain quantities of drugs as exceeding that amount is taken as evidence of trafficking. Those Singaporeans who return to Singapore and are required to provide urine samples at entry points and who are found to have consumed drugs outside Singapore can be prosecuted in Singapore. There are periodic raids on nightspots where people are required to provide urine samples. There are several drug rehabilitation centres in Singapore as well as homes for delinquent children.

Singapore's judicial system is regularly rated very highly by foreign surveys but these surveys are more concerned with the commercial and economic aspects of the legal system where speed, efficiency, low cost and fairness are important criteria. Lawyers have recently complained that attempts at achieving efficiency means that they have very short deadlines imposed on them and that the level of stress experienced has increased and this is given as the main reason for lawyers leaving their jobs. Up until October 2001, 355 lawyers had quit their jobs compared to 141 in the whole of 2000 and 114 in 1999 (*The Straits Times*, 7 October, 2001, p. 4).

It is notoriously difficult to compare crime rates across countries but the government recently produced comparative evidence of Singapore's crime rate in the booklet (*Singapore: The Last 10 Years*) distributed by the Prime Minister at the time of his National Day Rally Speech in August 2001. The booklet includes a chart on page 60 showing the 'Crime Rate' for 1997 for eleven countries. The source given was the *Sixth United Nations Survey of Crime Trends and Operations of Criminal Justice System Covering the Period 1995–1997* (United Nations, 2001). There was no clear definition of what the crime rate meant and numbers were given per 100 000 of population with Sweden recording 13 521 (the most) and China (130) the least. Singapore's rate was given as 1038, which was higher only than Malaysia (694), Thailand (464) and China (130). It was lower than Hong Kong (1070), Japan (1512), Taiwan (1961) and Korea (3041). In the original source, however, the numbers used were for the item 'Grand total of recorded crimes' and the United Nations report gives the figure for Singapore as 1833 (not 1038). Enquiries with the Department of Statistics, Singapore, revealed that they had substituted their own number which is based on the number of crimes divided by the whole population whereas the United Nation's method is to divide the crime rate by Singapore's resident population (citizens and permanent residents).[1] Presumably, the United Nations does that for all other countries as well so the numbers are not comparable.

This illustrates the problems of providing averages for a country when there are a large number of foreigners living there for longish periods but who are not counted in the resident population. The Singapore explanation of its murder rate, for example, is to note that some of these are committed by foreign workers, often in the construction industry, who live together on the building site or in wooden housing or containers and have very few recreation facilities. This often leads to fights and fatalities. Singapore's homicide rate is less than that in Malaysia, Hong Kong and China, for example.

6.5   EDUCATION

When reading the domestic press one cannot but get the impression that there is universal approval for the Singaporean education system – especially outside Singapore. Singapore students outperform those of most other countries in international competitions and Olympiads in the fields of mathematics and sciences. Singaporean students have won the Angus Ross Prize every year since its inception in 1987 for the best Cambridge University A-level English Literature paper taken by a student outside the United Kingdom. The schools are of recent vintage and are generally of a high architectural quality and well-equipped and the government's aim is that there will be one computer for every two students throughout all levels of education. Outsiders see only the results achieved by the best, perhaps 5 per cent of students who have been trained to do well, and do not know of the costs the education system is seen by many Singaporeans to impose on their family life and the happiness and welfare of their children. In Singapore the educational system is one aspect of society that is probably the most criticized. Students have to rise very early in the morning (5:30–6:00 a.m. is not uncommon) to get to the early sessions. They have to carry heavy bags. Myopia is very common amongst Singapore students, probably the highest rate in the world, and the number of students receiving psychological support has increased very significantly recently. Fear of school appears to be a main factor. In a very materialistic society like Singapore, more and more students are taking part-time jobs.

The main factors that are criticized are that students are streamed by perceived ability based on examinations at ten years of age. The Primary School Leaving Examination (the results of which are published for every pupil) is a crucial hurdle. This determines which secondary school one can enter – and standards and reputation do differ significantly – and that can affect which Junior College (pre-University two-year colleges) one enters, and standards there also vary a lot. Students are subjected to a heavy load of tests, revision examinations, preparation examinations and examinations, and performance in these can cause tension between students and parents. The schools and colleges that take the best students are reducing the reliance on examinations but nationwide it is a dominating factor in young people's lives. As teachers cannot cover most of the required syllabus there is a whole industry of private tutors who coach students. There are no large crammer colleges as in Japan but there is a huge amount of private tuition provided. Not all outsiders lavish praise on the system. Professor Roger Schank, Director of the Institute of Learning Sciences at Northwestern University said to Singapore: 'You don't have a great education. Your sense of a well-educated man is someone who has memorised all the facts' (from *The Straits Times*, 1994, quoted from Chee, 2001, p. 218). This can be illustrated by the comments of one student who knew he was not very good at English and would be required to discuss a certain book in a forthcoming public examination. His solution to the problem was to memorize the entire book! The government is trying to move away from this system by stressing creative and independent thinking amongst its students.

6.6 HEALTH

In 1960 the infant mortality rate per 1000 was 34.9. By 1999 it had been reduced to 3.2 per 1000. The overall death rate per 1000 in 1960 was 14.1. By 1999 it was 4.5 (Ministry of Health *Annual Report 2000* from http://www.gov.sg/moh/pub/ar 2000/AR2000-A1.html). Life expectancy at birth in 1970 was 65.1 years for males and 70 years for females. By 2000 it was 76 years for males and 80 years for females.

These are substantial improvements. Of Singapore's 26 hospitals half are private and half are public, but of the 11 798 hospital beds 81 per cent were in the public sector and of the 5577 doctors only 47 per cent were in the public sector. There is a shortage of doctors in the public sector and recently the government tried to rectify this by increasing their salaries. There is only one medical school in Singapore so the government can control the number of local graduates and puts a limit on the number of women who can study medicine as it is thought they are less likely to practice after they qualify. They also regulate the number of foreign qualified doctors allowed to practice in Singapore. There is a shortage of nurses and many are recruited from neighbouring countries. It is the policy of the government to build up the private sector to serve rich foreigners and has allowed foreign hospitals to operate in Singapore. At the time of writing both the King of Malaysia and General Ne Win from Burma are in Singapore for medical treatment. This policy could have some impact on the success of the attempts to build up the life sciences sector as a 'fourth pillar' of the economy. Research is conducted in traditional (mainly Chinese) and complementary medicines.

The government's philosophy towards payment for health care is one of 'individual responsibility coupled with help from the community and government' for those unable to pay on their own' (*Singapore 2001*, pp. 270–71). For CPF members, 6–8 per cent of their payments are put in the medisave account to be drawn on for hospitalization charges for the member or members of his or her family. The government also provides low-cost medical insurance that is intended for supporting people with long-term illnesses. One of the frequent complaints in Singapore is the increasing cost of health care, particularly for medicines, many of which can be bought a lot cheaper in Malaysia. With its rapidly aging population health costs have become an important issue and one that the political opposition has taken up with the government. Chee (2001, pp. 129–30) recounts the problems he had in bringing up this issue and quotes a medical practitioner who called on the government 'to put an end to the commercialisation of medical practice in Singapore' (Chee, 2001, p. 130). There are reports of Singaporeans going to hospitals in Malaysia for operations as they are significantly cheaper. Others go to China for kidney transplants. This is probably not motivated by cost differences, but because Singapore does not allow the sale of organs there is a chronic shortage of kidneys.

One aspect of developed country status that Singapore has achieved is the prevalence of developed country illnesses, especially among the young. The most serious of these is diabetes, of which Singapore has the fourth highest rate in the world. Every day, on average, two people lose a limb or digit to the effects of diabetes. It also has the third highest rate of kidney failure. These are costly illnesses to treat and will put a further burden on the health system and individuals' financial resources (Stephens, 2001, p. 59).

6.7   ENVIRONMENT AND LEISURE

Singapore is frequently described as vulnerable, and in terms of its location it might be thought to be vulnerable to the environmental disasters that hit other Asian countries and disrupt their economies, but this is not the case. It has never suffered the earthquakes that hit Japan, China and India. It does not experience the typhoons that frequently flatten large parts of the Philippines and reach the south coast of China and Taiwan. When a serious typhoon hits Hong Kong the city often stops work for a day or two and then has to spend time and money cleaning up. Billions of dollars of business are lost. Singapore has not experienced the devastation caused by volcanoes. It does suffer from tropical rain storms in the monsoon seasons but good city planning means there is usually no serious flooding. One consequence of its climate is that deaths by lightning strikes are more common than in most other countries. The major environmental damage it suffers that can have an affect on the economy is the smoke pollution caused by forest fires in Malaysia and Indonesia. The impact of these on Singapore was particularly serious in 1993 and 1997, causing health problems for many and affecting the tourist industry.

Terzani (1998) entitled his chapter on Singapore 'An Air-Conditioned Island', and George (2000) called Singapore 'The air-conditioned nation' in the subtitle of his book of essays. When *The Wall Street Journal* asked certain prominent people to name the most influential invention of the millennium, Lee Kuan Yew selected the air conditioner as it allowed those who lived in the tropics to recreate the climate of the advanced civilizations which have flourished in cooler climates. Singapore's buildings and public transport are fiercely air-conditioned and are very cold and Singapore's energy consumption is very high compared to that of developed countries. It is difficult to make international comparisons of Singapore with large nations and some such comparisons which rank Singapore very low in energy efficiency or sustainability are just wrong, as argued by Nathan (2001). However, it is admitted in Singapore that energy use is not very efficient. Comparative data from world development indicators show that energy use measured in kg of oil equivalent per dollar of GDP in Singapore in 1995 was 0.5 but only 0.185 in Hong Kong and 0.164 in Japan (quoted from http://www.info.gov.hk/planning). The government has accepted the estimates of the *2000 World Competitiveness Report* that ranked Singapore twenty-fifth out of 45 countries in energy intensity, showing greater inefficiency than in most developed countries (Press Release on the *Energy Efficiency in Singapore Report* from http://www.mnd.gov.sg/news 240500.htm and the report is available from http://www.gov.sg/mnd/ndhq/IACCE.htm).

So, given that Singapore is a generally unpolluted, humid, flat, safe, clean and green little island, how do Singaporeans spend their leisure time and benefit from the high level of GNP per capita?

In 1990, for which year we have census data, the median hours of leisure activities was 17.2 hours per week. Ho and Chua (1995, pp. 40–41), using the results of the 1990 Census, show that the leisure activity that consumes most of the time of Singaporeans is watching television and the most favourite leisure activity taken outside the home is shopping. Singapore has been described as 'a shopping mall with immigration control at both ends'. Certainly shopping and eating are the most observable leisure activities, but as we have seen, personal consumption is a very low ratio of total expenditures in Singapore as the government has done a lot to restrict consumption and the availability of personal credit through the use of credit cards. Nevertheless, Singapore is a very materialistic society where people are judged in terms of their ownership of branded consumer goods, cars, country club memberships and their type of housing. Its location just north of the equator means that every day there are about 12 hours of daylight with sunrise around 7:00 a.m. and sunset just after 7:00 p.m. This might tend to discourage outdoor leisure activities but swimming is popular. Singapore has a professional football league of 12 teams (see http://www.sleague.com) but Singaporeans seem to be more fanatical in their support of leading English teams. Both Manchester United FC and Liverpool FC thought it worth their while to visit and play in Singapore in 2001 and Manchester United opened its first shop/restaurant outside the United Kingdom in tiny Singapore. The government has a plan to get Singapore into the World Cup by the year 2010, but young footballers often complain about the lack of pitches for them to play and train on, especially on the weekends when many of the schools' pitches appear to be underutilized. Singapore has, however, many golf courses, mostly attached to country clubs. The nascent environmental movement has tried to influence the government not to expand their number but to retain more land for nature parks.

6.8   INCOME INEQUALITY

Finding good data to compare Singapore's income distribution with other countries is very difficult. Singapore has no entries in the United Nations Human Poverty Index included in its *Human Development Report* or in the World Bank *World Development Report* comparing international poverty and the distribution of income or consumption.

Advance data from the *Singapore Census of Population 2000* (Table 6.5) shows that average resident household income from work increased from

Table 6.5   Resident household income from work, 1990–2000

	Average monthly income ($)	Average annual change (%)
1990	3076	–
1990–95	4107	6.0
1995–97	4745	7.5
1998	4822	1.6
1999	4691	−2.7
2000	4943	5.4

	Total change 1990–2000 (%)	
	All resident households	Resident households with income earners
Lowest 10%	−83.5	39.6
Next 10%	22.6	58.9
Next 10%	40.9	59.9
Next 10%	50.4	64.3
Next 10%	55.9	65.8
Next 10%	58.8	66.7
Next 10%	61.0	67.2
Next 10%	62.1	66.9
Next 10%	63.4	67.5
Next 10%	73.8	77.5

Source: Computed from the *Singapore Census of Population 2000*, Tables 1, 6 and 7.

$3076 to $4943 per month between 1990 and 2000, or at an average rate of just under 5 per cent per year. In real terms, based on 1990 prices, the increase was still 3.1 per cent per year, since average inflation was relatively low over this period. All ethnic groups appear to have benefited from this growth but not in equal measure. Average Chinese household income was 62 per cent higher by 2000 compared to 1990, while for the other ethnic groups the corresponding figures were Malays (40 per cent), Indians (59 per cent) and 'others' (87 per cent). If resident households with at least one income earner are ranked by size of total income from work and are then divided into ten equal deciles (Table 6.5), all deciles saw an increase in incomes over the period, but higher decile groups tended to benefit more. If all resident households are included regardless of whether they contain an income earner or not, incomes actually fell for the bottom decile.

These changes in income were not, however, uniform over the whole period. In particular, household incomes fell by 2.7 per cent in 1999 due to the lagged effects of the economic slowdown in 1998 (Table 6.5). This left most Singapore families with lower earnings and widened the income gap between the richest and poorest households. In 1999, only the top 10 per cent of households saw an increase and the lower the income group the more their incomes fell. The bottom 10 per cent saw a 48 per cent fall in monthly earnings which meant they were worse off than in 1990 (*Singapore Census of Population 2000*, Table 6). By 2000, however, income growth had resumed at 5.4 per cent.

Household income inequality also appears to have increased in the latter part of the 1990s (Table 6.6) as a result of relatively faster income growth for higher income households. The Gini coefficient, a summary measure of income inequality, rose to 0.47–0.48 in 1999 and 2000 among all resident households, after remaining fairly stable between 1990 and 1997 at around 0.42–0.43. The Gini coefficient ranges between zero (perfectly equal distribution) and unity (perfectly unequal) so a rise in this coefficient implies a worsening of household income distribution. There was also an increase in the ratio of the average income of the top 20 per cent of households to the bottom 20 per cent (Table 6.6). Even if the top and bottom extremes of the distribution are removed, the ratio of the ninth to the second decile still increased sharply.

Table 6.6   Measures of household disparity, 1990–2000

	1990	1995	1997	1998	1999	2000
Gini coefficient	0.44	0.44	0.44	0.45	0.47	0.48
Excluding households with No income earner	0.41	0.41	0.41	0.41	0.42	0.43
Ratio of average income						
Top 20% to lowest 20%	11.4	13.8	13.6	14.6	17.9	20.9
Ninth decile to second decile	5.5	6.1	5.9	6.2	6.8	7.4

Source: Singapore Census of Population 2000, Table 8.

The strong link between educational attainment and gross monthly income is apparent from Table 6.7. Twenty-eight per cent of those persons earning $6000 or over were degree holders, whilst 18 per cent of those earning under $400 per month had never attended school or had only a lower primary education. Whether Singapore can stabilize the Gini coefficient thus depends a great deal on how the labour market changes with globalization and whether the authorities can maintain equal educational opportunities. Since primary and secondary education enrolment rates are already very high the main focus will be on continuing to expand the tertiary sector.

Table 6.7   Gross monthly income of employed persons according to highest educational attainment, 1999

Gross monthly income	Never attended school/ lower primary	Primary	% Secondary	Post secondary	Diploma	Degree
Under $400	17.5	8.9	5.6	10.2	5.6	0.5
$400–$999	36.1	27.0	10.4	7.2	3.2	1.1
$1000–$1999	36.1	47.4	40.8	27.0	26.1	7.0
$2000–$2999	7.1	12.0	25.0	24.2	29.0	21.5
$3000–$3999	1.8	2.9	10.2	12.7	15.8	19.0
$4000–$4999	0.4	0.8	3.7	7.8	8.8	12.2
$5000–$5999	0.5	0.4	2.1	4.4	4.8	11.1
$6000 and over	0.5	0.6	2.1	6.5	6.8	27.7
Total	100.0	100.0	100.0	100.0	100.0	100.0

Source: Adapted from Mukhopadhaya (2000).

Singapore has never espoused the welfare state as conventionally defined, since this might diminish the work ethic, but there has always been a sort of safety net for the very bottom of society and a policy of giving extra resources to disadvantaged groups, subject to stringent means tests. This may be changing as the allocation of subsidies has broadened to include the 'middle class' (Chua, 2001). Examples include the upgrading of private estates with government funds and the extension of HDB utilities rebates to those living in five-bedroomed flats instead of the lower income bracket which was assumed to occupy four-room or smaller dwellings.

But how does Singapore's income distribution compare with other countries? Using the rough and ready estimates in Table 6.6 as an indicator of Singapore's income inequality, Table 6.8 compares this with other countries in the 1990s. The Gini coefficient for Singapore between 0.44 and 0.48 is still high compared to developed countries, although it is not far from those countries, such as the USA and the UK, which have higher inequality than the average developed country. The ratio of the top 20 per cent of income earners to the bottom 20 per cent in the 1990s is also relatively high and seems to have increased since the 1980s. The United Nations estimate for 1981–93 was 9.6 (United Nations, 1996, Tables 17, 36).

The current picture compared to countries in the region is less clear-cut but the 'guesstimates' based on Gini coefficients from Rao (2001) suggest that inequality in Singapore is lower than for Malaysia and Hong Kong,

Table 6.8   Inequality in Singapore compared to other countries

	Period	Gini coefficient	Ratio of the top 20% to the lowest 20%
Singapore	1990, 2000	0.44, 0.48	11.4 – 20.9
Hong Kong	1991, 1996	0.48, 0.52	–
Korea	1988, 1993	0.34, 0.40	5.2
Malaysia	1992, 1995	0.48, 0.49	11.9
Taiwan	1991, 1997	0.31, 0.32	–
Thailand	1992, 1998	0.54, 0.41	7.6
USA	1997	0.41	8.9
UK	1991	0.36	6.5
Switzerland	1992	0.33	5.8
Canada	1994	0.32	5.2
Norway	1995	0.26	3.7
Australia	1994	0.35	7.0
Sweden	1992	0.25	3.6

Sources: The Singapore range is from Table 6.6; for the other East and South-east Asian countries the range is based on the World Bank (2000, Table 5) estimate, where available, and/or on Rao (2001, Chapter 3); for the developed countries the source is the World Bank (2000, Table 5).

similar to Thailand, but greater than for Taiwan and maybe Korea, but these estimates should be taken only as a rough guide since they differ in coverage and period.

To take a longer run perspective, Figure 6.1 plots the behaviour of the Gini coefficient (based on earnings) between 1975 and 1999. Between 1975 and 1980 the coefficient fell as unemployment fell and female labour market participation increased. The National Wages Council guidelines also tended to increase earnings equality by recommending a fixed quantum together with a percentage increase in wages, since the fixed component formed a larger proportion of an unskilled worker's wage. The 1980s, on the other hand, saw a steady rise in the Gini coefficient as the process of restructuring and upgrading the manufacturing sector, and the movement of resources into high income services, reduced the demand for unskilled workers and increased wage differentials in favour of professional and skilled workers. By the 1990s Singapore had managed to stabilize the coefficient at around 0.47–0.48 as spending on education increased educational opportunities, particularly at the tertiary level, but it remains relatively high as a result of the dualistic nature of the Singapore labour market. In the financial and business services sector, and in professional jobs, earnings are kept high by an excess demand for foreign 'talent' for which there is no obvious local substitute, whilst at the other end of the labour market wages are kept low by a steady inflow of unskilled labour from the region employed in manual jobs. The skills gap is also reflected in a higher incidence of training among professionals, executives and technicians compared to clerks, receptionists, chambermaids and waitresses (*Business Times*, 28 September, 2001, p. 13). These features of the Singapore labour market are likely to persist.

Source: Calculated from Mukhopadhaya (2000).

Figure 6.1   The Gini coefficient for Singapore, 1975–99

From time to time there are complaints about the inequalities in income distribution in Singapore and concern about foreign workers taking the jobs of locals, but controversy largely revolves around the accuracy or otherwise of the consumer price index in accounting for the differential effects of inflation on the various income groups and the size of ministerial salaries, which tend to be substantially higher than their counterparts in other countries. The latter issue surfaced again in July 2000 (*The Business Times*, 6 July, 2000) when the government announced a pay rise for ministers and senior civil servants by an average of 13 per cent and the amendment of a 1994 market-based formula to benchmark ministers' pay to top private sector salaries. This meant that a Junior Minister at Staff Grade 1, whose salary was pegged to two-thirds of the median income of the top eight earners in six professions, now earned approximately $1 million per year. Opposition Member of Parliament, Chiam See Tong, compared the Prime Minister's salary of $1.94 million to that of Bill Clinton, which was approximately one-third of this amount, and suggested $700 000 would be a more appropriate figure.

It is an article of faith for the PAP that ministers and civil servants should be paid in line with the private sector and sufficiently well to prevent corruption and to recruit good people. These salaries, as with most workers in Singapore, also contain a substantial variable component which is reduced when the economy fails to achieve a prespecified rate of growth. In defence of government policy the Prime Minister invoked the Chinese philosopher Sun Zi: 'it is impossible to have good people to come forward to serve without proper rewards; it is impossible to deter people from committing crimes without proper punishment' (*The Straits Times*, 21 August, 2000).

6.9   IS SINGAPORE A DEVELOPED COUNTRY?

Singapore's development status, as far as international organizations are concerned, is ambiguous. In January 1995 the Organization for Economic Cooperation and Development (OECD) decided to stop classifying Singapore as a developing country and reclassified the Republic along with Brunei, the Bahamas, Kuwait, Qatar and the United Arab Emirates as a 'more advanced developing country'. This was the follow up to a decision made in 1992 to remove these high income countries from the Development Assistance Committee list of developing countries eligible to receive foreign aid. In 1997 Korea applied for full membership of the OECD, which automatically brings with it developed country status, and was duly 'graduated' in October 1997. Singapore decided not to apply for OECD membership and so was not eligible for reclassification. Naturally this stimulated some discussion in Singapore and provoked an official justification.

The World Bank (1997) continued to classify Singapore as a 'high income economy' along with OECD countries such as the United States and Japan, but with a footnote qualification that it is one of the economies 'classified by the United Nations or otherwise regarded by their authorities as developing'. The World Bank (1999) regarded Singapore as a high income non-

OECD country in the same category as French Polynesia, with the corollary that 'classification by income does not necessarily reflect development status'. The International Monetary Fund (1997, p. 4) considered Singapore, together with Israel, Hong Kong, Korea and Taiwan, with the 'group of countries traditionally known as industrial countries'. Notwithstanding legal ambiguities, this reclassification reflects 'the advanced stage of economic development these economies have now achieved'.

What makes Singapore stand out as a developing country in the high income category (see Table 6.1) is the gap in per capita income between itself and other countries now regarded as fully developed such as Spain, Portugal, Korea and Greece. Singapore's income per capita of US$27 024 in 1999 is almost double that of Korea and Greece. Furthermore, there is no ambiguity about Singapore's sovereignty which might disqualify Taiwan or Israel, or exclusive dependence on a few natural resources, such as the middle east oil exporters.

Yet the official position in Singapore is that Singapore is still a developing country. Deputy Prime Minister Lee Hsien Loong restated this in November 1995 at the inauguration of a productivity campaign. The time frame the authorities have in mind is not very clear but 'promotion' is expected sometime between 2020 and 2030, presumably sometime after qualifying for the World Cup Finals in 2010! Why not accept promotion now?

One problem might be the loss of developing country privileges. There may still be some benefits, such as trade preferences under the European Union's General System of Preferences, but since Singapore has never been a recipient of foreign aid (although there have been indirect benefits from funds received by ASEAN, such as during bouts of haze generated by forest fires in neighbouring countries) and would be disqualified now anyway under the new OECD classification, this cannot be the issue.

It is also possible that Singapore's pro-China policy, membership of ASEAN, and earlier promotion of 'Asian values' as a counterweight to 'western liberalism' may have made the government reluctant to overtly align with the advanced developed countries (Haggard, 1999). But this has not stopped Singapore from participating in international forums, such as GATT, the WTO, IMF and the World Bank which are closely associated with the market-oriented development model of developed countries such as the USA. It is no coincidence that after hard lobbying, Singapore was rewarded with the honour of hosting the inaugural ministerial meeting of the WTO in December 1996.

There may be increasing pressure on the Singapore government from international organizations to accept developed country status, particularly if Singapore begins to play a more active role in the Asia–Pacific region. The irony here is that Singapore is currently trying hard to establish itself as a regional financial centre and business hub and to distance itself from the 'bad' economic policies of some 'less-developed' neighbours which surfaced after the 1997 Asian financial crisis. There is even the possibility that Singapore will be chosen to host the launching of a new round of WTO negotiations, in which case, Singapore will become immortalized along with previous hosts, such as Uruguay and Tokyo!

With the declining role of ASEAN as a political force and Singapore's frustration over the slow progress made by AFTA on implementing tariff reductions agreed in the past, Singapore has been seeking to form new economic relationships with countries and trading blocs outside of the region (see Section 7.8) even though this has incurred the obvious displeasure of ASEAN countries such as Malaysia, which has historically adopted a more belligerent attitude towards the non-Asian developed world.

A more subtle reason for Singapore's reluctance to accept reclassification is the need to retain the ultimate goal of development as a rallying cry and to legitimize the PAP's monopoly over political power and highly centralized development strategy and extensive state intervention in the economy. This is also consistent with the promotion of Asian values, the desire to manufacture a uniquely Singapore identity, and the PAP's obsession with campaigns. Singaporeans have been constantly urged not to drop 'killer' litter out of apartment blocks, to smoke in public places, to urinate in lifts or overfill plates at buffets, but have, on the other hand, been encouraged to speak Mandarin (not dialects), be more courteous, smile at tourists and keep fit. In fact, part of the official justification for retaining the developing country label stems from the belief (real or illusory) that Singapore has not yet reached a sufficient state of social graciousness. This was apparently the reaction of the Trade and Industry Minister, Yeo Cheow Tong, to the 1995 OECD reclassification of Singapore, as reported in the *The Business Times*, 17 January, 1996. Similar sentiments expressed by Prime Minister Goh Chok Tong are cited in *The Economist*, 11 January, 1997, p. 25. Singaporeans even have their own Chinese dialect word 'Kiasu' to sum up many of the selfish qualities which they find most distasteful about themselves. Literally translated 'Kiasu' means 'scared to lose' and is also the name of a cartoon character (Mr Kiasu) and the subject of a television situation comedy. For a Singaporean perspective on Kiasuism in a globalizing world in the form of a novel, see Tan (2001).

The reluctance on the part of the Singapore government to accept reclassification is thus puzzling but explicable when seen in the context of Singapore's history in the Asian region and its development strategy. The perception by its leaders that it is not yet a 'gracious society' is part and parcel of a longer-term campaigning psychology of 'striving to be the best'.

Such rallying calls are viewed as essential to create a society free of past racial tensions and to solidify a sense of national identity. Such goals remain fundamental to the PAP and are rationalized in terms of material prosperity and social and political stability.

Is there any substance to the argument that Singapore has special problems which preclude the Republic from joining the ranks of the developed nations, apart from a predilection towards a campaigning psychology, a nostalgia for Asian values from a past era, a reluctance to align itself openly with countries in the developed world, and the potential loss of some trading benefits?

The official view revolves around the perception that Singapore somehow lacks the depth and breadth of fully developed economies and is presently unable to compete with the advanced developed countries. So by conventional western standards it has yet to become developed. As Low (1999a, p. 376) puts it: 'Its [Singapore's] economic indicators as traditionally measured may reflect or even do better than those in developed countries. But its capability and technology to sustain the industrial structure and dynamism of a developed nation are more in doubt as it is extremely dependent on the global economy.'

Singapore undoubtedly exhibits some special characteristics which make classification in the development spectrum difficult, such as a lack of natural resources, a heavy reliance on foreigners for the creation of its domestic product and the economic and socio-political features of a small, densely populated island city-state. But none of these considerations justifies the label of developing country. Income per capita is high by current developed country standards, the structure of the economy is orientated towards high income services and the production of sophisticated manufactured goods, and the level of welfare of the indigenous population is higher than in many fully developed countries, especially if disaggregated socio-economic indicators are used rather than aggregate indexes such as the HDI.

Where Singapore undoubtedly performs badly is on comparisons which include non-economic criteria. In the Freedom House *Freedom in the World Index 2000*, where a sample of 192 countries is classified according to political rights and civil liberties, Singapore is classified along with countries such as Ethiopia, Malaysia, Russia and Togo, as 'Partly Free', as opposed to 'Not Free', or 'Free'. The final column in Table 6.3 lists the Dasgupta and Weale (1992) extension of the HDI incorporating a civil rights index and an index of political rights. Similar low rankings for Singapore are to be found in other studies. In the United Nations Human Freedom Index (United Nations, 1991, p. 99), which includes 40 'basic freedoms', Singapore was placed eleventh out of 40 and bottom of the 'medium freedom' category, below Columbia, Thailand, India and Sri Lanka and in the vicinity of Benin and Nigeria. In Barro's (1994a) Index of Human Rights Singapore scores 0.33 out of a possible 1.0, approximately the same as Peru and South Africa.

These rankings are in stark contrast to Singapore's rating in terms of the narrower concept of 'economic freedom' measured in terms of the magnitude of taxation, the orientation of trade policy, protection of property rights, and so on. The Heritage Foundation, for example, usually places Singapore top or second behind Hong Kong in it's annual *Index of Economic Freedom* (Johnson and Sheehy, 1996). The Washington-based Cato Institute and Canadian Fraser Institute *Economic Freedom of the World 2000* placed Singapore top, with near perfect scores for structure of the economy, use of markets, monetary policy and price stability, legal structures and security of private ownership. According to the Swiss-based Institute of Management Development *World Competitiveness Yearbook 2001*, Singapore is the most competitive Asian country and second overall after the USA, based on 286 criteria and a survey of some 3600 top global and local executives.

It is hard to sustain the view that Singapore 'lacks the depth and breadth of fully-developed economies' sufficient to mean disqualification from developed country status. It is true that Singapore's dependence on trade and factor flows (see Chapter 7) makes it vulnerable to external shocks, and a free-trading philosophy obliges a positive response to competitive pressures, rather than negative protectionism. But apart from the short-lived 1985–86 recession, the widely-experienced contagion effects of the 1997–98 Asian economic crisis, and the global slowdown in 2001, the record on growth and macroeconomic stability has been outstanding. The impotence of traditional macroeconomic policy tools has not prevented a successful exchange rate policy (see Section 8.3) and improvising where necessary with unconventional tools of domestic demand management through public building programmes, the termination of contracts for short-term foreign workers, or flexible wage arrangements. The Singapore economy does not operate in a vacuum. There are automatic stabilizers to help cushion swings in external demand. It has a triple 'A' rating in international financial markets and would not find it difficult to borrow funds in a crisis.

The view that Singapore is not yet able to compete with OECD countries is also unconvincing. Singapore worries about its capacity to compete globally in two senses. First, in its ability to deal with pressures on costs and prices with the limited conventional macroeconomic tools which the authorities have at their disposal (see Chapter 8), and secondly whether it can move away from an over-reliance on 'input-driven' growth and improve the quality of growth sufficiently – the total factor productivity debate

(Chapter 3). Singapore may be competitive according to many criteria but its small size constrains its technological capabilities and capacity to engage in research and development. The authoritarian nature of its political system and state-led institutions are in this sense a substitute for the private sector but, at least in the economic sphere, reforms since 1986 have reduced state involvement, and it has always been substantially more market-conforming than other countries with a similar level of government control over the economy, such as South Korea. The present style of management and politics and mix of western and Asian values are not incompatible with developed country status.

Competing with developed countries may be hard but Singapore's progression up the value-added ladder so far would give grounds for optimism. The more important issue is the extent to which this success will continue to depend on foreigners. Singapore's post-independence development strategy was never hampered by any pervasive ideological aversion to foreign labour, capital and technology or a 'dependency' psychology popular in Latin America in the 1960s and 1970s. Indeed, the fear in Singapore is just the opposite, that the foreigners will decide to leave. But even if one takes the low total factor productivity growth figures with a dose of salt, there is genuine concern about the speed with which Singapore can develop its own indigenous talent and innovation sufficient to compete successfully with advanced developed countries within the constraints of the existing political and educational system. The renewed emphasis on attracting 'foreign talent' is perhaps a recognition of the fact that Singapore may need to rely on foreigners in perpetuity and that local resources, including skilled labour, will continue to act as a complement to foreign resources rather than as a substitute, even over the longer run. On any reasonable application of conventional development criteria, therefore, Singapore is a developed country. Haggard (1999, p. 370) sums this up nicely: 'On any objective economic or social measure, Singapore has become broadly comparable to other developed countries. Moreover, although Singapore has developed a very distinctive style of economic management, there is nothing in that style which would differentiate it markedly from other small advanced industrial states.' Extensive state intervention in the economy and reliance on foreign capital have produced a highly selective but essentially pragmatic and market-conforming intervention.

NOTE

1. Letter to Gavin Peebles, 31st August, 2001.

7. Trade, trade policy and growth

In this chapter we look at the structure of Singapore's trade and how it has changed over time: its imports and exports and interdependence with other countries through trade flows, and its vulnerability to changes in external demand, including the cyclical ups and downs of the global electronics cycle and the regional slowdown induced by the Asian financial crisis of 1997–98. Despite a history of successful export-led growth and industrialization, there is a perception that Singapore has special characteristics and so lacks the depth and breadth of fully developed economies. From the trade perspective this means extreme openness to international trade and factor flows, heavy 'dependence' on imports of goods and services, export revenues, and foreign sources of labour and capital.

Singapore has always worried about its ability to continue to attract foreign direct investment and capacity to compete internationally both with other developing countries in the Asian region as they undergo rapid growth and structural change, and with the advanced developed countries in terms of high value-added and new economy goods and services. We look at empirical studies which suggest that Singapore may have lost export competitiveness in the last two decades, become over-specialized in electronics and chemicals, and too heavily oriented towards export markets in East and South-east Asia.

Since independence in 1965 there has been a remarkable degree of continuity in Singapore's trade policy: a commitment to free trade, an active export promotion strategy, an 'open arms' policy towards MNCs and the pursuit of multilateral trade liberalization through GATT and WTO, together with preferential trade arrangements through APEC, ASEAN and, more recently, AFTA. Nonetheless there have been key changes in the substance of Singapore's trade policy and a pragmatic approach to changes in the international environment. We shall look in particular at policy initiatives introduced in response to the 1985 recession to diversify Singapore's sources of income by 'growing its own MNCs' and helping them expand into the region as well as more recent initiatives to restructure the manufacturing sector to turn Singapore into an advanced and globally competitive knowledge-intensive economy; and to reduce dependence on Asian markets by encouraging local companies to 'sprout a third wing' and locate outside of Asia. More controversial has been the decision to instigate a series of bilateral trade agreements with countries outside the region, including a preferential trading arrangement with the United States, even though such arrangements have upset some of Singapore's ASEAN partners.

7.1 DEPENDENCE ON TRADE

Any inquiry about the role of trade in the Singapore economy inevitably elicits the standard local response: 'Singapore is a small open economy with no natural resources.' The implication is that Singapore must trade at prices set in international markets and is highly vulnerable to shocks emanating from the international arena, whether it be an oil price hike, a rise in world interest rates, the contagion effects from the Asian financial crisis, or the sharp fall in global electronics demand in 2001.

There is no doubt that on conventional criteria Singapore is extremely exposed to international trade in terms of both exports and imports, with a combined merchandise trade to GDP ratio in 1998 of 2.48, rising to 2.86 if services are included (Table 7.1). The total volume of trade is very large compared to annual production, making Singapore one of the most open economies in the world. Indeed, according to Sachs and Warner (1995), Singapore is one of only eight developing countries which have always been open since independence, where openness is measured more broadly to incorporate low tariffs and non-tariff barriers to trade, and the absence of a pervasive black market for foreign exchange, state monopolies over exports, or the trappings of a socialist economy.

Table 7.1   Dependence on trade and international comparisons, 1998

	Exports to GDP ratio (%)	Imports to GDP ratio (%)	Trade to GDP ratio (%)
Singapore	1.29 (1.52)	1.19 (1.34)	2.48 (2.86)
Hong Kong	1.10 (1.31)	1.18 (1.31)	2.28 (2.62)
South Korea	0.33 (0.39)	0.23 (0.28)	0.56 (0.67)
Indonesia	0.35 (0.39)	0.19 (0.31)	0.54 (0.70)
Malaysia	0.98 (0.96)	0.78 (0.80)	1.76 (1.76)
Thailand	0.44 (0.53)	0.35 (0.39)	0.79 (0.92)
Philippines	0.39 (0.49)	0.42 (0.53)	0.81 (1.02)
Japan	0.09 (0.10)	0.06 (0.08)	0.15 (0.18)
China	0.19 (0.21)	0.14 (0.17)	0.33 (0.38)

Notes: Numbers in parentheses refer to goods and services.

Source: *World Bank* (2000, Tables 12, 15, 20).

Of course the world itself has become a more open and 'interdependent' place in terms of the proportion of the world which lives in 'open' economies and the extent to which markets have become integrated across national borders, which is not the same thing as 'dependence' on trade. Dependence tends to imply additional vulnerability to threat or the use of power (Cooper, 1986), or 'exploitation' by outsiders. There has never been any pronounced 'dependence' psychology in Singapore or generalized resentment against foreigners as in many developing countries in the past, with the possible exception of water supplies. Singapore imports about half of its water needs from Malaysia and re-exports some of it back after treatment, but the continuation of this symbiotic arrangement is subject to periodic negotiation, which is highly politicized, to the extent that Singapore has declared itself ready to invest in expensive desalination plants to reduce dependence on Malaysia in the longer run.

Singapore's import 'interdependence' with the global economy is a direct consequence of extreme openness, very low level of protection, and resource deficiency. Almost all foodstuffs and raw materials (including water) are imported. But what makes Singapore unusual is its exceptionally high import content of exports. A dollar of final expenditure sucks in approximately 54 cents worth of imports in total, 60 cents worth for each dollar of exports, and 69 cents for manufactured exports (Table 4.1). The highest figure (90 cents) is for petroleum-based exports (mainly for ships and aircraft), which is not surprising, since all petroleum is imported.

The distinction between exports and imports has also become more blurred in recent years with the rise in the proportion of international trade which is 'intra-industry', that is two-way trade in similar categories of goods, rather than 'inter-industry' which is trade in different categories of goods. By 1990 almost half of Singapore's trade with the USA and European Economic Community (the predecessor of the European Union) in manufactured goods consisted of intra-industry trade and a fifth of the trade with Japan (Chow et al., 1994, Table 1). In the early years the Asian tigers were primarily engaged in supplying the industrial countries with labour-intensive industrial components and semi-finished manufactured goods which were subsequently transformed into more sophisticated manufactured goods for export or sale in the domestic market. The amount of trade they did with a given developed country tended to reflect historical links and the presence of foreign MNCs. By the 1990s, however, this had changed significantly with the broadening of the economic base and level of technological sophistication of the tigers, including the process of vertical integration by MNCs. The result was an increase in the value-added of exports and an increase in intra-industry trade. Singapore, in particular, has been a major beneficiary of this process.

Traditional measures of openness are, however, misleading as far as Singapore is concerned. Because much of its trade historically has taken the form of 'entrepot' trade, the published trade statistics sensibly distinguish between total exports and domestic exports, with re-exports or pure entrepot exports as the difference between the two series. A further distinction is made between domestic exports and non-oil domestic exports, given the rather special nature of the petroleum trade. To measure the true 'value-added' contribution of exports to GDP, however, even this distinction is too narrow because re-exports are officially defined as goods which are subject only to repacking, splitting into lots, sorting or grading. To take the high import content of exports into account Lloyd and Sandilands (1986) constructed an alternative export series by using the input–output tables to net out all imported inputs.

Table 7.2   Singapore as a very open re-export economy (% of GDP)

	Trade	Domestic exports	Oil exports	NODX	Entrepot exports	Total exports	Value-added exports
1970	212	32	19	13	50	82	11
1975	364	56	19	37	39	95	16
1980	370	107	59	48	64	171	27
1985	277	84	42	42	45	129	23
1990	302	93	26	67	48	141	32
1995	290	83	12	71	58	141	–
2000	296	85	14	71	64	149	–

Notes: Trade comprises merchandise exports plus merchandise imports; domestic exports are merchandise exports less officially defined re-exports; NODX are domestic exports less oil exports; Value-added exports are total exports less re-exports and imported intermediate inputs based on Lloyd and Sandilands (1986) and Tan (1995).

Source: Yearbook of Statistics, Singapore, various years; *Economic and Social Statistics, Singapore, 1960–82.*

Table 7.2 compares these export openness measures for Singapore since 1970. Removing traditional entrepot exports, oil and imported intermediate inputs does not change the basic picture that Singapore is an extraordinarily open economy, but the magnitude of the contribution of exports to GDP shrinks to a more meaningful size. Moreover, the fact that 'value-added' exports account for only 32 per cent of GDP in 1990 emphasizes the fact that Singapore is structurally still very much a re-export economy in the broad sense that there continues to be a heavy reliance on imported intermediate inputs as well as entrepot exports. It is precisely because of this that Lloyd and Sandilands described Singapore as a 'very open re-export economy'. For most economies the import content of exports is relatively small so this distinction is not important, but for Singapore almost all the output of goods and services by the private sector and almost all intermediate capital inputs are tradable goods. Even land is traded insofar as earth is imported from Indonesia and Malaysia and placed offshore for land reclamation.

Table 7.3 captures the direction of Singapore's trade: major export markets and sources of imports, and how they have changed since 1970. A problem in the reported data for some of Singapore's key trading partners arises from the different way in which these countries record entrepot trade (Sen, 2000). While Singapore supplies total export data, inclusive of re-exports, for international publications, its trading partners may not count such re-exports as part of their imports from Singapore. This leads to discrepancies between the reported data for the two countries and is likely to be more serious if there is a large amount of entrepot trade involved, such as that between Singapore and its ASEAN partners. There is a particular problem here with respect to Indonesia since Singapore's official trade statistics exclude Indonesian trade entirely since 1963, so the Indonesian figures reported in this chapter come from Indonesian sources and can only be taken as a rough approximation to the true figures. For this reason we have not included them in the ASEAN-4 aggregate.

The reason usually given for the absence of Indonesian data from the Singapore statistics is that the accounting systems used by the two countries are different, but what the problems are and why Indonesia should be singled out for special exclusion are not explained and this is all the more puzzling since Indonesia does publish its own trade data with respect to Singapore. The omission is serious because Indonesia is a key regional trading partner and member of ASEAN. Singapore's reluctance to publish trade data with Indonesia may also have something to do with political sensitivity over flows of capital from Chinese residents in Indonesia using Singapore as a safe haven from regional uncertainties.

The main destinations for Singapore's total exports in 2000 were the USA, Malaysia, and Japan. Compared to 1970 there has been a sharp redirection of total exports away from Europe as a whole and towards the North-east Asian economies of Hong Kong, Taiwan, South Korea and China. Notice the emergence of India as a market for Singapore's exports since 1980, although it is still small in relative terms. The share of exports destined for the ASEAN-4 (which does not include Indonesia) has remained fairly stable overall since 1970 but increased in the 1990s, particularly with respect to Malaysia.

Table 7.3 *Singapore's major export markets and sources of imports,*
1970–2000 (% of total exports or imports)

	Exports				Imports			
	1970	1980	1990	2000	1970	1980	1990	2000
USA	11.1	12.7	21.3 (26.6)	17.3 (24.6)	10.8	14.1	16.0	15.0
Japan	7.6	8.1	8.7 (9.9)	7.5 (7.7)	19.4	17.8	20.2	17.2
Australia	3.5	4.1	2.5 (2.6)	2.3 (2.6)	4.5	2.3	1.9	1.7
France	2.0	2.2	1.6 (1.9)	1.5 (2.0)	1.1	1.4	2.4	1.6
Germany	2.9	3.0	4.0 (4.5)	3.1 (3.3)	3.4	3.3	3.6	3.1
Netherlands	1.5	1.9	2.1 (2.1)	3.0 (4.1)	1.2	1.0	0.9	1.0
UK	6.8	2.6	3.2 (3.6)	2.6 (5.1)	7.6	3.4	3.1	2.0
Europe	23.9	16.0	17.4 (18.4)	14.6 (19.5)	18.6	13.7	15.9	14.2
Malaysia	21.9	15.0	13.1 (8.4)	18.2 (12.1)	18.6	13.9	13.6	17.0
Thailand	3.3	4.3	6.6 (7.3)	4.3 (3.7)	2.0	2.0	2.7	4.3
Philippines	0.3	1.4	1.3 (1.1)	2.5 (1.9)	0.4	0.3	0.5	2.5
Brunei	1.6	1.4	1.0 (0.5)	0.4 (0.2)	0.0	0.8	0.2	0.2
Indonesia	–	4.8	1.3 –	2.2	–	10.4	3.1	5.7
ASEAN-4	27.1	22.1	22.0 (17.3)	25.4 (17.9)	21.0	17.0	17.0	24.0
Hong Kong	4.1	7.7	6.5 (6.9)	7.9 (7.6)	2.5	2.1	3.1	2.6
Taiwan	0.8	1.7	3.6 (3.7)	6.0 (4.3)	1.7	2.4	4.3	4.4
South Korea	0.7	1.5	2.2 (2.1)	3.6 (2.5)	0.5	1.1	2.9	3.6
China	1.5	1.6	1.5 (1.4)	3.9 (3.4)	5.1	2.6	3.4	5.3
India	0.6	2.3	2.1 (1.3)	2.0 (1.7)	0.9	0.5	0.6	0.8
NEASIA-4	7.1	12.5	13.8 (14.1)	21.4 (17.8)	9.8	8.2	13.7	15.9

Note: Domestic exports in parentheses are for 1999; ASEAN-4 includes Malaysia, Thailand, Philippines, Brunei; NEASIA-4 comprises Hong Kong, Taiwan, South Korea, China; the data for Indonesia are from the *Direction of Trade Statistics*, various years, converted into the Singapore dollar at the prevailing exchange rate. The latest figure is for 1999.

Source: *Economic Survey of Singapore 2000.*

As far as imports are concerned, again the USA, Japan and Malaysia dominate and there has been a switch in origin away from Europe as a whole towards North-east Asia. The ASEAN-4 share, which had declined in 1980 and 1990, was higher by 2000. The share of Australian imports has stayed surprisingly small and has actually fallen in relative importance since 1970, and India was no more important in 2000 than it was in 1970. Saudi Arabia, which is not included in the table, supplied 3.2 per cent of Singapore's imports in 2000 but this is almost exclusively crude oil for refining and export. Japan is much more important as a supplier of imports (especially transport and machinery equipment) than as an export market. Singapore is not alone in experiencing difficulties when trying to penetrate the Japanese market.

One significant development in recent years has been the closer production and trade based integration between Malaysia and Singapore, particularly in electronics. In 2000 the proportion of total trade (exports plus imports) with Malaysia exceeded that with the USA, although the positions are reversed if domestic exports are used (Table 7.3). One reason for the rise in Singapore–Malaysia trade has been the increase in foreign direct investment in Malaysia by both Singapore-based companies and US and Japanese firms directly, which has led to increased production and hence bilateral trade. Another factor has been the upswing in the global electronics cycle since 1998. Both Singapore and Malaysia are major players in the electronics market and Singapore benefits directly from an increase in global demand, and also from the indirect increase in demand for exports to Malaysia of intermediate and capital goods, including such items as integrated circuits, parts of data processing machines and printed circuit boards. Petroleum-related products now also form a significant part of Singapore's domestic exports to Malaysia, exceeding 15 per cent of total exports in 2000 (*Economic Survey of Singapore 2000*, Table 5).

As far as the composition of Singapore's trade is concerned, Table 7.4 shows major exports and imports and how they have changed over time since the mid 1970s as Singapore was transformed from an entrepot trading economy producing labour-intensive goods, such as simple textiles and garments and household electrical goods, to capital-intensive petroleum refining in the 1970s, and to skill-intensive electronic goods and high income business and financial services in the 1980s and 1990s.

Since 1970 oil exports have fallen in significance after a peak in the early 1970s, as did traditional entrepot re-exports, leading to a steady rise in the importance of non-oil domestic exports, which accounted for about half of total exports by 1990. Crude materials and manufactured goods fell sharply after 1980 as Singapore's exports became dominated by machinery and equipment, particularly office machines and electronic components and parts which together made up nearly 60 per cent of total non-oil domestic exports in 2000. Chemicals are also a rising star at just under 10 per cent in 2000.

Parallel changes on the import side include the fall in the weight of food, beverages and tobacco, and crude materials, from approximately 30 per cent of the total in 1970 to less than 5 per cent by 2000. The decline in imports of manufactured goods has been less pronounced than on the

Table 7.4   Singapore's major exports and imports, 1970–2000

	1970	1980	1990	2000
(Percentage of total exports or imports)				
Oil exports	17.3	35.1	18.2	9.6
Non-oil domestic exports	21.9	28.0	47.9	47.5
Non-oil imports	86.5	71.0	84.2	87.9
(Percentage of non-oil domestic exports)				
Crude materials	2.9	1.3	1.0	0.6
Chemicals	4.7	4.9	7.9	9.5
Manufactured goods	30.2	27.6	15.3	11.6
Machinery and equipment:	19.0	56.5	70.9	75.9
Office machines	3.3	2.3	31.8	34.0
Electronics components and parts	–	18.9	11.3	24.7
(Percentage of non-oil imports)				
Food, beverages and tobacco	16.5	8.8	6.2	3.5
Crude materials	13.2	9.4	2.6	0.9
Chemicals	5.9	7.4	9.1	6.5
Manufactured goods	33.6	27.9	26.6	18.6
Machinery and equipment:	26.4	42.0	53.1	69.1
Electric generators	1.3	2.8	4.8	5.4
Electronic components and parts	–	7.5	9.7	27.3

Source: Economic Survey of Singapore 2000, Tables A6.1, A6.5, A6.7.

export side, but again machinery and equipment account for about 70 per cent of imports, with electronic parts and components individually contributing 27 per cent.

One facet of the change in the composition of trade over time has been the rising importance of tourism, which is now an important contributor to GDP in Singapore (Table 7.5) and in relative terms is one of the largest in the Asia–Pacific region. According to the World Tourism Organization (*Yearbook of Tourism Statistics, 2000*), Singapore ranked third in the top ten Asia–Pacific countries in 1998 in terms of visitor arrivals, exceeded only by Hong Kong and Thailand. By 2000 a record 7.7 million visitors were coming to the Republic (compared to a resident population of 3.3 million), and were increasingly more affluent 'short-haul' visitors from Asian countries such as Indonesia, Japan and Malaysia, which together accounted for 36 per cent of the total. China and India are now also beginning to have an impact, albeit from a low base. About half of the arrivals are holiday arrivals, as opposed to business arrivals, and 10 per cent are in 'transit'.

Table 7.5   Selected statistics on tourism in Singapore, 1970–2000

	Visitor arrivals (thousands)	Tourism receipts ($ millions)	% of GDP	% of exports
1970	579	280	4.8	7.9
1980	2 562	3 068	12.7	7.5
1990	5 323	8 428	11.5	8.9
2000	7 691	9 950	6.3	5.5
1995	7 137	10 837		
1996	7 293	10 552		
1997	7 198	9 445		
1998	6 242	8 228		
1999	6 958	8 807		
2000	7 691	9 950		

	Annual average percentage change in:	
	Visitor arrivals	Tourism receipts
1970–79	15	20
1980–89	7	9
1990–96	5	4
1997–2000	2	1
1990–2000	4	2

Notes: Visitor arrivals exclude Malaysian arrivals by land and, prior to 1978, other arrivals by land, as well as Malaysians coming directly to Singapore by air and sea; tourism receipts are proxied by travel receipts from the balance of payments data and represent the foreign currency inflow from international tourism; exports comprise domestic merchandise exports plus exports of services.

Sources: Data before 1990 is from Wilson (1994a, Table 1); from 1990 onwards the sources are the *Economic Survey of Singapore, various issues,* and *Balance of Payments Statistics Yearbook, 2000.*

Visitor arrivals have trended downwards during the 1990s with a steady decline in Singapore's share of tourist arrivals to the east Asian region, falling from around 9 per cent in 1990 to 5.5 per cent in 1999 (Monetary Authority of Singapore, 2001c, pp. 10–14). Most visitors are on holiday and Singapore appears to have lost some of its appeal as a shopping 'paradise'. The business segment has, however, remained stable at about 18 per cent with a small but growing proportion of arrivals (2.7 per cent) attending conferences, exhibitions and business meetings. A ten year Retail Master Plan is in place to woo tourists into the retail sector, Manchester United and Liverpool took part in exhibition soccer matches in August 2001, and Turkish-style ice-cream is on sale at Clarke Quay in the re-rejuvenated Mediterranean atmosphere of the Singapore River. How could it fail?

Despite a relative slowdown in the growth rates of both visitor arrivals and tourism receipts in the 1990s, and negative growth during the Asian financial crisis, both had recovered strongly by 1999. In 2000 travel receipts reached almost $10 billion (Table 7.5), contributing approximately 6 per cent to GDP. Moreover, travel receipts underestimate the contribution of tourism since they only measure the direct foreign exchange effects and ignore the strong multiplier linkages which the tourism sector has with the rest of the economy. According to Khan et al. (1989), regardless of a significant leakage of tourism spending through imports, Singapore's strong input–output linkages and high value-added tourist activities, including shipping, explain the significant contribution made by tourism to national output and employment. A more recent study (Monetary Authority of Singapore, 2001c, p. 11) using 1995 tourist expenditure and the 1990 Input–Output Tables found that tourism expenditure contributed $4.7 million in value-added or 3.9 per cent of GDP based on the value created in industries that directly provide goods and services to tourists. Of these industries, tourism expenditure contributed 42 per cent to the commerce sector (restaurants, hotels, wholesale and retail) and 19 per cent to transport and communications.

Table 7.6   Sources of export growth for Singapore, 1964–92

	Contribution from expansion in:		
	Exports	Domestic demand	Import substitution
Percentage of manufacturing GDP			
1964–70	24	121	−46
1970–80	76	44	−20
1980–92	98	44	−20
1964–92	89	42	−31
Percentage of GDP			
1964–70	35	99	−35
1970–80	76	50	−26
1980–92	58	29	12
1964–92	62	63	−26

Source: Tan (1995, Tables 3.4 and 3.8).

Singapore is often cited as a model of successful export-led growth. Table 7.6 identifies the sources of manufacturing growth and overall GDP growth for Singapore taking averages for a number of periods between 1964 and 1992 based upon a growth accounting methodology originally devised by

Chenery et al. (1986). Using value-added data to take into account Singapore's high import content of exports, the contribution to overall GDP growth and manufacturing growth is decomposed into export expansion, expansion of domestic demand and import substitution. The key observation from this table is the overwhelming contribution to growth from growth in exports, especially from the 1970s on. Domestic demand, on the other hand, was most important in the 1960s through infrastructure and housing expenditure. Import substitution is negative except for a small contribution to overall GDP growth between 1980 and 1992 as a result of a slowdown in export growth during this period. Negative import substitution is the counterpart to Singapore's heavy import penetration.

A problem here is that most studies looking at the link between export growth and GDP growth are based on cross-sections of countries (Balassa, 1978; Ram, 1987) which implicitly assume that all countries in the sample share a similar level of development. Resource-deficient economies, such as Singapore and Hong Kong, however, clearly do not fit into this category since export expansion itself requires a significant increase in imports to be successful. Tan (1984), for example, found Singapore to be overwhelmingly exporting natural resource-intensive goods in 1965, 1970 and 1992, yet Singapore has no natural resources! This puzzle is quickly resolved, however, when it is realized that exports such as petroleum and related products *appear* to have high natural resource content but are in fact largely made up of imports. When adjustments are made for this (Sandilands and Tan, 1986), the facts are broadly in line with an extended Heckscher–Ohlin framework insofar as Singapore's exports have become more capital- and skill-intensive over time, and when the link between imports and exports is taken into account (Khalid and Cheng, 1997) there is support for the export-led growth hypothesis for Singapore between 1978 and 1996.

7.2   DEPENDENCE ON FOREIGN RESOURCES

It is hard to overstate the importance of the role of foreign resources in the economic development of Singapore. Indeed Huff (1999) regards the attraction of mobile foreign capital, together with high subsidies to investment and infrastructure administered by the government, as the key to Singapore's success. A positive attitude early on towards foreign capital has also been an important feature of trade policy and the notion that dependence on foreign multinationals located in Singapore represents an Achilles heel for Singapore is a recurrent theme in the literature. For example Richardson concludes that: Singapore will be 'first-world' in terms of income and wealth and will also have a 'first-world' economic structure in that there will be a highly developed services sector, with a more specialized, high value-added manufacturing base. He continues:

> But Singapore will remain economically vulnerable in a way that 'first-world' countries are not. The predominance of foreign-owned firms in its manufacturing base will continue and a substantial proportion of these will remain US-owned. These firms have no underlying reasons to remain in Singapore and if economic or political circumstances forced them elsewhere, Singapore would find it difficult to fill the void. (Richardson, 1994, p. 97)

An ominous recent twist to this theme was the sharp fall in confidence in Singapore as a place for business after the September 2001 terrorist attacks in the USA. According to the Political and Economic Risk Consultancy (PERC), Singapore fell from the fourth safest place in the region to the second from last above Indonesia (*Business Times*, 18 October, 2001, p. 12). Although Singapore has always been seen as one of the safest places in Asia, this perception may be quite fragile, and underscores the island's vulnerability to social and political instability in neighbouring countries, such as Malaysia and Indonesia.

Table 7.7 shows how successful East Asia, and Singapore in particular, have been in attracting foreign direct investment compared to other developing countries since 1980, consistently accounting for almost half of the total destined for developing countries as a whole. Between 1980 and 1984 Singapore alone was responsible for almost 12 per cent, twice that of its nearest rival, Hong Kong. After 1985 China emerged as the biggest recipient and Singapore's share fell to 3–4 per cent after 1996, but unlike the other older tigers such as Taiwan, Korea and Hong Kong who have become net exporters, Singapore has remained a net importer. Singapore also stands out in terms of the share of foreign direct investment in gross fixed capital formation reaching almost 30 per cent between 1985 and 1996. This share also fell in the 1990s, but at around 20 per cent is higher than for China and Malaysia and has remained at the same level as in the early 1980s.

Singapore's success in attracting foreign direct investment undoubtedly has something to do with its strategic location in Asia, cheap but skilled labour force, social and economic stability, excellent infrastructure, tax incentives for research and development and exports and, crucially, a positive attitude by the government towards MNCs at an early stage in the development process. There is a consistency in treatment, a well-developed structure of administrative support and legal protection, and macroeconomic policies which have delivered low and stable inflation over decades and a relatively stable exchange rate. None of the negative features often

Table 7.7   Foreign direct investment into Singapore in a global context, 1980–99

US$ b	1980–84	1985–89	1990–96	1997	1998	1999
World	49.3	128.5	244.1	473.1	680.1	865.5
Developing countries	11.9	22.3	79.5	178.8	179.5	207.6
Share of developing countries total %						
Singapore	11.8	10.8	6.0	4.5	3.1	3.4
Hong Kong	5.9	7.2	5.2	6.4	8.2	11.1
Taiwan	1.7	3.6	1.4	1.2	0.1	1.4
China	4.2	11.2	22.4	24.7	24.4	19.5
Korea	0.8	3.1	1.2	1.7	2.9	5.0
Indonesia	1.7	1.7	2.7	2.6	0.0	−1.5
Malaysia	9.2	3.6	4.6	3.6	1.5	1.7
Philippines	0.0	1.8	1.0	0.7	1.0	0.3
Thailand	2.5	3.1	2.0	2.0	4.0	2.9
Total East Asia	37.8	46.1	46.5	47.4	45.2	43.8
Share of gross fixed capital formation %						
Singapore	18.9	29.3	27.4	22.1	17.6	18.5
Hong Kong	7.1	12.1	5.1	2.7	2.0	3.2
Taiwan	1.2	3.6	2.6	3.4	0.4	0.7
China	0.6	2.2	10.1	14.6	12.9	13.2
Korea	0.3	1.5	0.8	1.8	5.5	7.4
Indonesia	0.9	1.8	4.9	6.8	−0.8	−1.2
Malaysia	11.5	9.3	15.4	15.1	13.9	16.2
Philippines	0.4	6.2	7.0	6.2	12.8	13.1
Thailand	2.6	4.5	4.1	7.8	25.1	26.7

Note: Foreign direct investment is the sum of equity capital, reinvested earnings, and intra-company loans by foreign firms or their affiliates.

Sources: *World Investment Report*, various years, *International Financial Statistics*, various years.

associated with the presence of foreign MNCs appear to have been important in Singapore. Indeed the fear has been that they may decide to leave! Since 1980 the appeal of Singapore as a destination for foreign direct investment has not significantly diminished, despite rising production and living costs, and the removal of obstacles to foreign investment in other countries in the region. Few impediments are placed in the way.

Table 7.8 shows the stock of foreign direct equity investment in Singapore in 1990 and 1997 and net investment commitments in manufacturing in 1990 and 1999. Japan and the USA are the dominant individual

Table 7.8   Stock of foreign direct equity investment in Singapore and net investment commitments in manufacturing

	1990	1997
Total stock $ billion	49.8	112.1
Share % in:		
Manufacturing	39.7	34.7
Commerce	13.1	13.0
Financial/business services	43.2	47.7
Share % from:		
Japan	21.4	18.1
USA	17.2	18.4
Europe	27.0	30.2
UK	9.3	7.4
Netherlands	8.2	6.2
Germany	1.8	1.6
ASEAN	6.0	6.0
Malaysia	4.2	4.2
Indonesia	0.5	1.0

Net investment commitments in manufacturing $ billions	1990	1999
Total	2.5	8.0
Foreign	2.2	6.3
Share of foreign % in:		
Electronics	49.5	52.6
Chemicals	13.6	42.2
Machinery/equipment	13.8	7.8
Transport equipment	5.1	5.1
Share % from:		
USA	47.6	57.3
Japan	31.9	18.9
Europe	19.6	18.2
Germany	7.5	10.1
UK	4.1	1.5

Sources: *Yearbook of Statistics, Singapore*, various issues.

owners of this stock, but Europe (especially the UK, and the Netherlands) now accounts for about 30 per cent. The share from ASEAN is still small, with Malaysia being the only significant regional provider, but this understates the growing links between Singapore and Malaysia in terms of production and investment flows, especially in the electronics industry. We shall return to this issue in Section 7.6 below in connection with Singapore's outward foreign direct investment.

Although manufacturing accounts for a substantial share of foreign direct investment in the 1990s, almost half of the total stock is now in financial and business services. Within the manufacturing sector itself electronics accounts for over half of foreign investment commitments by 1999, but the proportion earmarked for chemicals has significantly risen since 1990. In recent years Singapore has adopted an explicit 'cluster' policy to channel foreign investment into areas where Singapore may have a comparative advantage within the manufacturing sector, including electronics, chemicals and biomedical. In 2000 the manufacturing sector attracted $9.2 billion in fixed assets investment which, if realized, will generate $8.5 billion worth of value-added and over 20 thousand new jobs (Table 7.9).

Table 7.9   Manufacturing investment commitments by cluster, 2000

Clusters	Fixed assets $m	Share %	Value-added $m	Share %	Employment	Share %
Electronics	4453	48	4627	55	12315	60
Chemicals	2187	24	1126	13	710	3
Biomedical	806	9	1140	13	566	3
Engineering	1586	17	1486	18	6402	31
General	175	2	102	1	674	3
Total	9208	100	8481	100	20667	100

Source: Economic Survey of Singapore 2000 (Table 9.2).

Of the total investment commitments in manufacturing in 1999 (Table 7.8) 79 per cent was still from foreign sources and this emphasizes once more the 'dependence' of Singapore on foreigners. By the early 1990s the problem of 'vulnerability' and 'dependence' became inextricably linked to the imperative over the longer run to diversify the structure of the economy away from exclusive reliance on a predominantly foreign manufacturing base and to increase domestic value-added. This was not seen as a negative reaction to foreigners or foreign capital per se but as a positive move towards a more diversified economy and developed country status. Changes in the education system would produce more creative workers, and centralized policy initiatives would reduce Singapore's propensity to rely on input-driven growth and increase the contribution from total factor productivity growth. This fitted in nicely with the concept of 'Asian values' and the view that Singapore could find an alternative Asian model of development different from the 'western' model:

> MNCs and borrowed technology have helped us rapidly leap from a poor trading village to an NIE, and in time to come to a developed economy . . . Foreign MNCs will continue to play a dominant part in our development. But to break through to the next level of development, we have to increasingly develop our home-grown talent and our own MNCs. (Prime Minister Goh Chok Tong, *The Business Times*, 25–26 March, 1995, p. 1)

By the late 1990s the debate over Asian values had largely receded into the background and emphasis in government policy reverted to the view that resources in Singapore are essentially complementary to foreign resources. Foreign talent is now actively sought and less stress is placed on the imperative of raising total factor productivity growth soon. This coincided with reforms to the financial sector to speed up Singapore's globalization and further integration into the world economy, a strategy which requires Singapore firms to form global alliances and compete on the world stage. In this sense, Singapore is returning to its original formula: to continue to make itself useful to the world and an attractive location for foreign capital, labour and technology. Huff (1995) in his perceptive longer-term assessment of the Singapore model of development observed that Singapore's income per capita at the end of the 1950s was already over a third of that of the UK and higher than anywhere else in Asia, yet in 1986 Singapore was still predominantly a manufacturing base, attractive to foreigners because of its pool of reliable and adaptable unskilled labour. Reliance on foreigners is not, therefore, a good reason for Singapore to delay reclassification as a fully developed country (see Chapter 6):

> But since Singapore, in this sense, is likely to lack the 'depth and breadth of fully developed countries' for some time to come (maybe in perpetuity!), especially if you subscribe to the view that its policy-driven initiatives to raise total factor productivity growth may not be very successful in the short run, then even if it continues to make itself useful to the world and an attractive location for foreign capital, labour, and technology, Singapore would be disqualified from the Super League on the grounds that the foreigners might decide to go home. This is as absurd as denying Chelsea Football Club promotion to the English Premier League on the grounds that its unusually high number of foreign players might decide to leave. (Wilson, 2000a, p. 121)

7.3   VULNERABILITY TO EXTERNAL SHOCKS

Given a high level of trade and financial openness and heavy reliance on foreign capital, Singapore is extraordinarily vulnerable to external shocks, whether it be a slowdown in export growth, a sharp exodus of short-term capital, a change in world interest rates, or an increase in imported inflation. On average, between 1992 and 2000, changes in external demand (exports) accounted for over three-quarters of the changes in real total demand, while changes in domestic demand accounted for less than a quarter (Table 7.10). In 2000, for example, external demand contributed 79 per cent (11/14) to total demand. This contrasts markedly with other economies such as Japan and the USA where domestic demand is the prime mover in total demand. No wonder forecasting the Singapore economy is so difficult and dependent on forecasts of external demand. Of course, total demand is not the same thing as GDP, which is total demand less imports. All the components in Table 7.10 are inclusive of imports except external demand (exports). To calculate the true 'value-added' contribution of exports and all other components to GDP would require deducting imports from the components separately from the input–output tables, but the numbers in Table 7.10 can be taken as an approximation to the relative importance of domestic and external sources of demand in total demand.

Table 7.10   *The contribution of domestic and external demand to growth in total demand, 1992–2000*

	Growth in total demand %	Contribution to growth in total demand %				
		Consumption spending	Investment spending	Increase in stocks	Domestic demand	External demand
1992	6.7	0.8	1.3	−0.2	1.9	4.8
1993	14.6	1.5	1.4	0.4	3.3	11.3
1994	15.4	0.9	1.0	−0.9	1.0	14.4
1995	12.7	1.0	1.1	0.3	2.4	10.3
1996	8.3	1.6	1.9	−0.7	2.8	5.5
1997	7.8	1.1	1.1	0.5	2.7	5.1
1998	−5.4	−0.2	−0.8	−1.3	−2.3	−3.1
1999	6.5	0.9	−0.5	1.1	1.5	5.0
2000	14.0	1.7	0.7	0.6	3.0	11.0
Mean	8.9	1.0	0.7	0.1	1.8	7.1

Source: *Economic Survey of Singapore*, various issues.

Singapore's growth cycle can be significantly affected by external swings in demand, such as the slowdown in the economy in the second and third quarters of 1996 and in 2001 (Abeysinghe and Wilson, 2001). In both cases a downswing in the global electronics cycle played a prominent part. Electronics accounts for about 15 per cent of Singapore's GDP, almost half of manufacturing output (47.8 per cent in 2000), and almost two-thirds of non-oil exports. Since almost half of Singapore's electronics exports are destined for the US market, swings in the demand for new orders of electronics in that market play a critical part in Singapore's business cycle. This affects Singapore directly through changes in domestic exports of electronic goods and re-exports of components to countries such as Malaysia, but also indirectly through the strong trade flows which link Singapore's GDP growth to income growth in its major trading partners in the region, such as South Korea, Hong Kong and Taiwan, which themselves are vulnerable to a fall in US electronics demand. The US demand for electronics appears to follow a 4–5 year cycle with cycles of smaller duration in between, and is significantly associated with cycles in Singapore in total exports, GDP and manufacturing output (Abeysinghe, 2000). Some insulation is given, however, by the finance and business services sector which displays an opposite cycle.

Notwithstanding this vulnerability Singapore is insulated to some degree from the impact of short-term fluctuations in export earnings on aggregate income and the balance of payments through the operation of in-built automatic stabilizers which act as a cushioning device. These stabilizers include high marginal propensities to save and import. The leakage through government taxes is itself quite small in Singapore, but the CPF system acts like a tax in the short run by locking up a significant amount of disposable income in compulsory savings. The size of the import leakage is obvious from Table 4.1, where a one dollar increase in final expenditure sucks in 54 cents' worth of total imports. For investment spending it is 63 cents, and for manufacturing exports 69 cents. Even exports of services, which usually require less imported inputs, draws in 29 cents' worth of imports.

Less obvious stabilizers operate through the 'damped' multiplier framework of MacBean (1966) and Lim (1991), including re-exports and repatriated profits. When calculating the effect of a fall in exports on domestic income and activity, re-exports should be omitted since, by definition, they do not add an equivalent dollar's worth of value to the income multiplier process, but only their value-added. The hypothesis about repatriated profits is that foreign-based companies may allow some of the profits which they might otherwise have expatriated to fall in tandem with a fall in export earnings (or vice versa), keeping operating costs and other payments to the host economy relatively constant. Whether this is what companies actually do has not been tested for Singapore, and there is an additional twist to this story since government investment abroad since the mid 1980s has itself generated a steady stream of income coming back to Singapore as investment income in the current account of the balance of payments, and this need not vary in any consistent manner with export performance in general and could be counter-cyclical. Another less obvious stabilizer arises from the fact that an increasing amount of Singapore's trade in the region consists of intra-firm transactions of intermediate inputs through MNCs to meet demand outside the region. Therefore, while exports destined for local consumption in the region were badly hit by the 1997–98 Asian financial crisis as domestic demand collapsed, those used as intermediate inputs and eventually re-exported to developed countries outside the region remained healthy. This had the effect of mitigating, to some extent, the effect of the crisis on Singapore's overall trade performance (*Economic Survey of Singapore 1997*, p. 101).

Taking some of these factors into account, Wilson (1995) found the trade multiplier to be heavily damped in the case of Singapore between 1972 and 1986. The negative impact that a fall in exports has on income is quickly cushioned by a fall in imports and re-exports and a feedback stimulus to real exports from a fall in real wage costs, itself induced by the fall in exports and economic activity. Singapore has also been protected (perhaps over-protected) from the adverse effects of falls in export earnings by a strong overall balance of payments and foreign exchange reserves position which has meant that emergency measures to finance a balance of payments deficit have not really been needed (see Chapter 8).

These stabilizers may partly explain why it has been so hard historically to knock Singapore off its sustained GDP growth path (Peebles and Wilson, 1996, pp. 170–71). The 1985–86 recession in Singapore, for example, is often used to illustrate Singapore's vulnerability to external shocks. But that recession, in fact, required a rather special combination of unfavourable circumstances. Recovery from the recession was also rapid, helped by an improvement in external factors, but important too was swift government action to reduce producer costs by cutting compulsory savings contribution rates and restraining wage increases. In fact Singapore has shown remarkable adaptability and resilience in the face of changes in the world environment.

Table 7.11 shows the relative impact of Singapore's trading partners on Singapore's real GDP growth from Abeysinghe (2001), using a quarterly model linking the GDPs of 12 economies or blocs through a matrix of bilateral export shares. Service exports are not included for data reasons but trade with Indonesia is factored into the model.

Table 7.11   Singapore's trading partners ranked by export shares and multiplier effects on Singapore's real GDP growth

Rank by export share in 1996 %			Rank by multiplier effect		
1	USA	18.4	1	ROECD	1.09
2	Malaysia	18.0	2	USA	0.92
3	ROECD	16.4	3	Japan	0.70
4	Hong Kong	8.9	4	Hong Kong	0.44
5	Japan	8.2	5	Malaysia	0.39
6	Thailand	5.7	6	China	0.29
7	Indonesia	3.7	7	South Korea	0.25
8	South Korea	3.0	8	Thailand	0.20
9	China	2.7	9	Taiwan	0.20
10	Taiwan	2.2	10	Indonesia	0.14
11	Philippines	1.8	11	Philippines	0.08

Notes: The multiplier effect measures the total direct and indirect effects on Singapore's real GDP growth of a 1 per cent shock to the real GDP of the foreign country or region concerned in the fourth quarter of 1997 after four quarters have elapsed. The multipliers are normalized in terms of the effect of the shock on the foreign country itself; ROECD is the OECD countries except Japan and the USA.

Source: Abeysinghe (2001).

As expected, shocks originating in Japan, the USA and the rest of the OECD have relatively strong effects. Less obvious, however, is the fact that countries with a larger trading volume generate more spin-off effects on other countries even though their direct trade links might be weak. This is because the multipliers take into account both the direct and indirect effects. Malaysia, for example, is Singapore's second largest market for total exports, but comes fifth in terms of the impact on Singapore's GDP growth while Hong Kong, which is half as important as a market for Singapore's exports, comes fourth. An increase in growth in GDP in Hong Kong stimulates imports from other countries including Singapore. This increases Singapore's exports directly and indirectly through Hong Kong's export markets that import intermediate products from Singapore, so the cumulative effect of the growth in Hong Kong on Singapore's GDP is larger than that resulting from an equivalent increase in growth in Malaysia.

It is for this reason that the contagion effects of the Asian financial crisis affected Singapore not so much through direct trade links with countries such as Thailand, Indonesia and Malaysia, but through indirect links with countries with large trade volumes, such as Japan, Hong Kong and Korea. Singapore is more trade diversified than Taiwan in terms of the proportion of its trade with the USA, Japan and ROECD, but was harder hit by the crisis with a multiplier value with respect to the direct victims of the contagion (Thailand, Korea, Indonesia and Malaysia) of 0.98 (Table 7.11) compared to the multiplier for Taiwan from those same countries of 0.51. Thus Singapore's extra diversification compared to Taiwan did not turn out to be a virtue after all.

In addition, this model confirms that a shock originating in Singapore itself has an immediate impact on Singapore's GDP but because of its openness and dependence on external demand, this drops off very fast over time. In other words, policy measures to stimulate the domestic economy, such as cost cutting exercises, will not be very effective unless they can generate positive feedback on Singapore's own GDP through the stimulus it gives to its trading partners, which in turn increase their demand for Singapore's exports.

7.4   INTERNATIONAL COMPETITIVENESS

There are two key senses in which Singapore worries about its present capacity to compete internationally (Abeysinghe and Wilson, 2002): whether Singapore can improve the quality of growth sufficiently to compete with advanced developed countries – the total factor productivity growth debate discussed in Chapter 3; and whether Singapore can cope effectively with pressures on costs and prices with the macroeconomic tools which the authorities have at their disposal (Chapter 8). In this chapter we look at competitiveness in the context of Singapore's trade structure and focus on more disaggregated trade performance indicators relevant to the competitiveness debate. The wider debate on Singapore's competitiveness is also addressed in Toh and Tan (1998).

Singapore has experienced rapid growth in its total exports in the last two decades, but this period also witnessed substantial growth and industrialization in East and South-east Asia and the emergence of a competitive group of Asian economies consisting of the older and more established tigers of Singapore, Taiwan, Korea and Hong Kong, together with Thailand and Malaysia, the two most dynamic ASEAN countries apart from Singapore. At the same time, Singapore has become more commodity concentrated in electronic and chemical exports and more geographically concentrated in regional markets in East and South-east Asia. This has raised concern in Singapore about its ability to compete sufficiently in the manufacturing sector in a changing global environment and whether there is a need to diversify away from over-reliance on regional markets, especially after the Asian financial crisis when the prospects for regional growth look more muted than before.

One way to capture these shifts in trade structure is to calculate trade intensity indices which measure bilateral or regional trade flows relative to the partner's share of trade with the rest of the world. This has the advantage of normalizing for large country effects and indicates whether trade growth is primarily the result of scale expansion or more intense commercial ties. The USA, for example, is Singapore's largest trading partner as far as domestic exports are concerned, but is also the largest trader in the world.

Table 7.12   Singapore's trade linkages

Trade intensity indices from/to in 1998	ASEAN-4	Developing East Asia	Industrial economies
ASEAN-4	1.5	2.4	0.9
Developing East Asia	2.2	2.3	0.9
Industrial economies	0.3	0.3	1.0

	Singapore's trade intensity average 1992–96		Singapore's intra-industry trade % total	
	Exports	Imports	1992	1996
With:				
ASEAN-3	7.0	7.9	52	65
North-east Asia	1.3	1.6	47	55
EU-13	0.3	0.3	32	38
North America	1.0	1.0	38	45

Notes: ASEAN-4 comprises Indonesia, Malaysia, Thailand, and the Philippines; developing East Asia includes ASEAN-4 plus China, Hong Kong, Singapore, Korea and Taiwan; the indices are based on 3-year averages of merchandise export flows.
Intra-industry trade is measured by the Grubel-Lloyd index; ASEAN-3 is Malaysia, Thailand and the Philippines; North-east Asia includes Japan, China, South Korea and Hong Kong; EU-13 refers to 13 members of the European Union.

Sources: Hill and Phillips (1993, Table 8), Monetary Authority of Singapore (1998c).

By 1988 (Table 7.12) developing East Asian countries were trading more intensively among themselves (2.3) than they did with the industrial countries (0.9), or than the latter did among themselves (1.0). On the other hand the relatively low indices for intra-ASEAN-4 trade (1.5), which excludes Singapore, compared to trade between ASEAN-4 and developing East Asia (which includes Singapore) underscores the relatively low value of intra-ASEAN trade and the key role Singapore plays in regional trade.

There is often a tendency to exaggerate intra-ASEAN trade by failing to take into account this pivotal role of Singapore in the trade matrix.

Table 7.12 also shows Singapore's average trade intensity between 1992 and 1996 with other trading groups. The relatively high trade intensity indices for Singapore's exports and imports with respect to ASEAN-3 and North-east Asia compared to the EU-13 and North America imply that Singapore's trade with these groups was significantly higher than their share of trade with the rest of the world, and are higher than the simple bilateral trade shares in Table 7.1 would suggest. Singapore's exports to ASEAN-3, for example, are seven times the latter's share of imports from the rest of the world.

Singapore has benefited from the rising share of its regional partners in world trade as they became more open and successfully pursued export-oriented industrialization, but does not seem to have benefited much from the upswing in trade flows in Europe and the strong growth between the EU and China and emerging markets in east and central Europe, such as Poland and the Czech Republic (*Economic Survey of Singapore 2000*, pp. 92–5). The main reason seems to be low 'special country bias' towards the Asian region indicating that the 'resistance' to Singapore's exports by the partner country or region, including the incidence of protection, is less than its resistance to exports from the rest of the world. This may have something to do with geographic proximity and the open regionalism practiced by ASEAN, and subsequently the ASEAN Free Trade Area (AFTA) insofar as Singapore has profited from its geographical proximity and hub activities as a port, strong bilateral ties, and investment links. For Europe and North America, however, Singapore has no geographical advantage and the resistance may have increased with the implementation of the North American Free Trade Agreement (NAFTA) and the European single market initiative in the early 1990s (Monetary Authority of Singapore, 1998c).

Another feature of Table 7.12 is the rise in the proportion of Singapore's trade with its partners which consists of intra-industry trade (IIT). Again this is higher with ASEAN-3 and North-east Asia than with the other groupings. Low special country bias towards the region may be one reason, but more important may be that industrialization and trade liberalization have brought these countries closer to Singapore's manufacturing structure, especially Malaysia, thus increasing the complementarity between Singapore and its regional partners, and the globalization of production has generated a significant increase in IIT in intermediate inputs, which make up a substantial proportion of Singapore's non-oil domestic exports.

One way to assess the implications of these structural developments for changes in Singapore's competitive position is to use shift–share analysis. This compares changes in Singapore's exports with the corresponding exports of a reference group of competitors. A positive net shift implies an improvement in competitiveness compared to the reference group in that year and a negative value constitutes a deterioration in competitiveness. This is a more relevant comparison than simply observing absolute changes in exports, which can overstate the importance of larger markets, or percentage changes which conversely overstate the importance of smaller markets. Shift–share is a relatively simple technique with a number of well documented shortcomings (see Wilson, 2000b) but it has proved to be a useful descriptive tool for isolating trends in relative export performance.

Table 7.13　Shift–share export performance for Singapore, 1983–95, compared to the dynamic Asian economies

	Years of positive net shifts (% of total)
To the USA:	
Organic chemicals	67
Office/data processing machines	92
Telecommunications/sound equipment	50
Electrical machinery	50
Apparel and clothing	33
To the European Union:	
Office/data processing machines	100
Telecommunications/sound equipment	25
Electrical machinery	42
Apparel and clothing	42
Miscellaneous manufactures	50
To Japan:	
Organic chemicals	58
Office/data processing machines	83
Telecommunications/sound equipment	75
Electrical machinery	58

Notes:　The Asian economies are Singapore, Thailand, Malaysia, Korea, Taiwan, Hong Kong.

Source:　Wilson (2000b).

When the more 'dynamic' Asian countries are used as the reference bloc over the period 1983–95 (Table 7.13), Singapore achieves predominantly positive net shifts in office and data processing machines (which includes electronics) and in chemicals, due principally to a favourable industrial structure which is biased towards industries which are growing rapidly, but has lost ground relatively in apparel and clothing, telecommunications and sound equipment, and in electrical machinery to the US and EU markets. The story is similar if ASEAN is used as the reference bloc (Wilson and Wong, 1999). Clothing and apparel is clearly a 'sunset' industry as far as Singapore is concerned but these results add credence to the perception that Singapore became more concentrated in chemicals and in the office and data processing sector over this period and lost ground in other areas of manufacturing to its emerging competitors in the region.

The Monetary Authority of Singapore (1998a) also used shift–share methods to look at Singapore's competitive position in the 1990s, but this time the objective was to identify which export markets were of growing (diminishing) importance to Singapore between 1991 and 1996 (excluding Indonesia). A positive net shift in this context signifies an increase in export earnings to a specific market greater than that implied by Singapore's overall export performance.

Table 7.14   Net export shifts for Singapore's total exports by destination, 1991–96 ($ billions)

Malaysia	5.4	Italy	−0.9
Hong Kong	2.9	Japan	−0.8
China	2.2	ASEAN-5	6.5
Ireland	1.5	North-east Asia	6.2
France	1.4	LAFTA	1.8
USA	−2.3	North America	−3.1
Germany	−1.9	EU-15	−2.6
Thailand	−1.1	South Asia	−1.1

Notes: ASEAN-5 comprises Malaysia, Thailand, Philippines, Brunei, Myanmar; North-east Asia is China, Hong Kong, Japan, South Korea, Taiwan; LAFTA is the Latin American Free Trade Association; EU-15 is the 15 members of the European Union.

Source: Monetary Authority of Singapore (1998a).

The highest net gains (Table 7.14) were to the markets of Malaysia, Hong Kong and China; while the biggest losses were to the USA, Germany and Thailand. The gains to ASEAN-5 and North-east Asia contrast with the loss of competitiveness in the USA, Japan and the EU-15, mirroring the trade intensity analysis referred to earlier. The increasing concentration of Singapore's competitive gains in office and data processing machines is also confirmed, especially electronics related items, even in those markets where the overall export shift was negative. Is Singapore becoming over-specialized in electronics and chemicals and too heavily oriented towards the region?

After the 1985–86 recession, there was a perception that Singapore was losing comparative advantage in low-skill labour-intensive goods and some capital-intensive goods relative to its competitors, but had not yet reached the stage at which Singapore could compete with the industrial developed countries in skill-intensive goods. The narrowness of its production base therefore left Singapore vulnerable to the threat of de-industrialization or the 'hollowing out' of the manufacturing sector as domestic costs rise and MNCs are tempted to re-locate their plants to lower wage economies. Another twist to this phenomenon was the fear that an across-the-board exodus by MNCs from the region to emerging markets such as eastern Europe might jeopardise Singapore's strategy to cushion the loss of lower end manufacturing by attracting the higher value-added end. So far this has not happened and the share of manufacturing in GDP was still 26 per cent in 2000 (*Economic Survey of Singapore 2000*, Table A1.1).

A shift to service provision, and an increase in value-added in the manufacturing that remains in Singapore would obviate this problem as long as the service sector expands to absorb the growing and retrenched labour force, but the fear in Singapore is that the workforce might not be able to adapt to the loss of manufacturing jobs and switch to those activities that service the overseas manufacturing base, such as design and marketing services and the provision of banking, insurance and transport services. Singapore's longstanding role as an entrepot for goods produced in Malaysia is also not so guaranteed as, in recent years, Malaysia has made it clear that it would like to 'encourage' local firms to use its own underutilized port facilities and attract transshipment firms away from the Port of Singapore. In 2000, Maersk Sealand, a major international shipping line accounting for 10 per cent of the annual throughput of the Port of Singapore, shifted its business to the Malaysian port of Tanjung Pelepas in nearby Johor. Others may follow, enticed by lower operating costs.

The spectre of de-industrialization is not peculiar to Singapore. As the share of manufacturing in total employment in rich countries fell from 28 per cent in 1970 to 18 per cent in 1994 (Rowthorn and Ramaswamy, 1997), similar fears were expressed in rich industrial countries and, arguably, the problem is likely to be more intractable for countries such as South Korea, where a substantial amount of manufacturing and employment has become structurally locked into inefficient production through the chaebol system and protectionist policies. If Rowthorn and Ramaswamy are correct, the problem is not due primarily to richer consumers wanting more services relative to manufactured goods, or to the export of jobs to lower wage countries, such as China and Vietnam, but is largely a result of faster productivity growth in manufacturing relative to services. It is inevitable that with development a smaller number of workers will be needed in manufacturing in newly-industrialized countries, as in developed countries in the past. The solution is to increase productivity growth in the service sector to absorb the labour released from manufacturing. Whether recent policies can achieve this is discussed in Section 8.5.

But do these regional and sectoral changes in Singapore's competitive position actually matter? Before answering this question we need to look at trade policy in Singapore.

7.5   SINGAPORE'S TRADE POLICY

Although there have been changes to the substance of Singapore's trade policy since 1965, there has also been a remarkable degree of continuity and a commitment to free trade in the fundamental sense of a low level of protection and continued exposure of consumers and producers to international price signals. In 1987 the World Bank classified Singapore as a strongly outward-oriented economy. An active export promotion strategy born out of necessity in the mid 1960s after the traumatic exodus of Singapore from the Malaysian Federation, primarily through improvements in infrastructure and selected fiscal incentives, has enabled Singapore to overcome the limitations imposed by a small domestic market by earning foreign exchange to purchase intermediate goods imports and an increasing quantity and variety of consumer goods from the international market at competitive prices.

Secondly, in sharp contrast to most developing countries at the time, an 'open arms' policy towards MNCs was extended at a very early stage in the industrialization process. This ensured that the transformation to an newly-industrialized economy, achieved by the 1980s, took place along the lines of shifting comparative advantage taking full advantage of the complementary resources provided by MNCs, especially in manufacturing and financial and business services.

Another integral part of trade policy in Singapore has been the pursuit of multilateral trade liberalization, but at the same time preferential trade arrangements, primarily through APEC, ASEAN and, more recently, AFTA. More recently Singapore has been pursuing bilateral preferential trade agreements with a number of countries, whilst at the same time continuing to press for further multilateral trade negotiations (see Section 7.8 below).

Finally, macroeconomic policy has been directed towards maintaining long-run external competitiveness and the flow of foreign investment into the Republic. From 1981 onwards this philosophy became enshrined in the managed floating exchange rate (see Chapter 8) regime in which the dollar is targeted primarily to achieve low and stable domestic price inflation as the bedrock for sustaining export competitiveness and inflows of foreign capital.

There is often a tendency to exaggerate the backwardness of the Singapore economy prior to 1960 but the colonial era did much to establish the basic preconditions for post-colonial growth. Unlike other staple ports such as Rangoon and Colombo Singapore was insulated from its hinterland and could pursue free trade and 'became rich because it was already relatively rich, and because it had good policies' (Huff, 1994, p. 369). From its inception as a trading port in the British Empire Singapore had always been a free port, initially exporting and processing staples: tin, rubber and petroleum, imported from regional neighbours such as Malaya and Indonesia. Free-trade policies, together with its strategic location and natural deepwater harbour, gave rise to a thriving entrepot trade and ancillary industries: shipping, insurance, banking, communications facilities and services, well into the 1950s and early 1960s.

With independence from the British in 1959, the ruling PAP intensified the process of industrialization to diversify away from the narrow entrepot base which was seen as being constraining in terms of potential income and employment growth as countries in the region industrialized and reduced their imports from Singapore and traded directly with industrialized countries, and was subject to high earnings instability.

Between 1960 and 1965 there was a brief period when trade strategy was geared towards import substitution rationalized in terms of the expected integration with the large Malaysian market nearby and standard 'infant industry' arguments for protection. Protective duties were introduced for the first time in 1960. This was accelerated when Singapore joined the Federation of Malaysia in 1963. Fiscal concessions were given to 'pioneer' industries, together with subsidies on factory sites, and quotas were imposed on selected import-competing industries. By May 1965, 230 commodities were subject to import quotas. When Singapore unexpectedly left the Federation of Malaysia in 1965 and became an independent Republic, it entered a transitional phase in its economic history as trade policy switched from inward to outward orientation. With no further guarantee of free access to the Malaysian market, and lacking a large pool of indigenous industrial entrepreneurs compared to other countries in the region, such as Hong Kong (from mainland China), import substitution was perceived to be unsustainable in an economy with such a small domestic market and dearth of natural resources.

The focus in trade policy therefore switched towards the promotion of labour-intensive exports, the attraction of foreign investment and the gradual lowering of protection, but even during the period of peak protection between 1965 and 1967, most ad valorem tariff rates were below 25 per cent and average nominal and effective tariff rates were low by international standards (Tan and Ow, 1982). In 1967 when the British government announced its intention to phase out its military bases in the Republic by 1971, nearly one-fifth of Singapore's GDP was at stake. This increased the imperative for rapid export-oriented and labour-intensive industrialization. At the present time most tariffs are below 5 per cent and are levied on selected items such as automobiles. Non-tariff barriers are negligible.

As far as trade promotion is concerned, in 1968 the Economic Development Board was reorganized and tax incentives given to encourage export promotion and foreign participation. The new strategy of export promotion combined with a lack of indigenous industrial entrepreneurs made the attraction of foreign investment a top priority. In 1967 tax incentives were encouraged to promote exports and in 1968 the Employment Act and Industrial Relations (Amendment Act) were introduced to foster a climate of 'harmonious' labour relations. Emphasis was placed on government-provided infrastructure. In 1968 Jurong Town Corporation was established to develop and manage industrial estates, offering prepared industrial land sites, ready made factories, and port and cargo-handling facilities nearby.

By the early 1970s export-oriented labour-intensive industrialization was well on track, with virtually full employment, and trade in services had also expanded in tandem with growth in manufacturing and policy initiatives to promote Singapore as a regional centre for transport and communications. Although MNCs located in Singapore had already begun to raise capital intensity, the domestic labour market became increasingly tight and the threat of competition from lower wage countries, together with the possibility of increased protectionism by developed countries, led to a shift of emphasis in trade policy towards the promotion of technology- and skill-intensive exports of goods and services with higher value-added – primarily transport and machinery. A restructuring programme, together with a 'high wage' policy was introduced in 1979 having been delayed by the 1973 oil shock and ensuing recession. Tax incentives were also introduced to increase research and development.

Following the second oil shock of 1979, the industrialized countries entered into recession between 1980 and 1982 with adverse effects on Singapore's commodity and service exports. Partly in response to these events, the National Productivity Board was established in 1981 to increase labour productivity, and in 1983 the Singapore Trade and Development Board was set up as a promotion agency to provide trade information, offer financial assistance to help companies globalize and, more recently, to introduce computers to speed up customs procedures and trade documentation.

The 1985 recession in Singapore led to further soul-searching as far as economic policy was concerned. A high-powered Economic Committee was established (*The Singapore Economy: New Directions*) to oversee a recovery package and in its Report, published in 1986, spelt out some new strategies. Instead of relying exclusively on Singapore as a manufacturing production base and export platform for MNCs, the goal was now to broaden the manufacturing and service base into a 'total business centre' providing conference facilities and industrial estates as self-contained business centres, to entice MNCs to use Singapore as their regional head-quarters, to shift production into higher value-added exports, including microelectronics and biotechnology, and to make Singapore a major exporter of financial and business services. Also part of this strategy was to 'grow a second wing' or encourage Singaporean firms to venture abroad in order to provide an extra source of income to the home economy from repatriated earnings to counterbalance any shortfall in export earnings.

7.6   GROWING A SECOND WING

Under the second wing policy, initiated after the 1985–86 recession, the Economic Development Board decided to 'grow its own MNCs' by nurturing a number of promising local enterprises over a ten-year period. Prominent early initiatives included an industrial park in Suchou in China, an information technology park in Bangalore, and the establishment of hotels and port facilities in Vietnam. More recent ventures are designed according to targeted industry clusters, such as electronics, precision engineering, heavy engineering and chemicals. Policy is now directed towards developing higher value-added manufacturing in areas such as marine biology, electronics, design and marketing.

Table 7.15 presents Singapore's direct investment abroad by major destination between 1981 and 1993 and the stock of Singapore's direct equity investment abroad by major destination and industry in the 1990s.

In 1981 total foreign direct investment abroad was quite small at $1.7 billion and overwhelmingly went to ASEAN countries. By 1993, however, it had increased eightfold to 13.1 billion. Most was still destined for the Asian region, but a fifth was now directed to Europe and the USA, mostly in financial services (especially investment holding companies). These flows tend to correlate with the increase in Singapore's trade with the region (see Section 7.1), but also the global rise in foreign direct investment to the Asia–Pacific in the 1990s attracted by fast growth, rising costs of production in investing countries such as Japan and NIEs, and the seemingly insa-

Table 7.15   Singapore's direct investment abroad and stock of direct equity investment abroad

	1981	1990	1993
Total investment abroad $ billions	1.7	7.8	13.1
Share %:			
ASEAN	64.3	29.4	26.4
NIEs	11.6	15.5	15.3
China	–	2.1	2.9
Europe	3.0	12.1	11.4
USA	1.9	4.9	10.5
	1990	1997	1998
Total stock abroad $ billions	13.6	57.2	52.9
Share %:			
Manufacturing	17.6	20.0	25.9
Commerce	11.0	7.2	7.5
Financial	53.6	58.7	52.3
Real estate	8.9	6.7	6.6
ASEAN	26.2	24.5	27.7
Malaysia	20.5	10.8	11.6
Indonesia	1.7	9.5	9.9
Hong Kong	16.6	10.1	9.5
China	1.8	13.9	16.8
Europe	8.0	14.2	6.4
UK	2.2	10.1	1.5
USA	5.1	4.6	5.5

Sources: Economic Survey of Singapore 1994, Table 6; *Yearbook of Statistics, Singapore*, various issues.

tiable demand for infrastructure development. Ironically this was instrumental in increasing Singapore's dependence on the region, since trade flows appear to be correlated with past investment flows, which were heavily biased towards the Asian region (Monetary Authority of Singapore, 1998a).

In terms of the stock data, the total increased markedly between 1990 and 1998, with the share going to China up from 1.8 per cent of the total to 16.8 per cent. ASEAN, together with Hong Kong and China, now accounts for over half of the total stock and financial services are the leading sector as companies became more internationalized and diversified away from manufacturing, real estate and commerce.

Once again the close links between Singapore and Malaysia are apparent from the outward foreign direct investment data. Singapore has become one of the most important investors in Malaysia, accounting for over 20 per cent of Singapore's direct equity investment abroad by 1990, falling to around 12 per cent by 1988, and second only to China in importance. Malaysia, with its natural resources and low-cost human capital, is also influencing the industrial restructuring of Singapore multinationals (Konstadakopulos, 2000). The industrial base in Johor Bahru (JB), the capital of Johor and closest Malaysian state to Singapore, is still relatively weak, especially in managerial 'know-how', so a major motive for multinational companies to locate in JB appears to be its geographical proximity to Singapore's managerial and professional expertise. This may be more important than other locational factors, such as the quality of the infrastructure and availability of cheap but skilled workers. On the other hand, a large proportion of high-tech Singapore-based firms have been expanding into Malaysia, and to JB in particular, looking for relatively well-developed infrastructure (the export processing free zone and expanding port facilities) and lower cost land and labour. This has not, however, reduced the extent of their operations in Singapore. In other words, firms on both sides of the causeway are taking advantage of complementarities between the two locations, with Singapore firms establishing manufacturing operations in JB whilst retaining their headquarters and research and development activities in Singapore.

It has not all been plain sailing, however. In May 2001 the China–Singapore–Suchou Industrial Park Development (CSSD) announced cumulative losses of US$77 million in its seven years of operation. It had been plagued with problems even though it was backed by the central Chinese government and was a high profile venture for both governments. Singapore investors include Statutory Boards, GLCs, and some foreign companies which form the Singapore-Suchou Township Development Consortium. The main problem seems to have been the diversion of foreign investment by the Chinese regional authorities to rival Suchou New District. More progress seems to have been made since the Chinese partners increased their control over the CSSID and reduced Singapore's stake from 65 per cent to 35 per cent and they might even recoup their investment if positive profits are made in the future. It has been a painful learning experience.

7.7 RESTRUCTURING THE EXTERNAL SECTOR

Although aggregate export performance has been robust since 1980 (see Chapter 8) there have certainly been significant changes in Singapore's trade structure at a more disaggregated level, as Singapore competes with the older tigers and the newly-industrializing economies in the Asian region. In this sense the shift–share and trade intensity calculations referred to above have been interpreted as indicating over-representation in Asia and some scope for diversification (Monetary Authority of Singapore, 1998a, 1998c). Globalization through regionalization in the 1990s also made Singapore vulnerable to the slowdown in Asian markets during the Asian financial crisis. In January 2000 the Singapore Trade Development Board launched its Trade 21 plan which, amongst other things, encouraged local companies 'to sprout a third wing' by locating beyond Asia. Singapore has also embarked on a series of bilateral trade negotiations extending beyond the region (see Section 7.8 below). But do these regional and sectoral changes in Singapore's competitive position justify such a new approach?

Singapore does well in aspects of international competitiveness which are directly controllable by government. Typical is the Lausanne-based International Institute for Management Development *World Competitiveness Yearbook 2001* (http://www.imd.ch/wcy/) which ranks Singapore second after the USA, with strong scores in economic performance, government efficiency, business efficiency and infrastructure. Singapore scores less highly in managerial entrepreneurship, the competency of local managers, the brain drain, new business start-ups, and the cost of living. Singapore was also well placed in the macroeconomic competitiveness rankings of the *World Economic Forum 1999* (http://www.imd.ch/wcy/), but this contrasts sharply, with its ranking of 12 in the *World Economic Forum* microeconomic competitiveness index and Singapore has lost some ground in the previous two years.

According to Cardarelli et al. (2000) the intensity of local competition is the most important single variable in the microeconomic competitiveness index, especially the quality and network of domestic suppliers and related industries, since this competition acts as a training ground for international competition. Yet this is a major weakness in Singapore. Examples cited include the lack of choice in media services and insufficient institutions in Singapore devoted to intermediating savings towards private sector entrepreneurial activities. Part of the reason for the weakness in the microeconomic environment is attributed to the high degree of government involvement in the economy through Statutory Boards and Government-Linked Companies. Although GLCs operate on a competitive basis and generate operating surpluses, they may have crowded out local private firms and this may partially explain why locally-controlled companies are smaller and less efficient than foreign-controlled companies, especially in manufacturing. There have also been recent high profile failures by GLCs to acquire large stakes in foreign companies, such as the Singapore Airlines bid for Air New Zealand and the attempted takeover of Cable and Wireless in Hong Kong by Singapore telecommunications. Estimated price-average cost margins also appear to be higher in Singapore than in Hong Kong, the OECD and the USA (Cardarelli et al., 2000).

The Singapore government is not unaware of these problems. A high level committee on Singapore's competitiveness presented its recommendations in November 1998 and outlined a vision of turning Singapore into an advanced globally-competitive knowledge-intensive economy revolving around a manufacturing and services hub and support services from which MNCs and local companies can manufacture high value-added products and provide related services to companies in the region. Targeted clusters under the Economic Development Board's 'Industry 21' blueprint (*Singapore 2000*, p. 123) launched in January 1999 include electronics, chemicals and petro-chemicals, info-communications and the media, logistics and supply chain management, healthcare and headquarters activities. As well as continuing to make Singapore an attractive base by providing generous tax concessions, industrial parks, prepared land sites and ready-made factories, special emphasis is now placed on housing and amenities for 'foreign talents'. Complementary trade policies are designed to improve market access through bilateral Preferential Trade Arrangements and facilitate trade logistics through electronic trade documentation and exhibition management.

'Hollowing out' has been subtly redefined as 'restructuring' as Singapore sheds its lower end manufacturing and moves up the ladder of value-added. A good example of this is the disk drive industry which accounted for about 27 per cent of electronics output in 1999, the latter making up about half of total manufacturing output (*Yearbook of Statistics Singapore 2001*, Table 10.4). This industry represents a classic case of successful globalization (McKendrick et al., 2000). In 1995 US firms had 80 per cent of the world market while South-east Asia had 70 per cent of the production. The US was able to compete despite its high wages due to deep technical infrastructure, world class tertiary education and a high level of research and development. Singapore did, nonetheless, develop a supporting industry infrastructure which helped the industry learn to move to volume production ensuring that it was not just a low-cost manufacturing base but a cluster of manufacturing and problem-solving expertise, which has spread to Malaysia and Thailand.

In 1999, however, the global disk drive industry came under severe pricing pressures as capacity increased and competition intensified. Seagate and Western Digital laid off workers in Singapore in 1998, and in 1999 Western Digital moved its manufacturing operations from Singapore to

Malaysia. The question is whether Singapore can continue to 'restructure' within this particular sector by raising the technical, engineering and management input and focus more on higher value-added semiconductors and telecommunications equipment.

An interesting comparison here is between Singapore and Israel, which has a sort of 'silicon valley', including Intel wafer fabrication plants, stretching out along the coastal strip between Tel Aviv and Haifa. Apart from the obvious difference in the level of political stability, Singapore and Israel share some common characteristics such as a small domestic market, an interventionist government, a location far from the USA, no natural resources, compulsory national service, a significant immigrant population and costs/wages which are not especially low. But Israel's silicon valley has, in contrast to Singapore, benefited from a sizeable pool of venture capitalists and large numbers of high technology new start-up companies. It has a large number of PhDs and engineers, a high level of investment in university research, and it boasts an environment in which it is relatively easy to raise funds for new business projects and produces a steady supply of budding entrepreneurs willing to take the risk after they complete their stint of national service.

Singapore hopes to emulate this process through a number of incentive schemes, such as the Skills Development Fund and Promising Enterprise Program, by attracting foreign talent and persuading successful Singaporean émigrés to return or at least 'network' with the mother country. To increase the supply of graduates, particularly in business, the Singapore Management University has now opened and foreign graduate schools are being set up by the University of Chicago, INSEAD, MIT and the Wharton School. The ratio of gross expenditure on research and development to GDP has also increased from 1.02 in 1991 to 1.87 in 1999 (*Economic Survey of Singapore 2000*, Table 9.3).

One must also put Singapore's international competitiveness into context. Of course one would expect some catching up here as the more mature tiger economies increasingly specialize in higher value-added manufactures and services or diversify into areas such as financial services. In this sense, the apparent loss of competitiveness by the older tigers, such as Singapore, in some areas of manufacturing might not be so important insofar as this reflects a natural process of changing comparative advantage as rising real wages and productivity lead to a restructuring away from labour-intensive industries. Ironically, Singapore's increased concentration in electronics exported to the region was a major factor in its success in the 1990s. A decline in exports to a specific market, such as the USA, also need not signify a loss of export competitiveness if at the same time aggregate exports are still buoyant and structural changes are taking place such as a diversification into chemicals exported to non-US markets, or away from disk drives to higher value-added semi-conductors and telecommunications devices.

The negative effects of the regional slowdown were also, to some extent, cushioned by substantial intra-industry flows to the region which sustained demand for intermediate imports from Singapore which were subsequently processed into goods exported outside the region where demand remained buoyant. Singapore's growing integration with its neighbours, especially Malaysia, is a natural consequence of the globalization of production and is easily concealed by conventional statistics which treat each sovereign country as a separate economic entity. What really matters as far as Singapore is concerned is not trade concentration or market diversification per se, but Singapore's sheer openness and dependence on international markets and the amount of trade Singapore does with countries or blocs with high trade volatility and significant direct and indirect trade links with Singapore.

So, rather like the Red Queen in Lewis Carroll's *Through the Looking Glass*, Singapore will have to keep running to stand still. Based on past experience, there are good grounds for optimism in view of Singapore's remarkable adaptability and resilience in the face of a changing international environment. There is no shortage of advice on how to transform the economy from 'investment-led' to 'innovation-led' growth. Harvard Business School Professor Michael Porter (*Business Times*, 6 August, 2001) has chastised Singapore for its pursuit of an activist industrial policy, heavy government involvement in the economy, and attempts to 'pick winners'. He suggested that the focus should shift much more towards services and creating the conditions for 'clusters' of activity to flourish, with stronger competition policies and more privatization of GLCs, and policies to 'create a more chaotic and heterogeneous society' which is more flexible and tolerant of different groups of people with new ideas, tastes and beliefs.

The continuity of a sound trade policy underpinned by the need to 'make Singapore useful to the world' combined with a pragmatic approach where necessary, should enable Singapore to sustain a small but high quality manufacturing base with ancillary high quality services requiring increasingly specialized inputs and customization. Whether government-based entrepreneurship and initiatives can be replaced quickly by a more competitive indigenous response remains to be seen. Certainly for the immediate future Singapore will continue to rely on foreign talent. Part of the problem stems from the low rate of technical progress as measured by total factor productivity growth and low industrial R&D compared to other industrialized countries (Bloch and Tang, 2000). The rapid growth in output in Singapore's industries has largely been due to increasing returns to scale and rapid growth of factor inputs in export-oriented foreign MNCs who do not engage in substantial R&D in Singapore.

7.8   OPEN REGIONALISM

Since the mid 1960s, the PAP has consistently advocated trade liberaliz-ation through multilateral institutions·such as GATT, its successor the WTO, and more recently at Asia-Europe Meetings (ASEM). At the same time Singapore has been a beneficiary of preferential trade arrangements extended by developed countries through the Generalized System of Preferences (GSP) and has pursued economic integration through mem-bership of regional groupings such as APEC, ASEAN, AFTA, and a 'growth triangle' with Indonesia and Malaysia.

Apart from clearing the way for China's entry into the WTO, multilat-eral initiatives appeared to have stalled by the middle of 2001. Despite calls for a new trade round by groups such as APEC, the Seattle Third Ministerial Conference of the WTO in November 1999 failed to agree on a new round of negotiations. Meanwhile at the 12 Ministerial and eight Leaders' Meeting in November 2000 in Brunei, APEC agreed some bilat-eral free trade deals begun in 1999 as building blocks for multilateral nego-tiations, but little progress has been made towards its ambitious goal of a free trade area for developed countries by 2010 and developing countries by 2020. It was about this time that Singapore began to step up its bilateral free trade initiatives with other countries and trading blocs. A further moti-vation was frustration over slow progress in AFTA.

From its inception in 1967 under the Bangkok Declaration, ASEAN has largely been a political organization established essentially to contain the rise of communism in South-east Asia. Its founding members (Indonesia, Malaysia, Singapore, Philippines and Thailand) were joined by Brunei in 1984, and more recently by Vietnam, Cambodia, Myanmar and Laos. It has undoubtedly been successful in containing intra-ASEAN conflict and in providing a forum for the discussion of regional matters, including dis-putes over territorial claims in the south China sea, but as a political force it has exerted little influence on the world stage given its heterogeneous character and the decline of the communist threat. The Asian financial crisis has further reduced its political consensus.

It is widely accepted that apart from providing some common policies on food, energy and tourism, ASEAN achieved little in terms of tangible eco-nomic benefits for its members in the first two decades of its existence (Wong, 1988; Yeung et al., 1999). Pomfret (1996) has described ASEAN as an 'enigma' in Asia by virtue of its longevity as a developing country trading bloc, but 'perpetually at the crossroads' in the sense that it fails to deliver and periodically something always needs to be done to revitalize the integration process. Intra-bloc trade between the original six members of ASEAN in 1999 was still only 21.7 per cent of their total trade, falling to 18.6 per cent if Singapore is excluded (calculated from the *Direction of Trade Statistics 2000*). Much of the gains would probably have been achieved without coordinated initiatives through ASEAN from unilateral trade liberalization after the mid 1980s (Singapore much earlier), driven by private enterprise, inward foreign direct investment and the mutual benefits from each country having 'growing neighbours'.

The underlying weakness of ASEAN from its inception was its hetero-geneous membership. While Singapore espoused export-oriented free trade policies, the other members chose import-substituting industrialization. In terms of economic structure, although all were developing countries seeking labour-intensive industrialization, there were significant structural differences between the resource-less Singapore, resource-rich Malaysia, the importance of agriculture in Thailand and the Philippines, and the oil-dominated Brunei. The gap between the more industrialized members of ASEAN, such as Malaysia and Singapore, and the emerging economies of Laos, Cambodia and Vietnam has only accentuated these differences in recent years. There is little evidence that the gap in income per capita among ASEAN countries has been narrowing (Park, 2000). Structural diversity has meant less scope for trade creation in the sense of shifting resources from inefficient to efficient producers within the bloc. Attempts to orchestrate this collectively were doomed to fail as governments resisted closing down their own factories. On the other hand, policies which were trade diverting by restricting lower cost competition from outside to protect infant industries within ASEAN (except Singapore) were politically feasible but were costly in the longer run by virtue of their inefficiency and came under increasing threat from advocates of trade liberalization.

Attempts to lower tariff rates collectively through preferential trading arrangements after 1977 were disappointing and hampered by the volun-tary listing of products for preferential treatment, and a cumbersome case-by-case approach. Not surprisingly, countries were reluctant to include items which afforded protection to domestic producers but were happy to include items which offered no threat. Using a seven-digit level classification, by 1981 9000 items had been submitted but this constituted less than 2 per cent of intra-bloc trade. Attempts to promote industrial cooperation after 1976 also largely failed, a classic example being Malaysia's decision to develop its own integrated automobile industry (Pomfret, 1996, p. 373).

Beginning in 1991, ASEAN members made a concerted effort to speed up the process of tariff reduction by committing themselves to an ASEAN free trade area (AFTA). There was no obligation for individual members to reduce protection against outsiders but only a common effective preferential tariff structure (CEPT). The goal was to reduce tariffs on manufactured goods and processed agricultural goods to between zero and 5 per cent by 2008, while some product categories were 'fast tracked' to reduce the implementation time to 2005. At the 1998 Hanoi Summit the end date was again brought forward to 2002 for the original six members to lower all import duties to between zero and 5 per cent and at the November 1999 Summit the target date of 2010 was set for all import duties to be eliminated, and the schedule for the new members (Cambodia, Laos, Myanmar and Vietnam) was reset from 2018 to 2015.

The AFTA goals were much more credible than earlier preferential tariff arrangements in ASEAN since there was evidence of political will at the highest level and the procedures were much more specific than in the past. There was a clear timetable and drawn out negotiations over inclusions were replaced by a list of exclusions. Forecasts of the potential gains from the tariff reductions were not especially optimistic, but member countries were growing fast and there was a common objective to make the region as a whole attractive to external foreign direct investment through initiatives such as the ASEAN Investment Area.

The Asian financial crisis seriously undermined both the political consensus in ASEAN and the shared benefits of economic growth. Since the crisis a two-track ASEAN has emerged amongst the original six with Indonesia, Thailand and the Philippines performing much less well than Malaysia and Singapore. By 2001 83 per cent of all tariff lines were covered by AFTA and average tariff rates were down to 4.59 per cent by 2000 (*Singapore 2000*, p. 131), but it still remains to be seen whether member countries, now performing less well economically, will open up their markets to the final consumer goods of their fellow AFTA members. The underlying problem is the same as before: governments are reluctant to lower protection on items which harm vested interests. An ominous sign in November 2000 was a protocol signed by ASEAN Economic Ministers setting up a temporary exclusion list for those countries facing economic difficulties, though they did reaffirm their commitment to realize AFTA by 2002. Malaysia has since been granted a reprieve until 2005 for its motor industry, which sets an alarming precedent for an important industry in ASEAN, and in March 2001 Indonesia postponed the lowering of import duties.

More successful, as far as Singapore is concerned, has been the establishment of an industrial park on the nearby Indonesian island of Batam which forms part of a 'growth triangle' linking Singapore, the State of

Johor in Malaysia and the Riau Islands in Indonesia. The term 'growth tri-angle' was first mooted by the then Deputy Prime Minister of Singapore, Goh Chok Tong in 1989 and agreements were signed in 1990 and 1991. Although there has been a long history of trade and tourism links between Singapore, Malaysia and the Riau, development had been severely ham-pered by lack of suitable infrastructure in Riau and political obstacles. The idea is to pool economic resources in a complementary fashion to stimulate growth. On Batam, for example, cheap Indonesian land and labour are combined with Singaporean infrastructure and management and financial services to produce labour-intensive manufactured goods. Activity has now been extended to other parts of the Riau, including Bintan, where light industries and tourism are promoted, and there is significant activity in shipyard and related activities and the petroleum industry dotted around the islands, such as Karimun. As at the end of 1998, the total number of Singapore projects in Riau was 66 amounting to some $3.2 billion, with 22 ($1.6 billion) presently under development. Notwithstanding current poli-tical uncertainties in Indonesia, the scale of activity in Riau looks set to increase as the Indonesian government has agreed to give Singapore access to provinces which will become more autonomous in the future, including Batam and the Rempang and Galang islands.

The Johor contribution to the Riau growth triangle is actually very small, so it is really a Singapore–Riau initiative, but Singapore and Johor have become much more integrated in recent years as Singapore firms relocate across the causeway to cut production costs, and both Malaysian and foreign (especially Japanese) companies locate in Johor motivated in part by the proximity of complementary services and managerial expertise in Singapore. Unlike the Singapore–Riau link, however, the role of govern-ment in initiating Singapore–Johor development has probably been minimal and 'demand following'. More important were liberalization reforms introduced in Malaysia from the mid 1980s onwards, and rational-ization of production by private enterprise. If anything, political and eco-nomic rivalries between Malaysia and Singapore have delayed integration. Malaysia has been determined to re-route Malaysian export traffic away from the super-efficient Port of Singapore to its own ports. The completion of the north–south highway linking Singapore to Northern Malaysia seemed to take an interminable length of time, and there are still unneces-sary impediments to the flow of goods and services across the causeways, including tedious customs and immigration procedures, and absurdly high toll charges on the Malaysian side of the second causeway link, which ensures that very little traffic has been diverted from the more congested Woodlands causeway. Like Siamese twins joined at the causeway(s), Malaysia and Singapore's destiny seems inextricably bound together. The

Sultan of Johor should immediately secede from Malaysia and join Singapore in a common market and monetary union!

In November 2000, at the end of the APEC Summit in Brunei, a surprise announcement was made that Singapore and the USA were to start negotiations on a bilateral free trade agreement modelled on that between the US and Jordan, which was to be concluded quickly. This was the first US–Asian or Asian–US bilateral initiative. Singapore had now emerged as the most important advocate of American 'bilateralism' in the region.

The USA had been converted to bilateralism, or the bilateral negotiation of preferential trading agreements, in 1982 after it had failed to get multilateral talks started in Geneva. The justification was that such agreements could form 'building blocks' to set standards to be carried over into multilateral negotiations or extended to other members, and in the meantime would keep the momentum for free trade going by providing a positive example of what could be done, or a means of exerting leverage on other countries or blocs to force them to the negotiating table. Bhagwati and Panagariya (1997) have labelled this 'second regionalism' as compared to the 'first regionalism' epitomized by blocs such as the European Economic Community (now the European Union). An example of the 'new regionalism' was the US–Canada Free Trade Agreement in 1989, then extended to Mexico under the North American Free Trade Agreement (NAFTA) in 1994. Is it a sensible trade strategy for Singapore?

As far as Singapore is concerned, the adoption of the second regionalism was partly motivated by frustration with the slow progress with AFTA and a desire to use such agreements as a catalyst to speed up trade liberalization in ASEAN: 'Those who can run faster should run faster. They should not be restrained by those who do not want to run at all' (Goh Chok Tong, quoted in the *The Business Times*, 23 April, 2001).

A key rationale behind AFTA was to attract foreign direct investment from outside the region, but since the Asian financial crisis, and with the exception of Singapore, more popular destinations now appear to be China and NAFTA. Even Japanese foreign direct investment to the region seems to be waning. There was also the realization that ASEAN had become less important and cohesive as a political force. Singapore's national interests now look rather different from its ASEAN partners. Singapore emerged relatively strong from the Asian financial crisis, is committed even more than ever to the cause of free trade, financial liberalization, and globalization, and is seeking to distance itself from the anti-western rhetoric of some of its neighbours. Indeed, the Singapore–US negotiations might be construed as part of a more general strategy to make international friends, a policy which does no harm at all to the chances of cash-rich GLCs making strategic investments in western countries such as Australia and New Zealand!

Another factor is the increasingly fluid nature of APEC. With so many members the 1994 Bogor goal to achieve free trade for developed countries by 2010 and developing countries by 2020 looks rather ambitious. Those members, such as Singapore, Australia and New Zealand, who want to move a little faster might well be looking, in the meantime, to make bilateral arrangements with similar minded countries such as the USA.

The official position as far as Singapore is concerned is based on the US philosophy that bilateral deals are a stepping stone to multilateral deals and a means to put pressure on less enthusiastic free traders without violating any pre-existing arrangements, such as AFTA. The negotiations with the USA are still ongoing as this book goes to print and there has been some pressure from American businesses and interest groups to remove existing barriers, notably in Singapore's service sector. Other obstacles include Singapore's high excise taxes on distilled spirits and wine, motor vehicles and gasoline, restrictions on the use of satellite receivers and on broadcasting for the local market and remaining discrimination in favour of domestic banks in retail services, such as the use and location of automatic teller machines.

To date little has been done to evaluate the economic costs and benefits of the Singapore–US proposal but Ramkishan et al. (2001) believe that the benefits would outweigh the costs given the importance of the US in Singapore's trade (see Table 7.3 above). Most of Singapore's exports to the USA already enter tariff free but there may be some gains in areas such as textiles and in transshipments via the Port of Singapore. Less obvious is that Singapore may gain some 'insurance' against any future rise in US protectionism and anti-dumping activities and it may enable Singapore to attract and retain US 'silicon valley' firms with large intra-firm trade from switching to other locations such as Hong Kong and China. These benefits would have to be offset against any costs from opening up the services and banking sectors too fast to US competition and the possibility of a political backlash in the US against a Singapore trade surplus, as with Japan in the 1980s.

Singapore is pressing ahead with other bilateral agreements. In August 2000 a free trade agreement was signed with New Zealand. All tariffs are abolished on goods and services, most of Singapore's main exports to New Zealand will qualify for preferential market access, and there will be common rules on investment and procurement, including access to government tenders above a threshold amount. Currently, negotiations are taking place with Japan, Australia and Mexico. The Mexican agreement, if it materializes, would be the first Asian–Latin American deal and a possible gateway into Latin America as a whole and, if an agreement can be reached with Japan, the benefits of preferential access to such a notoriously closed market where Singapore presently has a trade deficit would be obvious.

Singapore's bilateral strategy has not been above criticism from its ASEAN partners. Malaysia, in particular, has been vocal in expressing concern that deals with New Zealand and Australia might bring industrialized countries into AFTA through the backdoor as 'Trojan Horses' (*Business Times*, 7 August, 2001). It is certainly possible that cheap automotive parts might be imported into Singapore, processed up to the 40 per cent AFTA limit, before being exported legitimately to AFTA countries where duties on non-AFTA members are much higher. But Singapore is already a free port so most of the backdoor problem has existed for a long time, and it is not obvious that processing costs in Singapore are low enough to make this worthwhile. The Singapore authorities also correctly argue that such bilateral deals do not violate its commitments to AFTA, since any imports into Singapore subsequently exported to member countries will still have to pass the same local content rules as in the past. Singapore is simply running faster towards liberalization than its fellow members. Ironically it is the Americans who are concerned that Singapore's position as a transshipment hub may mean the redirection of textiles and dairy produce from countries such as Thailand, Indonesia and New Zealand, entering the USA at zero or reduced tariffs through Singapore.

Opponents of bilateralism at a general level, such as Mike Moore, the Secretary General of the WTO, and the prominent trade economist Jagdish Bhagwati (see Bhagwati and Panagariya, 1997), argue that such agreements have the effect of delaying the launch of a new round of multilateral talks and smack of self-interest and a return to the begger-thy-neighbour competitive protectionism of the 1930s to save domestic jobs and gain market access at the expense of other countries. Or, at the very least, such deals weaken the solidarity of groups such as ASEAN. The proliferation of bilateral deals also generates a 'spaghetti bowl' maize of rules of origin which differ by sector and country for each bilateral arrangement. This makes it costly to police and complicated for investors.

Moreover, such deals are inherently discriminatory and 'second best' compared to non-preferential trade liberalization. They are sold as free trade agreements, but in fact they are preferential trade agreements (PTAs) which violate the GATT principle of 'most favoured nation' under which no nation can be treated less favourably than the most favoured nation. But an exception can be made if it can be shown (Article 24 of GATT) that they cover all trade between the two countries, they are a step towards free trade within a reasonable period of time, and there are no barriers to third parties greater than before. Bhagwati also believes that the trade-diverting effects of PTAs, whereby imports are diverted from efficient outsider countries to a less efficient member, has been underestimated in the past and such deals give the wrong incentive structure to its members. Firms who are profiting from preferential market access will not want to encourage new members, and will lobby their governments to offset any fall in their home market share arising from the PTAs by increasing barriers against outsiders. Put bluntly, Singapore may export more to the USA by undercutting lower cost Malaysian goods which still have to pay US duties, and US importers who have lost home market share to Singapore firms may retaliate by lobbying their government to put further anti-dumping duties on Malaysian imports to restore their domestic market share.

The picture has been further complicated by the decision at the ASEAN Summit in Brunei in November 2001 to explore the possibility of an ASEAN–China free trade area, ostensibly 'to generate internal dynamism' within ASEAN and reduce dependence on the US economy following the September 11 terrorist bombings. The positions of Korea and Japan now look ambiguous. They have given tacit support to the idea and have not ruled out joining an ASEAN + 3 free trade area in the future, but Japan reacted coolly to the deal. Whether the agreement will materialize into substantive action or remain essentially a window-dressing exercise designed to demonstrate political solidarity in the face of an increasingly uncertain world environment remains to be seen.

8. International finance and growth

Between 1965 and the mid 1980s Singapore achieved rapid export-led growth and industrialization without encountering any significant balance of payments problems. The current account was in persistent deficit over this period but was more than covered by a high level of national savings and a continuous inflow of productive export-oriented foreign direct investment. Exchange rate policy has also been remarkably successful in the last two decades in delivering fast growth, low and stable price inflation, and a strong external position without the need for a deliberate weakening of the currency. At the same time, despite a small domestic resource base, Singapore has become a major foreign exchange and international banking centre and the location for the Asian Dollar Market (ADM), one of the largest offshore money markets in the world.

Yet Singapore still exhibits some of the features of an underdeveloped economy insofar as capital markets are relatively immature in terms of fixed income assets, equities and the fund management industry, and the impotence of conventional monetary and fiscal policy in such an open economy has limited the options available to the government to implement macro-stabilization policies. These features, together with the characteristics discussed in the previous chapter of extreme openness to trade and factor flows, 'dependence' on foreign resources, and vulnerability to external shocks, has provided the rationale for a development strategy based on high levels of forced saving through the CPF, high levels of centrally directed investment, a persistent build-up of official foreign exchange reserves and a strongly 'dirigiste' government in all sectors of the economy.

Since 1985, however, it has become harder to justify this development strategy, having already achieved the essential development infrastructure and given the opportunity costs in terms of private consumption and the over-centralization of savings and investment decisions. There have been large surpluses in the balance of payments, both on the current account and the capital account, and a relentless accumulation of reserve asserts. One would expect a higher than average level of reserves in view of Singapore's extreme openness to international trade and capital flows, the potential risk of speculative attacks on the currency, and the desire to enhance Singapore's credibility as an international financial centre. But the reserves are excessive as a 'war chest' against unforeseen contingencies or a doomsday scenario.

Similarly, the monetary authorities have been adamant that they will allow only a gradual internationalization of the dollar, even if this impedes the development of Singapore as a premier international financial centre with a wide range of activities. The tradition of looking to the government for initiatives, combined with a reputation for a tight regulatory framework and generally conservative approach, compared with other financial centres such as Hong Kong, has also led to complaints that the regulatory mechanism has complicated business practices and constrained private sector financial innovation and market development.

In this chapter we look at the structure of Singapore's balance of payments and how it has changed over time, the composition of the official foreign exchange reserves and their growth since 1960, and the argument that these reserves are excessively high by international standards. We also trace the evolution of exchange rate policy from the 'strong dollar' policy adopted in 1981 to the wider exchange rate band and more flexible management introduced in response to the Asian financial crisis. Related to this is the Singapore 'export puzzle' that despite episodes of substantial nominal and real appreciation of the Singapore dollar against most major currencies since the early 1970s, and a widely held perception that the relative costs of doing business in Singapore have increased over time, aggregate export performance has been very robust. We also examine Singapore's progress as an international financial centre, the controversial policy of not encouraging the internationalization of the Singapore dollar, and proposals which have been put forward, partly in response to the Asian financial crisis, to foster closer monetary union in Asia.

8.1   THE BALANCE OF PAYMENTS

Tables 8.1–8.3 highlight Singapore's balance of payments between 1960 and 2000. Table 8.1 shows the most important features on an annual average basis over key periods to take a long perspective. Tables 8.2 and 8.3 look more carefully at the 1990s and the years before and after the Asian financial crisis of 1997–98. Items marked as 'net' use a single entry for both inflows and outflows for convenience and the structure of the tables is based on a revised format (see Table 8.1) closer to the standard set by the International Monetary Fund than in the past, which makes interpretation of the numbers much easier than before (see Peebles and Wilson, 1996, pp. 171–5). Note, however, that the accounts are often subject to large revisions, particularly the financial account, and the net errors and omissions entry can be very large, averaging 10 per cent of GNP in the 1960s and 7.7 per cent in the 1970s. After 1986 it fell to less than 1 per cent but can still

Table 8.1   Trends in the balance of payments, 1960–2000

	Annual average $ billion					
	1960–69	1970–79	1980–85	1986–89	1990–96	1997–2000
Goods balance	−0.80	−4.57	−9.62	−4.01	−1.16	16.24
% GNP	−24.5	−36.6	−28.6	−8.3	−1.2	10.5
Services balance	0.52	3.19	8.35	6.11	12.77	9.48
% GNP	17.8	24.9	24.1	14.5	13.3	6.2
Goods and services (net)	−0.28	−1.38	−1.27	2.10	11.61	25.72
% GNP	−6.7	−11.7	−4.6	6.3	11.9	16.9
Income balance	0.06	−0.08	−0.22	0.92	1.96	10.02
% GNP	1.8	−0.6	−0.6	1.9	2.0	6.5
Current transfers (net)	−0.04	−0.06	−0.38	−0.55	−1.20	−1.97
% GNP	−1.2	−0.4	−1.1	−1.1	−1.2	−1.3
Current account	−0.26	−1.52	−1.87	2.47	12.37	33.77
% GNP	−8.0	−12.2	−5.6	5.1	12.7	21.9
Capital and financial account	0.10	1.49	3.82	0.73	−2.21	−26.16
% GNP	3.1	11.9	11.4	1.5	−2.3	−17.0
Net errors and omissions	0.34	0.96	0.43	−0.14	−0.28	1.39
% GNP	10.4	7.7	1.3	−0.3	−0.3	0.9
Overall balance	0.18	0.93	2.38	3.06	9.88	9.00
% GNP	5.5	7.4	7.1	6.3	10.1	5.8
Official reserves (net)	−0.18	−0.93	−2.38	−3.06	−9.88	−9.00

Notes: This table follows the latest (revised) format for the Singapore balance of payments. The figures prior to 1990 for the income balance refer to investment income and the capital and financial account was previously the capital account. The trade balance is now the goods balance and unrequited transfers are renamed current transfers.

Sources: Economic and Social Statistics, Singapore 1960–82, Table 4.10; *Yearbook of Statistics Singapore*, various issues.

be quite high in particular years, as in 1990 (−4.2 per cent) and 1998 (5.4 per cent).

From the mid 1980s the structure of the Singapore balance of payments changed dramatically (Table 8.1). Between 1960 and 1984 there were persistent current account deficits (reaching 12 per cent of GNP on average in the 1970s) with the surplus in services insufficient to offset the large negative goods balance. Current transfers were negative and the income balance was usually an outflow. On the other hand, the combined capital and financial account (CFA) was positive, largely due to inflows of foreign direct investment, generating an overall surplus and a steady accumulation of foreign exchange reserves. The size of the net errors and omissions term, however, means that the overall balance was often positive only when this

Table 8.2   The balance of payments, 1990–2000

	$ billion					
	1990	1996	1997	1998	1999	2000
Current account	5.66	18.08	26.62	34.03	36.87	37.58
% GNP	8.3	13.6	18.1	23.3	24.0	22.1
Goods balance	−2.96	3.14	1.67	24.74	18.91	19.66
% GNP	−4.3	2.4	1.1	16.9	12.3	11.6
Services balance	7.56	14.42	17.09	2.55	8.57	9.71
% GNP	11.1	10.8	11.6	1.7	5.6	5.7
Income balance	1.82	2.03	9.60	8.58	11.36	10.55
% GNP	2.7	1.5	6.5	5.9	7.4	6.2
Current transfers (net)	−0.76	−1.51	−1.74	−1.84	−1.97	−2.34
% GNP	−1.1	−1.1	−1.2	−1.3	−1.3	−1.4
Capital and financial account	7.12	−7.00	−16.55	−36.88	−31.31	−19.93
% GNP	10.4	−5.2	−11.2	−25.3	−20.4	−11.7
Direct investment (net)	6.42	5.00	5.36	9.64	5.40	3.65
% GNP	9.4	3.7	3.6	6.6	3.5	2.1
Portfolio investment (net)	−1.88	−16.48	−19.31	−11.73	−12.01	−23.89
% GNP	−2.8	−12.4	−13.1	−8.0	−7.8	−14.1
Other investment (net)	2.62	4.68	−2.34	−34.42	−24.38	0.59
% GNP	3.8	3.5	−1.6	−23.6	−15.9	0.3
Net errors and omissions	−2.87	−0.67	1.79	7.83	1.76	−5.81
% GNP	−4.2	−0.5	1.2	5.4	1.1	−3.4
Overall balance	9.91	10.41	11.86	4.98	7.32	11.84
% GNP	14.5	7.8	8.1	3.4	4.8	7.0
Official reserves (net)	−9.91	−10.41	−11.86	−4.98	−7.32	−11.84

Source: Economic Survey of Singapore 1998, 2000.

Table 8.3   The current account, 1997–2000

	1997	1998	1999	2000
Growth rate of real GDP %	8.5	0.1	5.9	9.9
Growth rate of real exports %	11.6	−0.3	5.4	16.8
Growth rate of real imports %	10.2	−12.9	9.5	14.8
Current account $ million	26 618	34 031	36 866	37 576
Current account balance % GNP	18.1	23.3	24.0	22.1

Sources: Economic Survey of Singapore 2000, TRENDS database, Singstat at http://www.singstat.gov.sg/FACT/HIST/trade1.html

item is added, making it difficult to unravel the precise relationship between the current account deficit and the overall surplus.

From 1985 onwards the balance of payments is characterized by current account surpluses (Table A.2) with the negative goods balance more than offset by the surplus on services. The trade balance actually became positive in the 1990s, rising to 12 per cent or more of GNP between 1998 and 2000 (Table 8.2). Current transfers remain negative but small as a percentage of GNP and the income balance turned positive as income from past investment abroad of the official foreign exchange reserves and public sector surpluses exceeded the repatriation of profits by foreign companies. This is why GNP exceeded GDP from 1989 onwards. On the other hand, the CFA was now negative in the 1990s reaching over 20 per cent of GNP in 1998 and 1999 (Table 8.2) due to firms investing abroad under the 'second wing' policy and further official investment abroad. Since the current account surplus is more than sufficient to offset this capital outflow the result is substantial overall surpluses (in excess of 10 per cent of GNP, 1990–96), and a continuing accumulation of reserves, averaging over $9 billion per year between 1990 and 2000 (Table 8.1).

Singapore emerged from the Asian financial crisis relatively well compared to other countries in the region in terms of growth, inflation and the balance of payments. The only important negative impact was on the financial sector with falling stock prices, property prices and asset wealth as the currency lost value and incomes fell (Tyabji, 1998). Export growth was negative in 1998 (Table 8.3) but had resumed its 1997 growth rate by 2000. At the height of the crisis in 1988, Singapore's overall balance of payments surplus fell to its lowest level of the 1990s (Table 8.2) but this was almost entirely due to a sharp outflow of 'other investment' or short-term capital, mostly bank related. The large net errors and omissions entry suggests caution, but by 2000 the surplus had returned to its 1997 level (Table 8.2). Taking the period as a whole from 1997 to 2000 as a percentage of GNP (Table 8.1) the Singapore balance of payments looks extraordinary strong. The average goods surplus (11 per cent) and net inflow on income account (6.5 per cent) ensured a hefty current account surplus (22 per cent) and an overall surplus averaging 6 per cent of GNP.

There are a number of reasons why Singapore escaped relatively unscathed from the Asian financial crisis. To begin with, the economy and balance of payments were 'fundamentally' strong. Capital inflows were dominated by productive investment in the form of foreign direct investment, which translated ultimately into exports rather than into domestic consumption. Fiscal conservatism also dampened liquidity from the inflow and pre-emptive regulations had been introduced in May 1996 to cool the property market ahead of the boom.

Singapore had also coped with the influx of foreign capital in the 1990s much better than its neighbours (Kwan et al., 1998). Large capital inflows through an open capital market make it very difficult for governments to maintain control over domestic monetary policy, as the extra liquidity spills into the banking system, and at the same time keep the home currency stable against foreign currencies. The inflow tends to appreciate the domestic currency and can cause a sharp loss of external competitiveness, unless the central bank acts to 'sterilize' the inflow by, for example, buying foreign assets to depreciate the local currency and simultaneously selling domestic assets to offset the impact of the capital inflow on the domestic money supply. Sterilized intervention in the foreign exchange market is used regularly by central banks, but is difficult to manage successfully if the banking and financial system is underdeveloped, as countries like Thailand found out to their cost. Singapore's early financial liberalization, absence of capital controls, and strong integration with international financial markets, with domestic interest rates set largely in international markets, ruled out the use of sterilized intervention to cope with capital inflows, and indeed any domestic monetary policy at all. Monetary policy effectively became a by-product of the policy to target the Singapore dollar exchange rate against a basket of currencies to achieve low and stable inflation. Unlike countries such as Thailand and Malaysia, Singapore did not fall into the trap of managing the currency too tightly against the US$ to maintain export competitiveness in the US market, but was prepared to allow the local currency to appreciate in the face of capital inflows, especially if this kept down import prices. The fact that Singapore had no foreign debt, the domestic banks did not build up large liabilities in foreign currency (interest rates were generally lower in Singapore) and the presence of restrictions on the lending of the dollar by domestic banks to foreigners also reduced the scope for a speculative attack. Does Singapore have a problem with its balance of payments?

Countries which grow fast and undergo a period of rapid economic development often find that excess demand for goods and services in an open economy tends to spill over into inflationary pressures at home, and deficits occur in the current account balance of payments as imports are sucked in faster than exports can be produced. Since developing countries have, until recently, tended to prefer fixed rather than flexible exchange rate systems, these deficits often resulted in a fall in foreign exchange reserves to critical levels and sharp cuts in government spending or a currency devaluation to 'cure' the underlying imbalances in the current account.

However, the mere fact that a sizeable and persistent current account deficit is observed need not imply that there is a 'problem' in the balance of payments, and indeed it may actually be a necessary and efficient concomitant of the development process itself. To begin with, if the deficit is a direct reflection of the excess of private investment over savings rather than a public sector excess of spending over revenue, then the deficit might be interpreted as a benign consequence of optimizing behaviour by the private sector. Secondly, from a trade perspective, much depends on what happens to the excess of imports over exports. If the imports are largely capital goods and intermediate inputs destined for final production and exports in the longer run, as opposed to private consumption, then the deficit may be justified as a necessary means to that end. Finally, if the current account deficit is temporary and financed by a fall in official foreign exchange reserves, or is persistent but matched by a net capital inflow which is long term in nature, such as foreign direct investment or portfolio debt with a long maturity date, then there need be little concern. If, on the other hand, the deficit is persistent and can only be financed by attracting short-term capital inflows, then this leaves the economy vulnerable to a financial crisis if there are no effective controls on capital outflows. This is one of the risks a country takes when it integrates its domestic financial markets with international financial markets.

Multilateral organizations estimated Singapore's external debt to GNP ratio at around 297 per cent in 1998, well above the Singapore Department of Statistics' own estimate of 10 per cent (*The Business Times*, 1 February, 2000), and at face value this looks unsustainable and suggests a high risk of a financial crisis. Since Singapore has never been a recipient of foreign aid, and much of the inflow of foreign capital is in the form of productive foreign direct investment, this looks puzzling. The Singapore view is that the international numbers exaggerate Singapore's vulnerability and do not take into account its unique role as an international hub and host for global funds. Foreign companies account for most of the debt and choose to raise capital from abroad. MNCs, for instance, often rely for their financing on loans and trade credits with their parent companies. If, therefore, interbank loans, non-resident bank holdings and secondary debt, such as trade credits, are omitted, the magnitude of Singapore's financial liabilities are much smaller and sustainable.

Seen in this light, Singapore's persistent current account deficit between 1965 and the mid 1980s was entirely sustainable (Monetary Authority of Singapore, 1997) and a natural consequence of rapid growth and development. The deficit largely reflected imports of long-term capital and intermediate goods rather than consumer goods as foreign investment-led industrialization transformed Singapore from an entrepot exporter to a manufacturing and high income service economy, and was balanced to some extent by the surplus in services, especially in transportation. The current account deficit was easily financed by the surplus on the CFA so the overall balance and reserve accumulation were positive. Short-term capital flows were probably less volatile than in more recent years, making it easier to handle during Singapore's critical development phase than for later developers in the region such as Malaysia and Thailand.

Thus even with three decades of fast growth and the absence of capital controls, there were few signs of a spillover into domestic inflation, and little need to constrain domestic spending. Indeed, the absence of frequent speculative attacks on the currency suggests that foreign exchange market participants regarded the Singapore balance of payments as 'fundamentally' sound. Also the opportunities for speculation were reduced by the determination not to internationalize the dollar too fast (see Section 8.6).

Between 1985 and 2000 the current account deficit switched to a surplus and the savings–investment resource balance became positive as the ratio of investment to GNP fell while the savings ratio increased (Table A.2). The trade deficit was easily offset by a surplus in services and income flows (largely official), resulting in a strong current account surplus now 'financed' by a CFA outflow and the investment of surplus savings in a mixture of foreign assets, mostly through official agencies or in 'second wing' initiatives.

From the trade and financing point of view, therefore, it is difficult to perceive Singapore's balance of payments as constituting a 'problem' at any time since the mid 1960s, but from the resource allocation perspective the situation is more controversial and needs to be seen within the wider context of Singapore's development strategy and the 'sacrifice' of private consumption through the CPF forced savings mechanism. It is legitimate to ask whether there was excess savings and investment over this critical development period. Indeed, savings increased over trend and government budgets were usually in surplus (except during the recession of the mid 1980s). During the first period when the current account was in deficit, investment exceeded savings (Table A.2), especially during the period of rapid construction of residential public housing during the late 1960s, and the building of manufacturing plant in the 1970s.

Huff (1995, p. 754) has also emphasized the implicit subsidization of foreign businesses who benefited from the ready-made factory sites, technical education and training, and education in English, and because government injections were strongly complementary to the private sector there was a degree of 'crowding-in' of private investment. The negative counterpart to this, however, was that the private sector investment crowded in was largely foreign and reinforced Singapore's longer-run dependence on foreigners.

One way to justify such resource mobilization (Sandilands, 1992) would be to see it as part of a successful non-inflationary development strategy geared towards specific normative goals, including the spread of home ownership and sufficient reserves to ensure external security. In effect, forced savings through the CPF mechanism were used to finance development infrastructure and public goods (port, airport, telecommunications and roads) whilst at the same time some of these savings were converted into a portfolio of foreign assets at the MAS and GIC to generate a diversified source of income from abroad. Singapore was thus able to finance development without recourse to deficit financing, foreign commercial debt, or foreign aid, whilst simultaneously achieving export-led growth based upon an efficient inflow of foreign direct investment.

This justification for the use of the nation's resources is, however, less plausible after the mid 1980s when the primary social infrastructure had been assembled after two decades of rapid growth and industrialization. There were now substantial surpluses on the current account balance of payments and rising foreign exchange reserves, while the primary responsibility for investing these reserves continued to be government agencies. The balance of payments surplus thus becomes entwined with the debate over the size and composition of the reserves, their returns over time, and whether it should continue to be the government's responsibility for investing them in a portfolio of domestic and foreign assets (see Section 8.4 below). The pressure on the dollar to appreciate on trends from the balance of payments surplus and reserve accumulation also had implications for export competitiveness by the late 1980s, although whether this mattered or not is still unclear and will be considered in the next section.

8.2 EXCHANGE RATES AND EXCHANGE RATE POLICY

In June 1973 Singapore moved to a floating exchange rate regime and in September 1975 the MAS began to actively manage the dollar in relation to an undisclosed basket of the currencies of its major trading partners. This was motivated, in part, by the desire to stop an appreciation from negatively impacting on export competitiveness. In the early part of the 1970s when inflation was high and the global economy was moving into recession, monetary policy was primarily directed towards containing inflation without sacrificing growth. In the second half of the 1970s, when growth in Singapore was moderate and inflation low by world standards, policy shifted towards re-injecting liquidity into the banking system. Over time the MAS began to rely more on foreign exchange market operations rather than the usual tools of monetary policy. The break-up of the interest rate cartel in 1975 and abolition of exchange controls by 1978 stimulated, to some degree, by the vision of making Singapore a major international financial centre, also speeded up this process. In 1981 monetary policy became almost exclusively allied to a policy of managed floating and a strong dollar policy to neutralize the effects of imported inflation and promote sustained non-inflationary growth.

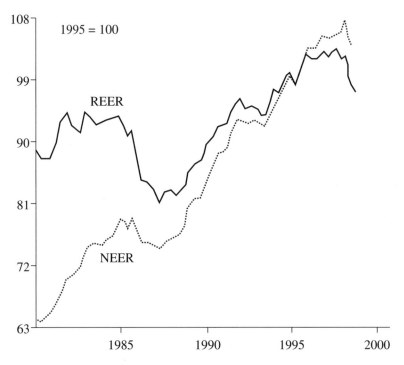

Notes: For definitions of *NEER* and *REER*, see Table 8.4.

Source: Abeysinghe and Wilson (2002).

Figure 8.1   Nominal and real effective exchange rates, 1980–99

Figure 8.1 plots the nominal effective exchange rate (NEER) and real effective exchange rate (REER) for Singapore since 1980, and Table 8.4 presents some statistics describing the behaviour of key trade and exchange rate variables.

What the data suggest are substantial periods of both nominal and real exchange rate appreciation since 1980, with a lull in the mid 1980s followed by a sustained rise in both the NEER and REER up to the Asian financial crisis of 1997. Periods of rapid appreciation tend to coincide with rapid

Table 8.4   Exchange rates and trade for Singapore, 1980–98

	1980–98	1980–89	1990–98	1986–95
Cumulative appreciation				
NEER	47	23	24	25
REER	9	−3	12	10
Annual average change (%)				
Real exports	7	8	6	12
Correlation coefficient with REER				
Real exports	0.73	−0.58	0.89	0.85
Real trade balance	0.20	−0.52	0.44	−0.16

Notes: NEER is a trade-weighted average of the exchange rates of Singapore's major trading partners. REER is the real effective exchange rate which converts the nominal exchange rates into real terms using consumer price indexes. Real exports and imports are total exports or imports in US$ converted at the market exchange rate into Singapore dollars and deflated by the consumer price index. The real trade balance is the difference between real exports and real imports.

Source: Abeysinghe and Wilson (2002).

growth and a tight labour market and the policy of managed appreciation of the NEER to contain consumer price inflation. On the other hand, the NEER tended to ease during the recession in the mid 1980s and during the Asian financial crisis. Cumulative appreciation is much higher for the NEER in the 1980s and over the whole period, compared to the REER, but not so much in the 1990s. In the 1980s there seems to be some adjustment in relative price levels to offset the nominal appreciation (the cumulative REER is actually negative), especially around the time of the 1985–86 recession, as the government reduced business and wage costs to restore international competitiveness and oil and commodity prices were relatively subdued. In the 1990s, however, this adjustment is less marked until after the 1997 crisis. Behind this trend appreciation is rapid economic growth, an exceptionally high savings rate, a strong overall balance of payments position, and productivity growth. Faster productivity growth in the traded goods sector compared to the non-traded goods sector may also have contributed through the familiar Balassa–Samuelson effect (Monetary Authority of Singapore, 2001a).

Singapore is very unusual in breaking the famous Tinbergen (1952) assignment rule in as much as the MAS has, since 1981, assigned one instrument – the nominal exchange rate – to the twin targets of low and stable inflation and external competitiveness. In essence, the MAS began to target the NEER on the basis of an undisclosed basket of currencies, with a close eye on inflationary pressures, on the grounds that both conventional fiscal and monetary policy tools are relatively ineffective for demand management purposes in Singapore, whilst external monetary policy is very effective. This is largely because the extreme openness of the Singapore economy means that policy-induced changes in the exchange rate have a powerful effect on domestic prices and costs. The Chairman of the MAS, Richard Hu Hsu Tau, put this succinctly in an interview with *Euromoney* in February 1995 (p. 85):

> We have only one monetary policy, which is the exchange rate. Because we have completely open financial markets without foreign-exchange controls or capital controls, we don't even control interest rates. Our only control is managing the exchange rate and that is basically to prevent the Singapore dollar from rising too fast.

The openness to trade and capital flows combined with the exceptionally high import content of domestic expenditures means that prices in Singapore are largely determined by world prices for a given exchange rate, and since non-oil domestic exports are the largest constituent of aggregate demand, neutralizing inflation through managed appreciation of the currency translates into export competitiveness by lowering the Singapore dollar prices of exports.

The impotence of monetary policy in Singapore follows largely from the high degree of financial integration of Singapore's financial markets with the rest of the world (Gan, 2000), including a prominent position for foreign financial institutions, an active offshore Asian dollar market, an absence of capital controls, and an open arms policy on foreign direct investment. Residents may borrow, lend and invest freely in foreign exchange and deal in spot/forward currency markets. The consequence of this openness to capital flows is that a large proportion of changes in the domestic quantity of money are attributable to flows of external sector net foreign assets. Hence, controlling the 'domestic' money supply is limited to narrow money aggregates such as M1, but this has little impact on ultimate targets such as inflation. M2 and M3, on the other hand, are neither stable nor controllable since they are dominated by international money markets. So as far as Singapore is concerned, there is almost perfect short-term capital mobility and asset substitutability. Interest rates in Singapore cannot be used as effective instruments either since they are tied to international rates and are almost entirely determined by offshore US$ interest rates adjusted for exchange rate expectations, and even if the MAS decided to use monetary policy for domestic goals, the effectiveness of open market operations is severely limited by the small domestic secondary market for government securities.

It is well known that fiscal policy is relatively ineffective as a stabilization tool in open economies with flexible exchange rates and high short-term capital mobility, but other factors come into play in Singapore. In particular, the wealth effect of tax policy is significantly reduced by the high compulsory contributions by employers and employees to the CPF. The capacity to 'crowd out' domestic investment through fiscal-induced changes in interest rates is also limited since interest rates are set by the world market; and the very high marginal propensity to import substantially reduces the multiplier effects on domestic income of any fiscal expansion or contraction. Singapore, like the other East Asian tigers, has tended to use fiscal policy more as a longer-term device to mobilize resources for exports, such as tax breaks to attract foreign MNCs, or for case-by-case social programmes, such as encouraging families to have more children, although sometimes tax cuts do indirectly stimulate investment and output by increasing business optimism, as did the cut in the corporate tax rate and in personal income taxes in the 1993 budget.

External monetary policy, on the other hand, has proved itself to be a very effective means of ensuring low and stable inflation in Singapore because of the strong link between import prices and domestic inflation, largely because of Singapore's very high import content of exports (see Section 7.1). Average consumer price inflation between 1980 and 2000 has been a remarkable 2.3 per cent (Table A.1). Recent simulations by the Monetary Authority of Singapore (2000b) have confirmed the relative importance of a one-off increase in import prices with a similar rise in wages on the CPI and GDP; and the stronger potency of a policy initiated a one-off rise in the trade-weighted exchange rate compared to an equivalent change in interest rates on GDP, non-oil domestic exports, and the CPI. A 2 per cent lower rate of appreciation of the trade-weighted dollar, however, produces no medium or long-run beneficial effects on GDP or exports, but does translate into a 2 per cent rise in the CPI. The view that exchange rate depreciation would not be an effective method of improving international competitiveness is also supported by Toh (1999) using Granger causality tests applied to data between 1978 and 1996. He finds that currency changes work principally through production prices, probably because of Singapore's dependence on imported intermediate inputs, rather than through consumer prices and the prices of services.

The essence of MAS policy (Monetary Authority of Singapore, 2001a) is to keep the NEER within an undisclosed target band based on quarterly assessments of the exchange rate position in relation to the targeted medium term policy path and band for the trade weighted exchange rate. A consensus decision is then made on the optimal policy path to ensure low and stable inflation given the level of world inflation and domestic price pressures consistent with sustainable growth. Periodically the MAS will intervene to smooth excess volatility ('lean against the wind') through spot intervention, currency swaps and so on, and at the same time use money market operations to control the level of liquidity in the banking system. The placing of the large CPF savings and government fiscal surpluses in deposits with the MAS withdraws liquidity from the banking system which can be offset by money market or foreign exchange intervention by the MAS. The policy band can, however, be fairly wide and there is no automatic intervention unless there are strong inflationary pressures or significant departures from fundamentals as, for example, when a 'speculative' capital inflow fuels a stock or property boom. As far as volatility is concerned, the standard deviation of the Singapore dollar NEER (1.48 per cent) has been lower than the US$ (3.52 per cent) and yen (4.61 per cent) between 1980 and 2000, but as with the other regional currencies, the dollar has not been spared significant major swings against these currencies, such as the 20 per cent depreciation against the US$ between mid 1997 and early 1998 (Monetary Authority of Singapore 2001a).

With the onset of the Asian financial crisis the dollar depreciated against the US$ but appreciated sharply against regional currencies, so the NEER actually increased initially. In mid 1998, as the domestic situation in Singapore deteriorated, exchange rate policy was weakened. In early 2000, against a background of a favourable external environment and strong rebound in the Singapore economy, policy switched to a modest appreciation of the trade-weighted dollar which reached the upper bound of the policy band by the end of the year. By the middle of 2001, however, with a sharp fall in external demand and the prospect of a recession, the MAS shifted to a neutral stance with a policy band centred on a zero per cent appreciation of the NEER (Monetary Authority of Singapore, 2001c).

In July 2000 the MAS announced that it was going to release regular monetary policy statements to increase the transparency of the monetary process, including the publication of movements in the trade-weighted index which forms the basis of its policy of managed floating (Monetary Authority of Singapore, 2001d). This is a significant departure from previous policy and is in line with reforms to the financial sector introduced after the Asian financial crisis (see Section 8.5).

Singapore's reliance on the exchange rate weapon to achieve the multiple goals of export competitiveness and low domestic inflation underscores the relatively underdeveloped character of its macroeconomic system and the difficult balancing act that external monetary policy has to perform. This explains why traditional macroeconomic tools of demand management have often been supplemented by less conventional measures, including the use of public construction projects as a countercyclical measure when external demand fell (as in 1992), pre-emptive measures in 1996 to cool the domestic property market, and the cutting back on imported labour as a stabilization device when unemployment rises, as during the 1985–86 recession. Of the net reduction of 96000 jobs, three-fifths were foreign (Huff, 1995, p. 753).

If costs in Singapore appear to be moving significantly out of line with regional competitors, as during the early stages of the 1997 Asian financial crisis, then direct action to reduce the real exchange rate by cutting costs is preferred to a large currency depreciation which would shake confidence in the currency, lower the value of savings, and would provide only a transitory improvement in competitiveness until import price rises are passed on to domestic prices and wages. The response by the MAS was to widen the exchange rate band and let the package of cost cuts introduced in January 1999 reduce the nominal and real effective exchange rate and relative unit labour costs compared to major competitors. The cost cuts lowered utility charges and reduced the employer rate of contribution to the Central Provident Fund by 10 per cent. These measures, together with productivity improvements and wage restraint, effectively cut unit business costs by an impressive 12 per cent in 1999 compared to the previous year. This is simply the latest example of an unorthodox, but highly successful, approach to macro-stabilization policy.

8.3 THE SINGAPORE DOLLAR AND INTERNATIONAL COMPETITIVENESS

Notwithstanding the rationale behind MAS policy, businessmen and economists increasingly expressed concern in the 1990s about the strength of the dollar and its potentially negative impact on exports, especially in competition with the other tigers (Taiwan, Hong Kong and South Korea) and newly-industrializing neighbours such as Malaysia and Thailand in manufactured goods. Yip (1994), for example, argued that the dollar was fundamentally overvalued relative to purchasing power parity between 1981 and 1985, and again from 1990 onwards. The MAS, on the other hand, has been adamant that the REER has been relatively stable compared to the NEER and that there is no real evidence of a net negative impact on exports. Manipulation of the nominal exchange rate to create a competitive advantage would not be effective in improving Singapore's export competitiveness. Rather, exchange rate policy should be directed towards achieving a longer run climate of macroeconomic stability by targeting the NEER to neutralize the effects of imported inflation, thereby achieving low and stable domestic price inflation. Singapore-based companies may have to learn to live with the inevitable swings in currencies and focus on maintaining long-run competitiveness by increasing productivity and successful marketing.

This has given rise to a curious puzzle or paradox. Despite episodes of substantial nominal and real appreciation of the Singapore dollar against most major currencies since the mid 1970s, and a widely held perception that the relative costs of doing business in Singapore have increased over time, aggregate export performance has been very robust in the last two decades. Yet the doubts persist that the dollar may historically have been too strong and that Singapore may have lost export competitiveness as a result.

One way to explore the relationship between the exchange rate and international competitiveness is to look at relative prices or relative costs expressed in a common currency using measures of the REER (see Abeysinghe and Wilson, 2002). One would expect movements in the real exchange rate to capture some aspects of relative competitiveness in the short run. Unfortunately there is no unique way of computing the REER since it depends on the choice of base period for the indexes, the weighting procedure behind the 'effective' or basket idea and, critically, on the choice of price or cost indices which are supposed to capture changes in relative competitiveness. Ideally for Singapore one would want a generalized measure of relative unit business costs in manufacturing since this most closely mirrors changes in the costs of traded goods and includes both labour and non-labour costs, such as the rental cost of capital. This is especially pertinent for a land-scarce economy, such as Singapore, in which rent is an important cost item. Unfortunately, at present, the published data series for unit business cost is not long enough for meaningful statistical analysis and there is, in any case, no readily available comparative series for Singapore's main competitors. There is, however, data on relative unit labour cost (RULC) and labour costs account for about half of manufacturing production costs. Whilst short-term fluctuations in RULC tend to be dominated by the nominal exchange rate, the longer term trend will be determined primarily by productivity growth, so RULC captures both aspects of international competitiveness.

Table 8.5 presents the annual average rate of change in a consumer price index version of the REER (RCPI) and one based on relative unit labour costs (RULC) for four members of ASEAN and four newly industrialized economies between 1993 and 1997. On the basis of the RCPI, Singapore lost competitiveness compared to South Korea and Taiwan, and maybe Malaysia and Thailand, but not relative to Hong Kong and the Philippines where price inflation has been high. But when the RULC is used, Singapore actually gained some competitiveness during the pre-crisis period compared to the ASEAN-4 and South Korea.

Table 8.5   RULC and RCPI compared for Singapore and regional competitors

ASEAN-4: 1993(1)–1997(2)	Malaysia	Indonesia	Thailand	Philippines
RULC	8.0	0.9	3.0	5.6
RCPI	−0.7	0.3	−0.4	2.4
NIE-4: 1993(1)–1997(2)	Hong Kong	S. Korea	Taiwan	Singapore
RULC	−3.4	−0.4	−4.4	−2.5
RCPI	3.0	−2.3	−5.1	0.3

Notes: Both RCPI and RULC are export-weighted geometric averages against the other seven countries in the table.

Source: Abeysinghe (2001).

If Abeysinghe and Lee (1998) are correct, Singapore's loss of competitiveness against the NIEs and its ASEAN partners between 1992 and 1997 was not primarily due to an increase in labour cost but rather to an appreciation of the dollar relative to regional currencies. When exchange rates are held constant, relative unit labour costs remained flat against the NIEs and trended downwards slightly against the ASEAN-3 (ASEAN-4 excluding Indonesia). It is especially important to separate out the exchange rate effect from the change in relative costs for Singapore since a rise in the dollar need not be a problem for competitiveness if this simultaneously lowers the costs of imported intermediate inputs into production.

This may help to explain why, after significant periods of nominal and real exchange rate appreciation, the real trade balance has not noticeably deteriorated and total real exports have grown fast at an annual average rate (Figure 8.2 and Table 8.4), especially after the recovery from the 1985–86 recession to the mid 1990s. This performance was very robust with few periods of negative change in real exports on a calendar year basis (1981–82, 1985, 1991 and 1998). Moreover, contrary to prior expectations, the real trade balance is *positively* correlated with the REER in the 1990s and over the whole period since 1980 (although it is negatively related in the 1980s). Real exports are negatively related to the REER only in the first part of the 1980s (Table 8.4).

A number of reasons have been put forward to explain the failure to find a relationship between the real exchange rate and trade performance for Singapore.

One possibility is that the process of purchasing power parity (PPP) has

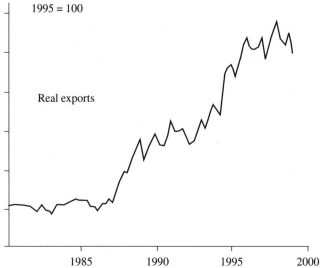

Notes: For definitions of the variables, see Table 8.4.

Source: Abeysinghe and Wilson (2002).

Figure 8.2   The real trade balance and real exports, 1980–99

been at work, such that the nominal exchange rate has primarily adjusted to offset changes in relative price levels between Singapore and the rest of the world. There is some evidence for PPP bilaterally with the USA (Abeysinghe and Lee, 1992; Chou and Shih, 1997) but not when more flexible fractional cointegration tests were applied, and the theory was not confirmed for other currencies relative to the Singapore dollar. Moreover, these results do not appear to generalize to effective exchange rates (Monetary Authority of Singapore, 1998b).

A problem here is that the MAS is not itself strictly neutral as far as the exchange rate is concerned, since the forex regime itself helps to ensure that the NEER adjusts to offset rises in import prices, thereby reinforcing PPP adjustment. This is particularly relevant to the bilateral relationship between Singapore and the USA since the US dollar has a significant (but unpublished) weight in the NEER basket used by the MAS as a guide to its policy of managed floating. Having said this, there is no direct evidence that exchange rate management to adjust for differences in relative price levels or currency misalignments plays an important role in the PPP adjustment mechanism for Singapore, and it is less likely insofar as the regime is closer to the floating end of the spectrum, than the more heavily managed foreign exchange regime in South Korea.

A second explanation stems from Singapore's very high import content of exports. In fact, Abeysinghe and Tan (1998) argue that this, in tandem with the policy of managed floating, is the most persuasive explanation of the 'export puzzle'. They find a close correlation between export prices and import prices (except for food and chemicals) over the period 1980–93, so a Singapore dollar appreciation lowers import prices measured in domestic currency and hence the domestic price of exports, effectively cushioning the conventional elasticities relationship between changes in the exchange rate and changes in export volumes. This relationship is weaker for services since they have a lower import content of exports, with the policy implication that the movement to a services-based economy will bring with it a greater need to increase productivity. This is also why, as we suggested earlier, it is so important to separate out the exchange rate effect from the change in relative labour costs for Singapore, since a rise in the dollar need not be a problem for competitiveness in general if this simultaneously lowers the costs of imported intermediate inputs used in production. This is also consistent with Toh's (1999) finding that changes in the $/US$ exchange rate work principally through production prices, because of Singapore's dependence on imported intermediate inputs, rather than through consumer prices and the prices of services.

Another, but not mutually exclusive, explanation of the puzzle focuses on the possibility of a low 'pass-through' from exchange rate changes to export prices. Low pass-through would make it possible for trade flows to stay relatively insensitive to currency changes even if export and import demand are highly price elastic. The time lag between the increase in imports of raw materials and machinery and subsequent production for export might also account for the coincidence of currency appreciation and robust export growth. The pass-through literature is particularly relevant to Singapore since 'pricing to market' is closely associated with MNCs, which account for a substantial portion of production for export in Singapore. Such enterprises also have the ability to manipulate internal exchange rates on intra-firm transactions as a way of hedging against exchange risks. Tongzon and Menon (1994) found the aggregate pass-through coefficient for Singapore to be quite low at 0.39, for the period 1978–93.

There remains the possibility that the pass-through effects on import and export prices are complete but that these changes are not translated into volume effects because of low export and import price elasticities of demand. The rationale behind this process is rooted in the 'elasticities' approach to balance of payments adjustment. Unfortunately empirical work on Singapore is rather scant on the magnitude of these elasticities. To test the relationship between the real trade balance and the real exchange rate more directly, Wilson and Kua (2001) looked at bilateral trade in merchandise goods between Singapore and the USA on a quarterly basis over the period 1970–96 and found that the real exchange rate does not have a significant impact on the real bilateral trade balance. In a broader comparative study using the same methodology and time period (Wilson, 2001), these negative findings were supported for bilateral trade between Singapore and Japan, and when the bilateral trade balance and real exchange rate were replaced by an aggregate trade balance and a trade-weighted REER. Excluding oil imports and exports, which a priori are less likely to be sensitive to exchange rate changes, also fails to reverse these results. The absence of a persuasive long-run relationship between the trade balance and the exchange rate has also been confirmed by Tongzon and Felmingham's (1998) analysis of bilateral trade flows between the USA, Japan, Singapore and Australia between 1977 and 1994, although they did find significant short-run bilateral relationships between Singapore and the USA and Japan.

There is also little hard evidence for the existence of so-called J-curve effects for Singapore (Wilson and Kua, 2001). These occur when a real currency depreciation worsens the trade balance in the short run as the value of imports measured in home currency rises by more than export revenues, but is successful in improving it in the longer run. Allowing for 'small country' effects does not appear to change the results. For small open economies where imports and exports are both predominantly invoiced in foreign currencies, such as the US$, the value of both might rise initially as the currency depreciates so no J-curve is observed. Singapore is surely a classic price taker in international markets, but the small country assumption does not appear to be the reason for the failure to find a J-curve for Singapore. There is some evidence that real exports increase at first when the currency depreciates, which would be expected if exporters price in US$, but this does not appear to be masking the J-curve effects of an initial rise in import values.

The failure to establish a close relationship between exchange rates and the trade balance is not peculiar to Singapore and is thus amenable to many explanations. It is possible that movements in the nominal exchange rate are determined largely by PPP differentials rather than by trade flows per se, although evidence for this at the aggregate level is very weak; and that this relationship is reinforced by the regime of managed floating in Singapore as the MAS offsets imported inflation by adjustments to the NEER. This is consistent with the view that the trade balance is essentially driven by external demand rather than by currency or price factors and that exchange rate-induced losses of competitiveness are compensated for by improvements in productivity as producers learn to anticipate long periods of currency strength. Singapore is not unique in achieving rapid export growth in the face of persistent nominal and real exchange rate appreciation, Japan managed the same feat between 1985 and 1995. It is also plausible that the very high import content of Singapore's exports, together with the MAS policy of managed floating, has kept domestic costs and prices from rising too fast and that exporters, particularly MNCs, have priced to market, thereby limiting the pass-through from currency changes to export price changes.

8.4   ARE SINGAPORE'S RESERVES TOO HIGH?

Table 8.6 shows the composition of Singapore's official foreign exchange reserves in 1999 and their growth since the mid 1960s. In 1999 total reserve assets were worth $128 billion, or about US$77 billion. Of these, 99 per cent were foreign exchange reserves (including gold) with negligible proportions of Special Drawing Rights or deposits at the IMF. These proportions have not changed since 1992 (Peebles and Wilson, 1996, Table 6.10). The reserves have grown rapidly since the mid-1960s in line with surpluses in the overall balance of payments. Growth slowed somewhat between 1997 and 2000 as a result of the Asian financial crisis, but was still 12 per cent on an annual average basis between 1990 and 2000.

Table 8.6   Composition of official foreign exchange reserves in 1999 and their growth, 1963–2000

	$ millions	
	1999	% of total
Deposits at the IMF	908.5	0.7
Special Drawing Rights	387.5	0.3
Gold and foreign exchange	127 161	99.0
Total reserves	128 457	100

Annual average growth %				
1963–69	1970–79	1980–89	1990–96	1997–2000
15	18	13	15	7

Notes: Reserves are gross official end-of-year total reserves.

Source: Economic and Social Statistics, Singapore, 1960–82; Yearbook of Statistics, Singapore, various issues.

Are the reserves too high?

The quantity of reserves held by a central bank should be sufficient to enable a country to meet its trade and payments obligations without liquidity crises or a loss of confidence in the currency. Countries which are very open to trade and investment flows, which experience relatively high volatility in such flows, and whose currency is subject to frequent and large speculative activity, would be wise to hold higher than average reserves. Having excessive reserves, however, is not only counterproductive but has opportunity costs in as much as these resources could have been invested in higher return physical or financial assets, or used for consumption purposes. The opportunity cost for developing countries tends to higher than for developed countries since they may be forced to hold reserves for precautionary reasons which could have been used to buy scarce capital goods imports essential for increasing growth.

Certainly Singapore is a very open economy (see Section 7.1) on any criteria, with few impediments to the free flow of goods and capital and the market plays a significant role in determining the external value of the currency. On the other hand, the fact that the dollar is not yet a truly international currency held in large quantities by non-residents or other central banks, means that speculative activity in the Singapore dollar has historically been very low. This may be due to the strong fundamentals of the Singapore economy, the high degree of credibility associated with the MAS and a currency which is not persistently over or undervalued. Of course, one could always argue that the decision not to internationalize the dollar too fast (see Section 8.6 below) has itself reduced the volatility of capital and currency flows, so *potential* volatility is a further justification for holding a high level of reserves.

The official view is that a high level of reserves is necessary given Singapore's import dependence, to instill confidence in Singapore as an international monetary centre, and to be able to intervene, when necessary, to combat inflation or improve export competitiveness through the policy of managed floating. They are also essential as a 'war chest' or a 'shock absorber' against an unexpected outflow of capital, as happened to Mexico in 1994, and to some Asian countries during the Asian financial crisis.

As far as import requirements are concerned, most developed countries would expect their reserves to be able to finance about 2–3 months of imports, while developing countries would prudently wish to hold, on average, about 3–4 months. In 1999 Singapore's reserves were sufficient to pay for about eight months of imports (Table 8.7), high by both developed and developing country standards, but not as high as China, Taiwan and Japan. On the other hand, China is still a relatively closed economy with excess demand for imports, Japan is still in a severe economic downturn with an artificially low level of imports, and Taiwan's political future is still highly uncertain. Moreover, if retained imports (proxied by total imports less entrepot exports in the absence of data on entrepot imports) are used to calculate import requirements instead of total imports, Singapore's reserves can buy 13.8 months of imports in 1999.

From a comparative perspective, Singapore does not have the highest absolute reserves in the world in 1999 (Table 8.7), coming fifth behind countries such as Japan, China and Taiwan, but it does have the highest per capita at almost US$26 000, well above its nearest rivals Hong Kong and Switzerland. Compared to the average of the top ten countries in Table 8.7, excluding Singapore, Singapore's reserves per capita are five times higher. This is a consequence of both a high level of absolute reserves and a relatively small population.

Of course one can always justify any level of reserves or savings on the grounds of a 'doomsday' scenario or extreme political insecurity (Taiwan), but it is not sound economics. Singapore has substantial in-built stabilizers to deal with export shocks (Section 7.3) and a low risk rating in international financial markets. Prudent government budgetary policies and financial credibility are, of course, important, but the analogy with households in debt or businesses going bankrupt is an inappropriate one in international finance. Sovereign governments cannot go bust and the international financial system is designed to accommodate individual countries experiencing temporary balance of payments crises.

Table 8.7   *Top ten ranking of countries by international reserves and reserves per head, 1999*

Country	Total reserves (US$ billions)	Months of imports	Increase in reserves, 1990–99 %
1 Japan	286.9	9.5	227
2 China	158.0	11.4	358
3 Taiwan	106.2	10.3	37
4 Hong Kong	96.2	5.6	29
5 Singapore	76.8	8.1	177
6 Korea	74.0	7.8	396
7 Germany	61.0	1.2	−42
8 USA	60.5	0.7	−65
9 France	39.7	1.4	−42
10 Switzerland	36.3	4.0	−41

Country	Reserves per head (US$)
1 Singapore	25 614
2 Hong Kong	13 748
3 Switzerland	5 189
4 Norway	5 100
5 Taiwan	4 827
6 Denmark	4 457
7 Israel	3 768
8 Botswana	3 150
9 Japan	2 259
10 Kuwait	2 412

Notes: Reserves are gross and comprise holdings of monetary gold valued at the year-end London price of US$290.25, Special Drawing Rights, reserves held at the International Monetary Fund and holdings of foreign exchange under the control of the monetary authorities; months of imports are calculated by dividing total reserves in 1999 by one-twelfth of the value of imports of goods and services in 1998.

Sources: *World Bank* (2000, Table 1 and Table 15); *Taiwan Statistical Data Book, 2000* (Table 2-2).

Singapore emerged from the Asian financial crisis relatively unscathed compared to its regional neighbours, not because of an exceptionally high level of reserves but because of its in-built stabilizers, good policies and sound fundamentals for the economy, including large surpluses on current account and long-term capital account. The MAS also allowed the dollar to appreciate to some extent in response to earlier capital inflows, especially when domestic inflation was threatening. Thailand and Indonesia, on the other hand, were overly dependent on foreign short-term capital without generating sufficient productive activity and exports. Moreover, their reserve positions looked better than they really were because their central banks had been busy in the years prior to the crisis sterilizing capital inflows to mop up the extra domestic liquidity to prevent inflationary pressures eroding their export competitiveness. They were intervening in the foreign exchange market to keep the domestic currency deliberately undervalued for the same reason. Ironically this put further upward pressure on domestic interest rates and attracted even more short-term capital.

A further justification for a high level of reserves in Singapore is the need for the reserves to grow in line with the increase in the (ageing) population and living standards, to provide a 'nest-egg' to cover future liabilities to CPF holders. The reserves have always been regarded in Singapore as a component of the nation's wealth with the government as the custodian, and an integral part of the broader development strategy translating forced savings through the CPF and budgetary surpluses into investment, whilst over time some of these funds were converted into a portfolio of foreign assets at the MAS and GIC. At times one might be forgiven for thinking that the objective is maximization of the reserves. In an interview with *Euromoney* in February 1995, Finance Minister Richard Hu explained the Government's policy as one of 'encouraging people not to spend too much on consumption' and 'to put aside every dollar we can lay our hands on'.

The question of the size of the reserves cannot be separated, therefore, from the broader issues of the size of the balance of payments surplus, the complaint that there has been over-saving and over-investment, and the opportunity costs of high savings and reserve accumulation in terms of domestic consumption and the alternative real returns that might have been earned on both domestic and foreign assets. If there is too much of a bias towards low-yielding liquid assets then this is akin to a firm with lots of cash in the bank rather than being invested in productive investment or being handed back to shareholders.

Yet the returns on public savings and reserve assets are not public information and it is virtually impossible to disentangle the flow of funds between the CPF, other statutory boards, the budget accounts, and the reserves at the MAS and GIC. For a brave attempt, see Low and Toh (1989). Access to the foreign media is often the only way to find out where the GIC has been investing. For example, in September 2000, the Dutch financial daily *Financieele Dag* reported that the GIC had bought a stake in Hegenmeyer and was now the biggest shareholder. This was later confirmed by the GIC as an 8 per cent stake and one of a string of investments including the purchase of the Korean Airlines office in Seoul (*The Business Times Online Edition,* 22 September, 2000).

From rare public disclosures, such as the interview given by Lee Kuan Yew to the *Asian Wall Street Journal* on 23 April 2001 (reported in the *The Business Times*, 27 April, 2001), we are able to glean together a rough picture of the principles of government investment. Three companies are involved: Temasek Holdings and MND Holdings invest the bulk of domestic assets and the GIC invests external assets. The GIC is a private investment management company with investment professionals, chaired by the Senior Minister. It manages a portfolio exceeding US$100 billion allocated across 30 or more countries and employs 221 professional staff, two-fifths of which are foreign. It takes a cautious stance on investment with approximately 40 per cent of the portfolio in equities, 40 per cent in bonds, and the rest in cash. It has a unit for real estate and another for technology start-ups. Mistakes have been made, such as the purchase of Guandong International Trust and Investment Corporation, which defaulted in 1999. The objective is to ensure a good long-term return on a sustainable basis and to protect the real value of government assets, not to take undue risks. Most government assets are therefore invested in shares and fixed income instruments such as bonds, since these are most liquid, with some holdings in real estate and venture capital funds. The government also invests in companies directly to avoid unnecessary competition with the private sector and to encourage local companies to expand overseas. The MAS has its own funds primarily to 'manage' the Singapore dollar.

We are periodically assured that the return on government investments has averaged well over 5 per cent in Singapore dollar terms over the last ten years (*The Business Times*, 15 March, 1996), the assets have steadily increased in value over the years (*The Business Times*, 23 April, 2001), and the GIC fund managers have out-performed the benchmarks they have set themselves (*The Business Times*, 24 May, 2001). This is comforting but a little inconsistent with the drive since 1997 to increase transparency and accountability in the private sector. Independent observers have been less complimentary. *The Economist* (*Financial Indicators*, 8 September, 1994) estimated the real return on pension funds in Singapore between 1983 and 1993 at 2.3 per cent per annum, the lowest of the 18 countries cited.

The secrecy surrounding the reserves is defended on a number of grounds. In the Senior Minister's interview with the *Asian Wall Street Journal* cited above, he reiterated the government's policy of not disclosing its investment performance:

> We are a special investment fund, the ultimate shareholders are the electorate. It is not in the people's interest, in the nation's interest, to detail our assets and their yearly returns. . . . If speculators knew the exact picture this would give them ammunition! They don't know the exact amount we have invested abroad and in what assets. . . . The sheer size of the reserves dictates secrecy, even stealth, it is

a must; it makes no sense for anyone who acquires wealth to advertise the fact – this is the first rule of wealth preservation.

Deputy Prime Minister Lee Hsien Loong, who is also GIC Deputy Chairman, in replying to a question in Parliament on behalf of the Senior Minister following the latter's interview with the *Asian Wall Street Journal* also pointed out that Singapore did not operate direct democracy in the fashion of ancient Greece. 'We operate a representative democracy in which the people elect the government . . . and here the government has decided that as a matter of policy, the reserves are a matter which are best not published and discussed every year and we have good reason for that . . .'. Public shareholders, it seems, are limited to voting once every five years, on a 'take it or leave it' basis. He added that the accounts of the GIC were checked by the Accountant-General, the Auditor-General and were examined by the Council of Presidential Advisors. The management staff of the GIC also took the opportunity of their twentieth anniversary in May 2001 (*The Business Times*, 24 May, 2001) to comment on their record and recent changes in their investment strategy away from country-specific portfolios, which tended to be suboptimal and compartmentalized, to a more integrated global approach, with increasing use of derivatives and less focus on G7 sovereign bonds and high grade corporate bonds.

Given the level of development that Singapore has now reached, one would have expected the reserves to have reached a plateau as there is less need for centralized investment and the concomitant large balance of payments and budgetary surpluses. The emphasis ought now to be on a competitive return to private savings as households are given more freedom over their pension and personal investment decisions, financial institutions are encouraged to hold less government debt and government bodies begin to rely more on commercial risk management services. The growth of a short-term debt market will also require less 'forced' holdings of government debt. The data in Table 8.6, however, give little indication of a slowdown in the growth of the reserves in the 1990s, once allowance is made for the Asian financial crisis.

It is true that the rapid growth in reserves in the 1990s has not been an exclusively Singaporean experience (Table 8.7). Indeed, developing countries now account for over half of the world's international reserves, and six Asian countries (Japan, China, Taiwan, Hong Kong, Singapore and Korea) alone accounted for 48 per cent in 1999. But often this is because of an inflow of foreign capital, which exceeds their current account deficits, and the purchase of foreign assets by the central banks as part of their sterilization policy to prevent an appreciation of the home currency negatively impacting on export competitiveness. In Singapore's case, however, the

reserves are rising because of large current account and budgetary surpluses as a direct manifestation of high (forced) private and government
savings.

Doubtless, the size of the reserves and the responsibility for managing
them will continue to be an important political issue in Singapore. Indeed
one of the reasons for the appointment of an elected President of the
Republic since 1993 is to act as a protector of the national reserves to
prevent a future elected government from squandering the nation's wealth
(Low and Toh, 1989). In mid 1999 public tension between President Ong
Teng Chong and the government surfaced over the President's power as the
holder of the 'second key' to the reserves (George, 2000, Chapter 4).

8.5   SINGAPORE AS AN INTERNATIONAL FINANCIAL CENTRE

Singapore satisfies many of the essential requirements for an international
financial centre (Tan, 1999). It has a strong domestic economy with a relatively well-developed transportation and communications infrastructure, a
stable currency, a strategic location on the world's main east–west sea and
air routes in a fast growing region of the world and bridges the time zone
between the major financial centres, making 24-hour trading possible. It
also boasts a substantial foreign presence, stretching back to British colonial days, in terms of political and legal institutions, banks and other
financial institutions and a long history of commercial trading in the
region. These are important reasons why Singapore ranks fourth behind
London, New York and Tokyo in foreign exchange dealing, with an average
daily turnover of US$100 billion (*Economic Survey of Singapore 2000*, p.
85), and fifth in terms of derivatives trading. It has an international reputation as a prudent financial centre with conservative banking and regulatory practices. In 1999 Singapore banks were ranked seventh in the world
and first in Asia by Moody's Investor Services.

Singapore also hosts one of the largest offshore financial markets in the
world, the Asian Dollar Market (ADM). This is the equivalent of the
Eurodollar market except that it is located in Asia and plays a key part in
channelling capital to corporations and government agencies for development in the Asian region. Although turnover in the ADM is small compared to the Eurodollar market, the number of units licensed in Singapore
to deal in US$ or other hard currencies, Asian Currency Units (ACUs),
reached 227 by 1998 (Tan, 1999, Table 7.1), with assets amounting to
US$486 billion (*Economic Survey of Singapore 2000*, Table A14.3). Growth
slowed in the late 1980s and contracted in the 1990s with the downturn in

Japan, but the ADM remains one of the largest offshore markets in the world. These assets are mostly short term (maturity of less than three months) and are predominantly lent and borrowed between banks. The market is attractive because ACUs are exempt from the usual reserve requirements imposed on domestic banks and favourable tax treatment is offered for ACU borrowers as well as opportunities for portfolio diversification.

Financial institutions in Singapore also deal in the Asian Dollar Bond Market (ADBM). This is the counterpart in Asia of the Eurobond market for medium- and long-term funds, where bonds are denominated in a foreign hard currency, usually the US$. In the 1970s there were six issues of Asian dollar bonds on average per year amounting to US$0.18 billion. In the 1980s these numbers had risen to 15 and US$1.24 billion, respectively, and to 18 (US$1.38 billion) between 1990 and 1997 (Tan, 1999, Table 8.1).

In contrast to Singapore's prominence in foreign exchange dealing and in international banking, both onshore and offshore, domestic capital markets are still relatively underdeveloped in terms of fixed-income and equity markets and the fund management industry. At the same time changes in global financial markets are leading to greater competition and consolidation of activity into fewer centres, and developments in technology, which ensure that money can be managed from a wider range of locations than in the past, are eroding Singapore's locational advantages. Not surprisingly, CPF holders are demanding a wider range of products with higher returns than are available in the local bank-dominated environment. The dilemma for Singapore is that it wants to be a premier international financial centre with a wide range of activities, and it is committed to globalization and the accompanying technological advances, such as e-commerce, but if it opens up the domestic market too quickly it may not be able to compete given its small home base. Has it achieved a critical mass for fund management? Does it have enough innovation?

Part of the problem arises from the dominant, but largely successful, role that the government has played in the creation of Singapore as a financial centre. Indeed, the development of financial and business services was the result of more deliberate planning than the manufacturing sector and it is unlikely Singapore could have reached its current position through its locational advantages alone. Unlike other major financial centres, such as New York and London, which developed largely in a spontaneous fashion to service the demand for financial services, the former enhanced by its role as a headquarters for MNCs after the Second World War and the latter through the commercial network associated with the British Empire and Commonwealth, the development of Singapore as a financial centre has been more the product of government initiative. The ADBM, for example, was started in 1971 by the Development Bank of Singapore (largely government-owned) when it floated bonds worth US$10 million for redemption in 1982, guaranteed by the Singapore government. Similarly, the ADM began operating in Singapore in 1968 when the Singapore branch of the Bank of America was given a license to set up an Asian Currency Unit to deal in US$ or other hard currencies. The removal of the 20 per cent liquidity requirement on foreign currency deposits enabled the ADM to compete with the Euromarkets. The result was rapid growth in the 1970s and early 1980s, intermediating savings from the rest of the world to faster-growing countries in Asia. Additional factors were the establishment of regional headquarters by MNCs in Singapore for financing operations in the region, and the attraction of regional banks generating large interbank transactions, largely to finance trade.

These were conscious political decisions to further Singapore's ambition to develop as a regional financial centre and to diversify away from manufacturing into services. The 1965 separation from Malaysia meant the loss of a reliable hinterland, and the winding up of the British bases in Singapore after 1967 further reduced the sources of Singapore's earnings. With few natural resources, and increasing political risks from regional neighbours, the decision was made to develop a modern financial centre which would serve its own industrialization needs but also those of the region.

Even by the 1980s, however, bond, equity and futures trading was very underdeveloped and the securities market was characterized by thin liquidity and low trade volume. Budget surpluses meant that there was no need for bond issues as a source of funding for GLCs and SBs and infrastructure projects were largely tax revenue financed, so the government securities market consisted mainly of primary issues to meet bank reserve requirements and to soak up excess CPF funds. Corporations, on the other hand, tended to rely on bank financing or parent companies rather than bond issues.

By 1985 the limited range of financial activities in Singapore and the reliance on government initiatives had been recognized. The Economic Committee, set up to re-examine economic policy in the light of the 1985 recession, recommended that Singapore take steps to develop itself into a risk management centre based upon a range of money market and capital market activities. This resulted in various fiscal reforms to remove existing obstacles to the development of domestic fund management services and changes in the funding practices of government ministries and SBs. CPF funds could now be used for a wider range of approved investments, a process which gathered momentum in the 1990s. GLCs and SBs were also encouraged to use capital markets for funding.

A tradition of looking to the government for initiatives, combined with a reputation for a tight regulatory framework and generally conservative approach by the MAS, also led to criticisms that the regulatory mechanism was complicating business practices and constraining private sector financial innovation and market development (Eschweiler, 1997), not least because such innovation would require time consuming consultations with the MAS. The comparison was often made with Hong Kong. Both are city-states with a good business and physical infrastructure, a sizeable English-speaking population and inherited British institutions. Both lack sizeable domestic populations so China became the hinterland for Hong Kong and Singapore looked to South-east Asia. Both built up a reputation for sound open financial systems and a large presence of foreign financial institutions. In Singapore, however, the authorities have been very proactive with tight controls and conservative prudential standards, while Hong Kong is altogether more laissez-faire with minimal controls, no reserve requirements, no central bank (until recently) and little government interference. Tax rates are lower, onshore and offshore markets are fully integrated and resident/non-resident activities are treated the same. Perhaps the old adage is correct: 'In Hong Kong anything not expressly forbidden is permitted, in Singapore anything not expressly permitted is forbidden'.

Ironically, Hong Kong began to introduce more controls after experiencing banking sector problems in the 1980s and the stock market crash of 1987, and now has a sort of central bank in the guise of the Hong Kong Monetary Authority, while Singapore began to relax controls and to establish a level playing field for local and foreign banks in the domestic market.

It was partly in response to such criticisms that the Singapore government set up the Financial Sector Review Group in 1997 and began to implement some of its sub-committee recommendations as they were made public during 1988 and early 1999 (see the summary in Peebles, 1998a, p. 1067 and Cardarelli et al., 2000). The result has been a comprehensive set of reforms to promote Singapore as a full service international financial centre.

These included further widening of the scope for investment of CPF funds by increasing investment limits on unit trusts, the lifting of fixed commissions in the stockbroking sector, a speeding up of the development of the domestic asset management industry by increasing the range of retirement products and allocating more government assets to selected fund managers located in Singapore, and a more proactive attempt to develop the local debt market. Long-term government bonds have been issued to increase liquidity in the government securities market and to set a benchmark for a corporate bond yield curve and this has been followed by a spate of bond issues by government-linked organizations, including the

Development Bank of Singapore and the Housing Development Board. This has already produced some success as assets managed in Singapore rose from $18 billion at the end of 1990 to $112 billion by the end of 1998, while the number of fund managers tripled to 157 (Cardarelli et al., 2000).

Reforms were also introduced to move Singapore companies closer to the US system of disclosure and to bring regulatory and supervisory practices in line with current best practice, shifting the emphasis from regulation to supervision and from a rules-based to a risk-management approach. Singapore now even has a Corporate Transparency Index (*Business Times* 15 October, 2000, p. 3) and a 'Most Transparent Company Award' (*Business Times*, 24 September, 2001, p. 20). The domestic banking sector has also been opened up to increased foreign participation and competition.

There is no doubt that these reforms are moving Singapore in the right direction towards its goal of becoming a full service international financial centre, but one issue remains controversial: the policy of discouraging the internationalization of the dollar. Although the government has encouraged the development of offshore financial markets, such as the ADM and the ADBM, it has preferred to keep these markets separate from the onshore financial system so that competition with the offshore market would not impede the progress of the domestic financial system. Tax exemptions on offshore income applied only to non-residents and domestic banking units were subject to stricter controls and restrictions on non-resident access to credit lines in the dollar. The objective was to discourage speculation and the build up of a large pool of dollars outside Singapore leading to a further loss of control over domestic monetary policy. This means that the dollar is not internationalized in the same way as the US$ or the yen, despite the fact that this may prevent the further progress of Singapore as a financial centre, not least by obstructing competition and synergies between the offshore centres and the domestic market (Eschweiler, 1997). Domestic institutions are shielded from competition and off-shore institutions are denied access to the domestic capital base. Should the dollar be internationalized?

8.6 THE INTERNATIONALIZATION OF THE SINGAPORE DOLLAR

In essence internationalization of the dollar would mean the development of a substantial market for the dollar outside Singapore analogous to the development of the Eurodollar and Eurocurrency markets. Non-residents would hold dollar deposits in Singapore, domestic banks could lend freely to non-residents, and non-residents would hold Singapore dollar-denominated government securities and corporate bonds without restriction. Foreign central banks could hold the dollar as a reserve asset and use it if they wished for day-to-day intervention in the currency market in the same way as the US$ and other major currencies are used at the present time.

There are significant advantages to having a currency internationalized. First the dollar could act as a settlement currency to facilitate trade and investment with major trading partners, particularly in the Asian region. For example, a Singapore-based firm might buy a factory in Indonesia with dollars instead of US$ or yen. This would be a convenient way for such companies, faced with limited investment opportunities at home, to use up some of their excess savings to finance 'second wing' or 'third wing' projects, but continue to use the banking and other financial services available in Singapore. Singapore has always done a significant amount of trade with neighbouring countries such as Malaysia and Indonesia, but the dollar is rarely used as the settlement currency (Ngiam and Tyabji, 1998).

A second benefit would come from a reduction in the transactions costs of settlement in multiple currencies. Singapore exporters and importers would be able to reduce their exchange rate risk if both exports and imports are invoiced in dollars and Singapore firms investing abroad would be able to match their dollar assets with dollar liabilities instead of foreign currency liabilities purchased to finance the investment, and they would no longer need to cover their foreign currency liabilities through forward hedges.

The internationalization of the dollar would also crucially help to boost Singapore as a major international financial centre beyond the narrow confines of banking-related activities, the ADM and ADBM, and foreign exchange transactions. By increasing the volume of financial transactions in Singapore and producing a deeper market in dollar-denominated assets, it will be able to attract business which might otherwise locate elsewhere. Singapore is the fourth largest foreign exchange trading centre in the world, but most of this is in Singapore dollar–US$ transactions and the market for instruments to manage interest and exchange rate risk, such as swaps and derivatives, is still small compared to rival monetary centres such as Hong Kong.

Internationalization would have the additional benefit of facilitating the development of a Singapore dollar debt securities market, which is currently very small and lacks a liquid secondary market. Most primary issues in dollars are instigated by SBs and GLCs and are held to maturity by insurance companies. Restrictions on non-resident access to the dollar also constrains the growth of a liquid repurchase (repo) market where a security can be sold and later bought back at an agreed price to enable investors to finance or hedge bond exposures. Urging SBs and GLCs to issue bonds is not enough. The participation of foreigners who have access to domestic sources of credit is crucial to deepen liquidity given the small domestic investor base. The need for such markets in Asia as a whole was clearly illustrated by the Asian financial crisis where private long-term domestic lending for activities such as real estate in Thailand was financed by short-term borrowing in foreign currency. A long-term debt market in domestic currency would be a major step towards correcting this liquidity mismatch.

There have always been restrictions on the amount non-residents can borrow to finance trading activities in dollar-denominated assets and on the lending of the dollar for activities deemed to be unrelated to the Singapore economy. This has tended to restrain financial institutions in Singapore from lending dollar financial instruments and constrains the growth of the bond market since access to domestic credit lines by non-residents is essential to deepen liquidity and encourage trading. For example, foreign companies have been encouraged to list in Singapore and issue debt but were obliged to swap the proceeds out of the dollar if they are not for use in Singapore. There was also some ambiguity until 1992 about the meaning of 'non-resident', for instance, whether the banks in Singapore were obliged to consult the MAS even for loans to residents for use outside Singapore.

The MAS has consistently resisted pressures to fully internationalize the dollar, regarding its policy as one of containment or a 'rearguard action', and the restrictions as being only minimal. The position was set out in the MAS Notice to Banks Act, Regulation 621 in November 1983: 'Banks should observe the Authority's policy of discouraging the internationaliz-ation of the Singapore dollar'. This position was reiterated by the Chairman of the MAS, Lee Hsien Loong in January 2001 (*The Business Times,* 19 January, 2001). He could not envisage full internationalization now although this did not mean that it would not happen at some time in the future. Singapore opposed the introduction of a dollar futures contract on the New York Cotton Exchange in 1997.

The fears as far as the monetary authorities are concerned are that faster internationalization would leave Singapore exposed to speculative money and capital flows with induced effects on real trade through larger fluctuations in dollar exchange rates, and the MAS would lose further control over monetary policy. Targeting the dollar to keep inflation low and stable, which is the primary objective of monetary policy, would be made more difficult if an increasing amount of the money supply were outside Singapore and was not controllable by the monetary authorities. Is the MAS too cautious?

The dollar has for some time been used as a regional currency, albeit on a small scale, for tourism services in the neighbouring Malaysian state of

Johor and in the Indonesian islands such as Batam and Bintan in the Riau province. Market-driven pressures for further liberalization are likely to increase as long as the cost of borrowing is low relative to other markets, there is a large pool of available dollars and the dollar remains a stable currency. In 1996, for example, the MAS succumbed to demands by foreign companies to relax the rules on foreign company listing of shares in dollars on the Stock Exchange of Singapore to reduce exchange rate exposure, and in April 1998 SIMEX began trading a Singapore dollar stock index futures contract.

It is also worth pointing out that the accumulation of balances in local banks by non-residents, which is permitted under MAS rules, did not appear to play a prominent role in the financial crises of 1985 or 1997. In any case, as internationalization is likely to be confined to the Asian region in the foreseeable future, the MAS should find little difficulty in 'mopping up' any excess dollars if necessary. Moreover, since the MAS cannot in reality distinguish between speculators and bona fide traders, it might be more sensible to let traders and investors borrow dollars without restriction but to have in place measures which would make it costly for speculators should the situation arise, for example, by imposing loan quotas on the domestic banks which are binding only during a crisis (Chan and Ngiam, 1996; Ngiam and Tyabji, 1998). Without access to new funds, it is unlikely that speculative activity would be significant enough to cause a lot of damage. Limited capital controls which could be effected quickly to deter short-term speculative inflows might be another option.

Further liberalization seems likely, and is consistent with the 'lighter touch' accompanying the comprehensive reforms to the financial sector set in motion during the Asian financial crisis. In August 1998 the MAS Notice to Banks on the internationalization of the dollar, which had been updated in 1992 was replaced by a new Notice 757. This clarified the meaning of 'residents', who can borrow dollars for use at home or abroad for any purpose, and 'foreigners' who were subject to restrictions. It also clarified what constitutes 'economic activity in Singapore' for which domestic banks can lend dollars to non-residents without seeking permission from the MAS. It is now legitimate, for example, to buy shares, bonds, and Singapore government securities (up to a maximum value), and to issue bonds and list dollar denominated shares on the Stock Exchange of Singapore, but the proceeds must still be swapped into foreign exchange before remitting. Singapore dollar credit is not allowed for direct or portfolio investment outside Singapore, for third country trade not involving Singapore, and for speculating in local financial or property markets in general.

The rules were further relaxed in December 2000 to stimulate the development of the domestic bond market. Foreigners can now borrow dollars freely to invest in dollar assets (with some safeguards) and can conduct asset swaps with local banks to finance/hedge bond exposure, and in February 2001 the offshore banks were permitted to participate in the dollar swap market without setting aside reserves on dollar funds received from non-bank customers.

8.7   MONETARY INTEGRATION IN ASIA?

Before the Asian financial crisis there had been an academic debate about the possibility of some Asian countries joining together in a currency bloc revolving around the yen, just as European countries had formed a bloc around the German mark in the 1980s (Kwan, 1998, and 2000). The objective would be to insulate Asian countries from fluctuations in the yen–US$ exchange rate, which tended to stimulate rapid growth and asset bubbles when the yen appreciated, and economic crises when it depreciated. Limited 'repo' agreements were already in place giving ASEAN countries access to hard currency loans from participating central banks in the Asian region during a crisis, but this was conditional on pledging US government securities as collateral, and there was no common defensive mechanism to fight speculative attacks on particular currencies or automatic help for economies with balance of payments problems. Asian countries still relied principally on programmes orchestrated by the IMF and its affiliates which were usually conditional on implementing policy reforms.

Paradoxically, the Asian crisis itself rekindled interest in the prospects for closer monetary integration in Asia. Pegging closely to the US$ had not enabled countries such as Thailand and Indonesia to overcome the 'triad of incompatibilities', that is managing the currency to stop an appreciation harming export performance, continuing to operate an independent monetary policy, and at the same time integrating the domestic capital market with global capital markets. On the other hand, the 'corner solutions' of fixing the currency absolutely, maybe with the backing of a currency board, or clean floating, did not look particularly attractive. Post-crisis governments, except Hong Kong (which was already on a fixed exchange rate system) were not in a hurry to give up their monetary policy and central banks (the fixed solution), and were not happy about the longer-term costs associated with a free float.

The search for a better system thus opened up the possibility of an intermediate type of regime operated unilaterally, such as a peg to a basket of currencies, or a collective solution such as the common basket peg proposed by John Williamson (1998) in which Asian countries would fix to a basket of currencies with the same weights based on their collective trade with outside countries or blocs. This would effectively insulate them against currency changes against each other, although not, of course, from changes against outside currencies. Another possibility would be to retain their own exchange rate regimes but explicitly cooperate to stabilize intra-bloc currency fluctuations as in the European Monetary System prior to full monetary union in 1999. The birth of the Euro also offered a concrete model showing that monetary integration was possible even if there was some dissimilarity in economic structures and a lack of synchronization in business cycles, providing the political will was there.

Another possibility, suggested by Nobel Laureate Robert Mundell (*Business Times*, 22 October, 2001) is to anchor regional currencies to the US$ as a first step towards a common Asian currency for the ASEAN + 3 (ASEAN plus Japan, China and South Korea), and to start with full dollarization of the Hong Kong dollar, since this currency is already pegged to the US$. In time this might bring with it the necessary economic convergence and political integration for the establishment of a single Asian currency akin to the Euro.

A series of initiatives on Asian monetary integration began in earnest at the ASEAN + 3 meeting in Chiang Mai in May 1999. An earlier Japanese proposal for an Asian Monetary Fund was shelved because of complaints from the IMF and USA that it would provide an inadequate framework for effective supervision and monitoring and would create a 'moral hazard' problem. Instead they agreed to set up a regional network of bilateral currency swaps, a monitoring framework based on macroeconomic indicators similar to that used by the IMF, and machinery for the surveillance of exchange rate movements and capital flows. However, these mechanisms would be complementary to IMF programmes in as much as the disbursement of funds would still be conditional on IMF funds being made available, except for 10 per cent, which could be given automatically for a short-term liquidity crisis.

In Kobe in January 2001 at the Third Asia–Europe Meeting (ASEM) of Finance Ministers, there was a surprising consensus on the need for new exchange rate mechanisms for Asian countries and measures to increase monetary cooperation. The outcome was a Japanese financed 'Kobe Research Project' to bring together think tanks on regional monetary cooperation and exchange rate regimes to study the feasibility of further monetary cooperation. At the same meeting France and Japan, supported by the Euro Group representing the European Central Bank, proposed an exchange rate basket containing the euro, yen and US dollar as reference currencies, with joint intervention based on a band with central parities, as a possible precursor to a European-type collective exchange rate mechanism.

In a follow up to the Chiang Mai initiative in May 2001 at the Asian

Development Bank meeting in Honolulu there was agreement to set up some surveillance/monitoring machinery supported by a Japanese secretariat. This was seen to be a first step towards further monetary cooperation which might ultimately include exchange rate mechanisms to limit currency fluctuations and full monetary union based on a single currency. A series of currency swap deals were also signed bilaterally between Japan and Thailand, Japan and Malaysia, and Japan and Korea. Unlike repo agreements these swaps involve a real credit risk for the lender. More of such arrangements are expected in the future, including a swap deal between Japan and China in which, for the first time, the Japanese yen would be exchanged for the renmimbi rather than the US$.

There is no doubt that these deals represent an important symbolic first step towards further monetary integration in the Asian region, but one needs to put them in perspective. The amount of reserves involved in these swap deals is still quite small and unlikely to make much difference in the event of a concerted speculative attack on a currency. The Thai government in 1997 called on a swap arrangement put in place after the Mexican crisis of 1994–95, but to little avail. Indeed it may even have exacerbated the problem since it looked like a sign of desperation. Is monetary integration in Asia a real possibility or just a pipedream?

In fact, Singapore already has a curious currency union with Brunei. Indeed, the Brunei ringgit is the only currency which can be obtained for Singapore dollars at a known and fixed rate, and the only sense in which Singapore operates a true currency Board system (Peebles and Wilson, 1996, p. 132). Under a 'currency interchangeability arrangement' introduced in June 1967, Brunei, Malaysia and Singapore adopted free interchangeability of their currencies. In 1973 Malaysia dropped out to focus on its own independent monetary policy, but Singapore and Brunei continue to accept each others' currency as 'customary tender' and exchange it at par into their own currency, periodically repatriating the accumulated stock of notes back to the country of origin. In essence, the arrangement is a currency union characterized by a one-for-one exchange rate and a joint managed floating exchange rate mechanism. There is no formal cooperative support mechanism but in practice a joint monetary policy is conducted by the MAS as a by-product of its policy of targeting the exchange rate.

Both countries seem to benefit from the arrangement as a common currency enhances trade and factor flows between the two countries and the effective pooling of the money stock and foreign exchange reserves reduces the threat from an outside speculative attack. Singapore benefits, in particular, from the attraction of Brunei funds into Singapore and the ADM through Singapore's offshore banks, and Brunei benefits from the credibility of Singapore's monetary policy keeping inflation low and the currency stable. There is little evidence of serious trade imbalances between the two countries or differential unemployment rates, even though there is limited inter-country labour mobility (Ngiam and Chan, 1992a). Brunei has given up its own monetary policy but seems happy to be the passive partner, and Singapore has little to lose.

For monetary integration to be feasible the countries concerned must have already achieved sufficient similarity in their economic structures and economic policies or demonstrate that they will converge fairly quickly once integration is underway. 'Similarity' in this sense increases the potential benefits of integration, such as the creation of a single homogeneous market for goods, services and assets, and minimizes the costs of giving up an independent monetary policy and exchange rate mechanism. It would be desirable, for example, to have a high level of labour mobility between the union members (Mundell, 1961), to permit a country experiencing a negative shock to its economy and rising unemployment, not affecting other members (an asymmetric shock), to use migration as a safety valve. It also helps if the countries are relatively open to international trade (McKinnon, 1963), since open economies with strong 'pass-through' effects from international prices to domestic prices would lose very little in a common monetary arrangement from abandoning their exchange rate weapon as a means of improving export competitiveness.

Monetary integration is also more likely to be successful if the countries involved have similar business cycles, inflation rates, unemployment levels, budget deficits, real interest rates and movements in exchange rates. High correlations of output movements and macro-indicators among the members signals similarity in economic structures, less need to retain independent policy instruments and greater potential success for common policies, as does evidence of symmetry or harmony in the type of economic shocks which affect their economies over time.

As far as Asia is concerned, the general conclusion (Bayoumi and Mauro, 1999; Eichengreen and Bayoumi, 1998) seems to be that the economic criteria for some sort of monetary integration are not as well fulfilled as for Europe or the USA in the past, but that the differences are not as great as one might have expected. There is, nonetheless, some ambiguity as to which particular subset of Asian countries would have the best chance of success, given the greater diversity in levels of development and economic objectives in the region. The belief that closer integration itself would bring about the necessary convergence (the 'endogeneity' argument), as in Europe after the signing of the Maastricht Treaty in 1991, would also have to apply even more strongly in the Asian case.

It is true that labour markets are relatively flexible in East and South-east Asia and there is a certain amount of labour migration measured in terms of the percentage of foreign workers in the labour force (Goto and Hamada, 1994), but most of the migration in the region is one way from poorer countries such as the Philippines to the richer countries of Brunei, Hong Kong, Malaysia and Singapore, or comes from outside the region as unskilled labour from Bangladesh to work in the construction industry in Singapore, or highly skilled labour from Europe and the United States to work in the business and financial services sectors in Singapore and Hong Kong.

Most countries in East Asia are also 'open' by international standards and intra-Asian trade has certainly increased since the 1980s. But it is less clear that the intensity of trade between Asian countries has grown as fast as for Western Europe in the past when allowance is made for the rapid growth in the size of trade as a whole (Frankel and Wei, 1994; Goto and Hamada, 1994). Intra-bloc trade in ASEAN is also exaggerated by the inclusion of sizeable re-exports for countries such as Singapore, Malaysia and Hong Kong, and the dominant role played by Singapore in bilateral trade within the bloc. Bilateral trade between other Asian countries, such as Thailand and the Philippines, can be quite small. There is also some doubt about the similarity of intra-Asian trade measured in terms of correlations between countries in the share or composition of imports and exports by product category (Kwan et al., 1998). ASEAN, in particular, is not as diversified as one would expect (Nicolas, 1999) and there are large differences between Singapore, which is well diversified, and more primary dependent economies such as Indonesia or Brunei.

The evidence is somewhat mixed on the confluence of major macroeconomic aggregates and similarity in business cycles in East Asia, and is sensitive to the choice of countries used. Mookerjee and Tongzon (1997), for instance found some evidence for common cycles in ASEAN countries linked to US and Japanese cycles. Kwan (1998) found less dispersion in inflation rates than for Europe, but Taguchi (1994) found low correlations in stock prices, interest rates and aggregate price levels. Looking at the inter-relationship between a range of macroeconomic variables simultaneously Goto and Hamada (1994) concluded that East Asia was at least as homogenous as Europe. More recent studies (Yuen, 2000; Kim and Chow, 2000) are less optimistic that a common monetary policy in East Asia would be able to cope with the type of shocks which are specific to each country.

For exchange rates specifically (Aggarwal and Mongoue, 1993), there is some evidence that the currencies of Japan, Hong Kong, Malaysia, the Philippines and Singapore move together over time (are cointegrated), but Tse (1997) concluded that this was only so if South Korea and Taiwan are added to the list. Eichengreen and Bayoumi (1998) found little support for an East Asian monetary bloc if the American dollar, German mark or the Japanese yen are used as the anchor currency, and the case was weaker than for the earlier European bloc based on the German mark. The tendency for East Asian countries in the past to independently peg their currencies quite closely to the US$ is likely of itself to increase the correlation between their currencies, but it is hard to believe that these countries have the same degree of similarity in their exchange rate objectives as the Europeans had by the 1980s.

Even if we were to accept that some form of monetary integration in East or South-east Asia was feasible on economic criteria, it is very doubtful that these countries have the requisite political will and institutional precondi- tions to pursue monetary integration beyond some minimal level of coop- eration in the foreseeable future. At the height of the economic uncertainty surrounding the breakdown of the Bretton Woods system of fixed exchange rates in the early 1970s, the commitment to ultimate monetary union in Europe was unrelenting and driven by a steady supply of influential statesmen committed to the European 'ideal' and they were willing to relinquish 'sovereignty' over monetary and fiscal policy, open up capital and labour markets, and adopt 'harmonized' policies. As Lee Kuan Yew suggested recently: first you must find a Helmet Kohl willing to give up his Deutschmark, or Nicolas (1999, p. 18) in relation to ASEAN's poor track record on joint economic initiatives: 'the chances of an ASEAN cur- rency unit getting off the ground are slim because countries are still too inward-looking and too inclined to pursue national interests above regional ones'. It is very difficult to believe, for example, that Singapore would be prepared to compromise its highly successful policy of managed floating in the interests of a common exchange rate policy in the foreseeable future.

Moreover, the fall-out from the Asian financial crisis, whilst stimulating some soul-searching, has probably increased socioeconomic disparities in the region and reduced the political solidarity of groups such as ASEAN. Singapore, for example, has recently begun to rethink its geopolitical posi- tion and sought to distance itself from some of the more dubious economic policies of neighbouring countries. Singapore has also been actively pursu- ing bilateral trade initiatives in spite of protests from some ASEAN partners (see Section 7.8 above). Gone has the consensus (if it ever really existed) on 'Asian values'. Can Japan really play the pivotal role in Asia that Germany has done in Europe, especially in view of the current poor shape of the economy? The Japanese government seems determined to promote Japan's role in the international monetary system and the idea of Asian monetary institutions independent of the IMF is appealing to the Malaysian govern- ment, but one wonders whether the enmity between Japan and its neigh- bours, such as Korea and China, over Japanese atrocities during the Second World War can be resolved quickly, at least until Japan follows the example of (West) Germany and apologizes unreservedly for its past actions.

9. Back to the future: continuity or real paradigm shift?

In this chapter we first examine how the Asian financial crisis affected the macroeconomic conditions in Singapore and the nature of the government's policy responses. We then summarize some of the main changes the economy is undergoing and the immediate short-term problems it faces and the nature of the government's responses. We identify the year 2001 as a possible pivotal year in the history of Singapore in which economic slow-down, continuing globalization and continuing liberalization within Singapore seem to have galvanized the government to formulate a vision of 'The New Singapore' which will have a new 'social compact' with the people and is to be achieved within ten years. Many of the features of this vision are very different from those we have seen to have supported economic growth so far and could create a new paradigm for development in Singapore. We conclude by examining some of the problems associated with this new paradigm.

9.1 THE RECENT RECESSIONS

Singapore emerged from the Asian financial crisis of 1997 relatively well compared to other countries in the region in terms of growth, inflation and the balance of payments. The only important negative impact was on the financial sector with falling stock prices, property prices and asset wealth as the currency lost value and incomes fell. Export growth was negative in 1998 but had resumed its 1997 growth rate by 2000.

There are a number of reasons why Singapore escaped relatively unscathed compared to Thailand, Indonesia, Malaysia and Hong Kong, including good policies and sound fundamentals for the economy. Capital inflows into Singapore tend to be dominated by productive foreign direct investment, which translates ultimately into exports, rather than short-term capital which may be more speculative in nature and fuel domestic consumption. Fiscal conservatism also dampened liquidity from the inflow and timely pre-emptive regulations had been introduced in May 1996 to cool the property market ahead of the boom. Singapore had also coped with the influx of foreign capital in the 1990s much better than did neighbouring countries and did not fall into the trap of trying to manage the currency too tightly against the American dollar to maintain export competitiveness in the US market, but was prepared to allow the local currency to appreciate in the face of capital inflows, especially if this kept down import prices. The fact that there were restrictions on the lending of the dollar by domestic banks to foreigners probably also reduced the scope for a speculative attack on the local currency.

Table 9.1 shows the quarterly development of important indicators of growth for the period 1997 to early 2001. Data are percentage changes over the same period of the previous. For 1998, a year in which annual growth was only 0.1 per cent, this slowdown was associated with four quarters of lower external demand. The annual growth rates for 1999 and 2000 were 5.9 per cent and 9.9 per cent, respectively, which were accompanied by much higher rates of external demand. In 2000, for example, exports of goods rose 22 per cent which led to the manufacturing sector being the largest contributor to growth.

Table 9.1   Quarterly macroeconomic indicators, 1997–2001

	GDP	Private consumption	Public consumption	Private GFCF	Public GFCF	External demand	CPI inflation	Unit labour cost
1997Q1	5.3	6.1	5.0	3.0	8.5	1.4	1.7	3.3
1997Q2	9.4	6.9	18.2	−3.0	32.9	10.0	1.8	−0.1
1997Q3	11.5	8.2	−7.3	25.5	31.7	10.5	2.3	−2.0
1997Q4	7.9	2.9	19.2	4.7	18.0	7.1	2.3	1.3
1998Q1	4.5	1.0	9.2	13.2	17.2	3.2	1.1	4.9
1998Q2	0.0	−1.7	10.1	−6.4	9.1	−6.0	0.1	7.1
1998Q3	−2.5	−6.7	1.9	−14.2	−1.5	−6.2	−0.9	5.4
1998Q4	−1.4	−4.1	10.4	−27.3	10.5	−7.6	−1.4	−0.9
1999Q1	1.3	−1.6	18.2	−26.4	24.3	−3.5	−0.7	−7.6
1999Q2	6.9	5.9	−2.7	−0.8	−1.9	6.8	0.0	−13.5
1999Q3	7.4	9.1	0.4	2.3	0.0	7.3	0.3	−11.3
1999Q4	7.7	7.9	−2.9	4.3	−5.1	16.9	0.5	−4.6
2000Q1	9.8	9.9	6.8	11.2	−11.6	16.9	1.1	−1.7
2000Q2	8.4	9.8	6.4	7.0	−2.3	12.6	0.8	−0.5
2000Q3	10.3	9.6	6.2	10.5	−0.1	19.5	1.5	−0.4
2000Q4	11.0	8.2	38.0	5.9	4.2	12.2	2.0	−1.1
2001Q1	4.7	7.2	−9.0	5.3	16.3	7.5	1.7	8.7
2001Q2	−0.9	3.0	28.1	−5.3	22.8	−4.2	1.7	12.5

Note: Data are percentage changes from the same period of the previous year.

Source: MAS Economics Department Quarterly Bulletin, March 2001, and October 2001. Tables 1, 2, 3, 4 and 6.

There is some evidence in the table that public expenditures, both for consumption and investment, were increased in those quarters, especially in 1998, when private expenditures fell. The fall in private fixed capital formation was significant in both 1998 and 1999 and on an annual basis fell 9.9 per cent and 6.1 per cent in each of these years. This reduced the share of investment in GNP to less than 30 per cent, its lowest level since the late 1960s. The changes in public expenditures might have had an effect in preventing a greater slowdown in 1998 when growth was essentially zero, but demand-side policies are not seen as effective in Singapore for all the reasons we have identified in previous chapters. The fall in the investment share in GNP after 1997 that was accompanied by an increasing saving rate contributed to the very large current account balances we have noted. We can see that by the second quarter of 2001 output and external demand had fallen at a time when unit labour costs were increasing. Again there is some evidence of public investment and consumption being used to offset falls or low growth in private expenditures. The MAS estimates that if public expenditures had not increased in the second quarter of 2001 GDP would have fallen by 1.4 per cent and not the 0.9 per cent registered. (Monetary Authority of Singapore, 2001d, p. 19).

The main thrust of the anti-recessionary policy in 1998 was cost-cutting to reduce the nominal and real effective exchange rate and relative unit labour costs compared to major competitors by widening the nominal exchange rate band and introducing a package of cost cuts, the first elements of which were announced in late 1998. Employers' CPF contributions were halved from the beginning of 1999, and many charges for services by GLCs and statutory boards were reduced. The total value of these cuts was about \$10000 million. As Table 9.1 shows, these measures, together with productivity improvements and wage restraint effectively reduced unit labour costs (ULC) significantly from the last quarter of 1998. In the manufacturing sector these cost reductions were more pronounced and in 1999 unit labour costs in manufacturing fell 17.3 per cent and by 7.1 per cent in 2000. As we have seen, ULC is an important determinant of domestic inflation and in the recessionary period inflation was very low as measured by the Consumer Price Index. These supply-side policy reactions were essentially a repeat of those used to deal with the 1985–86 recession. Unit labour costs rose in the first quarter of 2001 and this is partly attributable to the 4-percentage point restoration in employers' CPF contributions.

We have argued that 'cost-cutting' should best be seen as aimed at redistributing income to capital in the belief that this will sustain employment and prevent firms from moving from Singapore. We have also seen, in Chapter 4, that government statisticians believe that an increase in the remuneration (wage) share is a portent of recession. Table 9.2 shows the changes in the absolute amounts of the different forms of factor payments from the previous year and Table 9.3 shows their impact on the factor shares as a percentage of GDP at market prices so that indirect taxes (known here as taxes on production and on imports) can be thought of as one form of government income receipts. Compensation of employees includes wages and salaries in both cash and kind as well as employers' contributions to CPF and private pensions and insurance funds for their employees.

Table 9.2   Change in factor payments, 1996–2000

Percentage change over previous year	1996	1997	1998	1999	2000
Compensation of employees	10.0	9.2	4.1	−3.0	9.6
Gross operating surplus:	7.8	8.5	−6.4	11.3	11.9
Financial corporations	1.7	28.5	−6.1	26.3	3.3
Non-financial corporations	9.0	5.2	−5.9	9.9	14.4
Others	9.4	11.6	−1.8	4.5	3.5
Less imputed banks service charge	10.3	13.3	4.3	9.4	1.7
Taxes on production and on imports	5.5	9.1	−17.1	−1.5	22.6

Source: Calculated from *Yearbook of Statistics Singapore 2001*, Table 5.9.

Table 9.3   Factor shares in GDP, 1996–2000

Percentage of GDP	1996	1997	1998	1999	2000
Compensation of employees	43.3	43.2	45.9	43.1	42.2
Gross operating surplus:	46.6	46.2	44.1	47.5	47.5
Financial corporations	6.4	7.5	7.2	8.7	8.1
Non-financial corporations	36.3	34.9	33.5	35.6	36.4
Others	9.9	10.0	10.0	10.1	9.4
Imputed banks service charge	−6.0	−6.2	−6.6	−7.0	−6.4
Taxes on production and on imports	10.5	10.5	8.9	8.5	9.3

Note: Figures do not add to 100 as the statistical discrepancy has been omitted.

Source: Calculated from *Yearbook of Statistics Singapore 2001*, Table 5.9.

Table 9.2 shows that over the period 1996–98 the rate of growth of employees' compensation exceeded the growth of the operating surplus which increased the share of GDP earned as compensation. In 1998 the operating surplus of all sectors of the economy fell as did indirect tax receipts, and growth ceased, but that can better be attributed to external factors than to any domestic cause. 'Cost-cutting' measures were adopted in 1998 which, together with a slight increase in unemployment and wage restraint, produced a fall in the amount of remuneration in absolute terms and the operating surplus increased as a share of GDP in 1999. We cannot determine from these data how the 'cost-cutting' or redistributive policies affected local and foreign firms. The concern of the government was to maintain the incomes of possibly mobile foreign firms and prevent a rise in unemployment. In 1999 it was financial corporations that saw the largest increase in their operating surplus and in 2000 its was non-financial corporations which would include those in the manufacturing sector where foreign firms are most significant. In 1998 earnings of resident foreigners and resident foreign companies fell 2.7 per cent whereas the earnings of Singaporeans in Singapore fell 1.6 per cent. In 1999 these two items increased by 2.6 per cent and 3.8 per cent, respectively, but in 2000 foreigners' earnings increased by as much as 15.9 per cent when local earnings rose 9.9 per cent and nominal GDP rose 11.9 per cent. This increased the share of foreigners' earnings in GDP to 34.8 per cent (*Yearbook of Statistics Singapore 2001*, p. 61). These changes would be the product of both government measures and market forces but there is no doubt in most quarters that the government measures were a success in preventing a large increase in unemployment and larger falls in output. This is simply the latest example of an unorthodox, but highly successful, approach to macro-stabilization policy.

9.2   THE PRESENT IS THE PAST AGAIN

By the end of the year 2000 it looked as if Singapore had recovered rapidly from the affects of the Asian financial crisis. However, the very vulnerability of the economy that has been discussed in earlier chapters and was the concern of planners in the early 1990s ensured the progress of the economy during 2001 was very different from what had generally been expected, even early in that year. The slowdown in the American economy and its reduction in capital investment in information technology items, in particular, hit the electronics export markets of many Asian economies. Global electronics demand contracted sharply early in the year and continued to fall. In Singapore, chip sales are taken as an indicator of electronics demand and in the first quarter of 2001 global chip sales fell 20 per cent quarter-on-quarter, which was the largest fall in 20 years. Electronics production declined and other supporting parts of the manufacturing sector saw reductions in output. With such a weakening in manufacturing production and exports the transport sector, both in sea and air cargo shipments, experienced contractions. Prospects became more and more gloomy and the government cut its forecast for 2001's annual growth from a range of 5 to 7 per cent which it had maintained and defended as a reasonable forecast from November 2000 to February 2001, to 3.5 to 5.5 per cent in April and by July 2001 was forecasting annual growth of only 0.5 to 1.5 per cent. Some private sector forecasters were forecasting an absolute fall in GDP in 2001 for Singapore and in October 2001 the government announced a forecast for a 3 per cent fall in GDP for the whole of 2001 and predicted growth of between −2 per cent and 2 per cent for 2002. Many of these forecasters were, in contrast, expecting positive although slow growth for neighbouring Asian Countries for the whole of 2001. This was the pattern observed in the first quarter of 2001 (*The Economist*, 4 August, 2001, p. 84). If this turns out to be the actual pattern for the whole of 2001 then it would be in contrast with the events of 1998 when Singapore avoided recession but its neighbours suffered large output reductions. This is interpreted as highlighting 'Singapore's extreme vulnerability to the vagaries of world electronics demand' (Abeysinghe et al., 2001, p. 10). For an account of the beginning of the recession of 2001 and a comparison with earlier recessions and the government's response see Monetary Authority of Singapore (2001d). One of their conclusions is that the 2001 recession will be more prolonged than those of 1985 and 1998 (ibid., p. 83).

9.3   THE 2001 RECESSION IS DIFFERENT BUT THE POLICY REACTIONS WERE THE SAME

The February 2001 budget had not considered these events but was focused on tax reductions to benefit the domestic production sector and small local firms. The flexibility of the Singapore system and the extent of public sector involvement means that off-budget changes can be introduced quickly and on 25 July a whole range of cost-cutting and employment enhancement measures were announced in parliament. In addition, some social infrastructure projects were brought forward but such demand side measures are not expected to be sufficient to maintain demand (Yeo, 2001, p. 2). The expectation that low growth would cause higher than expected rates of retrenchment and unemployment meant that the package provided that government agencies (CPF and HDB in particular) would take circumstances into account and allow rescheduling of households' mortgage payments. Although significantly less than those of 1998 these measures were assessed to be as much as $2200 million over one year which is equivalent to 1.4 per cent of GDP. The minister made it clear that if 'the global economic situation worsens, we have the resources to do more, and will be ready to do so' (Yeo, 2001, p. 10).

One aspect of the measures was to cut labour costs by extending the earlier reduction in the foreign worker levy, not restoring the employers' CPF rate to its 20 per cent rate and relying on firms to cut wages and retain employees, as there now is a greater variable component in the wage. Property tax rebates and rental rebates were extended for companies and there was a 20 per cent cut in port duties. More funds were made available to the various public schemes to subsidize worker retraining and to help retrenched workers move into the services sector. It has been realized that of the expected 20000 retrenchments expected in 2001 many of these jobs will be in the manufacturing sector and will not remain in Singapore as some of the MNCs in electronics have announced transfers of some aspects of production to neighbouring countries. As the Minister for Trade and Industry put it:

> Workers should take this opportunity to train and upgrade ourselves so that we can switch quickly to new and better jobs. The Government will do everything possible to attract investment, promote development and help workers stay employable. We have weathered more serious economic crises before. Provided we respond cohesively and rationally, we have every reason to be confident of overcoming this downturn, and emerging more resilient and competitive than ever. (Yeo, 2001, p. 11)

In addition, the cooperative movement announced that its supermarkets would reduce the prices of basic items by up to 20 per cent. So, here we have a repeat of the policies that have been used to deal with earlier recessions. Despite the slowdown and a widely perceived deterioration in the stability of the region and increased interest in China as a destination for foreign investment, especially in electronics, all signs are that foreign investment commitments to Singapore remain strong. It is claimed that for manufacturing two-thirds of the targeted $9000 million commitment for 2001 was achieved in the first half of the year and commitments to the services sector continued at a high rate.

As the perception of the marked slowdown of the economy in 2001 was accepted the government announced another off-budget set of policies in October 2001. This set of policies was said to be equivalent in value to $11.3 billion (about 7 per cent of GDP), more than that used during the Asian financial crisis and as this package did not include cuts in CPF, it is significantly larger than the earlier policy in terms of extra expenditures, tax cuts and redistributive policies. It also included the issue of 'New Singapore' shares amounting to $2.7 billion (see below). Much of the package contained familiar and expected policies. Many construction projects are to be brought forward, individuals were given extra tax rebates as were companies, which would cost the government about $3 billion. Unemployed and poor people would get rebates on their utility bills, help to pay their mortgages for public houses and reductions in hospital fees. In addition a new scheme, the Economic Downturn Relief Scheme, was established to help those suffering severe difficulties through unemployment but the amount allocated was only $20 million. This sum would be distributed by citizens' consultation committees which are always headed by a PAP member of parliament on a discretionary basis and would be given to cover basic expenses such as school fees and transport fees but would be for a limited time period. Much more money would be put in retraining schemes for workers and one novel aspect of this package was the recognition that more people in middle management or able to earn about $4000 a month were unemployed and so would be eligible for support in retraining. Despite talk of moving to a market economy and having no subsidies, the government put a lot more money into the schemes that provides subsidized loans and 'micro-loans' for local companies, possible supporting companies that really should close down. The government also tightly restricted its sales of land for residential and industrial purposes. In the views of one commentator this was just the old familiar case of the government propping up the property and banking sectors when times were a bit difficult for them and that the government was just 'bailing them out' (Lee, H.S., 2001, p. 9). Although there were no cuts in the CPF contributions wages would be restrained, there would be no bonuses for civil servants and political appointees and senior civil servants would take a pay cut of 10 per cent and government ministers 17.3 per cent. Allowances of MPs and Nominated MPs would be cut by 10 per cent also. One clear feature of these measures is that there was no attempt to formalize a social security system to help the unemployed and they would benefit from a whole range of subsidies, rebates and ad hoc assistance provided by politicians on a discretionary basis.

9.4   A PARADIGM SHIFT?

From the vantage point of October 2001, Singapore has been remarkably successful in terms of its economic development since the mid 1960s. It is in the top seven countries in the world ranked by GNP per capita, and is one of the few countries to have achieved rapid growth in output over successive decades, even in the 1990s when expectations were that growth would fall to a more sustainable level as input-driven growth is replaced by 'quality' growth in total factor productivity. Moreover, Singapore's welfare achievements have probably been understated in international comparisons.

This has been achieved with a good deal of continuity in economic policy, together with a significant amount of pragmatism and unorthodoxy when required. Yet Singapore still exhibits many of the characteristics of an 'immature' or 'underdeveloped' economy and a reputation for an authoritarian style of politics. The characteristics of extreme openness to trade and factor flows, 'dependence' on foreign resources, and vulnerability to external shocks, has provided the rationale for a development strategy based on high levels of forced saving through the CPF, high levels of centrally directed investment, a persistent build-up of official foreign exchange reserves and a strongly 'interventionist' government in all sectors of the economy.

Since 1985, however, it has become harder to justify this development strategy, having already achieved the essential development infrastructure and given the opportunity costs in terms of private consumption and the over-centralization of savings and investment decisions. The strategy has undoubtedly worked well in the past but by the 1990s there surfaced new doubts that Singapore can continue to compete with both the newly-industrializing countries (including China) and the more advanced developed countries by increasing the quality of growth and responding to the economic and political pressures from globalization.

Perhaps it was time for a change in development strategy with more emphasis on a competitive return to private savings as households are given more freedom over their pension and personal investment decisions, financial institutions are encouraged to hold less government debt and government bodies begin to rely more on commercial risk management services. The growth of a short-term debt market also requires less 'forced' holdings of government debt.

Although liberalization in some sectors had been planned from about 1997 we can see that there is nothing like a recession in Singapore to produce considerations of the nature of policy and development strategy. The 1985–86 recession produced reports calling for more privatization but in the view of many this did not go very far and did not change the basic nature of the economy and the extent of government involvement. By the middle of 2001 very different views of the future of Singapore were being promoted. Whether they will be realized is another thing but they do sound revolutionary. One output for these new views was a conference organized in early August 2001 by the EDB on the New Economy where the Deputy Prime Minister spoke as did the main invited guest, Professor Michael Porter of Harvard University, who is probably best known for Porter (1990). In that work he observed of Singapore that:

While it has made substantial progress since its formation, Singapore remains a factor-driven economy. Singapore is largely a production base for foreign multinationals. Attracted by Singapore's relatively low-cost, well-educated workforce and efficient infrastructure including roads, ports, airports and telecommunications. Indigenous companies have yet to develop to a significant extent, nor have they been given much emphasis in economic policy. Singapore's improvement in living standards has come from upgrading the quality of human resources and infrastructure in order to upgrade the quality of jobs. (Porter, 1990, p. 566)

Eleven years after this judgement his current advice is aimed at overcoming some of these remaining and other weaknesses and proposing a new direction for the nature of economic policy. For example, he recommended a move towards a service-oriented economy as economies such as Taiwan, China and Korea, seen as competitors in manufacturing, are not so efficient in the potential supply of services such as health care, consulting and asset management. He remarked that domestic industries are not efficient enough which is partly the result of a low level of domestic competition. More business clusters based on existing sectors such as electronics, information technology, petrochemicals, health care and business services should be developed. One particularly noticeable suggestion was to develop deeper cooperation with Indonesia and Malaysia and this should be part of the creation of different industry clusters.

We have already seen that one of the side-effect changes in Singapore's trade pattern in the last decade has been the closer production and trade-based integration between Malaysia and Singapore, particularly in electronics. A major motive for multinational companies to locate in Johor Bahru appears to be its geographical proximity to Singapore's managerial and professional expertise, while at the same time some of Singapore's high-tech firms have been expanding into Malaysia, and to Johor Bahru in particular, looking for relatively well-developed infrastructure and lower cost land and labour. They have not, however, reduced the extent of their operations in Singapore. In other words, firms on both sides of the causeway are taking advantage of complementarities between the two locations, with Singapore-based firms establishing manufacturing operations in Johor Bahru whilst retaining their headquarters and research and development activities in Singapore. This could be seen as a challenging approach as it might reduce Singapore's involvement in the larger groups such as ASEAN and APEC.

Porter also stressed the need for the government to reduce its involvement in the economy, particularly as it has not been able to foster innovation, and he repeated the point being made in Singapore that association with the government has been a problem for some companies when trying to expand overseas.

One prescription of Porter's that attracted much comment for its vagueness (Khanna, 2001, p. 1) and marks a break with the perception of the very foundation of Singapore's success is that there was a need to 'create a more "chaotic" and heterogeneous [*sic*] society that is more flexible and tolerant of different groups of people with new ideas, tastes and beliefs' (*The Straits Times*, 3 August, 2001, p. S12). Presumably, the idea is that 'chaos' leads to freer thinking and therefore innovation and that perhaps the government has not been tolerant in the past of some groups that could have contributed more to Singapore.

At the same conference the deputy prime minister, Lee Hsien Loong, articulated what is probably the most pro-reform set of comments when he remarked that the government must allow the free market to work:

> We must free companies to make business decisions unencumbered by regulations and restrictions, and we must avoid distorting price signals through subsidies and taxes.
> A primary factor is whether we have the talent – people with the ideas, the dynamism and the risk-taking spirit to venture forth, seize a market opportunity, and create a business. (*The Straits Times*, 3 August, 2001, p. 1)

If future economic historians think it worthwhile to write full studies of the Singapore economy, either because it was then regarded as an outstanding success or because it had followed the fate of other trading city-states and had declined, then there will be certain key years in that history they will identify. The years 1965 and 1985 will, as we have seen in this study, be identified as important years. The Asian financial crisis might be given less prominence than expected but we think that the year 2001 might be considered as the key year when the extent of policy changes was revolutionary enough to indicate a strong desire to change the economy and society significantly. An event that reinforced the degree of commitment to earlier changes such as those introduced in the February 2001 budget and the continued commitment to reform in the financial sector might be seen in the Prime Minister's National Day address in August 2001 (Goh, 2001). Although revisiting in his speech many of the themes we have seen above he went much further and outlined the need to create a 'New Singapore' and to establish a new social compact with the population which was seen as more mobile than ever before. In getting to 'The New Singapore', which was defined as 'a global city with a strong social compact, . . . we will have to discard mindsets and old ways of doing things that have become irrelevant'. Many aspects of those mindsets had, of course, been proposed and enforced by the government itself in the 1980s and 1990s, in particular its attack on 'individualism'. Now it is stressing the need for innovation, risk-taking, not resenting businessmen 'who made it big' and giving 'a second, a third and further chance to those who have failed'. As Backman (1999, p. 15) puts it: 'Creativity is a highly individualistic endeavour – something that exposes one to potential ridicule.' How is the government going to unwind the mindsets that it itself has stressed as essentially Singaporean and characteristic of Asian values for years and are said by many to typify the Asian character?

The new economic strategy is to have five aspects and was expected to be implemented over the next ten years:

- The economy had to become global and to reach out to new markets in the region and the rest of the world.
- Ensure that Singaporeans become more enterprising and more willing to take risks.
- Singaporeans had to become more innovative.
- The domestic sector had to become more competitive as it was felt that it was far less competitive than the export sector.
- Increase the level of local talent and 'top it up from outside'.

Now, these are familiar themes but the press felt that the Prime Minister was seen to put a greater deal of urgency in his remarks than usual, especially as he introduced the idea of a new 'social compact' with the people. He announced the introduction of 'New Singapore' shares, a scheme under which every citizen would be given shares that would pay a guaranteed dividend with bonuses in those years when the economy was performing well. Details of the scheme were announced in October 2001. In essence the 'shares' are five-year government bonds each of a value of $1 to be given to all eligible adult Singaporeans with an active CPF account, about 1.98 million people altogether. The allocation and payments are to be administered by the CPF system. The 'shares' were distributed on 1 November 2001 and recipients could cash in up to half of their value from the next day. They could cash in all of them after November 2002. This indicates that the government was conscious that many households did need immediate cash relief, as top-ups to their CPF accounts, the usual form of redistribution, cannot be encashed. In fact, many people were already applying in October to encash their entitlement so they would be paid on 2 November. It seems that only 6.6 per cent of those receiving 'shares', or 130 000 people, cashed in what they could by 1 November. However, 12.7 per cent of those receiving the largest allocation, as they were the lowest income earners, cashed in what they could (*The Straits Times*, 3 November, 2001, p. 3). The 'shares' will pay a dividend of 3 per cent a year plus a rate equal to the real growth rate of GDP of the preceding year, as long as it was not negative, to be paid in bonus shares and to be tax free. Those who hold the 'shares' to term will be able to cash them in in March 2007. The 'shares' are not tradable or transferable. The amounts given varied according to age, income and occupational status of the citizen. Those with incomes of more than $4000 a month get 200 shares, those earning less than $1200 a month receive 1400 shares. There are three intermediate income bands which received 400, 600 or 1000 shares. Unemployed people were allocated shares on the basis of the type of house they lived in. Those in 1–3-room HDB flats received the maximum allocation of 1400 shares and those in executive flats 400 and those in private housing 200. Those above the age of 62 and active National Servicemen received an extra 200 shares and non-active servicemen 100. The scheme can be seen as redistributive and aimed at providing immediate cash payments for those in need as they could cash in half of their shares on 2 November. In November 2002 they can cash in the rest, if they wish. About 441 000 people would receive the maximum allocation of 1400 shares. The total amount, $2.7 billion, is 1.7 per cent of 2000's GDP and 2 per cent of mid 2000 official foreign reserves. It was also announced that there could be future issues of such shares and that the distribution would be more towards middle-income households. The money has not come out of these official reserves but from the reserves accumulated during the tenure of the existing government, that is since 1997. It was also announced that there might be further 'share' issues and that the middle class might get larger benefits as there were several letters of complaint in the local press on the criteria on which amounts distributed were based

Many saw this as a political move signalling an impending general election. The sequence of events might support this view. On a Tuesday the Minister of Finance announced who would be getting how many shares, the next day the Electoral Boundaries Committee announced the new boundaries, the next day (18 October) parliament was dissolved and 25 October was announced as nomination day and 3 November as polling day. This would give the legal minimum of nine days' of campaigning but the PAP was able to introduce new candidates on television and present its manifesto the very day after parliament was dissolved. Other parts of the timing of the election must have been pure coincidence. The New Singapore shares were to be distributed on 1 November, half of them could be cashed in the next day and the following day, 3 November, was to be polling day. It must be a coincidence as general elections must be held on a Saturday and 3 November is a Saturday.

Despite talk in the government of removing price-distorting taxes and subsidies, the government said it remained committed to continue heavy subsidies for housing, education and healthcare as an important part of the new social compact.

In order to foster innovation the government is to establish a National

Innovation Council because, in the words of the prime minister: 'Sporadic innovation by a few Singapore companies and the public sector is not good enough. The innovative spirit must permeate our whole society.' The Prime Minister acknowledged the irony of using a 'top-down approach' to change the people mindsets and even called for non-conformist thinking but mainly gave examples of this from the business world (Goh, 2001, p. 13).

There would even be innovations in the political sphere, with the prime minister saying:

> I know some people want even greater freedom. Where politics is concerned, I prefer to ease up slowly rather than open up with a big bang. When Gorbachev opened up the Soviet Union with 'Glasnost', the Soviet Union collapsed with a big bang. We should therefore pump the air into the political balloon slowly. I don't intend to change my name to 'Goh Ba Chev'. (Goh, 2001, p. 20)

The desire to make a pun in a public address might have been the reason for linking Singapore to the Soviet Union but, then again, it might reveal how he sees the main features of the current political system.

In the following sections we discuss some of the issues facing Singapore as it tries to introduce this 'New Singapore' and identify to what extent they are continuations of past policies or the extent they can be seen as a real paradigm shift in the government's approach to the economy and society.

9.5   THE POLITICAL FUTURE

The short-run political future is easy to predict: the PAP has won the 2001 General Election and that will ensure continuity of leadership and allow the identification of which new cadres are of ministerial calibre. How the election is perceived to have been conducted will be a test of the PAP's recent statements that it believes in the positive benefits of non-conformist thinking.

The slightly longer-run political future depends on how the PAP and the country react to the retirement of Lee Kuan Yew from politics. Mr Lee, at the age of 78, stood in the November 2001 general election in a six-member GRC and was returned unopposed. In other words, no one voted for him. He is not certain whether he will stand in what everyone refers to as the 2007 election. The Huntington thesis is that his retirement will lead to the decline of Singapore.

There are some other factors that have been identified as having possible effects on the dominant position of the PAP. If there is a permanent slow-down in growth then, as we have seen, there will be smaller budget surpluses. The Constitution allows any government to use the surpluses accumulated in its period in office without permission from the President. The government says its still wants to see the total reserves increase year after year so would not use all of the surpluses it generates in its term of office, whether to return to the population through CPF top-ups, dividends on the new proposed 'Singapore shares' or by upgrading public housing. This last promise, and threat to withhold upgrading form less than loyal constituencies, has been an important part of PAP control. It has been conjectured that if the amounts made available for upgrading are substantially reduced then support of the PAP might decline. This might make it even more authoritarian as it has not had much experience with an outspoken and disaffected electorate.

9.6   REGULATION NOT CONTROL

The government sees the future Singapore as a more market-controlled economy with a smaller role being played by GLCs and statutory boards. There is talk of further privatization of government companies but this is only likely to be partial in the short run and there is not likely to be a complete change of ownership and, more importantly, control of major state companies. More statutory boards might be corporatized and part of their equity will be sold on the stock exchange in an attempt to build up a general local shareholders stake in Singapore, the motivation for the government selling part of the equity of SingTel in 1993. The government has identified one major problem in full privatization: there are just not enough local businessmen with enough capital to take over and run these companies. So far they have been run by an interlocking group of civil servants and co-opted businessmen. The alternative of the complete sale of local government companies to foreign firms is still being debated. If there is a larger privately-owned corporate sector then this will require the government to learn how to regulate rather than directly control its enterprises. Some industries are likely to be duopolies or monopolies and regulating will be required. Telecommunications, electricity power generation and banking are areas where there will be a few private, non-competitive companies and regulation in these areas will be important.

Another consequence of privatization of government companies is that in the future they cannot be ordered to cut prices and charges as part of the 'cost-cutting' packages that have been the government's main anti-recessionary policy. Market forces will have to work and these take time and wage reductions often require rising unemployment. This might make the government more prone to use the exchange rate as an anti-recessionary tool if domestic prices and costs do not fall enough in a recession. Wage reductions will probably be secured by having a larger variable component in the wage so that employers will be exhorted to cut wages rather than sacking large numbers of people in economic downturns. During the Asian crisis some in Hong Kong argued that it was easier for the Singapore system to cut domestic costs whereas in Hong Kong such cost reductions were more important as the currency was linked to the American dollar and the necessary domestic deflation required unemployment, a fall in property prices, lower profit margins and so on.

9.7 SUPERVISION NOT REGULATION

In contrast to Singapore's prominence in foreign exchange dealing and in international banking, its capital markets are relatively underdeveloped in terms of fixed income assets, equities and the fund management industry. At the same time changes in global financial markets in the 1990s increased competition and led to pressures to consolidate activity into fewer financial centres and developments in technology, which ensure that money can be managed from a wider range of locations than in the past, are eroding Singapore's locational advantages. Singaporeans are also beginning to expect a wider range of products with higher returns than are available in the local bank-dominated environment.

The dilemma for Singapore is that it wants to be a premier international financial centre with a wide range of activities, and it is committed to globalization and the accompanying technological advances, such as e-commerce, but if it opens up the domestic market too quickly it may not be able to compete given its small home base, lack of critical mass for a fund management sector, and doubts about its capacity to generate sufficient innovation.

Part of the problem again arises from the dominant, but largely successful, role that the government has played in the development of Singapore as a financial centre. After 1965, with few natural resources, and increasing political risks from regional neighbours, the decision was made to develop a modern financial centre which would serve its own industrialization needs but also those of the region.

Reforms introduced after the 1985 recession were designed to transform Singapore into a risk management centre based upon a range of money market and capital market activities, but by the 1990s a tradition of looking to the government for initiatives, combined with a reputation for a tight regulatory framework and generally conservative approach by the MAS led to complaints that the regulatory mechanism was complicating business practices and constraining private sector financial innovation and market development. The comparison was made between Singapore, where the authorities have been very pro-active with tight controls and conservative prudential standards, and Hong Kong which was seen to be more laissez-faire with minimal controls and little government interference.

Although the authorities have emphasized the gradual nature of the financial reforms introduced since 1988, including the opening up of the domestic banking sector to greater foreign participation and a change in emphasis from regulation to supervision, one could easily be forgiven for thinking that they constitute a 'big bang'. In addition, the MAS has always resisted pressures to fully internationalize the dollar, but there has, in fact, been a significant relaxation of the rules and further liberalization seems likely. What is impressive is that these reforms were being introduced at the height of the Asian financial crisis when other countries in the region, such as Malaysia, were retreating from the principle of open capital and money markets. There is no doubt that these reforms are essential to move Singapore in the right direction towards its goal of becoming a full service international financial centre, but there are significant risks, including the possibility that global alliances and increased foreign participation will squeeze local financial institutions out of the domestic market.

9.8   PERSONAL SAVING PROBLEM

Singapore's rapid growth has been supported by an extremely high rate of investment financed after the early period of development by an even larger rate of domestic saving. The great paradox is that although Singapore has achieved the highest rate of national saving in the world the government has long been concerned that individuals are not saving enough and do not have enough saving to finance their retirement or even short periods of unemployment. So far, the policies adopted have been rather ad hoc by allowing CPF members to try to get a better return on their funds that the CPF offers by managing part of their own funds and by introducing supplementary saving systems. The recently announced scheme of 'New Singapore' shares indicates the government's desire for people to have a source of income other than labour income. The scheme reflects the government's concept of Singapore Inc, of course.

As the CPF scheme has been used to allow people to pay their mortgages on public housing one suggestion is that retirees should use their property for reverse mortgaging but there has been very little interest in providing such products by the private sector in Singapore. There needs to be a lot of imaginative thinking for the government to be able to cope with the problem of inadequate savings of retirees and probably lower incomes for older people who chose to defer their retirements.

9. 9   SERVICES NOT MANUFACTURING

Many of the international advisory panels advising the government have stressed the need to shift to a more service-oriented economy. The recent slowdown can be directly attributed to the fall in export demand for electronic products. The government has stressed the need to maintain manufacturing at about 25 per cent of GDP but has sought to encourage service sectors that will service the manufacturing sector.

After the 1985–86 recession there was a perception that the narrowness of the production base left Singapore vulnerable to the threat of de-industrialization or the 'hollowing out' of the manufacturing sector as domestic costs rose and MNCs were tempted to relocate their plants to lower wage economies. Since 1985 Singapore has become even more commodity concentrated in electronics and chemicals exports and more geographically concentrated in regional markets in East and South-east Asia. The irony here is that policies introduced in response to the 1985–86 recession, such as helping local firms to 'grow a second wing' and expand into the region, contributed directly to the increase in both commodity and geographic concentration in the 1990s which are now perceived as constituting 'overspecialization'. This has raised concern in Singapore whether Singapore is able to compete sufficiently in the manufacturing sector in a changing global environment and whether there is a need to diversify away from overreliance on regional markets and 'grow a third wing', especially after the Asian financial crisis when the prospects for regional growth look more negative than before.

A high level committee on Singapore's competitiveness presented its recommendations in November 1998 and outlined a vision of turning Singapore into an advanced globally-competitive knowledge-intensive economy based on a manufacturing and services hub and support services from which MNCs and local companies can manufacture high value-added products and provide related services to companies in the region. 'Hollowing out' has been redefined as 'restructuring' as Singapore sheds its lower end manufacturing and moves up the ladder of value-added. Incentive schemes such as the Skills Development Fund and Promising Enterprise Programme are aimed at encouraging local talent and persuading successful Singaporean émigrés to return or at least 'network' with the mother country. To increase the supply of graduates, particularly in business, the Singapore Management University has now opened and foreign graduate schools are being set up by the University of Chicago, INSEAD, MIT and the Wharton School.

There are grounds for optimism here given Singapore's remarkable adaptability and resilience in the face of a changing international environment, but it is much more difficult to change the entrepreneurial environment along the lines suggested earlier by business guru Michael Porter than it is to change some of the broader aggregates of economic policy. It is also more difficult for the government to 'pick winners' than in the past and there is no guarantee of success, even if the risks are spread over a 'cluster' of activities. Whether government-based entrepreneurship and initiatives can be replaced quickly by a more competitive indigenous response remains to be seen.

Singapore slipped to fourth place in the World Economic Forum competitiveness rankings for 2001, down from second position in the previous year (*World Economic Forum 2001* at http://www.imd.ch/wcy). Although no specific explanation was given for Singapore's downgrading, it did comment on the over-reliance by investment-driven economies such as Singapore and Taiwan on high levels of infrastructure investment, Original Equipment Manufacturer (OEM) manufacturing for multinationals and guidance by the government to boost efficiency, especially as their current levels of wages and domestic costs makes them vulnerable to competition from lower wage countries such as China and that 'many countries get stuck at critical junctures of economic transition . . . old strategies can become new weaknesses' (cited from *The Business Times*, 19 October, 2001, p. 2).

In the short run there is likely to be a shift to service sector employment as manufacturing firms, especially in electronics, lay off more and more workers in 2001. In the longer run a shift to service provision and an increase in the value-added in the manufacturing sector which remains would solve this problem as long as the service sector expands to absorb the growing and retrenched workforce, but only if the workforce is able to adapt to the loss of lower end manufacturing jobs and switch to more service-oriented new economy jobs. Many of these workers will be eligible for subsidized retraining but it is not likely that many of the older ones can move into high-end service sectors such as banking, finance, teaching, research, architecture and so on. The government has told older workers to be less choosy in taking up new jobs as many of the manufacturing jobs will have gone forever. Bank mergers are likely to reduce job opportunities in the longer run in this sector as well. This might mean that Singaporean workers will take up the jobs in low-end services such as retailing, working in fast-food outlets and hawker centres (foreign workers are not allowed to work in hawker centres) and cleaning and gardening. They would thus displace many foreign workers who are commonly found in these sectors. This trend is likely to widen even more the distribution of income.

It may be too early to say whether the Gini coefficient, which stabilized in the early 1990s, has been increasing but the same problem will arise as in the 1980s: a restructuring towards the services sector and increased use of foreign talent may increase the disparities between high- and low-income earners which is a consequence of the dualistic labour market. In the financial and business services sector and in professional jobs earnings are kept high by an excess demand for foreign 'talent' for which there is no local substitute, whilst at the other end of the labour market wages are kept low by a steady inflow of unskilled labour from the region employed in unskilled manual jobs. This feature of the Singapore labour market is likely to persist. Less clear is whether the widening gap between the richest and the poorest and the increase in household inequality in the latter part of the 1990s will be maintained. Given the strong links with educational attainment and pressures from globalization of the labour market, it will be important to maintain equal educational opportunities and expand the tertiary sector and continue giving extra resources to disadvantaged groups.

9.10 FOREIGN TALENT AND FOREIGN FIRMS ARE WELCOME

Singapore has been very successful in attracting foreign direct investment compared to other developing countries and the appeal of Singapore as a destination for foreign direct investment has not significantly diminished despite rising production and living costs and the removal of obstacles to foreign direct investment in other countries in the region, such as China. Total investment commitments in manufacturing still overwhelmingly come from abroad so Singapore is still heavily dependent on foreigners.

Attempts in the early 1990s to diversify the structure of the economy in the longer run away from exclusive reliance on a predominantly foreign manufacturing base was not seen as a negative reaction to foreigners or foreign capital per se but as a positive move towards a more diversified economy and higher domestic value-added. Changes in the education system would produce more creative workers, and central policies would guide the economy away from input-driven growth and increase the contribution from total factor productivity growth. This fitted in nicely with the concept of 'Asian values' and the view that Singapore could find an alternative 'Asian' model of development different from the 'American' model. However, by the late 1990s the debate over Asian values had largely receded into the background and the renewed emphasis on attracting 'foreign talent' is perhaps a recognition of the fact that Singapore may need to rely on foreigners in perpetuity and that local resources, including skilled labour, will continue to act as a complement to foreign resources rather than as a substitute, even over the longer run. It is difficult to imagine that

Singapore could have achieved such high growth over such a long period without the contribution of MNCs, but the MNCs have themselves obtained high returns. Compared to other NIEs, companies in Singapore have a relatively low remuneration share, which has helped to keep the Republic competitive, and a high profit share generating 48 per cent of GDP and exceeded only by Thailand (*The Business Times*, 31 August, 2001).

Despite the important role foreign workers play in the economy and the government's continually repeated support for the policy of recruiting from abroad at all levels when necessary the year 2001 did see an increase in negative comments on the policy in the press and in the political arena (Chee, 2001, pp. 10–13) to the extent that the *Asian Wall Street Journal* thought it necessary to summarise the views (Shu, 2001). Some of the resentment expressed is that foreigners do not have to do military service although their children might, that they make the workplace alien for Singaporeans and that they receive subsidized public housing. This became an issue in the general election as more and more Singaporeans lost their jobs throughout 2001. In the off-budget policies of October 2001 there was a tightening of the criteria for foreign workers to obtain an employment pass in terms of the education attainment and minimum monthly salary. The minimum salary was increased to $2500 a month which is just higher than the starting salaries of most tertiary-level graduates and would thus reduce foreign competition for their potential jobs. This might appease some of the local criticism of the policy. With immediate effect of the announcement of these policies foreigners would be allowed to borrow Singapore dollars to buy private housing.

The Prime Minister stressed the need to attract foreigners in his National Day Rally by noting that even though there would be increasing unemployment and foreign talent was necessary not least as 'our own talent is being creamed off'. He put it as 'a matter of life and death for us in the long term . . . If we do not top up our talent pool from outside, in ten years' time, many of the high-valued jobs we do now will migrate to China and elsewhere, for lack of sufficient talent here' (Goh, 2001, p. 20). Other ministers have stressed that talented foreign workers create jobs for Singaporeans and do not displace them.

9.11 'EDUCATION, EDUCATION, EDUCATION'

One aspect of the New Economy that was proposed a few years ago was that Singapore must be a 'knowledge-based economy' meaning that the economy must be able to create knowledge that can be used for producing new products, or reducing costs. This will require more emphasis on research and development and the creation of an education system that provides people who can innovate (Lim, 1999). The educational system can be influenced in terms of the courses it offers and currently there is a clear shift in schools and universities to stress biotechnology and related subjects in order to develop the 'fourth pillar' of the economy: life sciences. Work by JTC will soon start on building 'Biopolis', a science park that will specialize in providing homes for firms and researchers in the field of life sciences and to attract venture capitalist firms to the site as well as academics and journalists interested in the field. It is expected to house 1500 scientists and 63 per cent of the space will be occupied by public research institutes and 16 per cent by private enterprises. The fact that plans are for 1500 scientists and visits by as many as 50 foreign experts in related fields a year shows the size of the scheme, especially when we note that the merged Institute of Molecular Agrobiologic and the Institute of Molecular and Cell Biology will only have 200 scientists. Here again, we can see the traditional pattern of structural change. Public sector initiatives based on the advice of international advisors, a statutory board to provide the infrastructure, the public education system to try to guide Singaporeans into the relevant subjects and, no doubt, an international search for foreign scientists to fill the gap. This repeats the pattern that Alwyn Young hypothesized was the reason for Singapore's poor TFP performance: pushing the economy into new fields without realizing the productivity gains of existing production.

Teaching creative thinking is much more difficult and many teachers in Singapore still believe in the old-fashioned way of teaching through rote learning and telling students there is only one correct answer and only one way of reaching it. Many teachers are reluctant to accept non-conformist thinking. Examples of material the Ministry of Education has developed for teachers to introduce the nature of the Knowledge-Based Economy to students can be found at: http://www1.moe.edu.sg/etv/webbit99/ civics%20and%20moral%20education/KBE/content.html, for example. The intensive, stressful, examination-oriented nature of the Singapore school system is often given as the main reason by parents who choose to emigrate.

Students from Singapore's national university will be sent abroad to places that are thought to epitomize the innovation and creativity necessary for creating the New Singapore. These are Bangalore, Boston, Silicon Valley and Shenzhen in China. They will be given scholarships so if the assessors use traditional methods which have generally stressed academic success then they might be picking the wrong people. As we know, many entrepreneurial businessmen and inventors did not perform well at school.

The Singapore propaganda mechanism has realized this and newspapers, especially the one aimed at younger readers, have started featuring stories of people who were assessed as academic 'failures' at school but are now relatively successful self-employed businessmen.

9.12   FROM RATIONALIZATION TO GLOBALIZATION

In January 2000 the Singapore Trade Development Board launched its Trade 21 plan which, amongst other things, encouraged local companies 'to sprout a third wing' by locating beyond Asia. This coincided with reforms to the financial sector to speed Singapore's globalization and further integration into the world economy, a strategy which requires Singapore firms to form global alliances and compete on the world stage. In this sense, Singapore is returning to its original formula: to continue to make herself useful to the world and an attractive location for foreign capital, labour and technology. It is now impossible to travel down Tanglin Road towards Orchard Road without hearing the amplified sounds of 'Match of the Day'.

This 'globalization' of Singapore's trade policy is also a response to the perception of over-specialization in the region which increased Singapore vulnerability to the slowdown in Asian markets during the Asian financial crisis. Diversification is a good principle providing it is not at the expense of profitable opportunities in the region or a knee-jerk reaction to the Asian financial crisis. It is Singapore's openness and lack of indigenous resources which is the root of the 'vulnerability' problem which is not going to change significantly by selling more to markets in Latin America and Europe.

More controversial has been the decision by Singapore to instigate a series of bilateral preferential trading arrangements with countries outside the region, including New Zealand and the USA. These have upset Singapore's ASEAN partners who are worried that such deals might bring industrialized countries into AFTA through the backdoor as 'Trojan Horses' and may weaken the solidarity of ASEAN as an economic and political force. Singapore's conversion to 'bilateralism' was partly motivated by frustration with the slow progress with AFTA and a desire to use such agreements as a catalyst to speed up trade liberalization within ASEAN, which has been saddled lately with domestic political problems, and to sell the idea to the world as stepping stones towards multilateral initiatives, which appeared to have stalled by the middle of 2000. Singapore's national interests now look rather different from its ASEAN partners as it pursues the cause of free trade, financial liberalization and globalization (attracting foreign talent and investment), and is seeking to distance herself from the anti-western rhetoric of some neighbouring countries. Indeed, the Singapore–US negotiations might be construed as part of a more general change in the emphasis in trade policy to make more international friends. Maybe the ASEAN summit in Brunei at the end of 2001 will resuscitate the organization.

Singapore has also been a willing participant in a series of meetings among East and South-east Asian countries to consider proposals to further monetary integration in the region. The proposals agreed so far, including a network of bilateral currency swaps and surveillance machinery for regional exchange rate movements and capital flows (initiated by the Japanese), certainly represent the first steps towards greater monetary integration in Asia, but they require little commitment and are easy to achieve. It is hard to believe that Asian countries have become sufficiently similar in their economic structures and policies for more serious monetary integration to be feasible, or that they could 'converge' within a reasonable period of time, and there is much ambiguity over which particular subset of Asian countries would have the best chance of success, given their diversity in levels of development and economic objectives. Japan has been the most enthusiastic advocate of monetary integration but its domestic economic problems and former colonizing policies do not suggest that progress will be rapid. The rise of China as a major political and economic force in the region has also complicated the situation. Even if we were to accept that some form of monetary integration was feasible on economic criteria, it is very doubtful that these countries have the requisite political will and institutional preconditions to pursue monetary integration beyond some minimal level of cooperation in the foreseeable future. The Asian financial crisis might have rekindled interest in monetary union but has also increased socioeconomic disparities in the region and reduced the political solidarity of groups such as ASEAN.

Singapore's participation in Asian monetary initiatives to reduce the likelihood of, and damage from, regional currency crises and to encourage 'good behaviour' in macroeconomic policy is in its self-interest. It is also consistent with a broadening of the focus of Singapore's trade policy away from ASEAN and pressures to take on more responsibility as a more advanced country in the region. It is unlikely, however, that it is in its interest to pursue collective monetary arrangements which conflict with existing multilateral agencies such as the IMF and World Bank or compromise its own highly successful, albeit unusual, monetary policies. When Lee Hsien Loong was asked in 2001 whether Asia would ever become a homogeneous trading bloc like Europe or develop its own single currency, he clearly didn't think so: 'No it cannot be. The politics is very different. The political systems and the financial and economic philosophies are too

difficult. It cannot be harmonised. I cannot see it in my working lifetime
. . . will it be the yen or the renmimbi?' (*The Business Times,* 28 September,
2001).

9.13   A DEVELOPED COUNTRY AT LAST?

Singapore's development status remains strangely ambiguous. Despite
rapid growth and structural change, a high international ranking in income
per capita, and an absence of uncertainty about sovereignty which has
dogged countries such as Taiwan and Israel, the official position in
Singapore is that Singapore is still a developing country. This is because
they feel it somehow lacks the depth and breadth of fully developed economies and is presently unable to compete with advanced developed countries. Will Singapore soon apply to be called a fully-developed country as
Korea did in 1997?

Certainly geo-political pressures to resist reclassification in the past
appear to have lessened. The decline in ASEAN as a cohesive political force
has already encouraged Singapore to forge other alliances both within and
outside the region. Singapore is no longer exceptional in its pro-China
policy now that China has joined the WTO and is less likely to stand out
from other ASEAN members in its pro-Western stance in both economic
and political matters. Singapore was quick to give unconditional support
to the United States in the building of the anti-terrorist alliance after the
terrorist attacks in September 2001, with none of the domestic complica-
tions which faced Indonesia and Malaysia. This also fits in with Singapore's
shift in trade policy which has become more global and based on bilateral
deals with a range of countries outside the region and a desire to distance
itself from some of the 'bad' economic and political policies of neighbouring countries. The earlier commitment to 'Asian values' is no longer a
serious impediment.

Retaining the developing country classification, however, has been useful
to justify a heavily centralized economic policy to achieve the longer-run
goal of 'development' and to legitimize the PAP's monopoly over political
power. If Singapore is 'underdeveloped' it may require an authoritarian
political system and state-led economic institutions as a substitute for the
private sector.

The same argument could be made in terms of Singapore's vulnerability to social and political instability in neighbouring countries, such as
Malaysia and Indonesia. It is somewhat disconcerting to note that after the
terrorist attacks on America on 11 September, Singapore's ranking as a
safe place as far as perceptions of political and economic risks were con-

cerned fell substantially to its being ranked in one survey the second most unsafe country in the Asia–Pacific region only above Indonesia which was ranked the most unsafe (*The Business Times,* 18 October, p. 12). Another survey also reduced Singapore's ranking as a safe place. Although Singapore has always been seen as one of the safest places in Asia to do business, this perception has, in the short run at least, turned out to be very fragile. The safest country for business in one survey was Vietnam! Perhaps a one-party, communist state is necessary for foreign capitalism to flourish after all.

Developed country status is the logical outcome of Singapore's positive responses to the pressures of globalization and the recognition that to compete it may need further reforms. Yet the globalization of Singapore is being pursued along with a determination to make all aspects of economic, social and political life run like an efficient Town Council or City Hall. A computer literate and well-informed workforce is essential for the success-ful functioning of the new economy, but innovation and creativity are not easy to manufacture in a classroom or lecture theatre and do not exist in a social and political vacuum. Highly paid mandarins may be incorruptible and efficient but will they be able to adapt to competition which requires the encouragement of more disaggregated entrepreneurial activity and a reduction in their undisputed power in the economy?

Globalization is a double-edged sword. It offers a borderless world where companies compete but this necessitates the relinquishing of control as foreign companies come in and take over domestic enterprises. Foreign firms are wary of merging with 'state'-associated firms and Singapore's GLCs are encountering resistance when trying to venture abroad since they are seen as essentially government-controlled entities. The Singapore gov-ernment's vision of the twenty-first century is to transform the Republic into an 'intelligent island', meaning a society planned and co-coordinated with the universal use of computer networks. Singapore is enthralled by the commercial possibilities of the internet as a key to further exploiting its position as a regional communications hub. Singapore boasts one of the highest internet penetration rates in the Asia–Pacific and even had a 'Miss Internet' competition, where the participants were judged according to cerebral rather than purely physical qualities.

Developed country status would also introduce pressures for social and political change both from within and outside Singapore and the possibil-ity of scrutiny about the shortcomings of Singapore's economic and politi-cal system, in the same way as the bilateral trade negotiations with the USA exposed Singapore to criticism about lack of competition in the ser-vices sector, the media and the legal profession. If you are a developed country why do civil servants need to work on a Saturday morning? Why do you need the Internal Security Act? Why is so much economic information kept secret? Why does Singapore appear to score so low in international rankings based on non-economic criteria? Why are ministerial and judicial salaries so high? Why do some foreign news magazines still have their circulation restricted?

As a former Nominated Member of Parliament, Lee Tsao Yuan, put it: 'What is not certain is whether a political loosening is necessary to foster a more innovative culture, and if so, how to do it without embarking on the slippery descent into chaos' (*The Business Times*, 21 January, 1999). In contrast, a Singaporean former academic who has been marginalized in the political and academic arenas would argue that there is no inevitability of chaos if there is political loosening and more freedom leading to a democratic society which, in fact is a prerequisite for Singapore's future economic and cultural development (Chee, 2001). In the short run this will not be a main concern of the government as it has won the general election. It has to face the very strong possibility of the largest fall in GDP in its modern history in 2001 and possibly two years of falling output and increasing unemployment which could exceed that experienced during the Asian financial crisis. Much of this unemployment might be structural and long lasting and in a country that has no social welfare system to speak of. The structural reforms necessary to create the New Singapore have been entrusted to a high powered ministerial committee to be chaired by Lee Hsien Loong, just as after the 1985–86 recession he chaired a committee to help restructure the economy towards more private ownership. Much, much more needs to be done in the coming years than after the recession of the mid 1980s.

If the year 2001 is seen as pivotal in Singapore's modern history then the month of October of that year will stand out. In that month the government forecast that the economy could experience its sharpest recession in its history, it introduced the largest ever economic support and redistribute policy and announced the distribution of 'New Singapore' shares to bolster its new social compact with the people. In that month both the prime minister and senior minister gave televised speeches to trade unionists and young people. Interestingly, the younger of the two, the prime minister, who had outlined the need to create a new Singapore within ten years, seemed to emphasize the current problems of unemployment and the need to maintain social cohesion, especially after the terrorist attacks on the United States in the previous September (*The Straits Times*, 15 October, 2001, p. 1). In contrast, the senior minister appealed to the young that 'we have to remake Singapore over the next 10 to 20 years' and that Singapore has to reinvent itself for the 'New Age' (*The Straits Times*, 16 October, 2001, p. 1 and *The Straits Times,* 17 October, 2001, p. 20). Whether this can be done depends on whether the young have survived the over-regulated, conformist system that brought Singapore to the position it found itself in November 2001 – ostensibly rich, perhaps developed, but vulnerable and experiencing a serious recession.

Appendix A   Statistics and sources

RECENT REVISIONS TO THE DATA

Since the appearance of Peebles and Wilson (1996) Singapore's national accounts have been revised in a number of ways. One is that a new methodology has been adopted for estimating the output of parts of the financial services sector, a sector that is becoming more significant in the economy, and will provide more accurate measures of its output. This has had the affect of revising slightly the growth rates of GDP in recent years and they might differ from those that can be found in other sources that cover the same period. The department of statistics has adopted the suggestion to classify output into two broad sectors: that of the goods-producing industries and the service-producing industries. They are as follows:

Goods-producing industries
    Manufacturing
    Construction
    Utilities
    Other goods industries (agriculture, fishing and quarrying)
Service-producing industries
    Wholesale and retail trade
    Hotels and restaurants
    Transport and communications
    Financial services
    Business services
    Other service industries

The sum of these items plus the value of services of owner-occupied dwellings plus taxes and duties on imports, minus bank service charges equals GDP at market prices.

The Consumer Price Index was rebased using weights derived from the *Household Expenditure Survey 1997/1998* so that now the period November 1997–October 1998 = 100. This has the effect of reducing slightly the estimates of inflation in recent years compared to those implied by the former index that used weights for a period five years earlier.

We are grateful to the Econometric Studies Unit at the Department of Economics, National University of Singapore, for providing us with some consistent series of macroeconomic data from the Singapore Department of Statistics TRENDS (Time Series Retrieval and Dissemination) database.

Table A.1   Selected macroeconomic indicators, 1960–2000

	Real GDP growth rate %	CPI inflation rate %	Unemployment rate %	Indigenous GNP per capita $ per year	GNP per capita $ per year
1960	n.a.	n.a	n.a	n.a.	1330
1961	8.5	0.3	n.a	n.a.	1394
1962	7.1	0.5	n.a	n.a.	1464
1963	10.5	2.2	n.a	n.a.	1592
1964	−4.3	1.6	n.a	n.a.	1521
1965	6.6	0.3	n.a	n.a.	1618
1966	10.6	2.0	8.9	n.a.	1773
1967	13.0	3.3	n.a	n.a.	1945
1968	14.3	0.7	7.3	n.a.	2188
1969	13.4	−0.3	n.a.	n.a.	2499
1970	13.4	0.4	8.2 (census)	2478	2825
1971	12.5	1.8	n.a.	n.a	3233
1972	13.3	2.2	n.a.	n.a	3798
1973	11.3	19.6	4.4	n.a	4575
1974	6.8	22.3	3.9	n.a	5498
1975	4.0	2.6	4.5	n.a	5996
1976	7.2	−1.9	4.4	n.a	6353
1977	7.8	3.2	3.9	n.a	6817
1978	8.6	4.8	3.6	n.a	7558
1979	9.3	4.0	3.3	n.a	8577
1980	9.7	8.5	3.5 (census)	8343	9962
1981	9.6	8.2	2.9	9798	11067
1982	6.9	3.9	2.6	11027	11942
1983	8.2	1.2	3.2	12474	13574
1984	8.3	2.6	2.7	13515	14853
1985	−1.6	0.5	4.1	12973	14666
1986	2.3	−1.4	6.5	12842	14576
1987	9.7	0.5	4.7	13814	15515
1988	11.6	1.5	3.3	15692	18093
1989	9.6	2.4	2.2	17788	20381
1990	9.0	3.4	1.7 (census)	20075	22411
1991	7.1	3.4	1.9	21380	24021
1992	6.5	2.3	2.7	23887	25510
1993	12.7	2.3	2.7	25893	28200
1994	11.4	3.1	2.6	29500	31872
1995	8.0	1.7	2.7	30998	34420
1996	7.6	1.4	3.0	32489	35482
1997	8.5	2.0	2.4	35098	39494
1998	0.1	−0.3	3.2	34423	37226
1999	5.9	0.0	4.6	35928	38832
2000	9.9	1.3	4.4 (census)	38445	42212

Sources: GDP growth rate: http://www.singstat.gov.sg/FACT/HIST/gdp1.html CPI inflation rate: http://www.singstat.gov.sg/FACT/HIST/cpi.html

Table A.1 (continued)

Unemployment: 1966 and 1968 (Huff, 1993, Table 10.3). 1970 and after; official estimates from
http://www.singstat.gov.sg/FACT/HIST/unemployment.html
Per capita indigenous GNP: Up until 1995, calculated from IGNP and mid-year resident
population data from TRENDS data base. Published data for other years are not comparable.
1995–2000 from *Yearbook of Statistics Singapore 2001*, p. 61.
Per capita GNP from http://www.singstat.gov.sg/FACT/HIST/gnp.html

*Table A.2   Saving and investment as ratios of GNP, current account and
net factor income from abroad, 1960–2000*

	GNS/GNP %	I/GNP %	Current account balance $ million	Net factor income from abroad $ million
1960	−2.4	11.2	−244.7	39.4
1961	−2.3	11.4	−278.6	44.6
1962	5.8	15.3	−199.0	49.1
1963	3.7	17.0	−332.0	67.5
1964	8.9	194	−166.2	86.6
1965	11.2	21.2	−150.1	96.1
1966	15.7	21.3	3.3	106.2
1967	16.0	21.6	−209.4	97.8
1968	19.7	24.4	−408.2	87.2
1969	19.0	28.2	−585.3	84.7
1970	19.3	38.3	−1750.8	56.2
1971	18.8	40.7	−2205.4	−10.0
1972	24.5	41.5	−1392.4	−20.6
1973	27.6	40.3	−1275.0	−233.9
1974	26.3	46.6	−2489.6	−350.6
1975	29.4	39.6	−1385.2	123.5
1976	31.4	41.0	−1401.8	−81.3
1977	32.0	36.6	−719.8	−187.3
1978	33.3	39.1	−1029.0	−43.0
1979	35.7	43.5	−1600.1	−78.9
1980	34.3	48.4	−3375.8	−1044.2
1981	37.3	48.5	−3126.7	−1309.2
1982	40.9	49.5	−2731.6	−1065.3
1983	45.0	48.3	−1232.9	−338.8
1984	46.0	47.8	−754.8	533.7
1985	41.6	41.2	128.2	1202
1986	39.0	36.9	815.2	960.7
1987	37.3	37.9	−229.4	78
1988	41.2	33.7	3898.8	780.6
1989	43.8	34.1	5779.9	1545.8
1990	43.9	35.7	5659.2	1824.0
1991	45.4	34.2	8430.9	1307.7
1992	47.0	35.3	9634.9	2521.7
1993	45.0	37.7	6804.2	314.7
1994	48.7	32.7	17412.5	2383.8

Table A.2 (continued)

	GNS/GNP %	I/GNP %	Current account balance $ million	Net factor income from abroad $ million
1995	51.0	33.7	21 119.1	3 582.9
1996	50.4	36.5	18 079.5	2 031.3
1997	54.0	36.5	26 617.8	9 599.8
1998	54.0	30.7	34 031.2	8 578.9
1999	54.1	30.0	36 865.9	11 358.1
2000	51.5	29.3	37 576.1	10 554.7

Sources: Saving and investment ratios, calculated from TRENDS database. NFIA from TRENDS database. Current account balance: 1960–79 *Economic and Social Statistics, Singapore 1960–1982*, pp. 68–9. 1980–2000 from TRENDS database. These series are not strictly comparable.

MAIN STATISTICAL SOURCES USED THROUGHOUT THE BOOK

Economic and Social Statistics Singapore 1960–1982, Singapore: Department of Statistics Singapore, 1983.

Economic Survey of Singapore, Singapore: Ministry of Trade and Industry, Republic of Singapore, various annual issues.

Economic Survey of Singapore, Singapore: Ministry of Trade and Industry, Republic of Singapore, various quarterly issues.

Monetary Authority of Singapore Economics Department, *Quarterly Bulletin*, issues from 1999 to 2001.

Singapore Census of Population 2000: Advanced Releases: Singapore: Department of Statistics.

Singapore, 1965–1995: Statistical Highlights – A Review of 39 Years' Development, Singapore: Department of Statistics.

Singapore 2001, Singapore: Ministry of Information and the Arts, and earlier issues.

Singapore National Accounts 1987, Singapore: Department of Statistics, 1987.

Singapore National Accounts 1995, Singapore: Department of Statistics, 1995.

Yearbook of Statistics Singapore 2001, Singapore: Department of Statistics, Republic of Singapore, and earlier years.

The Annual Reports of the following organizations:

Board of Commissioners of Currency of Singapore.

Central Provident Fund.

Inland Revenue Authority of Singapore.

Ministry of Health.

Monetary Authority of Singapore.

Statistical web site: http://www.singstat.gov.sg

Appendix B Singapore election systems: results and implications

Singapore has a unicameral parliament and, since 1993, an elected President who holds the position for a maximum of six years. Members of parliament are elected either from single-member constituencies or from Group Representation Constituencies (GRCs) which were introduced for the 1988 General Election. GRCs require parties to put up a team that varies from four to six members depending on the constituency. One of the group must be from a minority community. In the 1997 election there were only nine single-member constituencies and 15 GRCs (from which 74 members were elected). Thus there are a total of 83 elected members of parliament. Forty-seven of the 83 seats were not contested. The number of each type of constituency and their geographical coverage is regularly revised by the Electoral Boundaries Review Committee which reports its rearrangements to the Cabinet so they are not discussed in parliament and are usually announced shortly before the general election is due to be held.

In addition to elected members of parliament there are a number of Nominated Members of Parliament, nine in 2000, appointed by the President for a period of two years. In addition there can be three (or up to a maximum of six) Non-Constituency MPs (NCMPs) who are the highest supported, non-elected candidates from an opposition party. The actual number of NCMPs is reduced by one for each candidate from an opposition party who is actually elected so, for example, after the 1997 General Election, as two opposition party members were returned, there was only one NCMP.

It must be remembered that as the opposition parties do not intend the PAP to be defeated they do not put forward (and probably cannot find) enough candidates to defeat the PAP even if they won all the seats they contested. This regularly gives the PAP a walkover and also means that there is no election in some constituencies, denying citizens a chance to express their feelings. More significantly, it also means that the PAP knows during election campaigning that it will be back in government and so its statements that if it does not receive a sufficient share of the votes in a particular constituency it will put them at the bottom of the list for redevelopment so that their houses will become slums, is not just electioneering but a real threat.

The 1997 campaign was particularly fierce when it seemed that the Workers' Party might win the five-member GRC of Cheng San which, ironically, means 'calm mountain' in Chinese. One opposition candidate, a lawyer, was sued by 11 members of the PAP including the Prime Minister, Senior Minister and other ministers with 13 defamation suits for remarks he made during the campaign. He left Singapore stating he had received death threats. He was subsequently investigated by the tax authorities and convicted of tax evasion and a warrant of arrest was issued against him. His wife's passport was cancelled. He was restrained from selling any assets he had in Singapore or using funds there for his defence and the courts controlled how much money his wife could spend on her support in Singapore. She was also made a defendant in the case by the courts. He was ordered to pay damages of more than $8.07 million, which was subsequently reduced to S$3.63 million by a judge who was misinformed as to who gave his police report to the police. The report had been obtained by the Prime Minister and Senior Minister from the Minister of Home Affairs and given to the local press. The judge thought the opposition party had done so and thus awarded huge damages to the plaintiffs. The politician now lives in Australia and his account of his experiences can be found at http://www.tang-talk.com/

Another opposition candidate from the same GRC faced nine defamation suits mainly from the same 11 PAP members. On election day 1997 a number of senior PAP members who were not candidates at that constituency, dressed in their all-white PAP uniforms and entered the polling station which act, in the view of many, was in clear violation of election laws. This showed the extent of their worry about losing this GRC. They were not admonished or prosecuted. The Workers' Party received 45.2 per cent of the votes which allowed them to select one of the group to become a non constituency MP. In mid 2001 this sole NCMP was declared bankrupt as he could not pay the damages awarded against him from a libel suit that was not initiated by the PAP, meaning that he could not contest the 2001 general election. This case could also mean the winding up of his political party, The Workers' Party. It also means that as an undischarged bankrupt he is not even allowed to make speeches at political rallies and he has put his support behind the Singapore Democratic Party.

In August 1993 Singapore elected its first elected President from a choice of two. The successful candidate, Ong Teng Cheong, had been associated with the PAP in his earlier political career mainly in the trade union movement and was a deputy prime minister. His opponent put up only a token campaign. In September 1999 there was only one candidate deemed suitable for election and so there was no election, making the sole candidate, S.R. Nathan, Singapore's first non-elected, elected President and therefore a selected President. Although largely a symbolic position the President has veto powers over the government's budget and over the appointment of certain public officials as well as examining the government's use of the Internal Security Act. For a discussion of the problems both the PAP and the elected President have in 'grappling with the paradoxes of Presidential power' see George (2000, pp. 57–64) and for a first-hand Singaporean criticism of the electoral system see Chee (2001, pp. 23–43).

In October 2001 the Electoral Boundaries Review Committee announced its changes in the constituencies. The number of elected seats was increased to 84 from 83 in line with total population growth. There are to be 14 GRCs, all of them either of five members (nine) or six members (five), meaning that four-member constituencies disappeared. Boundary lines were changed and the Cheng San GRC, which the PAP nearly lost in 1997, was abolished along with two other GRCs. The two opposition-held constituencies were left untouched. The required deposit of each candidate was increased by 62.5 per cent from the 1997 level to $13000. The deposit is forfeited if the candidate does not get one-eighth of the votes. A six-person group would thus have to deposit $78000 to contest such a GRC. On nomination day the PAP was uncontested in 55 seats so it was certain of forming the new government and only 29 seats were contested. The five-man Workers' Party team was disqualified from standing in its chosen GRC on a technicality as there was a mistake in the documents they submitted on Nomination Day. The Senior Minister, the Prime Minister and Deputy Prime Minister, Lee Hsien Loong, were all returned without a contest. This gave them the opportunity to concentrate on helping other PAP candidates defend their constituencies. Just as in the 1997 election the PAP picked out a particular GRC as essential for it to win as a test of its nationwide support and support for the Prime Minister personally. The constituency it concentrated on was a six-member GRC being contested by the Singapore Democratic Party led by Dr Chee Soon Juan. The PAP was worried he might get a seat in parliament as a NCMP if his group got the highest number of votes of a losing party and concentrated on ensuring his defeat. The PAP won this GRC easily.

ELECTION RESULTS, 1955–97

After 1988, changes in the overall share of votes for the PAP do not really tell a consistent story as the number of GRCs and individual-member constituencies has changed at each election time as has the number of them that has been contested (George, 2000, pp. 92–5).

The number of seats that were not contested is shown in brackets.

Legislative Assembly General Elections

2 April 1955
Number of seats: 25.
Parties: 5 plus 11 independent candidates.
Party returned: Labour Front with 10 seats forming a coalition government as no party had a clear majority.
Per cent of valid votes won: 27.06.
Four opposition parties including the PAP.

30 May 1959
Number of seats: 51.
Parties: 10 plus 39 independent candidates.
Party returned: PAP with 43/51 seats.
Per cent of valid votes won: 54.08.
Two opposition parties and one independent.

21 September 1963
Number of seats: 51.
Parties: 8 plus 16 independent candidates.
Party returned: PAP with 37 seats.
Per cent of valid votes won: 46.93.
Two opposition parties.

Parliamentary General Elections

13 April 1968
Number of seats: 58 (51).
Parties: 2 plus 5 independent candidates.
Party returned: PAP with 58/58 seats.
Per cent of valid votes won: 86.72.
Opposition members: None.
Prime Minister: Lee Kuan Yew.

2 September 1972
Number of seats: 65 (8).
Parties: 6 plus 2 independent candidates.
Party returned: PAP with 65/65 seats.
Per cent of valid votes won: 70.43.
Opposition members: None.
Prime Minister: Lee Kuan Yew.

23 December 1976
Number of seats: 69 (16).
Parties: 7 plus 2 independent candidates.
Party returned: PAP: with 69/69 seats.
Per cent of valid votes won: 74.09.
Opposition members: None.
Prime Minister: Lee Kuan Yew.

23 December 1980
Number of seats: 75 (37).
Parties: 8.
Party returned: PAP with 75/75 seats.
Per cent of valid votes won: 77.66.
Opposition members: None.
Prime Minister: Lee Kuan Yew.

22 December 1984
Number of seats: 79 (30).
Parties: 9 plus 3 independent candidates.
Party returned PAP: with 77/79 seats.
Per cent of valid votes won: 64.83.
Opposition members: Two.
Prime Minister: Lee Kuan Yew.

3 September 1988
Number of seats: 81 (11).
Parties: 8 plus 4 independent candidates.
Party returned: PAP: with 80/81 seats.
Per cent of valid votes won: 63.17.
Opposition members: One.
Prime Minister: Lee Kuan Yew until 28th November 1990 succeeded by Goh Chok Tong.

31 August 1991
Number of seats: 81 (41).
Parties: 6 plus 7 independent candidates.
Party returned: PAP with 77/81 seats.
Per cent of valid votes won: 60.97.
Opposition members: Four.
Prime Minister: Goh Chock Tong.

2 January 1997
Number of seats: 83 (47).
Parties: 6 plus 1 independent candidate.
Party returned: PAP with 81/83 seats.
Per cent of valid votes won: 64.98.
Opposition members: Two.
Prime Minister: Goh Chock Tong.

The 3 November 2001 general election is described in the text above. The PAP took 82 of the 84 elected seats and in those 29 contested seats received 75 per cent of the valid vote.

Sources: *Singapore 1994*; *Singapore 2000*, Pungalenthi (1996); *Lee Kuan Yew* (CD-Rom) Singapore: *Lianhe Zaobao* and Sony (n.d.).
For detailed results of all Singapore elections see:
http://www.elections.gov.sg/history/History.html

Table B.1   Percentage of voters who could not vote at general elections

1980	47
1984	37
1988	13
1991	50
1997	60

Source: *The Straits Times*,14 April, 2001, p. H8.

Appendix C   Suggestions for further reading

The following suggestions are the more important studies of particular issues covered in each chapter. We also recommend some non-economic readings.

CHAPTER 1

Turnbull (1989) remains the best general history of Singapore and Huff (1994) the best economic history, especially on the period before the Second World War. Peebles (2001b) is a short review of the history, institutions and strategy underlying Singapore's growth. The annual government report published by the Ministry of Information and the Arts with the latest title being *Singapore 2001* reviews the main events of the previous year and describes various institutions.

Froyen and Low (2001) is a macroeconomic textbook with applications to Asian economies, with some Singapore examples.

The other suggestions are general economic studies of Singapore's modern development. For a recent fictional account of life and political life in Singapore by an author who had her knuckles rapped by the government a few years ago for what they thought were remarks that put her in the political arena see Lim (2001). The book was not published in Singapore and it will be interesting to see what reaction it provokes as it will have people asking how much is fiction and how much is what she believes is fact. It is certain to be thought of as 'anti-Singapore' by many.

Lim Chong-Yah (1980), *Economic Development in Singapore*, Singapore, Kuala Lumpur, Hong Kong: Federal Publications.
Linda Low (1998), *The Political Economy of a City-State: Government-made Singapore*, Singapore: Oxford University Press.
Ooi Jim-Bee and Chiang Hai Ding (eds) (1969), *Modern Singapore*, Singapore: University of Singapore Press.
Kernial Singh Sandhu and Paul Wheatley (eds) (1989), *Management of Success: The Moulding of Modern Singapore*, Singapore: Institute of Southeast Asian Studies.
Gavin Peebles and Peter Wilson (1996), *The Singapore Economy*, Cheltenham and Brookfield: Edward Elgar.
Singapore 2001, Singapore: Ministry of Information and the Arts, and earlier editions.
C.M. Turnbull (2000), 'Singapore: History' in *The Far East and Australasia 2001*, London: Europa Publications.

CHAPTER 2

Chew (1996) is an important set of interviews with influential Singaporeans. Interestingly, Lee Kuan Yew declined to be interviewed for this volume by a fellow Singaporean, which would contain the recollections of several of his comrades. Mr Lee is not usually reluctant to give interviews, especially outside Singapore. The two volumes of Lee Kuan Yew's memoirs are invaluable. They can be read alongside the interviews with his comrades that are in Chew (1996) and with Barr (2000) for commentary.

Low et al. (1993) and Schein (1996) are two different perspectives on the Economic Development Board and Lim and Chew (1998) is a history of the National Wages Council.

The two volumes by Seow represent the analysis of Singapore by a former insider, Solicitor General of Singapore, chronicling the political use of the Internal Security Act, conditions experienced by political detainees and the laws used to suppress the domestic media. Seow (1994) contains a foreword by Singapore's third president.

Lam Peng Er and Kelvin Y.L. Tan (1999), *Lee's Lieutenants: Singapore's Old Guard*, St Leonards: Allen and Unwin.
Lee Kuan Yew (1998), *The Singapore Story: Memoirs of Lee Kuan Yew*, Singapore Press Holdings: Singapore.
Lee Kuan Yew (2000), *From Third World to First – The Singapore Story 1965–2000: Memoirs of Lee Kuan Yew*, Singapore Press Holdings: Singapore.

CHAPTER 3

Chen (1997) and Felipe (1999) are two recent surveys of the rapidly expanding literature on TFP in Asia and Singapore and the papers by Young which started the debate. Krugman (1994b) is still worth re-reading not just to re-establish what he actually said. Alwyn Young's papers (1992, 1994a, 1994b) brought the issue to the attention of Krugman and the Singapore government although a Singaporean economist had earlier pointed out the evidence for zero TFP in the manufacturing sector.

Jesus Felipe (2000), 'On the myth and mystery of Singapore's "Zero TFP"', *Asian Economic Journal*, **14** (2), June.
Koh Ai Tee (1990), *Booms and Busts in Modern Societies*, Singapore: Longmans.
Krugman, Paul (1994), at http:///web.mti/krugman/www/myth.html.

CHAPTER 4

Peebles (2002a, 2002b) discusses saving and investment in Singapore with the former paper reviewing more of the disputes about the nature of saving in Singapore and the implications of forecasts of future rates of saving on growth and the nature of the economy.

Chiu et al. (1995, 1997) compare the nature of industrialization in Hong Kong and Singapore. Early analysis of structural change can be found in Ooi and Chiang (1969).

Stephen W.K. Chiu, K.C. Ho and Tai-lok Lui (1995), 'A tale of two cities rekindled: Hong Kong and Singapore's divergent paths to industrialism', *Journal of Development Studies*, **11** (1).

Stephen W.K. Chiu, K.C. Ho and Tai-lok Lui (1997), *Global-States in the Global Economy: Industrial Restructuring in Hong Kong and Singapore*, Boulder Col.: Westview Press.

CHAPTER 5

For a review of Singapore's monetary experience when consistent sets of data were available see Peebles and Wilson (1996). Luckett et al. (1994) is a short textbook treatment of banking, finance and monetary policy in Singapore. Soh (1990) is a short, but interesting general history of money in Singapore and Monetary Authority of Singapore (2000a) presents its own overview of Singapore's monetary history.

Tan (1999) remains the standard overview of financial matters in Singapore. *The Annual Report* of the Monetary Authority of Singapore is highly recommended as is its much improved 'Quarterly Bulletin' from its Economics Department which often carries reports of interesting bits of recent research of theirs.

For taxation matters Asher and Tyabji (1996) is comprehensive but a bit dated and Asher (1999) is worthwhile.

Lee Hsien Loong's speeches on reforming the financial system are collected in Lee (2000b).

Mukul Asher and Susan Obsborne (eds) (1980), *Issues in Public Finance in Singapore*, Singapore: Singapore University Press.

CHAPTER 6

Huff (1995) looks at the Singapore model of development in the context of one of the most controversial aspects of the so-called 'Asian Miracle', namely the balance between planning and markets in the 'tiger' economies. Huff (1999) focuses more specifically on the difficulties Singapore is currently facing in trying to reduce her reliance on input-driven growth. A successful strategy in the past based on tax concessions and infrastructure spending geared up to attracting footloose foreign MNCs will not be sufficient if Singapore is to survive internationally in the future. As far as development indicators are concerned, Crafts (1997a) provides a longer-run perspective of Singapore's comparative performance based on the HDI. Rao (2001) looks at Singapore's income distribution compared to the other 'Dynamic Asian Economies' depicted as part of the 'Asian miracle' by the World Bank in 1993, and casts doubt on the view that income inequality was in fact reduced in these rapidly growing economies. Differing views on the controversy surrounding Singapore's development status can be found in Low (1999a) and Wilson (2000a).

Stan Sesser's essay 'The prisoner in the theme park' remains one of the best of foreigners' accounts of life in Singapore. It is chapter 1 of Sesser (1994).

CHAPTER 7

The best general background on Singapore's economic history as a trading nation is Huff (1994), and a reminder than Singapore's prosperity pre-dates independence in 1965. Sachs and Warner (1995) put Singapore's early conversion to free trade in the context of the global movement towards openness in international trade after the Second World War. Lloyd and Sandilands (1986) is a classic on the features which make Singapore unique as a 'very open re-export economy' and Abeysinghe (2001) provides a way of capturing the impact of Singapore's trading partners on Singapore's GDP growth through its trade links. Toh and Tan (1998) and Abeysinghe and Wilson (2002) look in much greater depth at the debate over Singapore's international competitiveness. Ramkishan and associates (2001) speculate on the potential benefits and costs of Singapore's current bilateral trade negotiations with the USA and Japan as part of the new policy of 'open regionalism', while Pomfret (1996) looks back at the inherent weaknesses of ASEAN as a political and economic organization.

CHAPTER 8

A useful starting-point for the background on the Singapore balance of payments and exchange rate policy is Peebles and Wilson (1996). For the reasons why Singapore emerged relatively unscathed from the Asian financial crisis, see Tyabji (1998). Abeysinghe and Wilson (2002) look in much greater detail at Singapore's cost competitiveness in terms of the aggregate relationships between costs, domestic and foreign price levels and the exchange rate, and also try to unravel the mysteries of the Singapore 'export puzzle'. The Monetary Authority of Singapore (2000a) has written its own history of external monetary policy, the principles behind its policy of managed floating since 1981, and the adoption of a more flexible policy of 'enlightened exchange rate management' in the aftermath of the Asian financial crisis. Cherian George (2000) applies a journalist's eye to uncover the rationale behind the government's management of the foreign exchange reserves. Tan Chwee Huat (1999) is the latest update on the financial system in Singapore. For a more critical evaluation of government policies, see Ngiam and Tyabji (1998) on the internationalization of the Singapore dollar, and the findings of a visiting team of economists from the International Monetary Fund in Cardarelli et al. (2000). The prospects for monetary integration in Asia are discussed from both an economic and political perspective in Eichengreen and Bayoumi (1998) and with greater scepticism by Nicolas (1999).

CHAPTER 9

The Prime Minister's National Day Rally 2001 Speech is worth consulting and is at: http://www.gov.sg.sgip/Amnnounce/NDR.html and is entitled 'New Singapore'. It was reported in the Singapore newspapers on 3 August 2001. It was accompanied for the first time with a booklet entitled *Singapore: The Last 10 Years* (Ministry of Information and the Arts, 2001) which can be found at http://www.gov.sg/SGIP/NDR/NDRsup.pdf

Another vision of the future Singapore can be found in Chee (2001) although some of the ideas there have been around for a while and now seem to be what the government is recommending to some extent.

For a fictional account of how a Singaporean sees Singapore's role in the world and its values see the novel by the up-and-coming writer Hwee Hwee Tan (2001).

Interactive versions of *The Business Times* and *The Straits Times* can be found at these sites:
http://business-times.asia1.com.sg/home
http://straitstimes.asia1.com.sg/home

Bibliography

Abeysinghe, T. (2000), 'Electronics cycles in Singapore', *Applied Economics*, **32**.

Abeysinghe, T. (2001), 'Thai meltdown and transmission of recession within ASEAN4 and NIE4', in S. Claessens (ed.), *International Financial Contagion*, Boston: Kluwer Academic Publishers.

Abeysinghe, T. and C. Lee (1992), 'Singapore's strong dollar policy and purchasing power parity', *The Singapore Economic Review*, **37** (1), April.

Abeysinghe, T. and Lee Hwee Chen (1998), 'Singapore's cost competitiveness in the region: A technical note on RULC', *Singapore Economic Review*, **43** (2), October.

Abeysinghe, T. and Tan Lin Yeok (1998), 'Exchange rate appreciation and export competitiveness: the case of Singapore', *Applied Economics,* **30**.

Abeysinghe, T. and Peter Wilson (2001), *Forecasts for the Singapore Economy*, Econometric Studies Unit, Department of Economics, National University of Singapore.

Abeysinghe, T. and Peter Wilson (2002), 'International Competitiveness', in W.T. Hui, A.T. Koh, Rao Bhanoji and K.L. Lim (eds), *The Singapore Economy in the Twenty-First Century: Issues and Strategies*, London: McGraw Hill.

Abeysinghe, Tilak, Reza Siregar and Choy Keen Meng (2001), 'Where is the illusive bottom of the electronics cycle?', Econometrics Studies Unit, Department of Economics, National University of Singapore, Press Release, August.

Adams, F. Gerard and Shinichi Ichimura (eds) (1998), *East Asian Development: Will the East Asian Growth Miracle Survive?*, Westport and London: Praeger.

Aggarwal, R. and M. Mougoue (1993), 'Cointegration among southeast Asian and Japanese Currencies', *Economic Letters*, **41**.

Alesina, Alberto and Lawrence H. Summers (1993), 'Central bank independence and macroeconomic performance', *Journal of Money, Credit and Banking*, May.

Alten, Florian von (1995), *The Role of Government in the Singapore Economy*, Frankfurt am Main: Peter Lang.

Arif, Mohamed and Ahmed M. Khalid (2000), *Liberalization, Growth and the Asian Financial Crisis: Lessons for Developing and Transitional*

Economies in Asia, Cheltenham and Northampton: Edward Elgar.

Arndt, H.W. (1991), 'Saving, investment and growth: Recent Asian experience', *Banca Nazionale Lavoro Quarterly Review*, No. 177, June.

Arndt, H.W. and Hal Hill (eds) (1999), *Southeast Asia's Economic Crisis: Origins, Lessons, and the Way Forward*, Singapore: Institute of Southeast Asian Studies, Singapore.

Asher, Mukul and Susan Obsborne (eds) (1980), *Issues in Public Finance in Singapore*, Singapore: Singapore University Press.

Asher, Mukul G. (1994), 'An analysis of Singapore's 1994–1995 budget', in Anthony Chin and Ngiam Kee Jin (eds), *Outlook for the Singapore Economy*, Singapore: Trans Global Publishing.

Asher, Mukul G. (1999), 'Tax Reform in Singapore', Working Paper No. 91, Asian Research Centre, Murdoch University, March.

Asher, Mukul G. and Amina Tyabji (eds) (1996), *Fiscal System of Singapore: Trends, Issues and Future Directions*, Centre for Advanced Studies, National University of Singapore; Singapore.

Asian Development Bank (2001), *Asia Recovery Report 2001*, (September update), Manila, Asian Development Bank, from http://aric.adb.org.

Backman, Michael (1999), *Asian Eclipse: Exposing the Dark Side of Business in Asia*, Singapore: John Wiley.

Balance of Payments Statistics Yearbook, Washington, DC: International Monetary Fund, various years.

Balassa, Bela (1978), 'Exports and economic growth: further evidence', *Journal of Development Economics*, **5**.

Baratham, Gopal (1994), *The Caning of Michael Fay*, Singapore: KRP publications.

Barr, Michael D. (2000), *Lee Kuan Yew: The Beliefs Behind the Man*, Washington, DC: Georgetown University Press.

Barro, Robert J. (1974), 'Are government bonds net wealth?', *Journal of Political Economy*, December.

Barro, Robert J. (1991), 'Economic growth in a cross section of countries', *Quarterly Journal of Economics,* May.

Barro, Robert J. (1994a), 'Democracy and Growth', paper presented at the Third Asian Development Bank Conference on Development Economics, Manila, 23–25 November 1994.

Barro, Robert J. (1994b), 'Democracy: A recipe for growth?', *Asian Wall Street Journal*, 2–3 December 1994, p. 6.

Barro, Robert J. (2001), 'Economic growth in East Asia before and after the Financial Crisis', National Bureau of Economic Research, Working Paper 8330, June.

Bayoumi, T. and Paulo Mauro (1999), 'The Suitability of ASEAN for a Regional Currency Arrangement', IMF Working Paper, WP/99/162.

Bautista, Romeo M. (1992), *Development Policy in East Asia: Economic Growth and Poverty Alleviation,* Singapore: ASEAN Economic Research Unit, Institute of Southeast Asian Studies.

Bercuson, Kenneth (ed.) (1995), *Singapore: A Case Study in Rapid Development*, IMF Occasional Paper No. 119, Washington, DC: International Monetary Fund.

Bhagwati, Jagdish and Arvind Panagariya (1997), 'Preferential Trading Areas and Multilateralism: Strangers, Friends or Foes?', Singapore, Department of Economics and Statistics, National University of Singapore.

Bird, Graham (1987), *International Macroeconomics: Theory, Policy and Applications*, London: Macmillan Press.

Blackwell, Roger D. (1994), *From the Edge of the World*, Columbus: Ohio State University Press.

Bloch, Harry and Sam Tang (2000), 'Estimating technical change, economies of scale and degree of competition for manufacturing industries in Singapore', *The Singapore Economic Review*, **45** (1) April.

Bodman, Philip M. and Mark Crosby (2000), 'Non-linearities in the Singapore business cycle', *The Singapore Economic Review*, **44** (2), October.

Bordo, Michael D. and Lars Jonung (1987), *The Long-run Behaviour of the Velocity of Circulation*, Cambridge: Cambridge University Press.

Brazil, David (1998), *No Money, No Honey: A Candid Look as Sex-for-Sale in Singapore*, 4th edn, Singapore: Angsana Books.

Brazil, David (1999), *Insider's Singapore: The Alternative City Guide*, Singapore: Times Editions.

Brown, Adam (1992), *Making Sense of Singapore English*, Singapore, Kuala Lumpur and Hong Kong: Federal Publications.

Bryant, Ralph C. (1989), 'The evolution of Singapore as a financial centre', in Kernial Singh Sandhu and Paul Wheatley (eds), *Management of Success: The Moulding of Modern Singapore*, Singapore: Institute of Southeast Asian Studies.

Bruton, Henry J. (1996), 'Review of Huff (1994)', *Journal of Regional Science*, **36** (2).

The Budget for the Financial Year 2001/2002, Command 3 of 2001, February.

Campos, Jose Edgardo and Hilton L. Root (1996), *The Key to the Asian Miracle: Making Shared Growth Credible*, Washington: The Brookings Institution.

Cao Yong and Stella Ng (1995), 'Voluntary Saving Behaviour in Singapore', in Chew Soon Beng and Jon D. Kendall (eds), *Regional Issues in Economics: Volume 1,* Singapore: Nanyang Business School, Nanyang Technological University.

Cardarelli, R., J. Gobat and J. Lee (2000), *Singapore: Selected Issues*, International Monetary Fund, Staff Country Report No. 00/83, Washington, DC: International Monetary Fund.

Caves, Richard E., Jeffrey A. Frankel and Ronald W. Jones (1993), *World Trade and Payments: An Introduction,* 3rd edn, New York: Harper Collins.

Chan, Kenneth S. and Ngiam Kee Jin (1992a), 'Currency interchangeability arrangement between Brunei and Singapore: A cost–benefit analysis', *The Singapore Economic Review,* **37** (2).

Chan, Kenneth S. and Ngiam Kee Jin (1992b), 'A tale of two currencies – Brunei and Singapore', in *Prudence at the Helm: Board of Commissioners of Currency, Singapore 1967–1992*, Singapore: Board of Commissioners of Currency, Singapore.

Chan, Kenneth S. and Ngiam Kee Jin (1996), *Currency Speculation and the Optimum Control of Bank Lending in Singapore Dollars: A Case for Partial Liberalization*, Washington, DC: International Monetary Fund, Working Paper WP/96/95.

Chan Kok Peng (1993), 'Effects of CPF liberalization and lower budget surplus', *Times Economic Link*, No. 1, July–September.

Chandavarkar, Anand (1993), 'Saving behaviour in the Asian-Pacific region', *Asian-Pacific Economic Literature,* **7** (1), May.

Chee Soon Juan (1994), *Dare to Change: An Alternative Vision for Singapore*, Singapore: Singapore Democratic Party.

Chee Soon Juan (1995), *Singapore: My Home Too*, Singapore: Melodies Press.

Chee Soon Juan (1998), *To Be Free: Stories from Asia's Struggle Against Oppression*, Clayton: Monash Asia Institute.

Chee Soon Juan (2001), *Your Future, My Faith, Our Freedom: A Democratic Blueprint for Singapore*, Open Singapore Centre: Singapore.

Chen, Edward K.Y. (1997), 'The total factor productivity debate', *Asian-Pacific Economic Literature*, **11** (1), May.

Chen Kang and Tan Khee-Giap (1998), 'Singapore', in *Domestic Savings in the Pacific Region: Trends and Prospects: Background Papers*, Osaka: Japan Committee for Pacific Economic Outlook.

Chen, Peter S.J. (ed.) (1983), *Singapore Development Policies and Trends*, Singapore: Oxford University Press.

Chenery, Hollis (1960), 'Patterns of industrial growth', *The Economic Journal*, **72**.

Chenery, Hollis, Sherman Robinson and Moshe Syrquin (1986), *Industrialization and Growth: A Comparative Study*, New York: Oxford University Press for the World Bank.

Cheung, Paul (1998), 'Needs and Challenges of New Demography', in

Linda Low (ed.), *The Political Economy of a City-State: Government-made Singapore*, Singapore: Oxford University Press.

Chew, Melanie (1996), *Leaders of Singapore*, Singapore: Resource Press.

Chew Soon Beng and Jon D. Kendall (eds) (1995), *Regional Issues in Economics: Volume 1,* Singapore: Nanyang Business School, Nanyang Technological University.

Chia Siow Yue (1986), 'The economic development of Singapore: A selective survey of the literature' in Basant K. Kapur (ed.), *Singapore Studies: Critical Surveys of the Humanities and Social Sciences*, Singapore: Singapore University Press.

Chia Siow Yue (1989), 'The character and progress of industrialization', in Kernial Singh Sandhu and Paul Wheatley (eds), *Management of Success: The Moulding of Modern Singapore*, Singapore: Institute of Southeast Asian Studies.

Chia Siow Yue (1994) (ed.), *APEC: Challenges and Opportunities*, Singapore: Institute of Southeast Asian Studies.

Chia Siow Yue (1999), 'The Asian financial crisis: Singapore's experience and response', in H.W. Arndt and Hal Hill (eds), *Southeast Asia's Economic Crisis: Origins, Lessons, and the Way Forward*, Institute of Southeast Asian Studies: Singapore.

Chou, W.L. and Y.C. Shih (1997), 'Long-run purchasing power parity and long-term memory: evidence from Asian newly industrialized countries', *Applied Economics Letters*, **4**.

Chow Hwee Kwan (1993), 'Performance of the official composite leading index in monitoring the Singapore economy', *Asian Economic Journal*, **7** (1).

Chow Hwee Kwan and Choy Keen Meng (1993), 'A leading economic index for monitoring the Singapore economy', *The Singapore Economic Review*, **38** (1), April.

Chow Hwee Kwan and Kim, Y. (2000*)*, 'Common Currency Peg in East Asia? Perspectives from Western Europe', Singapore: Department of Economics, Staff Seminar Series No. 14.

Chow Kit Boey and Ni Zhengchang (1997), 'The Singapore economy: Long-term forecasts (1996–2005)', in Mitsuru Toida and Daisuke Hiratsuka (eds), *Asian Industrialising Region in 2005*, Institute of Developing Economies: Tokyo.

Chow, P., M. Kellman and Y. Shachmurove (1994), 'East Asian NIC manufactured intra-industry trade 1965–1990', *Journal of Asian Economics*, **5** (3).

Chowdhury, A. (1993), 'External shocks and structural adjustments in East Asian newly industrializing economies', *Journal of International Development*, **5** (1).

Choy Keen Meng (1999), 'Sources of macroeconomic fluctuations in Singapore: Evidence from a structural VAR model', *The Singapore Economic Review*, **44** (1), April.

Chua Mui Hoong (2001), 'Singapore – a welfare state for the middle class?', *The Straits Times*, 25 March, from *The Straits Times Interactive* http://straitstimes.asia1.com.sg/

Clad, James (1989), *Behind the Myth: Business, Money and Power in Southeast Asia*, London: Unwin Hyman.

Cooper, Richard (1986), *Economic Policy in an Interdependent World*, Cambridge, Mass.: MIT Press.

Corden, Max (1999), *The Asian Crisis: Is There a Way Out?*, Institute of Southeast Asian Studies: Singapore.

Crafts, N.F.R. (1997a), 'The Human Development Index and changes in standards of living: Some historical comparisons', *European Review of Economic History*, **1**.

Crafts, N.F.R. (1997b), 'Economic growth in East Asia and Western Europe since 1950: Implications for living standards', *National Institute Economic Review*, 162.

Crafts, N.F.R. (1998), 'East Asian Growth Before and After the Crisis', Working Paper of the International Monetary Fund, WP/98/137.

Cukierman, Alex (1992), *Central Bank Strategy, Credibility, and Independence: Theory and Evidence*, Cambridge, Mass. and London: The MIT Press.

Dasgupta, P. and M. Weale (1992), 'On measuring the quality of life', *World Development*, **20**.

Daquila, Teofilio, C. and Alan Phua Kia Fatt (1993), 'Demand for money in Singapore revisited', *Asian Economic Journal*, **7** (2), July.

Davies, Rob (2001), 'Lee Hsien Loong outlines the challenges for Singapore's economy' *FinanceAsia.com*, 23 January from www.financeasia,com/Accessories.

Davies, Derek (1999), 'The Press', in Michael Haas (ed.), *The Singapore Puzzle*, Westport and London: Praeger.

De Long, J. Bradford and Lawrence H. Summers (1991), 'Equipment investment and economic growth', *Quarterly Journal of Economics*, **106** (2).

Deck, Richard A. (1999), 'Foreign Policy', in Michael Haas (ed.), *The Singapore Puzzle*, Westport and London: Praeger.

Delhasie, Philippe F. (1998), *Asia in Crisis: The Implosion of the Banking and Finance Systems*, Singapore: John Wiley.

Deluty, Philip J. and Perry L. Wood (1986), *Singapore: The Dynamics of Free Trade Regime*, Indianapolis: Hudson Institute.

Department of Statistics (1997a), 'Measuring Singapore's External

Economy', Occasional Paper on Economic Statistics, Singapore, September.

Department of Statistics (1997b), 'Multifactor Productivity Growth in Singapore: Concept, Methodology and Trends', Occasional Paper on Economic Statistics, Singapore, October.

Department of Statistics (1998a), 'Income Components of GDP: Trends and Analysis', Occasional Paper on Economic Statistics, Singapore, April.

Department of Statistics (1998b), *The Income Approach to Gross Domestic Product*, Singapore, Department of Statistics.

Department of Statistics (1999), 'Income, Expenditure, Saving and Investment of the Household Sector', Occasional Paper on Economic Statistics, Singapore, April.

Department of Statistics (2001), 'Contribution of Government-linked companies to Gross Domestic Product', Occasional Paper on Economic Statistics, Singapore, March.

Direction of Trade Statistics, Washington, DC: International Monetary Fund, various years.

Devan: Nation Builder, People's President (1981), Singapore: Singapore National Trades Union Congress.

Doessel D.P. and Rukmani Gounder (1991), 'International Comparisons of Levels of Living and the Human Development Index: Some Empirical Results', University of Queensland Department of Economics Discussion Paper No. 72, November.

Dolven, Ben (2000), 'Where's my nest egg?', *Far Eastern Economic Review*, 25 May, 69–70.

Dore, Mohammed H.I. (1993), *The Macrodynamics of Business Cycles: A Comparative Evaluation*, Cambridge Mass. and Oxford, UK: Blackwell.

Drake, P.J. (1981), 'The evolution of money in Singapore since 1819', in *Papers on Monetary Economics,* edited by the Economics Department, Monetary Authority of Singapore, Singapore: Singapore University Press for the Monetary Authority of Singapore.

Dutta, M. et al. (eds) (1995), *Research in Asian Economic Studies: Volume 6*, Greenwich, Conn. and London: JIA Press.

The Economist Intelligence Unit (1997), *Country Report, Singapore*, London: The Economist Intelligence Unit, 4th quarter 1997.

Eichengreen, B. and T. Bayoumi (1998), 'Is Asia an Optimum Currency Area? Can it Become One?', in Stefan Collignon, Jean Pisani-Ferry and Yung Chul Park (eds), *Exchange Rate Policies in Emerging Asian Countries*, London: Routledge.

Ermisch, J.F. and W.G. Huff (1999), 'Hypergrowth in an East Asian NIC: public policy and capital accumulation in Singapore', *World Development*, **27** (1), January.

Eschweiler, Bernhard (1997), 'The Singapore Economy: Near-Term Outlook and Long-Term Challenges', Paper presented at Workshop on Outlook for the Singapore Economy, Singapore: National University of Singapore, Department of Economics and Statistics.

Faruqee, Hamid and Aasim M. Husain (1998), 'Saving trends in Southeast Asia; A cross-country Analysis', *Asian Economic Journal*, **12** (3), September.

Felipe, Jesus (1999), 'Total factor productivity growth in East Asia: A critical survey', *Journal of Development Studies*, **35** (4), April.

Felipe, Jesus and J.S.L. McCombie (2001), 'Biased technical change, growth accounting, and the conundrum of the East Asian miracle', *Journal of Comparative Economics*, **29** (3), September.

Findlay, Ronald (1989), 'Theoretical notes on Singapore as a development model', in Kernial Singh Sandhu and Paul Wheatley (eds), *Management of Success: The Moulding of Modern Singapore*, Singapore: Institute of Southeast Asian Studies.

Findlay, Ronald and Basant Kapur (1992), 'An analytical growth model of the Singapore economy', *Asian Economic Journal*, **5** (1), March.

The Financial Structure of Singapore (1989), Singapore: Monetary Authority of Singapore.

Fleming, J. (1962), 'Domestic financial policies under fixed and floating exchange rates', *International Monetary Fund Staff Papers*, November 1962.

Frankel, Jeffrey A. and Shang-Jin Wei (1994), 'Yen Bloc or Dollar Bloc? Exchange rate policies of the East Asian economies', in Takatoshi Ito and Anne O. Krueger (eds), *Macroeconomic Linkages: Savings, Exchange Rates and Capital Flows*, Chicago: University of Chicago Press.

Froyen, Richard T. and Linda Low (2001), *Macroeconomics: An Asian Perspective*, Singapore: Prentice Hall.

Fu Tsu-Tan, Cliff Y. Huang and C.A. Knox Lovell (eds) (2000), *Economic Efficiency and Productivity Growth in the Asia-Pacific Region*, Cheltenham and Northampton: Edward Elgar.

Gan Wee Beng (2000), 'Financial market integration in Singapore: The narrow and the broad view', *The Singapore Economic Review*, **45** (1) April.

Gapinski, James H. (1999), *Economic Growth in the Asia Pacific Region*, New York: St Martin's Press.

Garnaut, Ross (1994), *Asian Market Economies: Challenges of a Changing International Environment*, Singapore: ASEAN Economic Research Unit, Institute of Southeast Asian Studies.

Garnaut, Ross (1999), 'Exchange Rates in the East Asian Crisis', in H.W

Arndt and Hal Hill (eds), *Southeast Asia's Economic Crisis: Origins, Lessons, and the Way Forward*, Institute of Southeast Asian Studies: Singapore.

Gayle, Dennis John (1988), 'Singaporean market socialism: Some implications for development theory', *International Journal of Social Economics*, **15** (7).

Geiger, Theodore and Frances M. Geiger (1973), *Tales of Two City-States: The Development Progress of Hong Kong and Singapore*, Washington, DC: National Planning Association.

Geiger, Theodore and Frances M. Geiger (1975), *The Development Progress of Hong Kong and Singapore*, London: Macmillan.

George, Cherian (2000), *Singapore: The Air-Conditioned Nation – Essays on the Politics of Comport and Control 1990–2000*, Singapore: Landmark Books.

George, T.J.S. (1984), *Lee Kuan Yew's Singapore*, Singapore: Eastern Universities Press.

Goh Chok Tong (2001), National Day Rally Speech, entitled 'New Singapore', August. From http://www.gov.sg/sgip/Announce/NDR.htm

Goh Keng Swee (1972), 'Socialism in Singapore', in Goh Keng Swee, *The Economics of Modernization*, Singapore, Kuala Lumpur, Hong Kong: Federal Publications.

Goh Keng Swee (1976), 'A socialist economy that works', in C.V. Devan Nair (ed.), *Socialism That Works: The Singapore Way*, Singapore, Kuala Lumpur, Hong Kong: Federal Publications also in Goh Keng Swee, *The Practice of Economic Growth*, Singapore, Kuala Lumpur, Hong Kong: Federal Publications.

Goh Keng Swee (1977), *The Practice of Economic Growth*, Singapore, Kuala Lumpur, Hong Kong: Federal Publications.

Goh Keng Swee (1995), *Wealth of East Asian Nations: Speeches and Writings by Goh Keng Swee arranged and edited by Linda Low*, Singapore, Kuala Lumpur, Hong Kong: Federal Publications.

Goh Keng Swee (1996), 'The technology ladder in development: The Singapore case', *Asian-Pacific Economic Literature*, **10** (1), May.

Goh Chok Tong (1969), 'Industrial Growth', in Ooi Jim-Bee and Chiang Hai Ding (eds), *Modern Singapore*, Singapore: University of Singapore Press.

Gomez, James (2000), *Self-censorship: Singapore's Shame*, Singapore: Think Centre.

Goodman, Roger, Gordon White and Huck-ju Kwon (eds) (2000), *The East Asian Welfare Model: Welfare Orientalism and the State*, London and New York: Routledge.

Gormely, P.J. (1995), 'The Human Development Index in 1994: impact of income on country rank', *Journal of Economic and Social Measurement*, **21**.

Goto, Junichi and Takatoshi Hamada (1994), 'Economic Preconditions for an Asian Regional Integration', in Takotoshi Ito and Anne O. Krueger (eds), *Macroeconomic Linkages: Savings, Exchange Rates and Capital Flows*, Chicago: University of Chicago Press.

Greenaway, David (ed.) (1988), *Economic Development and International Trade*, Basingstoke, Hants: Macmillan.

Grossman, Gene M. (ed.) (1996), *Economic Growth: Theory and Evidence*, volume II, Cheltenham: Edward Elgar.

Grubel, Herbert G. (1989), 'Singapore's Record of Price Stability, 1966–84', in Kernial Singh Sandhu and Paul Wheatley (eds), *Management of Success: The Moulding of Modern Singapore*, Singapore: Institute of Southeast Asian Studies.

Grubel, H. and P. Lloyd (1975), *Intra-industry Trade: The Theory and Measurement of International Trade in Differentiated Products*, London: Macmillan.

Gwartney, James and Robert Lawson (1997), *Economic Freedom of the World 1997: Annual Report,* Vancouver: Fraser Institute.

Gwartney, James and Robert Lawson with Dexter Samida (2000), *Economic Freedom of the World 2000: Annual Report* at: www.fraserinstitute.ca/publications/books/econ-free-2000.

Haas, Michael (ed.) (1999a), *The Singapore Puzzle*, Westport and London: Praeger.

Haas, Michael (1999b), 'The Singapore Puzzle', in Michael Haas (ed.), *The Singapore Puzzle*, Westport and London: Praeger.

Haas, Michael (1999c), 'Mass Society', in Michael Haas (ed.), *The Singapore Puzzle*, Westport and London: Praeger.

Haggard, Stephen (1999), 'An External View of Singapore's Developed Status', in Linda Low (ed.), *Singapore: Towards a Developed Status*, Oxford: Oxford University Press.

Hallwood, C. Paul and Ronald McDonald (1994), *International Money and Finance*, 2nd edn, Oxford and Cambridge, Mass.: Basil Blackwell.

Hamilton-Hart, Natasha (2000), 'The Singapore state revisited', *The Pacific Review*, **13** (3).

Han Kang Kong (1996), 'Savings and Investment in Singapore', in Lim (ed.), *Economic Policy Management in Singapore*, Singapore: Addison-Wesley.

Hanke, Steve H., Lars Jonung and Kurt Schuler (1993*)*, *Russian Currency and Finance: A Currency Board Approach to Reform*, London and New York: Routledge.

Harrigan, Frank (1998), 'Asian saving: Theory, evidence and policy', in F.

Gerard Adams and Shinichi Ichimura (eds) (1998), *East Asian Development: Will the East Asian Growth Miracle Survive?*, Westport and London: Praeger,

Heller, Peter S. and Steven Symansky (1998), 'Implications for savings of aging in the Asian "tigers" ', *Asian Economic Journal*, **12** (3).

Heller, R. (1978), 'Determination of exchange rate practices', *Journal of Money, Credit and Banking*, **10** (3).

Hiemenz, Ulrich (1996), 'Determinants of private investment in the Asia-Pacific region', in Kapur, Quah and Hoon (1996).

Hicks, George (1989), 'The four little dragons: An enthusiast's reading guide', *Asian-Pacific Economic Literature*, **3** (2), September.

Hill, Hal and Pang Eng Fang (1989), 'Technology Exports from a Small, very Open NIC: The Case of Singapore', Working Paper 89/6, National Centre for Development Studies, Australian National University, Canberra.

Hill, Michael (2000), '"Asian values" as reverse Orientalism: Singapore', *Asia Pacific Viewpoint*, **41** (2), August.

Hill, Hal and Prue Phillips (1993), 'Patterns of imports penetration in East Asian industrialisation', *Asian Economic Journal*, **7** (1), March.

Ho, K.C and B.H. Chua (1995), 'Cultural, social and leisure activities in Singapore', Monograph No. 3, Singapore: Department of Statistics, Census of Population 1990.

Holmes, Kim R. (1994), 'In search of free markets', *The Asian Wall Street Journal*, 15 December 1994.

Hooley, Richard (1995), 'Saving in Southeast Asia: Sources, rate and contribution to growth', in M. Dutta et al. (eds), *Research in Asian Economic Studies: Volume 6*, Greenwich, Conn. and London: JIA Press.

Hoon Hian Teck and Ho Kong Weng (1992), 'A short macroeconomic account of the Singapore economy', *Times Economic Link*, No. 3, October–December.

Hoon Hian Teck and Teo Kai Lin (1992), 'A model of the link between the fiscal system and Singapore's Central Provident Fund in general equilibrium', *The Singapore Economic Review*, **37** (2), October.

Hoon Hian Teck and Neo Mei Choo (1997), 'Taxes, the Central Provident Fund and retirement decisions', *The Singapore Economic Review*, **42** (2), October.

Hu, Richard Tsu Tau (2001), 'Budget Statements 20001: Printed Version', from http:www.mof.sg/bud20001_txt1.htm.

Huff, W.G. (1994), *The Economic Growth of Singapore: Trade and Development in the Twentieth Century*, Cambridge: Cambridge University Press.

Huff, W.G. (1995), 'What is the Singapore model of economic development?', *Cambridge Journal of Economics*, **19**.

Huff, W.G. (1999), 'Singapore's economic development: four lessons and some doubts', *Oxford Development Studies*, **27** (1).

Hung, Bill W.S. and Christopher S.P. Tong (1996), 'Financial integration of the East Asian economies: Evidence from the saving-investment correlation', *Hong Kong Economic Papers*, No. 24.

Husain, Aasim (1995), 'Determinants of private saving', in Bercuson (1995).

Ichimura, S. and Y. Matsumotoa (eds) (1994), *Econometric Models of Asian-Pacific Countries*, Tokyo: Springer-Verlag.

Income Components of GDP: Trends and Analysis, Occasional Paper on Economic Statistics, April 1998.

Inland Revenue Authority of Singapore (2000), *I Respond and Serve: Annual Report 1999*, Singapore: Inland Revenue Authority of Singapore.

International Financial Statistics: Washington, DC: The International Monetary Fund, various issues.

International Monetary Fund (1997), *World Economic Outlook*, Washington, DC: The International Monetary Fund, May.

Ito, Shoichi and Tay Boon Nga (1994), 'The impact of the oil shock on the Singaporean economy: Simulation results of a CGE model', *Asian Economic Journal*, **8** (1), March.

Jao Y.C., Victor Mok and Ho Lok-sang (eds) (1989), *Economic Development in Chinese Societies: Models and Experiences*, Hong Kong: Hong Kong University Press.

Jajoura, Greg (1994), 'Capital goods sector in small open economies: Cuba and Singapore', *Journal of Contemporary Asia*, **24** (3).

Jayasankaran, S. (2000), 'Time for change', *Far Eastern Economic Review*, **163** (26), 29 June, 48–50.

Johnson, Bryan T. and Thomas P. Sheehy (1996), *The 1996 Index of Economic Freedom*, Washington, DC: The Heritage Foundation.

Johnson, Bryan T., Kim R. Homes and Melanic Kirkpatrick (1999), *The 1999 Index of Economic Freedom*, Washington, DC: The Heritage Foundation.

Jones, Alun (1995), 'Who killed Rajan Pillai?', *The Spectator*, 15 July.

Kapur, Basant K. (1981), 'Exchange rate flexibility and monetary policy', in *Papers on Monetary Economics*, edited by the Economics Department, Monetary Authority of Singapore, Singapore: Singapore University Press for the Monetary Authority of Singapore.

Kapur, Basant K. (ed.) (1986), *Singapore Studies: Critical Surveys of the Humanities and Social Sciences*, Singapore: Singapore University Press.

Kapur, Basant K. (1996), 'Comment on "Stabilisation policy in Singapore" by Koh Ai Tee', in Mukul G. Asher and Amina Tyabji (eds), *Fiscal System of Singapore: Trends, Issues and Future Directions*, Singapore: Centre for Advanced Studies, National University of Singapore.

Kapur, Basant K., Euston T.E. Quah and Hoon Hian Teck (eds) (1996), *Development, Trade and the Asia-Pacific: Essays in Honour of Professor Lim Chong Yah*, Singapore; Prentice-Hall.

Kasa, Kenneth (1997), 'Does Singapore invest too much?', *Federal Reserve Board of San Francisco, Economic Newsletter* No. 97–15 May. From their web site. www.frbsf.org/econrsrch/wklyltr

Keenan, Faith (1997), 'What economic crisis? Vietnam needs faster reform but it's set to apply the brakes instead', *Far Eastern Economic Review*, 18 December.

Kendall, Jon D., Park Donghyun and Randolph Tan (eds) (1997), *East Asian Economic Issues*, Volume III, Singapore: World Scientific.

Kernial Singh Sandhu and Paul Wheatley (eds) (1989), *Management of Success: The Moulding of Modern Singapore*, Singapore: Institute of Southeast Asian Studies.

Khalid, Ahmed, M. and Bay Teck Cheng (1997), 'Imports, exports and economic growth, cointegration and causality tests for Singapore', *The Singapore Economic Review*, **42** (2).

Khan, H., Seng, C. and W. Cheong (1989), *The Sociological Impact of Tourism on the Singapore Economy*, National University of Singapore, Multidisciplinary Research on Tourism.

Khan, Habibullah (1988), 'Role of agriculture in a city-state economy', *ASEAN Economic Bulletin*, **5** (2), November.

Khan, Moshin S. (1981), 'The dynamics of money demand and monetary policy in Singapore', in *Papers on Monetary Economics*, edited by the Economics Department, Monetary Authority of Singapore, Singapore: Singapore University Press for the Monetary Authority of Singapore.

Khanna, Vikram (2001), 'The Porter medicine will be hard to swallow', *The Business Times*, 6 August 2001, pp. 1 and 2.

Kim, L.-L. and Laurance Lau (1994), 'The sources of economic growth in the East Asian Newly Industrialising countries', *Journal of the Japanese and International Economies*, **8**.

Kim Yoonbai and Hwee Kuan Chow (2000), 'Exchange rate policy in Singapore: Prospects for a common currency peg in East Asia', *The Singapore Economic Review*, **45** (2), October.

Koh Ai Tee (1987), 'Saving, Investment and Entrepreneurship', in Lawrence B. Krause, Koh Ai Tee and Lee Tsao Yuan (eds), *The Singapore Economy Reconsidered*, Singapore: Institute of Southeast Asian Studies.

Koh Ai Tee (1989), 'Diversification of Trade', in Kernial Singh Sandhu and Paul Wheatley (eds), *Management of Success: The Moulding of Modern Singapore*, Singapore: Institute of Southeast Asian Studies.

Koh Ai Tee (1990), *Booms and Busts in Modern Societies*, Singapore: Longmans.

Koh Ai Tee (1992a), 'Singapore: Monetary and Financial System', in Peter Newman, Murray Milgate and John Eatwell (eds), *The New Palgrave Dictionary of Money and Finance*, Volume 3, London: Macmillan.

Koh Ai Tee (1992b), 'How much do we know about Singapore's business cycles', *Times Economic Link*, No. 1, April–June.

Koh Seng Khon (1988), 'Demand for money in Singapore', Academic exercise in part fulfilment for the Honours Bachelor of Social Science degree, Department of Economics and Statistics, National University of Singapore, academic year 1988/89.

Kolar, Elizabeth (1993), 'Toward a cash-less society', *The Freeman*, **43** (10), October, from http://www.libertyhaven.com/regulationandproperty-rights/bankingmoneyorfinance/freebanking/towardcashless.shtml

Konstadakopulos, Dimitrios (2000), 'Learning behaviour and co-operation of small high technology firms in the ASEAN region', *ASEAN Economic Bulletin*, **17** (1).

Krause, Lawrence B., Koh Ai Tee and Lee Tsao Yuan (1987), *The Singapore Economy Reconsidered*, Singapore: Institute of Southeast Asian Studies.

Krugman, Paul (1994a), *Peddling Prosperity: Economic Sense and Nonsense in the Age of Diminished Expectations*, New York and London: W.W. Norton.

Krugman, Paul (1994b), 'The myth of Asia's miracle', *Foreign Affairs*, **73**, November–December, 62–78.

Krugman, Paul (1996), 'Cycles of conventional wisdom on economic development', *International Affairs*, **72** (1).

Krugman, Paul (1999), *The Return of Depression Economics*, Harmondsworth: Penguin.

Kwan, C.H. (1998), 'The possibility of forming a yen bloc in Asia', *Journal of Asian Economics,* **9** (4).

Kwan, C.H. (2000), 'The possibility of forming a yen bloc revisited', *ASEAN Economic Bulletin*, **17** (2).

Kwan, C.H., Donna Vanderbrink and Chia Siow Yue (eds) (1998), *Coping with Capital Flows in East Asia*, Singapore: Nomura Research Institute (Tokyo) and Institute of Southeast Asian Studies.

Kwon, Huck-ju (2000), 'Democracy and the Politics of Social Welfare: A comparative analysis of welfare systems in East Asia', in Roger Goodman, Gordon White and Huck-ju Kwon (eds), *The East Asian Welfare Model: Welfare Orientalism and the State*, London and New York: Routledge.

Lam Peng Er and Kelvin Y.L. Tan (1999), *Lee's Lieutenants: Singapore's Old Guard*, St Leonards: Allen and Unwin.

Latif, Asad (1994), *The Flogging of Singapore: The Michael Fay Affair*, Singapore: Times Books International.

Lau, Albert Khoong Hwa (1981), 'Pragmatism: A history of the ideas of socialism on the People's Action party (1954–1976)', B.A. Honours Thesis, Department of History, National University of Singapore.

Lau, Lawrence J. (1998), 'The Sources of East Asian Economic Growth', in F. Gerard Adams and Shinichi Ichimura (eds), *East Asian Development: Will the East Asian Growth Miracle Survive?*, Westport and London: Praeger.

Lee Han Shih (2001), 'Aid for captains of industry', *The Business Times*, 16 October, p. 9.

Lee Hsien Loong (2000a), 'Speech at the 2000 Singapore Business Awards' from Ministry of Trade website. www.mti.gov.sg.

Lee Hsien Loong (2000b), *Policy Statements: Speeches on Singapore's Key Financial Strategies 1997–2000*, Monetary Authority of Singapore: Singapore.

Lee Kuan Yew (1998), *The Singapore Story: Memoirs of Lee Kuan Yew*, Singapore: Singapore Press Holdings.

Lee Kuan Yew (2000), *From Third World to First – The Singapore Story 1965–2000: Memoirs of Lee Kuan Yew*, Singapore: Singapore Press Holdings.

Lee, Sheng-yi (1984), 'The demand for money in Singapore, 1968–82', *ASEAN Economic Bulletin*, **1** (2), November.

Lee, Sheng-yi (1985), *Demand for and Supply of Money in Singapore, 1968–1982*, Taipei, Taiwan: Chung-Hua Institution for Economic Research Monograph Series No. 4.

Lee, Sheng-yi (1990), *The Monetary and Banking Development of Singapore and Malaysia*, 3rd edn, Singapore: Singapore University Press.

Lee, S.Y. and Y.C. Jao (1982), *Financial Structures and Monetary Policies in Southeast Asia*, London: Macmillan.

Lee, S.Y. and W.K. Li (1983), 'Money, income and prices and their lead-lag relationships in Singapore', *The Singapore Economic Review*, **28** (1), April.

Lee Tsao Yuan (1987), 'The government in macroeconomic management', in Lawrence B. Krause, Koh Ai Tee and Lee Tsao Yuan (eds), *The Singapore Economy Reconsidered*, Singapore: Institute of Southeast Asian Studies.

Lee Tsao Yuan (1987), 'The government in the labour market' in Lawrence B. Krause, Koh Ai Tee and Lee Tsao Yuan (eds), *The Singapore Economy Reconsidered*, Singapore: Institute of Southeast Asian Studies.

Lee Tsao Yuan (1994), *Overseas Investment: Experience of Singapore Manufacturing Companies*, Singapore: Institute of Policy Studies, McGraw-Hill.

Leeson, Nick with Edward Whitely (1996), *Rogue Trader*, London: Little Brown.

Leyland, J. (1997), *World-wide Business Cost Comparisons: The Costs of Setting up a Business in 27 Countries*, London: Economist Intelligence Unit.

Lian, Daniel (2001a), 'Changing Singapore's Model', *The Asian Wall Street Journal*, 3–5 August 2001, p. 8.

Lian, Daniel (2001b), 'Singapore must deal with structural unemployment', *The Business Times*, 22 August, p. 14.

Li Yeow Ju (1993), 'Domestic Resource Mobilization in Singapore', in Y.M.W.B. Weerasekera (ed.), *Domestic Resource Mobilization in the Seacan Countries*, Kuala Lumpar: The South East Asian Central Banks (SEACAN) Research and Training Centre.

Lim, Catharine (2001), *Following the Wrong God Home*, London: Orion.

Lim Chong Yah (1980), *Economic Development in Singapore*, Singapore, Kuala Lumpur, Hong Kong: Federal Publications.

Lim Chong Yah (1986), 'Singapore: resources and growth – an introductory overview', in Lim Chong Yah and Peter Lloyd (eds), *Resources and Growth in Singapore*, Singapore: Oxford University Press.

Lim Chong Yah (1989), 'From High Growth Rates to Recession', in Kernial Singh Sandhu and Paul Wheatley (eds), *Management of Success: The Moulding of Modern Singapore*, Singapore: Institute of Southeast Asian Studies.

Lim Chong Yah (ed.) (1996), *Economic Policy Management in Singapore*, Singapore: Addison-Wesley.

Lim Chong Yah (1998), 'The national wages council: Targets and goals', in Lim Chong Yah and Rosalind Chew (eds), *Wages and Wages Policies: Tripartism in Singapore*, Singapore: World Scientific.

Lim Chong Yah (2001), *Economic Essays by Lim Chong Yah*, Singapore: World Scientific.

Lim Chong Yah and Peter Lloyd (eds) (1986), *Resources and Growth in Singapore*, Singapore: Oxford University Press.

Lim Chong Yah and Associates (1988), *Policy Options for the Singapore Economy*, Singapore: McGraw-Hill.

Lim Chong Yah and Rosalind Chew (eds) (1998), *Wages and Wages Policies: Tripartism in Singapore*, Singapore: World Scientific.

Lim, D. (1974), 'Export instability and economic development: the example of West Malaysia', *Oxford Economic Papers*, **26**.

Lim, D. (1991), *Export Instability and Compensatory Financing*, London: Routledge.

Lim Kian Guan, Chow Kit Boey and Tsui Kai Chong (1996), 'Estimating Singapore's import function using demand systems theory', *The Singapore Economic Review*, **41** (1).

Lim, L.Y.C. (1989), 'Social welfare', in Kernial Singh Sandhu and Paul

Wheatley (eds), *Management of Success: The Moulding of Modern Singapore*, Singapore: Institute of Southeast Asian Studies.

Lim Swee Say (1999), 'Speech by Mr Lim Swee Say, Minister of State for Trade and Industry and Communications and Information Technology at the Rotary-ASME Entrepreneur of the year Award 1999 Presentation Ceremony', 18 August.

Lingle, Christopher (1996), *Singapore's Authoritarian Capitalism: Asian Values, Free Market Illusions, and Political Dependency*, Barcelona and Farifax: Edicions Sirocco and the Locke Institute:

Lingle, Christopher (1998), *The Rise and Decline of the Asian Century: False Starts on the Path to the Global Millennium*, 3rd revised edn, Asia 2000: Hong Kong.

Lingle, Christopher and Kurt Wickman (1999), 'Political Economy', in Michael Haas (ed.), *The Singapore Puzzle*, Westport and London: Praeger.

Liu Pak-wai (1992), 'Economic Development of the Four Little Dragons: Lessons for LDCs and China', Hong Kong Institute of Asia-Pacific Affairs, Chinese University of Hong Kong, Occasional Paper No.12.

Lloyd, Peter J. (1998), 'A long-term view of labour migration, foreign investment and growth in the Singapore economy', in Lim Chong Yah and Rosalind Chew (eds), *Wages and Wages Policies: Tripartism in Singapore*, Singapore: World Scientific.

Lloyd, Peter J. and Roger J. Sandilands (1986), 'The trade sector in a very open re-export economy', in Lim Chong-Yah and Peter Lloyd (eds), *Resources and Growth in Singapore*, Singapore: Oxford University Press.

Love, J. (1987), 'Export instability in less developed countries: consequences and causes', *Journal of Economic Studies*, **14** (2).

Lovell, C.A. Knox and Yih Pin Tang (1999), 'An alternative tale of two cities', in Fu Tsu-Tan, Cliff Y. Huang and C.A. Knox Lovell (eds), *Economic Efficiency and Productivity Growth in the Asia-Pacific Region*, Cheltenham, UK and Northampton, USA: Edward Elgar.

Low, Linda (1991), *The Political Economy of Privatisation in Singapore: Analysis, Interpretation and Evaluatio*n, Singapore: McGraw-Hill.

Low, Linda (1993), 'Conclusion', in Low, Linda, Toh Mun Heng, Soon Teck Wong, Tan Kong Yam and Helen Hughes, *Challenges and Response: Twenty-Five Years of the Economic Development Board*, Singapore: Times Academic Publishers.

Low, Linda (1998), *The Political Economy of a City-State: Government-made Singapore*, Singapore: Oxford University Press.

Low, Linda (1999a), 'The Elusive Developed Country Status', in Linda Low (ed.), *Singapore: Towards a Developed Status,* Centre for Advanced Studies, National University of Singapore and Oxford University Press.

Low, Linda (ed.) (1999b), *Singapore: Towards a Developed Status,*

Singapore: Centre for Advanced Studies, National University of Singapore and Oxford University Press.

Low, Linda and T.C. Aw (1996), 'High savings in Singapore: not by decree but by choice', *Singapore Management Review*, **18** (2).

Low, Linda and T.C. Aw (1997), *Housing a Healthy, Educated and Wealthy Nation Through the CPF*, Singapore: Times Academic Press.

Low, Linda and Ngiam Tee Liang (1999), 'An underclass among the overclass', in Low (ed.), *Singapore: Towards a Developed Status*, Singapore: Centre for Advanced Studies, National University of Singapore and Oxford University Press.

Low, Linda and Toh Mun Heng (1989), 'The Elected Presidency as a Safeguard for Official Reserves: What is at Stake?', Singapore: Institute of Policy Studies Occasional Paper No. 1, Times Academic Press.

Low, Linda and Toh Mun Heng (eds) (1992), *Public Policies in Singapore: Changes in the 1980s and Future Signposts*, Singapore: Times Academic Press.

Low, Linda, Toh Mun Heng, Soon Teck Wong, Tan Kong Yam and Helen Hughes (1993), *Challenges and Response: Twenty-Five Years of the Economic Development Board*, Singapore: Times Academic Publishers.

Low, Vincent (1994), 'The MAS Model: Structure and some policy simulations', in Anthony Chin and Ngiam Kee Jin (eds), *Outlook for the Singapore Economy*, Singapore: Trans Global Publishing.

Luckett, Dudley G., David L. Schulze and Raymond W.Y. Wong (1994), *Banking, Finance and Monetary Policy in Singapore*, Singapore: McGraw-Hill.

Mahadevan, Renuka and Kali Kalirajn (2000), 'Singapore's manufacturing sector's TFP growth: A decomposition analysis', *Journal of Comparative Economics*, **28** (4), December.

Margolin, Jean-Louis (1988), *Singapour: Genese d'un Noveau Pays Industriel*, Paris: Editions L'Harmattan.

Maddison, A. (1995), *Monitoring the World Economy: 1820–1992*, Paris: OECD.

MacBean, A. (1966), *Export Instability and Economic Development*, London: Allen and Unwin.

McKendrick, David G., Richard F. Doner, Stephan Haggard with Poh Kam Wong (2000), 'Singapore', in David G. McKendrick, Richard F. Doner and Stephan Haggard (eds), *From Silicon Valley to Singapore: Location and Competitive Advantage in the Hard Disk Drive Industry*, Stanford: Stanford University Press.

McKinnon, R. (1963), 'Optimum currency areas', *American Economic Review*, **53**.

McNulty, Sheila (2000), 'Preparing to Compete in a Wider World', in

Financial Times Survey: Singapore 2000/Government, from 13http:// www.ft.com.ftsurveys/country/sc232aa.htm.

Medhi Krongkaew (1994), 'Income distribution in East Asian developing countries', *Asian-Pacific Economic Literature*, **8** (2), November.

Mellor, William (2001), 'The risks of playing it safe', *Asiaweek,* 4 May, pp. 29–35.

Milne, R.S. and Diane K. Mauzy (1990), *Singapore: The Legacy of Lee Kuan Yew*, Boulder, San Francisco, Oxford: Westview Press.

Minchin, James (1990), *No Man is an Island: A Portrait of Singapore's Lew Kuan Yew*, 2nd edn, Sydney: Allen & Unwin.

Ministry of Trade and Industry (1991), *The Strategic Economic Plan: Towards a Developed Nation*, Singapore: Economic Planning Committee, Ministry of Trade and Industry.

Ministry of Trade and Industry (1999), 'The burgeoning role of the electronics industry in East Asia', November, at http://www.mti.gov.sg/ public/econodata/econodata.cfm.

Mirza, Hafiz (1986), *Multinationals and the Growth of the Singapore Economy*, New York: St. Martin's Press.

Monetary Authority of Singapore (1997), *Current Account Deficits in the ASEAN-3. Is there Cause for Concern?*, Occasional Paper No. 1, June.

Monetary Authority of Singapore (1998a), 'Growth in Singapore's Export Markets, 1991–96: A Shift-Share Analysis', Singapore: Monetary Authority of Singapore, Economics Department, Occasional Paper No. 4, February.

Monetary Authority of Singapore (1998b), 'What Lies Behind Singapore's Real Exchange Rate? An Empirical Analysis of the Purchasing Power Parity Hypothesis', Singapore: Monetary Authority of Singapore, Economics Department, Occasional Paper No. 6, May.

Monetary Authority of Singapore (1998c), 'Singapore's Trade Linkages, 1992–96: Trends and Implications', Singapore: Monetary Authority of Singapore, Economics Department, Occasional Paper No. 7, August.

Monetary Authority of Singapore (1999a), 'Capital Account and Exchange Rate Management in a Surplus Economy: The Case of Singapore', Singapore: Economics Department, Occasional Paper No. 11, March.

Monetary Authority of Singapore (1999b), 'Money, Interest Rates and Income in the Singapore Economy', Singapore: Economics Department, Occasional Paper No. 15, July.

Monetary Authority of Singapore (2000a), 'A Survey of Singapore's Monetary History', Singapore: Economics Department Occasional Paper No. 18, January.

Monetary Authority of Singapore (2000b), 'Enlightened Discretion in

Monetary Policy: Singapore's Experience', Economics Department, National University of Singapore, Staff Seminar, 24 March.

Monetary Authority of Singapore (2000c), *Staying the Course: Monetary Authority of Singapore Annual Report 1999/2000.*

Monetary Authority of Singapore (2000d), *Quarterly Bulletin,* Volume II, No. 4, Economics Department, December.

Monetary Authority of Singapore (2001a), *Singapore's Exchange Rate Policy,* February.

Monetary Authority of Singapore (2001b), *Quarterly Bulletin,* Volume III, No. 1, Economics Department, March.

Monetary Authority of Singapore (2001c), *Quarterly Bulletin,* Volume III, No. 2, Economics Department, June.

Monetary Authority of Singapore (2001d), *Quarterly Bulletin,* Volume III, No. 3, Economics Department, October.

Monetary Authority of Singapore (2001e), *Innovation, Enterprise, Credibility: Monetary Authority of Singapore Annual Report 2000/2001.*

Mookerjee, Raajen and Jose L. Tongzon (1997), 'Do the ASEAN countries have a common business cycle?', *Journal of the Asia Pacific Economy,* **2** (1).

Moreno, Ramon (1989), 'Exchange rates and monetary policy in Singapore and Hong Kong', *Hong Kong Economic Papers,* No. 19.

Mori, Kazuo (1991), 'Business Cycles in Asian Countries', in Hiroshi Osada and Dasuke Hiratsuka (eds), *Business Cycles in Asia,* Tokyo: Institute of Developing Economies.

Mukhopadhaya, Pundarik (2000), 'Income Gap and Educational Opportunity in Some Southeast Asian Countries: Government Efforts in Bridging Inequality', Singapore: National University of Singapore, Department of Economics, Economic Policy Forum, October.

Mukhopadhaya, Pundarik (2001a), 'Education policies as means to tackle income disparity: The Singapore case', *International Journal of Social Economics,* forthcoming.

Mukhopadhaya, Pundarik (2001b), 'Changing labour force gender composition and male-female income diversity in Singapore' *Journal of Asian Economics,* **12** (4), forthcoming.

Mullineux, Andy, David G. Dickson and Peng Wensheng (1993), *Business Cycles: Theory and Evidence,* Oxford, UK and Cambridge, USA: Blackwell.

Mundell, R.A. (1961), 'A Theory of Optimum Currency Areas', *American Economic Review,* **51**.

Mundell, R.A. (1963), 'Capital mobility and stabilization under fixed and flexible exchange rates', *Canadian Journal of Economics and Political Science,* **29**, November.

Murray, Geoffrey and Audrey Perera (1996), *Singapore: The Global City-State*, Folkstone: China Library.

Myint, H. (1972), *Southeast Asia's Economy: Development Policies in the 1970s*, Harmondsworth: Penguin.

Nadal de Simone, Francisco (2000), 'Monetary and fiscal policy interaction in a small open economy: the case of Singapore', *Asian Economic Journal*, **14** (2) June.

Nadiri, M. Ishaq and Wanpyo Son (2000), 'Sources of Growth in East Asian Economies', in Fu Tsu-Tan, Cliff Y. Huang and C.A. Knox Lovell (eds), *Economic Efficiency and Productivity Growth in the Asia-Pacific Region*, Cheltenham and Northampton: Edward Elgar.

Nair, C.V. Devan (ed.) (1976), *Socialism That Works: The Singapore Way*, Singapore, Kuala Lumpur, Hong Kong: Federal Publications.

Nair, C.V. Devan (1982), *Not by Wages Alone: Selected Speeches and Writings of C.V. Devan Nair 1959–1981*, Singapore: Singapore National Trades Union Congress.

Nair, C.V. Devan (1994), 'Foreword', in Francis T. Seow, *To Catch a Tatar: A Dissident in Lee Kuan Yew's Prison*, Yale Southeast Asia Studies Monograph No. 42, New Haven: Yale Center for International and Area Studies.

Nathan, Dominic (2001), 'Singapore: Green paradise or polluted city?', *The Straits Times Interactive Edition*, 29 January, from http://www.ecologyasia.com/NewsArchive.

Ng, Chee Yuen (1989), 'Privatization in Singapore: Divestment with control', *ASEAN Economic Bulletin,* **5** (3), March.

Ngiam Kee Jin and Amina Tyabji (1998), 'Liberalizing the use of Singapore dollars: benefits, problems and prospects', Kuala Lumpur: 23 Federation of ASEAN Economic Associations (FAEA) Conference, 15 October.

Nicolas, Francoise (1999), 'Is there a case for a single currency within ASEAN?', *The Singapore Economic Review*, **44** (1), April.

Noland, Marcus (1998), 'The Asian financial crisis: Looking forward', *Singapore Economic Review*, **43** (2), October.

Nordhaus, W.D. and J. Tobin (1972), *Is Growth Obsolete*, New York: Columbia University Press.

Nuaw Mee Kau (1979), *Export Expansion and Industrial Growth in Singapore, Hong Kong*, Kingsway International Publications.

O'Driscoll, Gerald P., Kim R. Holmes and Melanie Kirkpatrick (1999), *2000 Index of Economic Freedom: Executive Summary* from www.heritage.org/index/execsum and the volume from http://www.heritage.org/index/2001/

O'Driscoll, Gerald P. Jr., Kim R. Holmes and Melanie Kirkpatrick (2001),

The 2001 Index of Economic Freedom, Washington, DC: The Heritage Foundation. Also at http://www.heritage.org/index/2001/

Okposin, Samuel Bassey (1999), *The Extent of Singapore's Investments Abroad*, Aldershot: Ashgate.

Ong Chin Huat and David Wan Tai Wai (2000), 'Money, output and causality: The case of Singapore', *ASEAN Economic Bulletin*, **17** (1), April.

Ooi Jim-Bee and Chiang Hai Ding (eds) (1969), *Modern Singapore*, Singapore: University of Singapore Press.

Osada, Hiroshi and Dasuke Hiratsuka (eds) (1991), *Business Cycles in Asia*, Tokyo: Institute of Developing Economies.

Ow Chin-Hock (1986), 'The role of government in economic development: The Singapore experience', in Lim Chong-Yah and Peter Lloyd (eds), *Resources and Growth in Singapore*, Singapore: Oxford University Press.

Owyong, David and Bhanoji Rao (1998), 'Total factor productivity growth in the Singapore economy: Some econometric estimates', *Singapore Economic Review*, **43** (1), April.

Park Donghyun (2000), 'Intra-Southeast Asian income convergence', *ASEAN Economic Bulletin*, **17** (3).

Peebles, Gavin (1988), *Hong Kong's Economy: An Introductory Macroeconomic Analysis*, Hong Kong and New York: Oxford University Press.

Peebles, Gavin (1993), 'National income accounting and the case of Singapore', *Times Economic Link*, No. 6, July–September.

Peebles, Gavin (1994), 'Review of Russian Currency and Finance: A Currency Board Approach to Reform by Steve H. Hanke, Lars Jonung and Kurt Schuler', in *Europe–Asia Studies*, **46** (6).

Peebles, Gavin (1996), 'Money demand in Singapore revisited: a comment with implications', *Asian Economic Journal*, **10** (3).

Peebles, Gavin (1997), 'Review of Toh and Tan (1998)', *Singapore Economic Review*, **42** (2).

Peebles, Gavin (1998a), 'Singapore: Economy', in *The Far East and Australasia 1999*, London: Europa Publications.

Peebles, Gavin (1998b), 'Values and Development: An Economist's Historical and Comparative Perspective with reference to Singapore', in Hank Lim and Ranjit Singh (eds), *Values and Development: A Multidisciplinary Approach with Some Comparative Studies*, Singapore: Centre for Advanced Studies, NUS.

Peebles, Gavin (1999a), 'Singapore: Economy', in *The Far East and Australasia 2000*, London: Europa Publications.

Peebles, Gavin (1999b), 'Review Article: "Economists and the Asian Miracle" a review of *The Key to the Asian Miracle: Making Shared Growth Credible* by Jose Edgardo Campos and Hilton L. Root', *The Journal of Southeast Asian Studies*, March.

Peebles, Gavin (2000a), 'Singapore: Economy', in *The Far East and Australasia 2001*, London: Europa Publications.

Peebles, Gavin (2000b), 'Saving and Investment in Singapore: An Overview', unpublished typescript: Singapore.

Peebles, Gavin (2001), 'Singapore: Economy', in *The Far East and Australasia 2002*, London: Europa Publications.

Peebles, Gavin (2002), 'Saving and Investment in Singapore: Implications for the economy in the early twenty-first century', in W.T. Hui, A.T. Koh, Rao Bhanoji and K.L. Lim (eds), *Singapore Economy in the Twenty-First Century: Issues and Strategies*, Singapore: McGraw-Hill.

Peebles, Gavin and Peter Wilson (1996), *The Singapore Economy*, Cheltenham and Brookfield: Edward Elgar.

Peh Kian-heng and Wong Fot-Chyi (2000), 'Singapore trade linkages, 1992–96: A trade intensity analysis', *The Singapore Economic Review*, **44** (2), October.

Phang Sock-Yong (1996), 'Economic development and the distribution of land rents in Singapore: A Georgist implementation', *American Journal of Economics and Sociology*, **55** (4), October.

Phua Kia Fatt, Alan (1989), 'Demand for money specifications and its stability in Singapore', Academic exercise in part fulfilment for the Honours Bachelor of Social Science degree, Department of Economics and Statistics, National University of Singapore, academic year 1989/90.

Pillai, Philip N. (1983), *State Enterprises in Singapore: Legal Importation and Development*, Singapore: Singapore University Press.

Pomfret, Richard (1996), 'ASEAN – always at the crossroads?', *Journal of the Asia Pacific Economy*, **1** (3).

Porter, Michael E. (1990), *The Competitive Advantage of Nations*, London: Macmillan.

Prudence at the Helm: Board of Commissioners of Currency Singapore 1967–1992, Singapore: Board of Commissioners of Currency, 1992.

Przeworski, Adam and Fernando Limongi (1993), 'Political regimes and economic growth', *Journal of Economic Perspectives*, **7** (3).

Pugh, Cedric (1986), 'Housing in Singapore', *International Journal of Social Economics*, **13** (4/5).

Quah, Jon S.T. (1998), 'Singapore's model of development: Is it transferable?', in Henry S. Rowen (ed.), *Behind East Asian Growth: The Political and Social Foundations of Prosperity*, London and New York: Routledge.

Ram, R. (1987), 'Exports and economic growth in developing countries: evidence from time-series and cross-section data', *Economic Development and Cultural Change*, **36**.

Ramesh, M. (2000), 'The politics of social security in Singapore', *The Pacific Review*, **13** (2).

Ramesh, M. and M. Asher (2000), 'Social Security', in Ramesh and Asher (2000), *Welfare Capitalism in Southeast Asia: Social Security, Health and Education Policies,* London: Macmillan.

Ramkishan, Rajan, Rahul Sen and Reza Siregar (2001), *Singapore and Free Trade Agreements: Economic Relations with Japan and the United States,* Singapore: Institute of Southeast Asian Studies, ICEA28.

Ramstetter, Eric D. (1999), 'Comparisons of foreign multinationals and local firms in Asian manufacturing over time', *Asian Economic Journal,* **13** (2), June.

Rana, Pradumna B. (1984), 'Inflationary effects of exchange rate changes: The case of the ASEAN countries, 1973–1979', *ASEAN Economic Bulletin,* **1** (1), July.

Rao, V.V. Bhanoji (1988), 'Income distribution in East Asian developing countries', *Asian–Pacific Economic Literature,* **1**.

Rao, V.V. Bhanoji (1990), 'Income distribution in Singapore: trends and issues', *The Singapore Economic Review,* **35** (1), April.

Rao, V.V. Bhanoji (1993), 'A primer on income inequality', *Times Economic Link,* October–December.

Rao, V.V. Bhanoji (2001), *East Asian Economies: The Miracle, a Crisis and the Future,* Singapore: McGraw-Hill.

Rao, V.V. Bhanoji and M.K. Ramakrishnan (1980), *Income Inequality in Singapore,* Singapore: Singapore University Press.

Rao, V.V. Bhanoji and Christopher Lee (1995), 'Sources of growth in the Singapore Economy and its manufacturing and the service sectors', *The Singapore Economic Review,* **40** (1), April.

Rao, V.V. Bhanoji and David Owyong (1998), 'Total Factor Productivity growth in the Singapore economy: Some econometric estimates', *The Singapore Economic Review,* **43** (1) April.

Report of the Public Sector Divestment Committee (1987), Singapore.

Reynolds, C. (1963), 'Domestic consequences of export instability', *American Economic Review,* **53**.

Richardson, Graham (1994), *Singapore to 2003: Aspiring to the First World,* London: The Economist Intelligence Unit.

Richardson, Michael (2001), 'Singapore's habits are found to stall innovation', *International Herald Tribune,* 24–25 March 2001, p. 24.

Rodan, Garry (1989), *The Political Economy of Singapore's Industrialization: Nation State and International Capital,* London: Macmillan.

Rodan, Garry (2000), 'Asian crisis, transparency and the international media in Singapore', *The Pacific Review,* **13** (2).

Rodan, Garry, Kevin Hewison and Richard Robinson (eds) (1997), *The Political Economy of South-East Asia,* Melbourne: Oxford University Press.

Rowen, Henry S. (ed.) (1998), *Behind East Asian Growth: The Political and Social Foundations of Prosperity*, London and New York: Routledge.

Rowthorn, Robert and Ramana Ramaswamy (1997), 'Reindustrialization: Causes and Implications', IMF Working Paper, April.

Sachs, Jeffrey D. and Larrain B. Felipe (1993), *Macroeconomics in the Global Economy*, New York: Harvester Wheatsheaf.

Sachs, Jeffrey D. and Andrew Warner (1995), 'Economic reform and the process of global integration', *Brookings Papers on Economic Activity*, **1**.

Sandilands, Roger J. (1992), 'Savings, investment and housing in Singapore's growth, 1965–1990', *Savings and Development*, **15** (2).

Sandilands, Roger J. and Tan Ling Hui (1986), 'Comparative advantage in a re-export economy: The case of Singapore', *The Singapore Economic Review*, **31** (2), October.

Sarel, Michael (1997), 'Growth and Productivity in ASEAN Countries', Working Paper of the International Monetary Fund, WP/97/97.

Saywell, Trish (2001), 'Mental health: Suffer the children: In Singapore, as in much of Asia, stress starts early', *Far Eastern Economic Review*, 9 August.

Schein, Edgar H. (1996), *Strategic Pragmatism: The Culture of Singapore's Economic Development Board*, Cambridge, Mass., London: MIT Press.

Schulze, David L. (1986), 'Monetization in ASEAN: 1970–1984', *The Singapore Economic Review*, **31** (2), October.

Schulze, David L. (1990), 'Domestic Financial Institutions in Singapore: Public Sector Competition', Centre for Advanced Studies, National University of Singapore, Occasional Paper, Singapore: Times Academic Press.

Seah, Linda (1983), 'Public enterprise and economic development', in Peter S.J. Chen (ed.), *Singapore Development Policies and Trends*, Singapore: Oxford University Press.

Sen, Amartya (1997), 'Human rights and Asian values', *The New Republic*, 14–21 July.

Sen, Rahul (2000), 'Analysing international trade data in a small open economy: The case of Singapore', *ASEAN Economic Bulletin*, **17** (1), April.

Seow, Francis T. (1994), *To Catch a Tatar: A Dissident in Lee Kuan Yew's Prison*, Yale Southeast Asia Studies Monograph No. 42, New Haven: Yale Center for International and Area Studies.

Seow, Francis T. (1998), *The Media Enthralled: Singapore Revisited*, Boulder and London: Lynne Rienner.

Seow, Francis T. (1999), 'The Judiciary', in Michael Haas (ed.), *The Singapore Puzzle*, Westport and London: Praeger.

Sesser, Stan (1994), *The Lands of Charm and Cruelty*: *Travels in Southeast Asia*, London: Picador.

Shameen, Assif and Alejandro Reyes (2000), 'Creative destruction city', *Asiaweek*, **26** (11), 42–6.

Shimada, Hiromitsu (1996), 'Impact of DFI on the supply side of the Singapore economy', *ASEAN Economic Bulletin*, **12** (3).

Shu Shih Luh (2001), 'Work policy worries some Singaporeans', *The Asian Wall Street Journal*, 9 October, pp. 12 and 14.

Simkin, Colin (1984), 'Does money matter in Singapore?', *The Singapore Economic Review*, **29** (1), April.

Sinclair, T. and A. Tsegaye (1988), 'International tourism and export instability', University of Kent Studies in Economics, 88/4.

Singapore Census of Population (2000), Advance Data Release no. 7.

Singapore 1,000 1993: Industrial (1993), Singapore: Datapool Ltd.

Singapore 1,000 1993: Services (1993), Singapore: Datapool Ltd.

Singapore 1000: Year 2000/2001, Singapore: DP Information Network Pte Ltd.

Singapore: The Last 10 Years, Singapore: Ministry of Information and the Arts from http://www.gov.sg/SGIP/NDR/NDRsup.pdf

'Singapore Briefing No. 29: Singapore's Export Competitiveness vis-a-vis other Dynamic Asian Economies', DBS Bank, Economic Research Department, June 1992.

'Singapore Economic Trends Report', American Embassy, Singapore, July 2000 from http://www.usembassysingapore.org.sg/embassy/politics/Trends 2001.html and http://infiserve2.ita.gov/apweb.nsf (International Trade Administration of the US Department of Commerce, June 2000).

'Singapore Economic Trends Report', American Embassy, Singapore, July 2001 from http://www.usembassysingapore.org.sg/embassy/politics/Trends 2001.html.

Singh, Ajit (1998), 'Savings, investment and the corporation in the East Asian miracle', *The Journal of Development Studies*, **34** (6), August.

Siriwardana, Mahina and David Schulze (2000), 'Singapore and the Asian economic crisis: An assessment of policy responses', *ASEAN Economic Bulletin*, **17** (3), December.

Smith, Peter (1993), 'Measuring human development', *Asian Economic Journal*, **7** (1), March.

Soesastro, Hadi (1994), 'Military expenditure and the arms trade in the Asian-Pacific region', *Asian–Pacific Economic Literature*, **8** (1), May.

Soh, Doreen (1990), *From Cowries to Credit Cards: Stories of Singapore's Money*, Singapore: Federal Publications.

Soon Teck Wong, Linda Low and Toh Mun Heng (1990), 'On using statistics in Singapore', *Singapore Journal of Statistics*, **1**, October.

Stephen, W.K., Chiu, K.C. Ho and Tai-lok Lui (1995), 'A tale of two cities rekindled: Hong Kong and Singapore's divergent paths to industrailism', *Journal of Development Studies*, **11**(1)

Stephen, W.K., Chiu, K.C. Ho and Tai-lok Lui (1997), *Global-States in the Global Economy: Industrial Restructuring in Hong Kong and Singapore*, Boulder Col: Westview Press.

Stephens, Jacintha (2001), 'The hidden peril', *Asiaweek*, **27** (4), 19 October.

Taguchi, H. (1994), 'On the Internationalization of the Japanese Yen', in Takotoshi Ito and Anne O. Krueger (eds), *Macroeconomic Linkages: Savings, Exchange Rates and Capital Flows*, Chicago: University of Chicago Press.

Taiwan Statistical Data Book (2000), Taiwan: Council for International Economic Cooperation and Development.

Tamboer, Kees (1996), 'Albert Winsemius, "founding father of Singapore"', *IAAS Newsletter*, at http://iias.leidenuniv.nl/iiasn/iiasn9/soueasia/winsemiu.html

Tamney, Joseph B. (1995), *The Struggle Over Singapore's Soul: Western Modernization and Asian Culture*, Berlin and New York: de Ruyter.

Tan, A. (1984), 'Changing Patterns of Singapore Foreign Trade and Investment since 1960', in You Poh Seng and Lim Chong Yah (eds), *Twenty-five Years of Development*, Singapore: Nanyang Xingzhou Lianhe Zaobao.

Tan, A. and Ow Chin Hock (1982), 'Singapore', in Bela Balassa and associates, *Development Strategies in Semi-Industrial Economies*, Baltimore: The Johns Hopkins University Press for the World Bank.

Tan Chwee Huat (1999), *Financial Markets and Institutions in Singapore*, 10th edn, Singapore: Singapore University Press.

Tan Hwee Hwee (2001), *Mammon Inc.*, London: Michael Joseph.

Tan Kim Heng (1996), 'A New View of Macroeconomic Stabilization: The Singapore perspective', in Lim Chong Yah (ed.), *Economic Policy Management in Singapore*, Singapore: Addison-Wesley.

Tan Kin Lian (1998), 'Impact of current economic crisis on the region and the way co-operatives adjust to the changing environment – view from Singapore (1998)', *Co-op Dialogue*, **8** (2) July–September.

Tan Kong Yam (1993), 'Comparative development experience with the other NIEs', in Linda Low, Toh Mun Heng, Soon Teck Wong, Tan Kong Yam and Helen Hughes (eds), *Challenges and Response: Twenty-Five Years of the Economic Development Board*, Singapore: Times Academic Publishers.

Tan Sook Yee (1998), *Private Ownership of Public Housing in Singapore*, Singapore: Times Academic Press.

Tan Teck Yoong (1995), 'An analysis of Singapore's external trade in the light of the new (1988) input–output tables', unpublished M.Soc. Science dissertation, Department of Economics and Statistics, National University of Singapore.

Tay Boon Nga (1992), 'The Central Provident Fund: Operation and schemes', in Linda Low and Toh Mun Heng (eds), *Public Policies in Singapore: Changes in the 1980s and Future Signposts*, Singapore: Times Academic Press.

Teh Kok Peng and Tharman Shanmugaratnam (1992), 'Exchange rate policy: Philosophy and conduct over the past decade', in Linda Low and Toh Mun Heng (eds), *Public Policies in Singapore: Changes in the 1980s and Future Signposts*, Singapore: Times Academic Press.

Terzani, Tiziano (1998), *A Fortune-teller Told Me: Earthbound Travels in the Far East*, London: Flamingo.

Thanagevelu, S.M. (2000), 'TFP growth in the electronics industry in Singapore', *The Singapore Economic Review*, **44** (2), October.

Thanisorn Dejthamrong (1993), *The Budget Deficit: Its Impact on Money Supply and Output in Selected SEACEN Countries*, Kuala Lumpur: The South East Asian Central Banks (SEACEN), Research and Training Centre.

Theroux, Paul (1976), *Saint Jack*, London: Penguin.

Thornton, John (1993), 'A test of the rational expectations-permanent income hypothesis for Singapore', *Asian Economic Journal*, **7** (1), March.

Tinbergen, J. (1952), *On the Theory of Economic Policy*, Amsterdam: North-Holland.

Toh Mun Heng (1986), 'Income redistribution and trade policy effects on Macroeconomic aggregates: A simulation study of the Singapore economy based on an extended input-output model', *Journal of Economic Development*, **11** (1), July.

Toh Mun Heng (1990), 'Developments in econometric modelling in Singapore', *Singapore Journal of Statistics*, **1**, October.

Toh Mun Heng (1993), 'Partnership with multinational corporations', in Linda Low, Toh Mun Heng, Soon Teck Wong, Tan Kong Yam and Helen Hughes (eds), *Challenges and Response: Twenty Five Years of the Economic Development Board*, Singapore: Times Academic Publishers.

Toh Mun Heng (1994), 'Cost of living, price impact on income distribution and consumption tax in Singapore', *The Singapore Economic Review*, **39** (2), October.

Toh Mun Heng (1997), 'Saving, Capital Formation, and Economic Growth in Singapore', East-West Center Working Paper, No. 88–8, August.

Toh Mun Heng (1999), 'Exchange rates and domestic prices in Singapore: An empirical study', *The Singapore Economic Review*, **44** (1), April.

Toh Mun Heng and Linda Low (1990), *An Economic Framework of Singapore*, Singapore: McGraw-Hill.

Toh Mun Heng and Linda Low (1994), 'Capital Stock, Latent Resource and Total Factor Productivity in Singapore', paper presented at the Workshop on Measuring Productivity and Technological Progress, Faculty of Business Administration, National University of Singapore, August.

Toh Mun Heng and Eric D. Ramstetter (1994), 'A Structural Model of Singapore for Asian Link', in S. Ichimura and Y. Matsumotoa (eds), *Econometric Models of Asian-Pacific Countries*, Tokyo: Springer-Verlag.

Toh Mun Heng and Tan Kong Yam (eds) (1998), *Competitiveness of the Singapore Economy: A Strategic Perspective*, Singapore: Singapore University Press and World Scientific.

Toh Mun Heng and Ng Wai Choong (2000), 'Efficiency of Investments in Asian Economies: Has Singapore over-invested?', Paper presented at the 7th Convention of the East Asian Economic Association, Singapore, November 2000.

Toida, Mitsuru (1985), 'A monetarist small econometric model for Singapore', in *Econometric Link System for ASEAN*, ELSA Final Report, Vol. 1, Tokyo: Institute of Developing Economies.

Toida, Mitsuru and Daisuke Hiratsuka (eds) (1997), *Asian Industrialising Region in 2005*, Tokyo: Institute of Developing Economies.

Tongzon, Jose L. and Jayant Menon (1994), 'Exchange rates and export pricing in a small open NIC: The Singapore experience', *The Singapore Economic Review*, **39** (2), October.

Tongzon, Jose L. and Bruce S. Felmingham (1998), 'Bilateral trade in the Asia-Pacific: a case study for Australia, USA, Japan and Singapore', *Asian Economic Journal*, **12** (4).

Tremewan, Christopher (1994), *The Political Economy of Social Control in Singapore*, New York: St Martin's Press in association with St. Antony's College, Oxford.

Tremewan, Christopher (2000), 'Welfare and Governance: Public housing under Singapore's party-state', in Roger Goodman, Gordon White and Huck-ju Kwon (eds), *The East Asian Welfare Model: Welfare Orientalism and the State*, Routledge: London and New York.

Tsao Yuan (1985), 'Growth without productivity: Singapore manufacturing in the 1970s', *Journal of Development Economics*, **19** (1/2), September–October.

Tsao Yuan (1986), 'Sources of growth accounting for the Singapore economy', in Lim Chong-Yah and Peter Lloyd (eds), *Resources and Growth in Singapore*, Singapore: Oxford University Press.

Tse, Y.K. (1997), 'The cointegration of Asian Currencies Revisited', *Japan and the World Economy*, **9** (1).

Tumnong Dasri (1991), *Open Market Operations: Its Nature and Extent in the SEACEN Countries*, Kuala Lumpur: The South East Asian Central Banks (SEACEN), Research and Training Centre.

Turnbull, C.M. (2000), 'Singapore: History' in *The Far East and Australasia 2001*, London: Europa Publications.

Tyabji, Amina (1998), 'Capital Flows and Macroeconomic Stabilization in Singapore', in C.H. Kwan, Donna Vanderbrink and Chia Siow Yue (eds), *Coping With Capital Flows in East Asia*, Singapore: Institute of South-east Asian Studies and Japan Nomura Research Institute.

Turnbull, C.M. (1969), 'Constitutional development 1819–1968', in Ooi Jim-Bee and Chiang Hai Ding (eds), *Modern Singapore*, Singapore: University of Singapore Press.

Turnbull, C.M. (1989), *A History of Singapore 1819–1988*, 2nd edn, Singapore: Oxford University Press.

United Nations (1991), *Human Development Report 1991*, Oxford: Oxford University Press.

United Nations (1996), *Human Development Report 1996*, Oxford: Oxford University Press.

United Nations (2000), *Human Development Report 2000*, Oxford: Oxford University Press.

United Nations (2001), *Sixth United Nations Survey of Crime Trends and Operations of Criminal Justice System Covering the Period 1995–1997* available from: http://www.undcp.org/crime_cicp_survey_sixth.html

United States State Department (2001), *Report on Human Rights Practices in Singapore*, Bureau of Democracy, Human Rights and Labour, February.

Vasil, Raj (1992), *Governing Singapore*, Singapore: Mandarin.

Walters, A.A. (1987), 'Currency boards', in Peter Newman, Murray Milgate and John Eatwell (eds), *The New Palgrave: A Dictionary of Economics*, Vol. 1, London: Macmillan.

Wan Jr., Henry (1998), 'The Singaporean economy: Prospects for the 21st century', *The Singapore Economic Review*, **43** (2), October.

Weerasekera, Y.M.W.B. (1993), *Domestic Resource Mobilization in the Seacan Countries*, Kuala Lumpur: The South East Asian Central Banks (SEACAN), Research and Training Centre.

Wescott, Robert F. (1998), 'East Asian saving patterns in a global context', in F. Gerard Adams and Shinichi Ichimura (eds), *East Asian Development: Will the East Asian Growth Miracle Survive?*, Praeger: Westport and London.

Williamson, John (1998), 'The case for a common basket peg for East Asia?', in Stefan Collignon, Jean Pisani-Ferry and Yung Chul Park (eds), *Exchange Rate Policies in Emerging Asian Countries*, London: Routledge.

Wilson, Peter (1983), 'The consequences of export instability for developing countries', *Development and Change*, **14**.

Wilson, Peter (1986), *International Economics: Theory, Evidence and Practice*, London: Wheatsheaf.

Wilson, Peter (1993), 'The transmission of export shocks to domestic economic variables in a very open reexport economy; the case of Singapore 1970–1986', unpublished manuscript, National University of Singapore.

Wilson, Peter (1994a), 'Tourist earnings instability in Singapore, 1972–1988', *Journal of Economic Studies*, **21** (1).

Wilson, Peter (1994b), 'Is managed floating the best exchange rate policy for Singapore?', *Global Economic Digest*, **1** (2), July–August.

Wilson, Peter (1994c), 'Export earnings instability of Singapore, 1957–1988: A time series analysis', *Journal of Asian Economics*, **5** (3).

Wilson, Peter (1995), 'Export instability in Singapore 1972 to 1986: A time series simulation approach', *Asian Economies*, **24** (3), September.

Wilson, Peter (2000a), 'The dilemma of a more advanced developing country: Conflicting view on the development strategy of Singapore', *The Developing Economies*, **38** (1), March.

Wilson, Peter (2000b), 'The export competitiveness of dynamic Asian economies 1983–95: a dynamic shift–share approach', *Journal of Economic Studies,* **27** (6).

Wilson, Peter (2001), 'Exchange rates and the trade balance for dynamic Asian economies – does the J-curve exist for Singapore, Malaysia, and Korea?', *Open Economies Review*, **12** (4).

Wilson, Peter and Kua Choon Tat (2001), 'Exchange rates and the trade balance: the case of Singapore 1970–96', *Journal of Asian Economics,* **12**.

Wilson, Peter and Wong Yin Mei (1999), 'The export competitiveness of ASEAN economies 1986–95', *ASEAN Economic Bulletin*, **16** (2).

Winsemius, Albert (1962), 'Organising for industrial development', in Albert Winsemius and John A. Pincus (eds), *Methods of Industrial Development with Special Reference to Less Developed Areas*, Paris: Organisation for Economic Co-operation and Development.

Winsemius, Albert (1982), 'Foreword', in C.V. Devan Nair, *Not by Wages Alone: Selected Speeches and Writings of C.V. Devan Nair 1959–1981*, Singapore: Singapore National Trades Union Congress.

Winsemius, Albert and John A. Pincus (eds) (1962), *Methods of Industrial Development with Special Reference to Less Developed Areas*, Paris: Organisation for Economic Co-operation and Development.

Wong Chung Ming (1984), 'Trends and patterns of Singapore's trade in manufactures', Paper presented to a conference on the global implications of the trade pattern of East and Southeast Asia, Kuala Lumpur, Malaysia, January.

Wong, Daniel Chi Hoong and Park Donghyun (1997), 'The adequacy of CPF for Old-Age support', in Jon D. Kendall, Park Donghyun and Randolph Tan (eds), *East Asian Economic Issues, Volume III*, Singapore: World Scientific.

Wong Fot-chyi (1993), 'Patterns of labour productivity growth and employment shift in the Singapore manufacturing industries', *The Singapore Economic Review*, **38** (2), October.

Wong Fot-chyi (1997), 'Quality of employment growth in Singapore: 1983–96', *The Singapore Economic Review*, **42** (2), October.

Wong Fot-chyi and Gan Wee-beng (1994), 'Total factor productivity growth in the Singapore manufacturing industries during the 1980s', *Journal of Asian Economics*, **5** (2).

Wong, John (1988), 'The Association of Southeast Asian Nations', in Ali M. El-Agraa (ed.), *International Economic Integration*, London: Macmillan.

Wong, John (1989), 'Singapore's recent economic set-back: Lessons for the NICS', in Y.C. Jao, Victor Mok and Ho Lok-Sang (eds), *Economic Development in Chinese Societies: Models and Experiences*, Hong Kong: Hong Kong University Press.

Wong Kum Poh (1986), 'Saving, capital inflow and capital formation', in Lim Chong Yah and Peter Lloyd (eds), *Resources and Growth in Singapore*, Singapore: Oxford University Press.

Woon Kin Chung (1991), 'Net exports and economic growth: An assessment of the applicability of the export-led growth hypothesis to Singapore', unpublished M.Soc. Science dissertation, Department of Economics and Statistics, National University of Singapore.

World Bank (1993), *The East Asian Miracle: Economic Growth and Public Policy*, New York: Oxford University Press for the World Bank.

World Bank (1997), *World Development Report 1997*, Washington, DC: Oxford University Press for the World Bank.

World Bank (1999), *World Development Report 1998/9*, Washington, DC: Oxford University Press for the World Bank.

World Bank (2000), *World Development Report 2000/20001: Attacking Poverty*, New York: Oxford Press for the World Bank.

World Health Organization (2000), http://www.who.int/mental_health/Topic/Suicide_rates.html

World Economic Forum 1999, www.reforum.org

World Competitiveness Yearbook 2001, Institute for Management Development, www.imd/ch/wcy.

World Investment Report, New York: United Nations, Various years.

Yeo, George (2001), 'Cushioning the impact of the downturn: Statements by Minister for Trade and Industry to Parliament, 25 July', from www.gov.sg/sgip/announce/250701gy.htm.

Yeung, May T., Nicholas Perdikis and William A. Kerr (1999), *Regional Trading Blocks in the Global Economy: The EU and ASEAN*, Northampton, MA: Edward Elgar.

Yip, P. (1994), 'The Singapore dollar: Where do we stand? An application of the relative PPP on the valuation of a currency', National University of Singapore, Department of Economics and Statistics, Staff Seminar Series no. 11.

Yoshihara, Kunio (2000), *Asia Per Capita: Why National Incomes Differ in East Asia*, London and Singapore: Curzon Press and New Asian Library.

You Poh Seng and Lim Chong Yah (eds) (1984), *Twenty-five Years of Development*, Singapore: Nanyang Xingzhou Lianhe Zaobao.

Young, Alwyn (1992), 'A tale of two cities: Factor accumulation and technical change in Hong Kong and Singapore', in Stanley Fischer and Olivier Blanchard (eds), *NBER Macroeconomics Annual 1992*, Number 7, Cambridge: MIT Press. Also in Grossman (1996 chapter 3).

Young, Alwyn (1994a), 'The tyranny of numbers: Confronting the statistical realities of the East Asian growth experience', National Bureau of Economic Research Working Paper No. 4680, March.

Young, Alwyn (1994b), 'Lessons from the East Asian NICS: A contrarian view', *European Economic Review*, **38**.

Young, Alwyn (1995), 'The tyranny of numbers: Confronting the statistical realities of the East Asian growth experience', *Quarterly Journal of Economics*, **110** (3) August.

Youngson, A.J. (1982), *Hong Kong: Economic Growth and Policy*, Hong Kong: Oxford University Press.

Yuen, Hazel (2000), *Is Asia An Optimum Currency Area? Shocking Aspects of Output Fluctuations in East Asia*, Singapore: National University of Singapore, Department of Economics, Staff Working Paper Series.

Zhang, Peter G. (1995), *Barings Bankruptcy and Financial Derivatives*, World Scientific: Singapore.

Index